The Editor

Suzanne Raitt is the author of *Virginia Woolf's "To the Lighthouse," Vita and Virginia: The Work and Friendship of V. Sackville-West and Virginia Woolf,* and *May Sinclair: A Modern Victorian.* She is professor of English at the College of William and Mary, where she teaches courses on Virginia Woolf, nineteenth-century fiction, psychoanalytic theory, and sexuality.

A NORTON CRITICAL EDITION

Virginia Woolf

JACOB'S ROOM

AUTHORITATIVE TEXT
VIRGINIA WOOLF AND THE NOVEL
CRITICISM

Edited by

SUZANNE RAITT
THE COLLEGE OF WILLIAM AND MARY

W · W · NORTON & COMPANY · *New York* · *London*

W. W. Norton & Company has been independent since its founding in 1923, when William Warder Norton and Mary D. Herter Norton first published lectures delivered at the People's Institute, the adult education division of New York City's Cooper Union. The Nortons soon expanded their program beyond the Institute, publishing books by celebrated academics from America and abroad. By mid-century, the two major pillars of Norton's publishing program—trade books and college texts—were firmly established. In the 1950s, the Norton family transferred control of the company to its employees, and today—with a staff of four hundred and a comparable number of trade, college, and professional titles published each year—W. W. Norton & Company stands as the largest and oldest publishing house owned wholly by its employees.

The text of this book is composed in Fairfield Medium
with the display set in Bernhard Modern.
Book design by Antonina Krass.
Composition by Binghamton Valley Composition.
Manufacturing by the Maple-Vail Book Group, Binghamton.
Production manager: Benjamin Reynolds.

Library of Congress Cataloging-in-Publication Data

Woolf, Virginia, 1882–1941.
Jacob's room: authoritative text, Virginia Woolf and the novel, criticism /
Virginia Woolf; edited by Suzanne Raitt.
p. cm. — (A Norton critical edition)
Includes bibliographical references

ISBN-13: 978-0-393-92632-3 (pbk.)
ISBN-10: 0-393-92632-X (pbk.)

1. Woolf, Virginia, 1882–1941 Jacob's room.   2. World War,
1914–1918—England—Fiction.   3. Young men—Fiction.   4. Psychological
fiction.   5. Experimental fiction.   I. Raitt, Suzanne,   II. Title.

PR6045.O72J3 2006
823'.912—dc22
2006047303

W. W. Norton & Company, Inc., 500 Fifth Avenue,
New York, N.Y. 10110-0017
www.wwnorton.com

W. W. Norton & Company Ltd., Castle House,
75/76 Wells Street, London W1T 3QT

1 2 3 4 5 6 7 8 9 0

Contents

Criticism

Preface

On Sunday, July 23, 1922, Leonard Woolf, Virginia Woolf's husband, read through the final draft of *Jacob's Room*, his wife's third novel. Apart from the typist, Leonard was always the first person to read her manuscripts, and his opinion was enormously important to her. She reported herself "on the whole pleased" with his response, although she argued with him when he said it was her best work.[1] Neither of them was very sure how it would be received: Virginia had felt all along that she was experimenting with techniques she had used only in short stories so far; and Leonard commented that it was "unlike any other novel."[2] But Virginia was satisfied that her attempt to evolve "a new form for a new novel" had resulted in something that was more radical, and more authentic, than some of her earlier efforts: "There's no doubt in my mind that I have found out how to begin (at 40) to say something in my own voice; & that interests me so that I feel I can go ahead without praise."[3]

One reason that Woolf felt able to adopt this bolder, less compromising approach was that *Jacob's Room* was the first of her novels to be published by the Woolfs themselves at the Hogarth Press. This meant that she did not have to bow to the demands of an outside editor, who might have been worried about taking a risk on such an unusual book, and pressed for revisions she was unwilling to make. Virginia and Leonard were completely in control of the final form of the book, and she chose a woodcut by her artist sister, Vanessa Bell, to go on the dust cover. The novel was published in Britain on October 27, 1922, with a print run of 1,200 copies; about 2,000 more were printed the following month. Reviews were mixed, but Virginia's friends, many of them writers, were impressed and told her so. By the time the first American edition was published, by Harcourt Brace on February 8, 1923, with an initial print run of 1,500 copies, Virginia had received plenty of praise, and she made hardly any alterations to the American edition, apart from corrections of two tiny errors. The only major difference between the two editions was that

---

1. *The Diary of Virginia Woolf*, 5 vols., ed. Anne Olivier Bell and Andrew McNeillie (New York: Harcourt Brace, 1977–84), II: 186.
2. *Diary*, II: 186.
3. January 26, 1920, *Diary*, II: 13; *Diary*, II: 186.

vii

in a number of places, where the British edition had blank spaces
on the page, between paragraphs or sometimes even between sentences, the American edition closed up those gaps and had the text
simply run on without interruption. Woolf seems never to have
objected to this, even though it can be assumed that she was responsible for the gaps in the British edition. The copy-text used in this
volume is the first British edition, with the gaps reinstated.[4] The first
editions were re-issued as the "Uniform Edition" in 1929 (UK) and
1931 (US), but these volumes were photo-offsets of the original
pages. There were no further editions in Woolf's lifetime.

Virginia Woolf was often the best critic of her own work, and her
comments on *Jacob's Room* are no exception to this rule. I have
selected for this Norton Critical Edition a series of excerpts from
Woolf's diary for the years 1920 to 1922, when she was working on
the novel, as well as two letters she wrote to friends commenting on
the novel. She also wrote a brief outline of her plans for the novel
at the beginning of the notebook that contains the handwritten draft
of the first part of the novel, and in another notebook she seems to
have toyed with the idea of an epigraph in memory of her brother
Thoby, who died in 1906 at the age of twenty-six. I have included
both these items here.

While she was working on *Jacob's Room* and the short stories that
led up to it, and evolving what she thought of as her "new form" for
the novel, Woolf was also writing and publishing essays that reflected
on her own methods as a novelist, and on those of her contemporaries. One of these essays, "Modern Novels" (1919), is included
here.[5] She also saw three of her early short stories as experiments in
the style of *Jacob's Room*, and deliberately modeled the novel on
them: "Whether I'm sufficiently mistress of things—thats the doubt;
but conceive mark on the wall, K[ew]. G[ardens]. & unwritten novel
taking hands & dancing in unity."[6] Those stories—"The Mark on the
Wall" (1917), "Kew Gardens" (1919), and "An Unwritten Novel"
(1920)—are all reprinted here. "A Woman's College from Outside"
originally came between what are now Chapters 3 and 4 of *Jacob's
Room*, as the holograph makes clear, but when Woolf's method in
the novel shifted away from the description of a series of rooms, she

4. See Edward L. Bishop, "Mind the Gap: The Spaces in *Jacob's Room*," *Woolf Studies Annual*
   10 (2004): 31–49, reprinted in this volume on pp. 303–16, for a detailed discussion of
   this issue.
5. A later version of "Modern Novels," "Modern Fiction" (1925; *The Essays of Virginia Woolf*,
   ed. Andrew McNeillie, 4 vols., New York: Harcourt Brace Jovanovich, 1989–91, IV: 157–
   65) is often taken to be Woolf's "manifesto" as a novelist. I have reprinted the original
   version here, since it reflects her thinking as she prepared to work on *Jacob's Room*.
6. "The Mark on the Wall," originally published in *Two Stories* (London: Hogarth, 1917);
   "Kew Gardens," originally published as a separate pamphlet by the Hogarth Press in May
   1919; "An Unwritten Novel," originally published in *London Mercury* (July 1920). All three
   are reprinted in this volume on pp. 183–203.

cut this section from the novel and turned it into a separate sketch, which was published in *Atalanta's Garland: Being the Book of the Edinburgh University Women's Union* (1926) and is reprinted here.

   Jacob's Room was widely reviewed when it came out, and many of its reviewers were Virginia Woolf's friends and associates. I have included a selection of contemporary reviews here, and excerpts from a number of the letters Woolf received from friends who were also writers: Lytton Strachey, the biographer; Rebecca West, the journalist; T. S. Eliot, the poet; E. M. Forster, the novelist; and Clive Bell, art critic and Virginia Woolf's brother-in-law. Few of the published reviews were glowing, but most were complimentary and respectful, even as they noted, as Arnold Bennett did in *Cassell's Weekly*, the failure of the central character truly to come to life.

   Over the years, the volume of academic literary criticism of Virginia Woolf's work has swelled to hundreds of thousands of books, articles, and conference papers. *Jacob's Room* has to some degree escaped the intensity of attention devoted to some of her later novels (*Mrs Dalloway* and *To the Lighthouse*, for example). But nonetheless there has been a steady flow of work discussing Woolf's manuscript revisions, her narrative methods, her use of painterly techniques, and the novel's attitude to women and to sexuality. I have reprinted a cross-section of the most useful of these articles here.

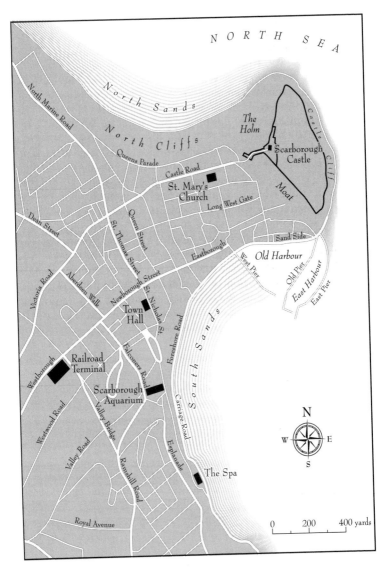

Scarborough in 1899.

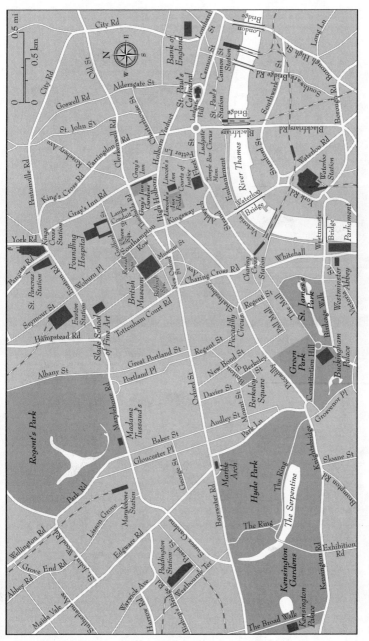

Central London in 1911.

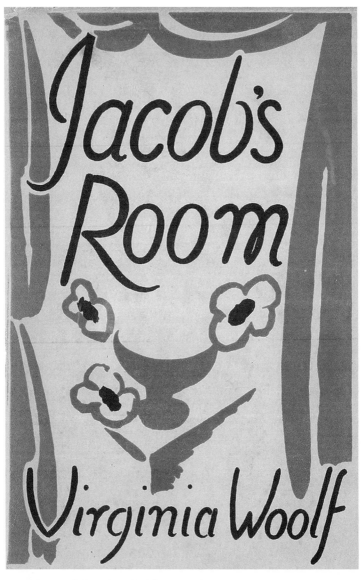

Dust Cover of First British Edition, 1922.
Courtesy of the Mortimer Rare Book Room, Smith College.

A Note on the Text

There are very few differences between the first British edition of October 27, 1922, printed by R. & R. Clark of Edinburgh, and the first American edition, published by Harcourt Brace over three months later on February 8, 1923. Harcourt Brace seems to have typeset their edition from a set of proofs sent to them by R. & R. Clark in early October 1922, three weeks before publication of the British edition, and for the most part the American edition follows the British edition extremely closely. Most of the variants are in capitalization, hyphenation, and spelling, and, apart from two minor changes requested by Woolf, were presumably introduced by the typesetter (often to conform to American spelling conventions).[1] Readers interested in the details of the differences between the American and the British editions can consult James M. Haule and Philip H. Smith, Jr., *Concordance to the Novels of Virginia Woolf* (New York: Garland, 1991).

Because the two editions are so similar, I have chosen the first British edition for this volume, since Woolf was far more involved in the preparation and printing of this book than of its American counterpart. The only substantial difference between the British and American editions is in the number of space breaks in the text. The British edition has far more blank spaces, of varying sizes, than the American edition. It seems that the American typesetters simply closed many of them up, sometimes because they were hard to identify (at the top or bottom of a page, for example) and sometimes, presumably, to save space and paper. If Woolf objected to this change, any record of her objection has not survived, but the spaces in the British edition are so numerous, and so carefully calibrated, that it must be assumed that the space breaks were intentional, especially since Woolf corrected the proofs of the British edition herself. For this reason, the blank spaces are reproduced here, exactly as they appear in the first British edition.

No proofs of *Jacob's Room* have survived. The holograph draft, contained in three notebooks housed in the Henry W. and Albert A.

---

1. For details of Woolf's requested changes, see Virginia Woolf, *Jacob's Room*, ed. Edward L. Bishop (Oxford: Blackwell, 2004), xxxvi–xxxvii, 176.

Berg Collection of English and American Literature at the New York Public Library, has been published in *Virginia Woolf's "Jacob's Room": The Holograph Draft*, transcribed and edited by Edward L. Bishop (New York: Pace University Press, 1998). The novel was substantially revised between the holograph manuscript and the final version, and where the holograph draft has significant and interesting material that was deleted from the published version, I have included it here in the section "Extracts from the Holograph Draft." I have also reprinted in *Virginia Woolf and the Novel* a short story called "A Woman's College from Outside," which was originally inserted between Chapters 3 and 4 of the novel (Chapter 10 in the holograph), but which Woolf cut from the novel and published separately in *Atalanta's Garland: Being the Book of the Edinburgh University Women's Union* (1926).

Eight nonconsecutive pages of the typescript, with a few corrections and insertions in Woolf's handwriting, are housed in Special Collections at the University of Sussex, Monk's House Papers, File B12.

The Text of
JACOB'S ROOM

I

"So of course," wrote Betty Flanders,[1] pressing her heels rather deeper in the sand, "there was nothing for it but to leave."

Slowly welling from the point of her gold nib, pale blue ink dissolved the full stop; for there her pen stuck; her eyes fixed, and tears slowly filled them. The entire bay quivered; the lighthouse wobbled; and she had the illusion that the mast of Mr. Connor's little yacht was bending like a wax candle in the sun. She winked quickly. Accidents were awful things. She winked again. The mast was straight; the waves were regular; the lighthouse was upright; but the blot had spread.

". . . nothing for it but to leave," she read.

"Well, if Jacob doesn't want to play" (the shadow of Archer, her eldest son, fell across the notepaper and looked blue on the sand, and she felt chilly—it was the third of September already), "if Jacob doesn't want to play"—what a horrid blot! It must be getting late.

"Where *is* that tiresome little boy?" she said. "I don't see him. Run and find him. Tell him to come at once." ". . . but mercifully," she scribbled, ignoring the full stop, "everything seems satisfactorily arranged, packed though we are like herrings in a barrel, and forced to stand the perambulator which the landlady quite naturally won't allow . . ."

Such were Betty Flanders's letters to Captain Barfoot—many-paged, tear-stained. Scarborough is seven hundred miles from Cornwall:[2] Captain Barfoot is in Scarborough: Seabrook is dead. Tears made all the dahlias in her garden undulate in red waves and flashed the glass house in her eyes, and spangled the kitchen with bright knives, and made Mrs. Jarvis, the rector's wife, think at church, while the hymn-tune played and Mrs. Flanders bent low over her little boys' heads, that marriage is a fortress and widows stray solitary in the open fields, picking up stones, gleaning a few golden straws, lonely, unprotected, poor creatures. Mrs. Flanders had been a widow these two years.

"Ja—cob! Ja—cob!" Archer shouted.

"Scarborough," Mrs. Flanders wrote on the envelope, and dashed a bold line beneath; it was her native town; the hub of the universe. But a stamp? She ferreted in her bag; then held it up mouth down-

---

1. The Flanders region of Belgium was the site of some of the bloodiest battles on the Western Front of the First World War.
2. Actually about four hundred miles. Scarborough, where the Flanders family lives, was one of the most popular beach resorts in the north of England in the nineteenth and early twentieth centuries.

wards; then fumbled in her lap, all so vigorously that Charles Steele in the Panama hat[3] suspended his paint-brush.

Like the antennae of some irritable insect it positively trembled. Here was that woman moving—actually going to get up—confound her! He struck the canvas a hasty violet-black dab. For the landscape needed it. It was too pale—greys flowing into lavenders, and one star or a white gull suspended just so—too pale as usual. The critics would say it was too pale, for he was an unknown man exhibiting obscurely, a favourite with his landladies' children, wearing a cross on his watch chain, and much gratified if his landladies liked his pictures—which they often did.

"Ja—cob! Ja—cob!" Archer shouted.

Exasperated by the noise, yet loving children, Steele picked nervously at the dark little coils on his palette.

"I saw your brother—I saw your brother," he said, nodding his head, as Archer lagged past him, trailing his spade, and scowling at the old gentleman in spectacles.

"Over there—by the rock," Steele muttered, with his brush between his teeth, squeezing out raw sienna,[4] and keeping his eyes fixed on Betty Flanders's back.

"Ja—cob! Ja—cob!" shouted Archer, lagging on after a second.

The voice had an extraordinary sadness. Pure from all body, pure from all passion, going out into the world, solitary, unanswered, breaking against rocks—so it sounded.

Steele frowned; but was pleased by the effect of the black—it was just *that* note which brought the rest together. "Ah, one may learn to paint at fifty! There's Titian[5] . . ." and so, having found the right tint, up he looked and saw to his horror a cloud over the bay.

Mrs. Flanders rose, slapped her coat this side and that to get the sand off, and picked up her black parasol.

The rock was one of those tremendously solid brown, or rather black, rocks which emerge from the sand like something primitive. Rough with crinkled limpet[6] shells and sparsely strewn with locks of

---

3. Wide-brimmed straw hat.
4. Yellowish-brown.
5. Italian painter (c. 1487–1576). In the early 1540s Titian's style changed under the influence of central and north Italian mannerism.
6. Shellfish that clings to rocks.

dry seaweed, a small boy has to stretch his legs far apart, and indeed to feel rather heroic, before he gets to the top.

But there, on the very top, is a hollow full of water, with a sandy bottom; with a blob of jelly stuck to the side, and some mussels. A fish darts across. The fringe of yellow-brown seaweed flutters, and out pushes an opal-shelled crab——

"Oh, a huge crab," Jacob murmured——and begins his journey on weakly legs on the sandy bottom. Now! Jacob plunged his hand. The crab was cool and very light. But the water was thick with sand, and so, scrambling down, Jacob was about to jump, holding his bucket in front of him, when he saw, stretched entirely rigid, side by side, their faces very red, an enormous man and woman.

An enormous man and woman (it was early-closing day) were stretched motionless, with their heads on pocket-handkerchiefs, side by side, within a few feet of the sea, while two or three gulls gracefully skirted the incoming waves, and settled near their boots.

The large red faces lying on the bandanna handkerchiefs stared up at Jacob. Jacob stared down at them. Holding his bucket very carefully, Jacob then jumped deliberately and trotted away very nonchalantly at first, but faster and faster as the waves came creaming up to him and he had to swerve to avoid them, and the gulls rose in front of him and floated out and settled again a little farther on. A large black woman was sitting on the sand. He ran towards her.

"Nanny! Nanny!" he cried, sobbing the words out on the crest of each gasping breath.

The waves came round her. She was a rock. She was covered with the seaweed which pops when it is pressed. He was lost.

There he stood. His face composed itself. He was about to roar when, lying among the black sticks and straw under the cliff, he saw a whole skull—perhaps a cow's skull, a skull, perhaps, with the teeth in it. Sobbing, but absent-mindedly, he ran farther and farther away until he held the skull in his arms.

"There he is!" cried Mrs. Flanders, coming round the rock and covering the whole space of the beach in a few seconds. "What has he got hold of? Put it down, Jacob! Drop it this moment! Something horrid, I know. Why didn't you stay with us? Naughty little boy! Now put it down. Now come along both of you," and she swept round, holding Archer by one hand and fumbling for Jacob's arm with the other. But he ducked down and picked up the sheep's jaw, which was loose.

Swinging her bag, clutching her parasol, holding Archer's hand, and telling the story of the gunpowder explosion in which poor Mr. Curnow had lost his eye, Mrs. Flanders hurried up the steep lane, aware all the time in the depths of her mind of some buried discomfort.

There on the sand not far from the lovers lay the old sheep's skull without its jaw. Clean, white, wind-swept, sand-rubbed, a more unpolluted piece of bone existed nowhere on the coast of Cornwall. The sea holly would grow through the eye-sockets; it would turn to powder, or some golfer, hitting his ball one fine day, would disperse a little dust.—No, but not in lodgings, thought Mrs. Flanders. It's a great experiment coming so far with young children. There's no man to help with the perambulator. And Jacob is such a handful; so obstinate already.

"Throw it away, dear, do," she said, as they got into the road; but Jacob squirmed away from her; and the wind rising, she took out her bonnet-pin, looked at the sea, and stuck it in afresh. The wind was rising. The waves showed that uneasiness, like something alive, restive, expecting the whip, of waves before a storm. The fishing-boats were leaning to the water's brim. A pale yellow light shot across the purple sea; and shut. The lighthouse was lit. "Come along," said Betty Flanders. The sun blazed in their faces and gilded the great blackberries trembling out from the hedge which Archer tried to strip as they passed.

"Don't lag, boys. You've got nothing to change into," said Betty, pulling them along, and looking with uneasy emotion at the earth displayed so luridly, with sudden sparks of light from greenhouses in gardens, with a sort of yellow and black mutability, against this blazing sunset, this astonishing agitation and vitality of nature, which stirred Betty Flanders and made her think of responsibility and danger. She gripped Archer's hand. On she plodded up the hill.

"What did I ask you to remember?" she said.

"I don't know," said Archer.

"Well, I don't know either," said Betty, humorously and simply, and who shall deny that this blankness of mind, when combined with profusion, mother wit, old wives' tales, haphazard ways, moments of astonishing daring, humour, and sentimentality—who shall deny that in these respects every woman is nicer than any man?

Well, Betty Flanders, to begin with.

She had her hand upon the garden gate.

"The meat!" she exclaimed, striking the latch down.

She had forgotten the meat.

There was Rebecca at the window.

The bareness of Mrs. Pearce's front room was fully displayed at ten o'clock at night when a powerful oil lamp stood on the middle of the table. The harsh light fell on the garden; cut straight across the lawn; lit up a child's bucket and a purple aster[7] and reached the hedge. Mrs. Flanders had left her sewing on the table. There were her large reels of white cotton and her steel spectacles; her needlecase; her brown wool wound round an old postcard. There were the bulrushes and the *Strand* magazines;[8] and the linoleum sandy from the boys' boots. A daddy-long-legs shot from corner to corner and hit the lamp globe. The wind blew straight dashes of rain across the window, which flashed silver as they passed through the light. A single leaf tapped hurriedly, persistently, upon the glass. There was a hurricane out at sea.

Archer could not sleep.

Mrs. Flanders stooped over him. "Think of the fairies," said Betty Flanders. "Think of the lovely, lovely birds settling down on their nests. Now shut your eyes and see the old mother bird with a worm in her beak. Now turn and shut your eyes," she murmured, "and shut your eyes."

The lodging-house seemed full of gurgling and rushing; the cistern overflowing; water bubbling and squeaking and running along the pipes and streaming down the windows.

"What's all that water rushing in?" murmured Archer.

"It's only the bath water running away," said Mrs. Flanders.

Something snapped out of doors.

"I say, won't that steamer sink?" said Archer opening his eyes.

"Of course it won't," said Mrs. Flanders. "The Captain's in bed long ago. Shut your eyes, and think of the fairies, fast asleep, under the flowers."

"I thought he'd never get off—such a hurricane," she whispered to Rebecca, who was bending over a spirit-lamp[9] in the small room next door. The wind rushed outside, but the small flame of the spirit-lamp burnt quietly, shaded from the cot by a book stood on edge.

"Did he take his bottle well?" Mrs. Flanders whispered, and Rebecca nodded and went to the cot and turned down the quilt, and Mrs. Flanders bent over and looked anxiously at the baby, asleep,

7. Perennial plant with daisylike flowers.
8. Illustrated magazine, founded 1891, offering an American-style combination of entertainment and informed debate, aimed at a family readership.
9. Lamp fed by methylated spirits.

but frowning. The window shook, and Rebecca stole like a cat and wedged it. The two women murmured over the spirit-lamp, plotting the eternal conspiracy of hush and clean bottles while the wind raged and gave a sudden wrench at the cheap fastenings.

Both looked round at the cot. Their lips were pursed. Mrs. Flanders crossed over to the cot.

"Asleep?" whispered Rebecca, looking at the cot.

Mrs. Flanders nodded.

"Good-night, Rebecca," Mrs. Flanders murmured, and Rebecca called her ma'm, though they were conspirators plotting the eternal conspiracy of hush and clean bottles.

Mrs. Flanders had left the lamp burning in the front room. There were her spectacles, her sewing; and a letter with the Scarborough post-mark. She had not drawn the curtains either.

The light blazed out across the patch of grass; fell on the child's green bucket with the gold line round it, and upon the aster which trembled violently beside it. For the wind was tearing across the coast, hurling itself at the hills, and leaping, in sudden gusts, on top of its own back. How it spread over the town in the hollow! How the lights seemed to wink and quiver in its fury, lights in the harbour, lights in bedroom windows high up! And rolling dark waves before it, it raced over the Atlantic, jerking the stars above the ships this way and that.

There was a click in the front sitting-room. Mr. Pearce had extinguished the lamp. The garden went out. It was but a dark patch. Every inch was rained upon. Every blade of grass was bent by rain. Eyelids would have been fastened down by the rain. Lying on one's back one would have seen nothing but muddle and confusion—clouds turning and turning, and something yellow-tinted and sulphurous in the darkness.

The little boys in the front bedroom had thrown off their blankets and lay under the sheets. It was hot; rather sticky and steamy. Archer lay spread out, with one arm striking across the pillow. He was flushed; and when the heavy curtain blew out a little he turned and half-opened his eyes. The wind actually stirred the cloth on the chest of drawers, and let in a little light, so that the sharp edge of the chest of drawers was visible, running straight up, until a white shape bulged out; and a silver streak showed in the looking-glass.

In the other bed by the door Jacob lay asleep, fast asleep, profoundly unconscious. The sheep's jaw with the big yellow teeth in it lay at his feet. He had kicked it against the iron bed-rail.

Outside the rain poured down more directly and powerfully as the wind fell in the early hours of the morning. The aster was beaten to the earth. The child's bucket was half-full of rain-water; and the opal-shelled crab slowly circled round the bottom, trying with its weakly legs to climb the steep side; trying again and falling back, and trying again and again.

II

"Mrs. Flanders"—"Poor Betty Flanders"—"Dear Betty"—"She's very attractive still"—"Odd she don't marry again!" "There's Captain Barfoot to be sure—calls every Wednesday as regular as clockwork, and never brings his wife."

"But that's Ellen Barfoot's fault," the ladies of Scarborough said. "She don't put herself out for no one."

"A man likes to have a son—that we know."

"Some tumours have to be cut; but the sort my mother had you bear with for years and years, and never even have a cup of tea brought up to you in bed."

(Mrs. Barfoot was an invalid.)

Elizabeth Flanders, of whom this and much more than this had been said and would be said, was, of course, a widow in her prime. She was half-way between forty and fifty. Years and sorrow between them; the death of Seabrook, her husband; three boys; poverty; a house on the outskirts of Scarborough; her brother, poor Morty's, downfall and possible demise—for where was he? what was he? Shading her eyes, she looked along the road for Captain Barfoot— yes, there he was, punctual as ever; the attentions of the Captain— all ripened Betty Flanders, enlarged her figure, tinged her face with jollity, and flooded her eyes for no reason that any one could see perhaps three times a day.

True, there's no harm in crying for one's husband, and the tombstone, though plain, was a solid piece of work, and on summer's days when the widow brought her boys to stand there one felt kindly towards her. Hats were raised higher than usual; wives tugged their husbands' arms. Seabrook lay six foot beneath, dead these many years; enclosed in three shells; the crevices sealed with lead, so that, had earth and wood been glass, doubtless his very face lay visible beneath, the face of a young man whiskered, shapely, who had gone out duck-shooting and refused to change his boots.

"Merchant of this city," the tombstone said; though why Betty Flanders had chosen so to call him when, as many still remembered, he had only sat behind an office window for three months, and before that had broken horses, ridden to hounds, farmed a few fields, and run a little wild—well, she had to call him something. An example for the boys.

Had he, then, been nothing? An unanswerable question, since even if it weren't the habit of the undertaker to close the eyes, the light so soon goes out of them. At first, part of herself; now one of a company, he had merged in the grass, the sloping hillside, the thousand white stones, some slanting, others upright, the decayed wreaths, the crosses of green tin, the narrow yellow paths, and the lilacs that drooped in April,[1] with a scent like that of an invalid's bedroom, over the churchyard wall. Seabrook was now all that; and when, with her skirt hitched up, feeding the chickens, she heard the bell for service or funeral, that was Seabrook's voice—the voice of the dead.

The rooster had been known to fly on her shoulder and peck her neck, so that now she carried a stick or took one of the children with her when she went to feed the fowls.

"Wouldn't you like my knife, mother?" said Archer.

Sounding at the same moment as the bell, her son's voice mixed life and death inextricably, exhilaratingly.

"What a big knife for a small boy!" she said. She took it to please him. Then the rooster flew out of the hen-house, and, shouting to Archer to shut the door into the kitchen garden, Mrs. Flanders set her meal down, clucked for the hens, went bustling about the orchard, and was seen from over the way by Mrs. Cranch, who, beating her mat against the wall, held it for a moment suspended while she observed to Mrs. Page next door that Mrs. Flanders was in the orchard with the chickens.

Mrs. Page, Mrs. Cranch, and Mrs. Garfit could see Mrs. Flanders in the orchard because the orchard was a piece of Dods Hill enclosed; and Dods Hill dominated the village. No words can exaggerate the importance of Dods Hill. It was the earth; the world against the sky; the horizon of how many glances can best be computed by those who have lived all their lives in the same village, only leaving it once to fight in the Crimea,[2] like old George Garfit, leaning over his garden gate smoking his pipe. The progress of the sun was measured by it; the tint of the day laid against it to be judged.

"Now she's going up the hill with little John," said Mrs. Cranch to Mrs. Garfit, shaking her mat for the last time, and bustling indoors.

Opening the orchard gate, Mrs. Flanders walked to the top of Dods

---

1. As Virginia Woolf points out in her letter to C. P. Sanger (see p. 171), this is inaccurate: lilacs usually bloom later in the spring.
2. Crimean War, fought 1853–56 between Russia and Turkey, Britain, France, and Piedmont.

Hill, holding John by the hand. Archer and Jacob ran in front or lagged behind; but they were in the Roman fortress[3] when she came there, and shouting out what ships were to be seen in the bay. For there was a magnificent view—moors behind, sea in front, and the whole of Scarborough from one end to the other laid out flat like a puzzle. Mrs. Flanders, who was growing stout, sat down in the fortress and looked about her.

The entire gamut of the view's changes should have been known to her; its winter aspect, spring, summer, and autumn; how storms came up from the sea; how the moors shuddered and brightened as the clouds went over; she should have noted the red spot where the villas were building; and the criss-cross of lines where the allotments were cut; and the diamond flash of little glass houses in the sun. Or, if details like these escaped her, she might have let her fancy play upon the gold tint of the sea at sunset, and thought how it lapped in coins of gold upon the shingle. Little pleasure boats shoved out into it; the black arm of the pier hoarded it up. The whole city was pink and gold; domed; mist-wreathed; resonant; strident. Banjoes strummed; the parade smelt of tar which stuck to the heels; goats suddenly cantered their carriages through crowds. It was observed how well the Corporation had laid out the flower-beds. Sometimes a straw hat was blown away. Tulips burnt in the sun. Numbers of sponge-bag trousers[4] were stretched in rows. Purple bonnets fringed soft, pink, querulous faces on pillows in bath chairs.[5] Triangular hoardings were wheeled along by men in white coats. Captain George Boase had caught a monster shark. One side of the triangular hoarding said so in red, blue, and yellow letters; and each line ended with three differently coloured notes of exclamation.

So that was a reason for going down into the Aquarium,[6] where the sallow blinds, the stale smell of spirits of salt, the bamboo chairs, the tables with ash-trays, the revolving fish, the attendant knitting behind six or seven chocolate boxes (often she was quite alone with the fish for hours at a time) remained in the mind as part of the monster shark, he himself being only a flabby yellow receptacle, like an empty Gladstone bag[7] in a tank. No one had ever been cheered by the Aquarium; but the faces of those emerging quickly lost their dim, chilled expression when they perceived that it was only by stand-

---

3. Remains of a Roman signal station in the ruins of medieval Scarborough Castle on Castle Cliff. Dods Hill is fictitious, although there is a "Dodd's Hill" (the spelling in the manuscript of *Jacob's Room*) in Nutley, near Rodmell, where the Woolfs had a house.
4. Men's checked trousers, patterned in the same style as many sponge-bags (wash-bags).
5. Wheelchairs.
6. Scarborough Aquarium, built in 1877 in the Indo-Moorish style, included a concert hall, reading room, dining room, and fernery, as well as the largest fish tank in the world. A swimming pool, theater, and skating rink were added in the early twentieth century. The Aquarium closed in 1914 and is now destroyed.
7. Piece of luggage that opens out flat.

ing in a queue that one could be admitted to the pier. Once through the turnstiles, every one walked for a yard or two very briskly; some flagged at this stall; others at that. But it was the band that drew them all to it finally; even the fishermen on the lower pier taking up their pitch within its range.

The band played in the Moorish kiosk.[8] Number nine went up on the board. It was a waltz tune. The pale girls, the old widow lady, the three Jews lodging in the same boarding-house, the dandy, the major, the horse-dealer, and the gentleman of independent means, all wore the same blurred, drugged expression, and through the chinks in the planks at their feet they could see the green summer waves, peacefully, amiably, swaying round the iron pillars of the pier.

But there was a time when none of this had any existence (thought the young man leaning against the railings). Fix your eyes upon the lady's skirt; the grey one will do—above the pink silk stockings. It changes; drapes her ankles—the nineties; then it amplifies—the seventies; now it's burnished red and stretched above a crinoline—the sixties; a tiny black foot wearing a white cotton stocking peeps out. Still sitting there? Yes—she's still on the pier. The silk now is sprigged with roses, but somehow one no longer sees so clearly. There's no pier beneath us. The heavy chariot may swing along the turnpike road, but there's no pier for it to stop at, and how grey and turbulent the sea is in the seventeenth century! Let's to the museum. Cannon-balls; arrow-heads; Roman glass and a forceps green with verdigris.[9] The Rev. Jaspar Floyd dug them up at his own expense early in the forties in the Roman camp on Dods Hill—see the little ticket with the faded writing on it.

And now, what's the next thing to see in Scarborough?

Mrs. Flanders sat on the raised circle of the Roman camp, patching Jacob's breeches; only looking up as she sucked the end of her cotton, or when some insect dashed at her, boomed in her ear, and was gone.

John kept trotting up and slapping down in her lap grass or dead leaves which he called "tea," and she arranged them methodically but absent-mindedly, laying the flowery heads of the grasses together, thinking how Archer had been awake again last night; the

---

8. Scarborough pier was destroyed by a gale in 1906; the "Moorish kiosk" echoes the style of the Aquarium architect Eugenius Birch, who was heavily influenced by Hindu temples.
9. Green coating that forms when copper, brass, or bronze is exposed to air or moisture for a long period.

church clock was ten or thirteen minutes fast; she wished she could buy Garfit's acre.

"That's an orchid leaf, Johnny. Look at the little brown spots. Come, my dear. We must go home. Ar—cher! Ja—cob!"

"Ar—cher—Ja—cob!" Johnny piped after her, pivoting round on his heel, and strewing the grass and leaves in his hands as if he were sowing seed. Archer and Jacob jumped up from behind the mound where they had been crouching with the intention of springing upon their mother unexpectedly, and they all began to walk slowly home.

"Who is that?" said Mrs. Flanders, shading her eyes.

"That old man in the road?" said Archer, looking below.

"He's not an old man," said Mrs. Flanders. "He's—no, he's not—I thought it was the Captain, but it's Mr. Floyd. Come along, boys."

"Oh, bother Mr. Floyd!" said Jacob, switching off a thistle's head, for he knew already that Mr. Floyd was going to teach them Latin, as indeed he did for three years in his spare time, out of kindness, for there was no other gentleman in the neighbourhood whom Mrs. Flanders could have asked to do such a thing, and the elder boys were getting beyond her, and must be got ready for school, and it was more than most clergymen would have done, coming round after tea, or having them in his own room—as he could fit it in—for the parish was a very large one, and Mr. Floyd, like his father before him, visited cottages miles away on the moors, and, like old Mr. Floyd, was a great scholar, which made it so unlikely—she had never dreamt of such a thing. Ought she to have guessed? But let alone being a scholar he was eight years younger than she was. She knew his mother—old Mrs. Floyd. She had tea there. And it was that very evening when she came back from having tea with old Mrs. Floyd that she found the note in the hall and took it into the kitchen with her when she went to give Rebecca the fish, thinking it must be something about the boys.

"Mr. Floyd brought it himself, did he?—I think the cheese must be in the parcel in the hall—oh, in the hall——" for she was reading. No, it was not about the boys.

"Yes, enough for fish-cakes to-morrow certainly—Perhaps Captain Barfoot——" she had come to the word "love." She went into the garden and read, leaning against the walnut tree to steady herself. Up and down went her breast. Seabrook came so vividly before her. She shook her head and was looking through her tears at the little shifting leaves against the yellow sky when three geese, half-running, half-flying, scuttled across the lawn with Johnny behind them, brandishing a stick.

Mrs. Flanders flushed with anger.

"How many times have I told you?" she cried, and seized him and snatched his stick away from him.

"But they'd escaped!" he cried, struggling to get free.

"You're a very naughty boy. If I've told you once, I've told you a thousand times. I won't *have* you chasing the geese!" she said, and crumpling Mr. Floyd's letter in her hand, she held Johnny fast and herded the geese back into the orchard.

"How could I think of marriage!" she said to herself bitterly, as she fastened the gate with a piece of wire. She had always disliked red hair in men, she thought, thinking of Mr. Floyd's appearance, that night when the boys had gone to bed. And pushing her work-box away, she drew the blotting-paper towards her, and read Mr. Floyd's letter again, and her breast went up and down when she came to the word "love," but not so fast this time, for she saw Johnny chasing the geese, and knew that it was impossible for her to marry any one— let alone Mr. Floyd, who was so much younger than she was, but what a nice man—and such a scholar too.

"Dear Mr. Floyd," she wrote.—"Did I forget about the cheese?" she wondered, laying down her pen. No, she had told Rebecca that the cheese was in the hall. "I am much surprised . . ." she wrote.

But the letter which Mr. Floyd found on the table when he got up early next morning did not begin "I am much surprised," and it was such a motherly, respectful, inconsequent, regretful letter that he kept it for many years; long after his marriage with Miss Wimbush, of Andover;[1] long after he had left the village. For he asked for a parish in Sheffield,[2] which was given him; and, sending for Archer, Jacob, and John to say good-bye, he told them to choose whatever they liked in his study to remember him by. Archer chose a paper-knife, because he did not like to choose anything too good; Jacob chose the works of Byron[3] in one volume; John, who was still too young to make a proper choice, chose Mr. Floyd's kitten, which his brothers thought an absurd choice, but Mr. Floyd upheld him when he said: "It has fur like you." Then Mr. Floyd spoke about the King's Navy (to which Archer was going); and about Rugby[4] (to which Jacob was going); and next day he received a silver salver and went—first to Sheffield, where he met Miss Wimbush, who was on a visit to her uncle, then to Hackney—then to Maresfield House, of which he became the principal, and finally, becoming editor of a well-known series of Ecclesiastical Biographies, he retired to Hampstead with his wife and daughter, and is often to be seen feeding the ducks on Leg of Mutton Pond.[5] As for Mrs. Flanders's letter—when he looked

1. Small agricultural town in the south of England near Southampton.
2. Large industrial city about two hundred miles south of Scarborough.
3. English Romantic poet (1788–1824), author of *Childe Harold's Pilgrimage* (1812) and many other works.
4. Famous public (private) school for boys, founded 1567.
5. On the western side of Hampstead Heath; Hackney: working-class suburb in east London; Hampstead: affluent suburb in northwest London.

for it the other day he could not find it, and did not like to ask his wife whether she had put it away. Meeting Jacob in Piccadilly[6] lately, he recognized him after three seconds. But Jacob had grown such a fine young man that Mr. Floyd did not like to stop him in the street.

"Dear me," said Mrs. Flanders, when she read in the *Scarborough and Harrogate Courier*[7] that the Rev. Andrew Floyd, etc., etc., had been made Principal of Maresfield House, "that must be our Mr. Floyd."

A slight gloom fell upon the table. Jacob was helping himself to jam; the postman was talking to Rebecca in the kitchen; there was a bee humming at the yellow flower which nodded at the open window. They were all alive, that is to say, while poor Mr. Floyd was becoming Principal of Maresfield House.

Mrs. Flanders got up and went over to the fender and stroked Topaz on the neck behind the ears.

"Poor Topaz," she said (for Mr. Floyd's kitten was now a very old cat, a little mangy behind the ears, and one of these days would have to be killed).

"Poor old Topaz," said Mrs. Flanders, as he stretched himself out in the sun, and she smiled, thinking how she had had him gelded, and how she did not like red hair in men. Smiling, she went into the kitchen.

Jacob drew rather a dirty pocket-handkerchief across his face. He went upstairs to his room.

The stag-beetle[8] dies slowly (it was John who collected the beetles). Even on the second day its legs were supple. But the butterflies were dead. A whiff of rotten eggs had vanquished the pale clouded yellows[9] which came pelting across the orchard and up Dods Hill and away on to the moor, now lost behind a furze[1] bush, then off again helter-skelter in a broiling sun. A fritillary basked on a white stone in the Roman camp. From the valley came the sound of church bells. They were all eating roast beef in Scarborough; for it was Sun-

---

6. Major thoroughfare in central London, starting at the south-west corner of Hyde Park.
7. A fictitious local newspaper.
8. Large black or reddish-brown European beetle.
9. Species of butterfly. A number of different species are mentioned in the following pages, including "fritillary," "death's head moth," "red underwing," "straw-bordered underwing," "blues," "painted ladies," "commas," and "white admiral."
1. More commonly known as "gorse"; spiny evergreen shrub with small yellow flowers, common on wastelands and moorlands in Britain.

day when Jacob caught the pale clouded yellows in the clover field, eight miles from home.

Rebecca had caught the death's-head moth in the kitchen.

A strong smell of camphor[2] came from the butterfly boxes.

Mixed with the smell of camphor was the unmistakable smell of seaweed. Tawny ribbons hung on the door. The sun beat straight upon them.

The upper wings of the moth which Jacob held were undoubtedly marked with kidney-shaped spots of a fulvous[3] hue. But there was no crescent upon the underwing. The tree had fallen the night he caught it. There had been a volley of pistol-shots suddenly in the depths of the wood. And his mother had taken him for a burglar when he came home late. The only one of her sons who never obeyed her, she said.

Morris[4] called it "an extremely local insect found in damp or marshy places." But Morris is sometimes wrong. Sometimes Jacob, choosing a very fine pen, made a correction in the margin.

The tree had fallen, though it was a windless night, and the lantern, stood upon the ground, had lit up the still green leaves and the dead beech leaves. It was a dry place. A toad was there. And the red underwing had circled round the light and flashed and gone. The red underwing had never come back, though Jacob had waited. It was after twelve when he crossed the lawn and saw his mother in the bright room, playing patience,[5] sitting up.

"How you frightened me!" she had cried. She thought something dreadful had happened. And he woke Rebecca, who had to be up so early.

There he stood pale, come out of the depths of darkness, in the hot room, blinking at the light.

No, it could not be a straw-bordered underwing.

The mowing-machine always wanted oiling. Barnet turned it under Jacob's window, and it creaked—creaked, and rattled across the lawn and creaked again.

Now it was clouding over.

Back came the sun, dazzlingly.

It fell like an eye upon the stirrups, and then suddenly and yet very gently rested upon the bed, upon the alarum clock, and upon the butterfly box stood open. The pale clouded yellows had pelted over the moor; they had zigzagged across the purple clover. The fritillaries flaunted along the hedgerows. The blues settled on little

---

2. Strong-smelling substance used to kill moths.
3. Yellowish.
4. Francis Orpen Morris, author of *A History of British Butterflies* (1853) and *A Natural History of British Moths* (1872), both of which went into many editions.
5. Solitaire, a card game played by one person.

bones lying on the turf with the sun beating on them, and the painted ladies and the peacocks feasted upon bloody entrails dropped by a hawk. Miles away from home, in a hollow among teasles beneath a ruin, he had found the commas. He had seen a white admiral circling higher and higher round an oak tree, but he had never caught it. An old cottage woman living alone, high up, had told him of a purple butterfly which came every summer to her garden. The fox cubs played in the gorse in the early morning, she told him. And if you looked out at dawn you could always see two badgers. Sometimes they knocked each other over like two boys fighting, she said.

"You won't go far this afternoon, Jacob," said his mother, popping her head in at the door, "for the Captain's coming to say good-bye." It was the last day of the Easter holidays.

Wednesday was Captain Barfoot's day. He dressed himself very neatly in blue serge,[6] took his rubber-shod stick—for he was lame and wanted two fingers on the left hand, having served his country— and set out from the house with the flagstaff precisely at four o'clock in the afternoon.

At three Mr. Dickens, the bath-chair man, had called for Mrs. Barfoot.

"Move me," she would say to Mr. Dickens, after sitting on the esplanade for fifteen minutes. And again, "That'll do, thank you, Mr. Dickens." At the first command he would seek the sun; at the second he would stay the chair there in the bright strip.

An old inhabitant himself, he had much in common with Mrs. Barfoot—James Coppard's daughter. The drinking-fountain, where West Street joins Broad Street, is the gift of James Coppard, who was mayor at the time of Queen Victoria's jubilee,[7] and Coppard is painted upon municipal watering-carts and over shop windows, and upon the zinc blinds of solicitors'[8] consulting-room windows. But Ellen Barfoot never visited the Aquarium (though she had known Captain Boase who had caught the shark quite well), and when the men came by with the posters she eyed them superciliously, for she knew that she would never see the Pierrots, or the brothers Zeno, or Daisy Budd and her troupe of performing seals.[9] For Ellen Barfoot in her bath-chair on the esplanade was a prisoner—civilization's prisoner—all the bars of her cage falling across the esplanade on sunny

6. Strong fabric, usually made of wool, with a surface pattern of diagonal ridges.
7. Queen Victoria's Golden Jubilee was in 1887 and her Diamond Jubilee in 1897.
8. Lawyers.
9. Fictitious circus acts. Pierrots: clowns.

days when the town hall, the drapery stores, the swimming-bath, and
the memorial hall striped the ground with shadow.

An old inhabitant himself, Mr. Dickens would stand a little behind
her, smoking his pipe. She would ask him questions—who people
were—who now kept Mr. Jones's shop—then about the season—
and had Mrs. Dickens tried, whatever it might be—the words issuing
from her lips like crumbs of dry biscuit.

She closed her eyes. Mr. Dickens took a turn. The feelings of a
man had not altogether deserted him, though as you saw him coming
towards you, you noticed how one knobbed black boot swung trem-
ulously in front of the other; how there was a shadow between his
waistcoat and his trousers; how he leant forward unsteadily, like an
old horse who finds himself suddenly out of the shafts drawing no
cart. But as Mr. Dickens sucked in the smoke and puffed it out again,
the feelings of a man were perceptible in his eyes. He was thinking
how Captain Barfoot was now on his way to Mount Pleasant; Captain Barfoot, his master. For at home in the little sitting-room above
the mews, with the canary in the window, and the girls at the sewing-
machine, and Mrs. Dickens huddled up with the rheumatics—at
home where he was made little of, the thought of being in the employ
of Captain Barfoot supported him. He liked to think that while he
chatted with Mrs. Barfoot on the front, he helped the Captain on
his way to Mrs. Flanders. He, a man, was in charge of Mrs. Barfoot,
a woman.

Turning, he saw that she was chatting with Mrs. Rogers. Turning
again, he saw that Mrs. Rogers had moved on. So he came back to
the bath-chair, and Mrs. Barfoot asked him the time, and he took
out his great silver watch and told her the time very obligingly, as if
he knew a great deal more about the time and everything than she
did. But Mrs. Barfoot knew that Captain Barfoot was on his way to
Mrs. Flanders.

Indeed he was well on his way there, having left the tram, and
seeing Dods Hill to the south-east, green against a blue sky that was
suffused with dust colour on the horizon. He was marching up the
hill. In spite of his lameness there was something military in his
approach. Mrs. Jarvis, as she came out of the Rectory gate, saw him
coming, and her Newfoundland dog, Nero, slowly swept his tail from
side to side.

"Oh, Captain Barfoot!" Mrs. Jarvis exclaimed.

"Good-day, Mrs. Jarvis," said the Captain.

They walked on together, and when they reached Mrs. Flanders's
gate Captain Barfoot took off his tweed cap, and said, bowing very
courteously:

"Good-day to you, Mrs. Jarvis."

And Mrs. Jarvis walked on alone.

She was going to walk on the moor. Had she again been pacing her lawn late at night? Had she again tapped on the study window and cried: "Look at the moon, look at the moon, Herbert!"

And Herbert looked at the moon.

Mrs. Jarvis walked on the moor when she was unhappy, going as far as a certain saucer-shaped hollow, though she always meant to go to a more distant ridge; and there she sat down, and took out the little book hidden beneath her cloak and read a few lines of poetry, and looked about her. She was not very unhappy, and, seeing that she was forty-five, never perhaps would be very unhappy, desperately unhappy that is, and leave her husband, and ruin a good man's career, as she sometimes threatened.

Still there is no need to say what risks a clergyman's wife runs when she walks on the moor. Short, dark, with kindling eyes, a pheasant's feather in her hat, Mrs. Jarvis was just the sort of woman to lose her faith upon the moors—to confound her God with the universal that is—but she did not lose her faith, did not leave her husband, never read her poem through, and went on walking the moors, looking at the moon behind the elm trees, and feeling as she sat on the grass high above Scarborough . . . Yes, yes, when the lark soars; when the sheep, moving a step or two onwards, crop the turf, and at the same time set their bells tinkling; when the breeze first blows, then dies down, leaving the cheek kissed; when the ships on the sea below seem to cross each other and pass on as if drawn by an invisible hand; when there are distant concussions in the air and phantom horsemen galloping, ceasing; when the horizon swims blue, green, emotional—then Mrs. Jarvis, heaving a sigh, thinks to herself, "If only some one could give me . . . if I could give some one . . ." But she does not know what she wants to give, nor who could give it her.

"Mrs. Flanders stepped out only five minutes ago, Captain," said Rebecca. Captain Barfoot sat him down in the arm-chair to wait. Resting his elbows on the arms, putting one hand over the other, sticking his lame leg straight out, and placing the stick with the rubber ferrule[1] beside it, he sat perfectly still. There was something rigid about him. Did he think? Probably the same thoughts again and again. But were they "nice" thoughts, interesting thoughts? He was a man with a temper; tenacious; faithful. Women would have felt, "Here is law. Here is order. Therefore we must cherish this man.

1. Rubber cap protecting the tip of a walking-stick.

He is on the Bridge at night," and, handing him his cup, or whatever it might be, would run on to visions of shipwreck and disaster, in which all the passengers come tumbling from their cabins, and there is the captain, buttoned in his pea-jacket;[2] matched with the storm, vanquished by it but by none other. "Yet I have a soul," Mrs. Jarvis would bethink her, as Captain Barfoot suddenly blew his nose in a great red bandanna handkerchief, "and it's the man's stupidity that's the cause of this, and the storm's my storm as well as his" . . . so Mrs. Jarvis would bethink her when the Captain dropped in to see them and found Herbert out, and spent two or three hours, almost silent, sitting in the arm-chair. But Betty Flanders thought nothing of the kind.

"Oh, Captain," said Mrs. Flanders, bursting into the drawing-room, "I had to run after Barker's man . . . I hope Rebecca . . . I hope Jacob . . ."

She was very much out of breath, yet not at all upset, and as she put down the hearth-brush which she had bought of the oil-man, she said it was hot, flung the window further open, straightened a cover, picked up a book, as if she were very confident, very fond of the Captain, and a great many years younger than he was. Indeed, in her blue apron she did not look more than thirty-five. He was well over fifty.

She moved her hands about the table; the Captain moved his head from side to side, and made little sounds, as Betty went on chattering, completely at his ease—after twenty years.

"Well," he said at length, "I've heard from Mr. Polegate."

He had heard from Mr. Polegate that he could advise nothing better than to send a boy to one of the universities.

"Mr. Floyd was at Cambridge . . . no, at Oxford . . . well, at one or the other," said Mrs. Flanders.

She looked out of the window. Little windows, and the lilac and green of the garden were reflected in her eyes.

"Archer is doing very well," she said. "I have a very nice report from Captain Maxwell."

"I will leave you the letter to show Jacob," said the Captain, putting it clumsily back in its envelope.

"Jacob is after his butterflies as usual," said Mrs. Flanders irritably, but was surprised by a sudden afterthought, "Cricket begins this week, of course."

2. Short overcoat of coarse wool, usually worn by sailors.

"Edward Jenkinson has handed in his resignation," said Captain Barfoot.

"Then you will stand for the Council?" Mrs. Flanders exclaimed, looking the Captain full in the face.

"Well, about that," Captain Barfoot began, settling himself rather deeper in his chair.

Jacob Flanders, therefore, went up to Cambridge in October, 1906.

III

"This is not a smoking-carriage," Mrs. Norman protested, nervously but very feebly, as the door swung open and a powerfully built young man jumped in. He seemed not to hear her. The train did not stop before it reached Cambridge, and here she was shut up alone, in a railway carriage, with a young man.

She touched the spring of her dressing-case, and ascertained that the scent-bottle and a novel from Mudie's[1] were both handy (the young man was standing up with his back to her, putting his bag in the rack). She would throw the scent-bottle with her right hand, she decided, and tug the communication cord with her left. She was fifty years of age, and had a son at college. Nevertheless, it is a fact that men are dangerous. She read half a column of her newspaper; then stealthily looked over the edge to decide the question of safety by the infallible test of appearance. . . . She would like to offer him her paper. But do young men read the *Morning Post*?[2] She looked to see what he was reading—the *Daily Telegraph*.[3]

Taking note of socks (loose), of tie (shabby), she once more reached his face. She dwelt upon his mouth. The lips were shut. The eyes bent down, since he was reading. All was firm, yet youthful, indifferent, unconscious—as for knocking one down! No, no, no! She looked out of the window, smiling slightly now, and then came back again, for he didn't notice her. Grave, unconscious . . . now he looked up, past her . . . he seemed so out of place, somehow, alone with an elderly lady . . . then he fixed his eyes—which were blue— on the landscape. He had not realized her presence, she thought.

1. Popular circulating library, known for its strict moral standards in the selection of its books.
2. Right-wing daily newspaper, popular with retired officers.
3. Founded in 1855 as a cheaper rival daily newspaper to the *Times*, aimed at the lower middle-class.

Yet it was none of *her* fault that this was not a smoking-carriage—if that was what he meant.

Nobody sees any one as he is, let alone an elderly lady sitting opposite a strange young man in a railway carriage. They see a whole—they see all sorts of things—they see themselves. . . . Mrs. Norman now read three pages of one of Mr. Norris's novels.[4] Should she say to the young man (and after all he was just the same age as her own boy): "If you want to smoke, don't mind me"? No: he seemed absolutely indifferent to her presence . . . she did not wish to interrupt.

But since, even at her age, she noted his indifference, presumably he was in some way or other—to her at least—nice, handsome, interesting, distinguished, well built, like her own boy? One must do the best one can with her report. Anyhow, this was Jacob Flanders, aged nineteen. It is no use trying to sum people up. One must follow hints, not exactly what is said, nor yet entirely what is done—for instance, when the train drew into the station, Mr. Flanders burst open the door, and put the lady's dressing-case out for her, saying, or rather mumbling: "Let me" very shyly; indeed he was rather clumsy about it.

"Who . . ." said the lady, meeting her son; but as there was a great crowd on the platform and Jacob had already gone, she did not finish her sentence. As this was Cambridge, as she was staying there for the week-end, as she saw nothing but young men all day long, in streets and round tables, this sight of her fellow-traveller was completely lost in her mind, as the crooked pin dropped by a child into the wishing-well twirls in the water and disappears for ever.

They say the sky is the same everywhere. Travellers, the shipwrecked, exiles, and the dying draw comfort from the thought, and no doubt if you are of a mystical tendency, consolation, and even explanation, shower down from the unbroken surface. But above Cambridge—anyhow above the roof of King's College Chapel—there is a difference. Out at sea a great city will cast a brightness into the night. Is it fanciful to suppose the sky, washed into the crevices of King's College Chapel, lighter, thinner, more sparkling than the sky elsewhere? Does Cambridge burn not only into the night, but into the day?

---

4. Frank Norris (1847–1925), popular American novelist. Woolf reviewed two of his novels in 1920 and 1921.

Look, as they pass into service, how airily the gowns blow out, as though nothing dense and corporeal were within. What sculptured faces, what certainty, authority controlled by piety, although great boots march under the gowns. In what orderly procession they advance. Thick wax candles stand upright; young men rise in white gowns; while the subservient eagle bears up for inspection the great white book.

An inclined plane of light comes accurately through each window, purple and yellow even in its most diffused dust, while, where it breaks upon stone, that stone is softly chalked red, yellow, and purple. Neither snow nor greenery, winter nor summer, has power over the old stained glass. As the sides of a lantern protect the flame so that it burns steady even in the wildest night—burns steady and gravely illumines the tree-trunks—so inside the Chapel all was orderly. Gravely sounded the voices; wisely the organ replied, as if buttressing human faith with the assent of the elements. The white-robed figures crossed from side to side; now mounted steps, now descended, all very orderly.

. . . If you stand a lantern under a tree every insect in the forest creeps up to it—a curious assembly, since though they scramble and swing and knock their heads against the glass, they seem to have no purpose—something senseless inspires them. One gets tired of watching them, as they amble round the lantern and blindly tap as if for admittance, one large toad being the most besotted of any and shouldering his way through the rest. Ah, but what's that? A terrifying volley of pistol-shots rings out—cracks sharply; ripples spread—silence laps smooth over sound. A tree—a tree has fallen, a sort of death in the forest. After that, the wind in the trees sounds melancholy.

But this service in King's College Chapel—why allow women to take part in it? Surely, if the mind wanders (and Jacob looked extraordinarily vacant, his head thrown back, his hymn-book open at the wrong place), if the mind wanders it is because several hat shops and cupboards upon cupboards of coloured dresses are displayed upon rush-bottomed chairs. Though heads and bodies may be devout enough, one has a sense of individuals—some like blue, others brown; some feathers, others pansies and forget-me-nots. No one would think of bringing a dog into church. For though a dog is all very well on a gravel path, and shows no disrespect to flowers, the way he wanders down an aisle, looking, lifting a paw, and approaching a pillar with a purpose that makes the blood run cold with horror (should you be one of a congregation—alone, shyness is out of the question), a dog destroys the service completely. So do these women—though separately devout, distinguished, and vouched for by the theology, mathematics, Latin, and Greek of their husbands. Heaven knows why it is. For one thing, thought Jacob, they're as ugly as sin.

Now there was a scraping and murmuring. He caught Timmy Durrant's eye; looked very sternly at him; and then, very solemnly, winked.

"Waverley," the villa on the road to Girton[5] was called, not that Mr. Plumer admired Scott or would have chosen any name at all, but names are useful when you have to entertain undergraduates, and as they sat waiting for the fourth undergraduate, on Sunday at lunch-time, there was talk of names upon gates.

"How tiresome," Mrs. Plumer interrupted impulsively. "Does anybody know Mr. Flanders?"

Mr. Durrant knew him; and therefore blushed slightly, and said, awkwardly, something about being sure—looking at Mr. Plumer and hitching the right leg of his trouser as he spoke. Mr. Plumer got up and stood in front of the fireplace. Mrs. Plumer laughed like a straight-forward friendly fellow. In short, anything more horrible than the scene, the setting, the prospect, even the May garden being afflicted with chill sterility and a cloud choosing that moment to cross the sun, cannot be imagined. There was the garden, of course. Every one at the same moment looked at it. Owing to the cloud, the leaves ruffled grey, and the sparrows—there were two sparrows.

"I think," said Mrs. Plumer, taking advantage of the momentary respite, while the young men stared at the garden, to look at her husband, and he, not accepting full responsibility for the act, nevertheless touched the bell.

There can be no excuse for this outrage upon one hour of human life, save the reflection which occurred to Mr. Plumer as he carved the mutton, that if no don[6] ever gave a luncheon party, if Sunday after Sunday passed, if men went down, became lawyers, doctors, members of Parliament, business men—if no don ever gave a luncheon party——

"Now, does lamb make the mint sauce, or mint sauce make the lamb?" he asked the young man next him, to break a silence which had already lasted five minutes and a half.

"I don't know, sir," said the young man, blushing very vividly.

5. Women's college at Cambridge, established 1869 in Hitchin, moved to a location in Cambridge a few miles up Girton Road in 1873. "Waverley": historical novel by Sir Walter Scott (1771–1832), published in 1814.
6. University professor at Oxford or Cambridge; mutton: meat from an adult sheep.

At this moment in came Mr. Flanders. He had mistaken the time. Now, though they had finished their meat, Mrs. Plumer took a second helping of cabbage. Jacob determined, of course, that he would eat his meat in the time it took her to finish her cabbage, looking once or twice to measure his speed—only he was infernally hungry. Seeing this, Mrs. Plumer said that she was sure Mr. Flanders would not mind—and the tart was brought in. Nodding in a peculiar way, she directed the maid to give Mr. Flanders a second helping of mutton. She glanced at the mutton. Not much of the leg would be left for luncheon.

It was none of her fault—since how could she control her father begetting her forty years ago in the suburbs of Manchester?[7] and once begotten, how could she do other than grow up cheese-paring,[8] ambitious, with an instinctively accurate notion of the rungs of the ladder and an ant-like assiduity in pushing George Plumer ahead of her to the top of the ladder? What was at the top of the ladder? A sense that all the rungs were beneath one apparently; since by the time that George Plumer became Professor of Physics, or whatever it might be, Mrs. Plumer could only be in a condition to cling tight to her eminence, peer down at the ground, and goad her two plain daughters to climb the rungs of the ladder.

"I was down at the races yesterday," she said, "with my two little girls."

It was none of *their* fault either. In they came to the drawing-room, in white frocks and blue sashes. They handed the cigarettes. Rhoda had inherited her father's cold grey eyes. Cold grey eyes George Plumer had, but in them was an abstract light. He could talk about Persia and the Trade winds, the Reform Bill and the cycle of the harvests.[9] Books were on his shelves by Wells and Shaw; on the table serious sixpenny weeklies[1] written by pale men in muddy boots—the weekly creak and screech of brains rinsed in cold water and wrung dry—melancholy papers.

"I don't feel that I know the truth about anything till I've read them both!" said Mrs. Plumer brightly, tapping the table of contents with her bare red hand, upon which the ring looked so incongruous.

---

7. Industrial town in the north of England.
8. Mean with money.
9. The three Reform Bills formed the series of parliamentary acts in 1832, 1867, and 1884–85 that extended voting rights among British men; Persia: modern-day Iran; trade winds: easterly winds, named by sailors who depended on them for voyages in trading ships.
1. H. G. Wells (1866–1946), British novelist and journalist, author of *The Time Machine* (1895), and member of the Fabian society, a middle-class socialist organization; George Bernard Shaw (1856–1950), Irish playwright and journalist, author of *Mrs Warren's Profession* (1902) and many other works, and founder of the Fabian society in 1884. Sixpence was the standard price for a weekly magazine. Woolf may have been thinking of *The New Statesman*, a sixpenny weekly founded by the Fabian society, including Shaw, in 1913 (although it did not exist in the year during which this scene is set, 1907).

"Oh God, oh God, oh God!" exclaimed Jacob, as the four under-graduates left the house. "Oh, my God!"

"Bloody beastly!" he said, scanning the street for lilac or bicycle—anything to restore his sense of freedom.

"Bloody beastly," he said to Timmy Durrant, summing up his discomfort at the world shown him at lunch-time, a world capable of existing—there was no doubt about that—but so unnecessary, such a thing to believe in—Shaw and Wells and the serious sixpenny weeklies! What were they after, scrubbing and demolishing these elderly people? Had they never read Homer, Shakespeare, the Elizabethans? He saw it clearly outlined against the feelings he drew from youth and natural inclination. The poor devils had rigged up this meagre object. Yet something of pity was in him. Those wretched little girls——

The extent to which he was disturbed proves that he was already agog.[2] Insolent he was and inexperienced, but sure enough the cities which the elderly of the race have built upon the skyline showed like brick suburbs, barracks, and places of discipline against a red and yellow flame. He was impressionable; but the word is contradicted by the composure with which he hollowed his hand to screen a match. He was a young man of substance.

Anyhow, whether undergraduate or shop boy, man or woman, it must come as a shock about the age of twenty—the world of the elderly—thrown up in such black outline upon what we are; upon the reality; the moors and Byron; the sea and the lighthouse; the sheep's jaw with the yellow teeth in it; upon the obstinate irrepressible conviction which makes youth so intolerably disagreeable—"I am what I am, and intend to be it," for which there will be no form in the world unless Jacob makes one for himself. The Plumers will try to prevent him from making it. Wells and Shaw and the serious sixpenny weeklies will sit on its head. Every time he lunches out on Sunday—at dinner parties and tea parties—there will be this same shock—horror—discomfort—then pleasure, for he draws into him at every step as he walks by the river such steady certainty, such reassurance from all sides, the trees bowing, the grey spires soft in the blue, voices blowing and seeming suspended in the air, the springy air of May, the elastic air with its particles—chestnut bloom, pollen, whatever it is that gives the May air its potency, blurring the trees, gumming the buds, daubing the green. And the river too runs

2. Very interested and excited.

past, not at flood, nor swiftly, but cloying the oar that dips in it and drops white drops from the blade, swimming green and deep over the bowed rushes, as if lavishly caressing them.

Where they moored their boat the trees showered down, so that their topmost leaves trailed in the ripples and the green wedge that lay in the water being made of leaves shifted in leaf-breadths as the real leaves shifted. Now there was a shiver of wind—instantly an edge of sky; and as Durrant ate cherries he dropped the stunted yellow cherries through the green wedge of leaves, their stalks twinkling as they wriggled in and out, and sometimes one half-bitten cherry would go down red into the green. The meadow was on a level with Jacob's eyes as he lay back; gilt with buttercups, but the grass did not run like the thin green water of the graveyard grass about to overflow the tombstones, but stood juicy and thick. Looking up, backwards, he saw the legs of children deep in the grass, and the legs of cows. Munch, munch, he heard; then a short step through the grass; then again munch, munch, munch, as they tore the grass short at the roots. In front of him two white butterflies circled higher and higher round the elm tree.

"Jacob's off," thought Durrant, looking up from his novel. He kept reading a few pages and then looking up in a curiously methodical manner, and each time he looked up he took a few cherries out of the bag and ate them abstractedly. Other boats passed them, crossing the backwater from side to side to avoid each other, for many were now moored, and there were now white dresses and a flaw in the column of air between two trees, round which curled a thread of blue—Lady Miller's picnic party. Still more boats kept coming, and Durrant, without getting up, shoved their boat closer to the bank.

"Oh-h-h-h," groaned Jacob, as the boat rocked, and the trees rocked, and the white dresses and the white flannel trousers drew out long and wavering up the bank.

"Oh-h-h-h!" He sat up, and felt as if a piece of elastic had snapped in his face.

"They're friends of my mother's," said Durrant. "So old Bow took no end of trouble about the boat."

And this boat had gone from Falmouth to St. Ives Bay,[3] all round the coast. A larger boat, a ten-ton yacht, about the twentieth of June, properly fitted out, Durrant said . . .

"There's the cash difficulty," said Jacob.

"My people'll see to that," said Durrant (the son of a banker, deceased).

---

3. Distance of approximately sixty miles, around the western tip of Cornwall.

"I intend to preserve my economic independence," said Jacob stiffly. (He was getting excited.)

"My mother said something about going to Harrogate,"[4] he said with a little annoyance, feeling the pocket where he kept his letters.

"Was that true about your uncle becoming a Mohammedan?"[5] asked Timmy Durrant.

Jacob had told the story of his Uncle Morty in Durrant's room the night before.

"I expect he's feeding the sharks, if the truth were known," said Jacob. "I say, Durrant, there's none left !" he exclaimed, crumpling the bag which had held the cherries, and throwing it into the river. He saw Lady Miller's picnic party on the island as he threw the bag into the river.

A sort of awkwardness, grumpiness, gloom came into his eyes.

"Shall we move on . . . this beastly crowd . . ." he said.

So up they went, past the island.

The feathery white moon never let the sky grow dark; all night the chestnut blossoms were white in the green; dim was the cow-parsley in the meadows.

The waiters at Trinity[6] must have been shuffling china plates like cards, from the clatter that could be heard in the Great Court. Jacob's rooms, however, were in Neville's Court;[7] at the top; so that reaching his door one went in a little out of breath; but he wasn't there. Dining in Hall, presumably. It will be quite dark in Neville's Court long before midnight, only the pillars opposite will always be white, and the pavement. A curious effect the gate has, like lace upon pale green. Even in the window you hear the plates; a hum of talk, too, from the diners; the Hall lit up, and the swing-doors opening and shutting with a soft thud. Some are late.

Jacob's room had a round table and two low chairs. There were yellow flags[8] in a jar on the mantelpiece; a photograph of his mother; cards from societies with little raised crescents,[9] coats of arms, and initials; notes and pipes; on the table lay paper ruled with a red margin—an essay, no doubt—"Does History consist of the Biogra-

---

4. Popular spa town on the edge of the Pennine Hills in the north of England, about forty-five miles from Scarborough.
5. Obsolete term for Muslim.
6. One of the largest and most prestigious colleges of Cambridge University, attended by Virginia Woolf's brother Thoby Stephen between 1899 and 1902.
7. Misspelling of "Nevile's Court."
8. Irises.
9. Symbol in heraldry.

phies of Great Men?" There were books enough; very few French books; but then any one who's worth anything reads just what he likes, as the mood takes him, with extravagant enthusiasm. Lives of the Duke of Wellington, for example; Spinoza; the works of Dickens; the *Faery Queen*; a Greek dictionary with the petals of poppies pressed to silk between the pages; all the Elizabethans.[1] His slippers were incredibly shabby, like boats burnt to the water's rim. Then there were photographs from the Greeks, and a mezzotint from Sir Joshua—all very English. The works of Jane Austen, too, in deference, perhaps, to some one else's standard. Carlyle was a prize. There were books upon the Italian painters of the Renaissance, a *Manual of the Diseases of the Horse*, and all the usual text-books. [2] Listless is the air in an empty room, just swelling the curtain; the flowers in the jar shift. One fibre in the wicker arm-chair creaks, though no one sits there.

Coming down the steps a little sideways [Jacob sat on the window-seat talking to Durrant; he smoked, and Durrant looked at the map], the old man, with his hands locked behind him, his gown[3] floating black, lurched, unsteadily, near the wall; then, upstairs he went into his room. Then another, who raised his hand and praised the columns, the gate, the sky; another, tripping and smug. Each went up a staircase; three lights were lit in the dark windows.

If any light burns above Cambridge, it must be from three such rooms; Greek burns here; science there; philosophy on the ground floor. Poor old Huxtable can't walk straight;—Sopwith, too, has praised the sky any night these twenty years; and Cowan still chuckles at the same stories. It is not simple, or pure, or wholly splendid, the lamp of learning, since if you see them there under its light (whether Rossetti's on the wall, or Van Goch[4] reproduced, whether

1. Duke of Wellington (1769–1852), commander of British troops during the Napoleonic Wars (1807–14) against the French, defeated Napoleon at Waterloo in 1815; Baruch Spinoza (1632–1677), Dutch philosopher, one of the leading figures of seventeenth-century rationalism; Charles Dickens (1812–1870), British novelist, author of *Oliver Twist* (1837–89), *Our Mutual Friend* (1862–65), etc.; *Faerie Queene*, allegorical epic poem in six books published in 1590 and 1596, written by Edmund Spenser (c. 1552–1599).
2. Mezzotint: a print made from an engraved copper plate original; Sir Joshua Reynolds (1723–1792), British portrait painter Jane Austen (1776–1817), British novelist, author of *Pride and Prejudice* (1813) and other works; Thomas Carlyle (1795–1881), British writer and social critic; no book with the exact title *Manual of the Diseases of the Horse* exists.
3. Academic robe.
4. Dante Gabriel Rossetti (1828–1882), British painter, one of the founders of the pre-Raphaelite brotherhood; Van Goch, alternative spelling of (Vincent) Van Gogh (1853–1890), Dutch post-impressionist painter.

there are lilacs in the bowl or rusty pipes), how priestly they look!
How like a suburb where you go to see a view and eat a special cake!
"We are the sole purveyors of this cake." Back you go to London; for
the treat is over.

Old Professor Huxtable, performing with the method of a clock
his change of dress, let himself down into his chair; filled his pipe;
chose his paper; crossed his feet; and extracted his glasses. The
whole flesh of his face then fell into folds as if props were removed.
Yet strip a whole seat of an underground railway carriage of its heads
and old Huxtable's head will hold them all. Now, as his eye goes
down the print, what a procession tramps through the corridors of
his brain, orderly, quick-stepping, and reinforced, as the march goes
on, by fresh runnels, till the whole hall, dome, whatever one calls it,
is populous with ideas. Such a muster takes place in no other brain.
Yet sometimes there he'll sit for hours together, gripping the arm of
the chair, like a man holding fast because stranded, and then, just
because his corn twinges, or it may be the gout, what execrations,
and, dear me, to hear him talk of money, taking out his leather purse
and grudging even the smallest silver coin, secretive and suspicious
as an old peasant woman with all her lies. Strange paralysis and
constriction—marvellous illumination. Serene over it all rides the
great full brow, and sometimes asleep or in the quiet spaces of the
night you might fancy that on a pillow of stone he lay triumphant.

Sopwith, meanwhile, advancing with a curious trip from the fireplace, cut the chocolate cake into segments. Until midnight or later
there would be undergraduates in his room, sometimes as many as
twelve, sometimes three or four; but nobody got up when they went
or when they came; Sopwith went on talking. Talking, talking, talking—as if everything could be talked—the soul itself slipped through
the lips in thin silver disks which dissolve in young men's minds like
silver, like moonlight. Oh, far away they'd remember it, and deep in
dulness gaze back on it, and come to refresh themselves again.

"Well, I never. That's old Chucky. My dear boy, how's the world
treating you?" And in came poor little Chucky, the unsuccessful pro-
vincial, Stenhouse his real name, but of course Sopwith brought
back by using the other everything, everything, "all I could never
be"—yes, though next day, buying his newspaper and catching the
early train, it all seemed to him childish, absurd; the chocolate cake,
the young men; Sopwith summing things up; no, not all; he would
send his son there. He would save every penny to send his son there.
Sopwith went on talking; twining stiff fibres of awkward speech—
things young men blurted out—plaiting them round his own smooth
garland, making the bright side show, the vivid greens, the sharp

thorns, manliness. He loved it. Indeed to Sopwith a man could say anything, until perhaps he'd grown old, or gone under, gone deep, when the silver disks would tinkle hollow, and the inscription read a little too simple, and the old stamp look too pure, and the impress always the same—a Greek boy's head. But he would respect still. A woman, divining the priest, would, involuntarily, despise.

Cowan, Erasmus Cowan, sipped his port alone, or with one rosy little man, whose memory held precisely the same span of time; sipped his port, and told his stories, and without book before him intoned Latin, Virgil, and Catullus,[5] as if language were wine upon his lips. Only—sometimes it will come over one—what if the poet strode in? "*This* my image?" he might ask, pointing to the chubby man, whose brain is, after all, Virgil's representative among us, though the body gluttonize, and as for arms, bees, or even the plough, Cowan takes his trips abroad with a French novel in his pocket, a rug about his knees, and is thankful to be home again in his place, in his line, holding up in his snug little mirror the image of Virgil, all rayed round with good stories of the dons of Trinity and red beams of port. But language is wine upon his lips. Nowhere else would Virgil hear the like. And though, as she goes sauntering along the Backs, old Miss Umphelby sings him melodiously enough, accurately too, she is always brought up by this question as she reaches Clare Bridge: "But if I met him, what should I wear?"—and then, taking her way up the avenue towards Newnham,[6] she lets her fancy play upon other details of men's meeting with women which have never got into print. Her lectures, therefore, are not half so well attended as those of Cowan, and the thing she might have said in elucidation of the text for ever left out. In short, face a teacher with the image of the taught and the mirror breaks. But Cowan sipped his port, his exaltation over, no longer the representative of Virgil. No, the builder, assessor, surveyor, rather; ruling lines between names, hanging lists above doors. Such is the fabric through which the light must shine, if shine it can—the light of all these languages, Chinese and Russian, Persian and Arabic, of symbols and figures, of history, of things that are known and things that are about to be known. So that if at night, far out at sea over the tumbling waves, one saw a haze on the waters, a city illuminated, a whiteness even

5. Virgil (70–19 B.C.E.), Roman poet, author of the classical epic *Aeneid* (started 29 B.C.E., unfinished at his death) and of the *Eclogues*, a series of pastoral poems (42–37 B.C.E.); Catullus (84–54 B.C.E.), Roman poet, best known for his love poems to Lesbia. Virginia Woolf quotes from Catullus in the canceled epigraph to *Jacob's Room* (see p. 165).
6. Backs: grounds of a number of Cambridge colleges that back onto the river Cam; Clare Bridge: oldest surviving (mid-seventeenth century) bridge across the Cam; Newnham: a women's college, founded 1880, a brief walk up Sidgwick Avenue from the Backs.

in the sky, such as that now over the Hall of Trinity where they're still dining, or washing up plates, that would be the light burning there—the light of Cambridge.

"Let's go round to Simeon's room," said Jacob, and they rolled up the map, having got the whole thing settled.

All the lights were coming out round the court, and falling on the cobbles, picking out dark patches of grass and single daisies. The young men were now back in their rooms. Heaven knows what they were doing. What was it that could *drop* like that? And leaning down over a foaming window-box, one stopped another hurrying past, and upstairs they went and down they went, until a sort of fulness settled on the court, the hive full of bees, the bees home thick with gold, drowsy, humming, suddenly vocal; the Moonlight Sonata[7] answered by a waltz.

The Moonlight Sonata tinkled away; the waltz crashed. Although young men still went in and out, they walked as if keeping engagements. Now and then there was a thud, as if some heavy piece of furniture had fallen, unexpectedly, of its own accord, not in the general stir of life after dinner. One supposed that young men raised their eyes from their books as the furniture fell. Were they reading? Certainly there was a sense of concentration in the air. Behind the grey walls sat so many young men, some undoubtedly reading, magazines, shilling shockers[8] no doubt; legs, perhaps, over the arms of chairs; smoking; sprawling over tables, and writing while their heads went round in a circle as the pen moved—simple young men, these, who would—but there is no need to think of them grown old; others eating sweets; here they boxed; and, well, Mr. Hawkins must have been mad suddenly to throw up his window and bawl: "Jo—seph! Jo—seph!" and then he ran as hard as ever he could across the court, while an elderly man, in a green apron, carrying an immense pile of tin covers, hesitated, balanced, and then went on. But this was a diversion. There were young men who read, lying in shallow arm-chairs, holding their books as if they had hold in their hands of something that would see them through; they being all in a torment, coming from midland towns, clergymen's sons. Others read Keats.[9]

7. Piano sonata by Ludwig von Beethoven (1770–1827) in C sharp minor, op. 27, No. 2, 1801.
8. Novels about violence or crime, very popular in late Victorian and Edwardian England, costing one shilling.
9. John Keats (1795–1821), British Romantic poet who died tragically young of tuberculosis.

And those long histories in many volumes—surely some one was now beginning at the beginning in order to understand the Holy Roman Empire, as one must. That was part of the concentration, though it would be dangerous on a hot spring night—dangerous, perhaps, to concentrate too much upon single books, actual chapters, when at any moment the door opened and Jacob appeared; or Richard Bonamy, reading Keats no longer, began making long pink spills[1] from an old newspaper, bending forward, and looking eager and contented no more, but almost fierce. Why? Only perhaps that Keats died young—one wants to write poetry too and to love—oh, the brutes! It's damnably difficult. But, after all, not so difficult if on the next staircase, in the large room, there are two, three, five young men all convinced of this—of brutality, that is, and the clear division between right and wrong. There was a sofa, chairs, a square table, and the window being open, one could see how they sat—legs issuing here, one there crumpled in a corner of the sofa; and, presumably, for you could not see him, somebody stood by the fender, talking. Anyhow, Jacob, who sat astride a chair and ate dates from a long box, burst out laughing. The answer came from the sofa corner; for his pipe was held in the air, then replaced. Jacob wheeled round. He had something to say to *that*, though the sturdy red-haired boy at the table seemed to deny it, wagging his head slowly from side to side; and then, taking out his penknife, he dug the point of it again and again into a knot in the table, as if affirming that the voice from the fender spoke the truth—which Jacob could not deny. Possibly, when he had done arranging the date-stones, he might find something to say to it—indeed his lips opened—only then there broke out a roar of laughter.

The laughter died in the air. The sound of it could scarcely have reached any one standing by the Chapel,[2] which stretched along the opposite side of the court. The laughter died out, and only gestures of arms, movements of bodies, could be seen shaping something in the room. Was it an argument? A bet on the boat races? Was it nothing of the sort? What was shaped by the arms and bodies moving in the twilight room?

A step or two beyond the window there was nothing at all, except the enclosing buildings—chimneys upright, roofs horizontal; too much brick and building for a May night, perhaps. And then before one's eyes would come the bare hills of Turkey—sharp lines, dry earth, coloured flowers, and colour on the shoulders of the women, standing naked-legged in the stream to beat linen on the stones. The stream made loops of water round their ankles. But none of that

1. Thin strips of twisted paper used to light fires, candles, etc.
2. Runs along the northern side of Great Court.

could show clearly through the swaddlings and blanketings of the
Cambridge night. The stroke of the clock even was muffled; as if
intoned by somebody reverent from a pulpit; as if generations of
learned men heard the last hour go rolling through their ranks and
issued it, already smooth and time-worn, with their blessing, for the
use of the living.

Was it to receive this gift from the past that the young man came
to the window and stood there, looking out across the court? It was
Jacob. He stood smoking his pipe while the last stroke of the clock
purred softly round him. Perhaps there had been an argument. He
looked satisfied; indeed masterly; which expression changed slightly
as he stood there, the sound of the clock conveying to him (it may
be) a sense of old buildings and time; and himself the inheritor; and
then to-morrow; and friends; at the thought of whom, in sheer confidence and pleasure, it seemed, he yawned and stretched himself.

Meanwhile behind him the shape they had made, whether by argument or not, the spiritual shape, hard yet ephemeral, as of glass
compared with the dark stone of the Chapel, was dashed to splinters,
young men rising from chairs and sofa corners, buzzing and barging
about the room, one driving another against the bedroom door,
which giving way, in they fell. Then Jacob was left there, in the
shallow arm-chair, alone with Masham? Anderson? Simeon? Oh, it
was Simeon. The others had all gone.

". . . Julian the Apostate.[3] . . ." Which of them said that and the
other words murmured round it? But about midnight there sometimes rises, like a veiled figure suddenly woken, a heavy wind; and
this now flapping through Trinity lifted unseen leaves and blurred
everything. "Julian the Apostate"—and then the wind. Up go the elm
branches, out blow the sails, the old schooners[4] rear and plunge, the
grey waves in the hot Indian Ocean tumble sultrily, and then all falls
flat again.

So, if the veiled lady stepped through the Courts of Trinity, she
now drowsed once more, all her draperies about her, her head
against a pillar.

"Somehow it seems to matter."

The low voice was Simeon's.

The voice was even lower that answered him. The sharp tap of a
pipe on the mantelpiece cancelled the words. And perhaps Jacob
only said "hum," or said nothing at all. True, the words were inau-
dible. It was the intimacy, a sort of spiritual suppleness, when mind
prints upon mind indelibly.

3. Roman emperor from 361 to 363 C.E., who announced his conversion to paganism in 361.
4. Fast sailing-ships with at least two masts.

"Well, you seem to have studied the subject," said Jacob, rising and standing over Simeon's chair. He balanced himself; he swayed a little. He appeared extraordinarily happy, as if his pleasure would brim and spill down the sides if Simeon spoke.

Simeon said nothing. Jacob remained standing. But intimacy— the room was full of it, still, deep, like a pool. Without need of movement or speech it rose softly and washed over everything, mollifying, kindling, and coating the mind with the lustre of pearl, so that if you talk of a light, of Cambridge burning, it's not languages only. It's Julian the Apostate.

But Jacob moved. He murmured good-night. He went out into the court. He buttoned his jacket across his chest. He went back to his rooms, and being the only man who walked at that moment back to his rooms, his footsteps rang out, his figure loomed large. Back from the Chapel, back from the Hall, back from the Library, came the sound of his footsteps, as if the old stone echoed with magisterial authority: "The young man—the young man—the young man—back to his rooms."

IV

What's the use of trying to read Shakespeare, especially in one of those little thin paper editions whose pages get ruffled, or stuck together with sea-water? Although the plays of Shakespeare had frequently been praised, even quoted, and placed higher than the Greek, never since they started had Jacob managed to read one through. Yet what an opportunity!

For the Scilly Isles[1] had been sighted by Timmy Durrant lying like mountain-tops almost a-wash in precisely the right place. His calculations had worked perfectly, and really the sight of him sitting there, with his hand on the tiller, rosy gilled, with a sprout of beard, looking sternly at the stars, then at a compass, spelling out quite correctly his page of the eternal lesson-book, would have moved a woman. Jacob, of course, was not a woman. The sight of Timmy Durrant was no sight for him, nothing to set against the sky and worship; far from it. They had quarrelled. Why the right way to open a tin of beef, with Shakespeare on board, under conditions of such splendour, should have turned them to sulky schoolboys, none can tell. Tinned beef is cold eating, though; and salt water spoils biscuits; and the waves tumble and lollop much the same hour after hour— tumble and lollop all across the horizon. Now a spray of seaweed floats past—now a log of wood. Ships have been wrecked here. One or two go past, keeping their own side of the road. Timmy knew

1. Small group of islands twenty-eight miles off the western tip of Cornwall.

where they were bound, what their cargoes were, and, by looking
through his glass, could tell the name of the line, and even guess
what dividends it paid its shareholders. Yet that was no reason for
Jacob to turn sulky.

The Scilly Isles had the look of mountain-tops almost a-wash. . . .
Unfortunately, Jacob broke the pin of the Primus stove.[2]

The Scilly Isles might well be obliterated by a roller sweeping
straight across.

But one must give young men the credit of admitting that, though
breakfast eaten under these circumstances is grim, it is sincere
enough. No need to make conversation. They got out their pipes.

Timmy wrote up some scientific observations; and—what was the
question that broke the silence—the exact time or the day of the
month? anyhow, it was spoken without the least awkwardness; in
the most matter-of-fact way in the world; and then Jacob began to
unbutton his clothes and sat naked, save for his shirt, intending,
apparently, to bathe.

The Scilly Isles were turning bluish; and suddenly blue, purple,
and green flushed the sea; left it grey; struck a stripe which vanished;
but when Jacob had got his shirt over his head the whole floor of the
waves was blue and white, rippling and crisp, though now and again
a broad purple mark appeared, like a bruise; or there floated an entire
emerald tinged with yellow. He plunged. He gulped in water, spat it
out, struck with his right arm, struck with his left, was towed by a
rope, gasped, splashed, and was hauled on board.

The seat in the boat was positively hot, and the sun warmed his
back as he sat naked with a towel in his hand, looking at the Scilly
Isles which—confound it! the sail flapped. Shakespeare was knocked
overboard. There you could see him floating merrily away, with all
his pages ruffling innumerably; and then he went under.

Strangely enough, you could smell violets, or if violets were impossible in July, they must grow something very pungent on the mainland then. The mainland, not so very far off—you could see clefts
in the cliffs, white cottages, smoke going up—wore an extraordinary
look of calm, of sunny peace, as if wisdom and piety had descended
upon the dwellers there. Now a cry sounded, as of a man calling
pilchards[3] in a main street. It wore an extraordinary look of piety and
peace, as if old men smoked by the door, and girls stood, hands on
hips, at the well, and horses stood; as if the end of the world had
come, and cabbage fields and stone walls, and coast-guard stations,
and, above all, the white sand bays with the waves breaking unseen
by any one, rose to heaven in a kind of ecstasy.

But imperceptibly the cottage smoke droops, has the look of a

2. Portable paraffin camping stove.
3. Street-vendor selling fish.

mourning emblem, a flag floating its caress over a grave. The gulls, making their broad flight and then riding at peace, seem to mark the grave.

No doubt if this were Italy, Greece, or even the shores of Spain, sadness would be routed by strangeness and excitement and the nudge of a classical education. But the Cornish hills have stark chimneys standing on them; and, somehow or other, loveliness is infernally sad. Yes, the chimneys and the coast-guard stations and the little bays with the waves breaking unseen by any one make one remember the overpowering sorrow. And what can this sorrow be?

It is brewed by the earth itself. It comes from the houses on the coast. We start transparent, and then the cloud thickens. All history backs our pane of glass. To escape is vain.

But whether this is the right interpretation of Jacob's gloom as he sat naked, in the sun, looking at the Land's End,[4] it is impossible to say; for he never spoke a word. Timmy sometimes wondered (only for a second) whether his people bothered him. . . . No matter. There are things that can't be said. Let's shake it off. Let's dry ourselves, and take up the first thing that comes handy. . . . Timmy Durrant's notebook of scientific observations.

"Now . . ." said Jacob.

It is a tremendous argument.

Some people can follow every step of the way, and even take a little one, six inches long, by themselves at the end; others remain observant of the external signs.

The eyes fix themselves upon the poker; the right hand takes the poker and lifts it; turns it slowly round, and then, very accurately, replaces it. The left hand, which lies on the knee, plays some stately but intermittent piece of march music. A deep breath is taken; but allowed to evaporate unused. The cat marches across the hearth-rug. No one observes her.

"That's about as near as I can get to it," Durrant wound up.

The next minute is quiet as the grave.

"It follows . . ." said Jacob.

Only half a sentence followed; but these half-sentences are like flags set on tops of buildings to the observer of external sights down below. What was the coast of Cornwall, with its violet scents, and mourning emblems, and tranquil piety, but a screen happening to hang straight behind as his mind marched up?

"It follows . . ." said Jacob.

"Yes," said Timmy, after reflection. "That is so."

Now Jacob began plunging about, half to stretch himself, half in

4. Western tip of Cornwall.

a kind of jollity, no doubt, for the strangest sound issued from his lips as he furled the sail, rubbed the plates—gruff, tuneless—a sort of pæan,[5] for having grasped the argument, for being master of the situation, sunburnt, unshaven, capable into the bargain of sailing round the world in a ten-ton yacht, which, very likely, he would do one of these days instead of settling down in a lawyer's office, and wearing spats.[6]

"Our friend Masham," said Timmy Durrant, "would rather not be seen in our company as we are now." His buttons had come off.

"D'you know Masham's aunt?" said Jacob.

"Never knew he had one," said Timmy.

"Masham has millions of aunts," said Jacob.

"Masham is mentioned in Domesday Book,"[7] said Timmy.

"So are his aunts," said Jacob.

"His sister," said Timmy, "is a very pretty girl."

"That's what'll happen to you, Timmy," said Jacob.

"It'll happen to you first," said Timmy.

"But this woman I was telling you about—Masham's aunt——"

"Oh, do get on," said Timmy, for Jacob was laughing so much that he could not speak.

"Masham's aunt . . ."

Timmy laughed so much that he could not speak.

"Masham's aunt . . ."

"What is there about Masham that makes one laugh?" said Timmy.

"Hang it all—a man who swallows his tie-pin," said Jacob.

"Lord Chancellor[8] before he's fifty," said Timmy.

"He's a gentleman," said Jacob.

"The Duke of Wellington was a gentleman," said Timmy.

"Keats wasn't."

"Lord Salisbury[9] was."

"And what about God?" said Jacob.

The Scilly Isles now appeared as if directly pointed at by a golden finger issuing from a cloud; and everybody knows how portentous that sight is, and how these broad rays, whether they light upon the Scilly Isles or upon the tombs of crusaders in cathedrals, always shake the very foundations of scepticism and lead to jokes about God.

"Abide with me:
Fast falls the eventide;

---

5. Song of triumph and celebration.
6. Cloth coverings worn over shoes, to protect them from splashes.
7. William the Conqueror's survey of England, conducted in 1086 and listing the names of all land-holders.
8. Head of the judiciary and chief administrator of the legal system in Britain.
9. Conservative prime minister of Britain in 1885–86, 1886–92, and 1895–1902.

The shadows deepen;
Lord, with me abide,"[1]

sang Timmy Durrant.

"At my place we used to have a hymn which began

Great God, what do I see and hear?"[2]

said Jacob.

Gulls rode gently swaying in little companies of two or three quite near the boat; the cormorant, as if following his long strained neck in eternal pursuit, skimmed an inch above the water to the next rock; and the drone of the tide in the caves came across the water, low, monotonous, like the voice of some one talking to himself.

"Rock of Ages, cleft for me,
Let me hide myself in thee,"[3]

sang Jacob.

Like the blunt tooth of some monster, a rock broke the surface; brown; overflown with perpetual waterfalls.

"Rock of Ages,"

Jacob sang, lying on his back, looking up into the sky at mid-day, from which every shred of cloud had been withdrawn, so that it was like something permanently displayed with the cover off.

By six o'clock a breeze blew in off an icefield; and by seven the water was more purple than blue; and by half-past seven there was a patch of rough gold-beater's skin round the Scilly Isles, and Durrant's face, as he sat steering, was of the colour of a red lacquer box polished for generations. By nine all the fire and confusion had gone out of the sky, leaving wedges of apple-green and plates of pale yellow; and by ten the lanterns on the boat were making twisted colours upon the waves, elongated or squab,[4] as the waves stretched or humped themselves. The beam from the lighthouse strode rapidly across the water. Infinite millions of miles away powdered stars twinkled; but the waves slapped the boat, and crashed, with regular and appalling solemnity, against the rocks.

1. English hymn, popular at funerals, written by Henry Francis Lyte, c. 1847.
2. Traditional English hymn, additional verses composed by William Collyer, 1812.
3. English hymn, written by Augustus Toplady in 1776.
4. Short and fat.

Although it would be possible to knock at the cottage door and
ask for a glass of milk, it is only thirst that would compel the intru-
sion. Yet perhaps Mrs. Pascoe[5] would welcome it. The summer's day
may be wearing heavy. Washing in her little scullery,[6] she may hear
the cheap clock on the mantelpiece tick, tick, tick . . . tick, tick, tick.
She is alone in the house. Her husband is out helping Farmer Hos-
ken; her daughter married and gone to America. Her elder son is
married too, but she does not agree with his wife. The Wesleyan[7]
minister came along and took the younger boy. She is alone in the
house. A steamer, probably bound for Cardiff,[8] now crosses the horizon, while near at hand one bell of a foxglove swings to and fro with
a bumble-bee for clapper.

These white Cornish cottages are built on the edge of the cliff;
the garden grows gorse more readily than cabbages; and for hedge,
some primeval man has piled granite boulders. In one of these, to
hold, an historian conjectures, the victim's blood, a basin has been
hollowed, but in our time it serves more tamely to seat those tourists
who wish for an uninterrupted view of the Gurnard's Head.[9] Not
that any one objects to a blue print dress and a white apron in a
cottage garden.

"Look—she has to draw her water from a well in the garden."

"Very lonely it must be in winter, with the wind sweeping over
those hills, and the waves dashing on the rocks."

Even on a summer's day you hear them murmuring.

Having drawn her water, Mrs. Pascoe went in. The tourists regret-
ted that they had brought no glasses, so that they might have read
the name of the tramp steamer.[1] Indeed, it was such a fine day that
there was no saying what a pair of field-glasses might not have
fetched into view. Two fishing luggers,[2] presumably from St. Ives
Bay, were now sailing in an opposite direction from the steamer, and
the floor of the sea became alternately clear and opaque. As for the
bee, having sucked its fill of honey, it visited the teasle[3] and thence
made a straight line to Mrs. Pascoe's patch, once more directing the
tourists' gaze to the old woman's print dress and white apron, for she
had come to the door of the cottage and was standing there.

There she stood, shading her eyes and looking out to sea.

5. The Pascoes were in charge of the bathing tents on the beach at St. Ives, where Virginia
   Woolf spent her childhood summers.
6. Room attached to the kitchen where basic chores, such as washing dishes, were carried
   out.
7. British Methodist.
8. Large Welsh port on the Bristol Channel.
9. Rocky promontory on the north coast of Cornwall west of St. Ives.
1. Cargo boat with no fixed route.
2. Small boats with square sails.
3. Old spelling of "teasel," a plant with flowers and prickly leaves.

For the millionth time, perhaps, she looked at the sea. A peacock butterfly now spread himself upon the teasle, fresh and newly emerged, as the blue and chocolate down on his wings testified. Mrs. Pascoe went indoors, fetched a cream pan, came out, and stood scouring it. Her face was assuredly not soft, sensual, or lecherous, but hard, wise, wholesome rather, signifying in a room full of sophisticated people the flesh and blood of life. She would tell a lie, though, as soon as the truth. Behind her on the wall hung a large dried skate. Shut up in the parlour she prized mats, china mugs, and photographs, though the mouldy little room was saved from the salt breeze only by the depth of a brick, and between lace curtains you saw the gannet[4] drop like a stone, and on stormy days the gulls came shuddering through the air, and the steamers' lights were now high, now deep. Melancholy were the sounds on a winter's night.

The picture papers were delivered punctually on Sunday, and she pored long over Lady Cynthia's wedding at the Abbey.[5] She, too, would have liked to ride in a carriage with springs. The soft, swift syllables of educated speech often shamed her few rude ones. And then all night to hear the grinding of the Atlantic upon the rocks instead of hansom cabs and footmen whistling for motor cars. . . . So she may have dreamed, scouring her cream pan. But the talkative, nimble-witted people have taken themselves to towns. Like a miser, she has hoarded her feelings within her own breast. Not a penny piece has she changed all these years, and, watching her enviously, it seems as if all within must be pure gold.

The wise old woman, having fixed her eyes upon the sea, once more withdrew. The tourists decided that it was time to move on to the Gurnard's Head.

Three seconds later Mrs. Durrant rapped upon the door.

"Mrs. Pascoe?" she said.

Rather haughtily, she watched the tourists cross the field path. She came of a Highland race, famous for its chieftains.

Mrs. Pascoe appeared.

"I envy you that bush, Mrs. Pascoe," said Mrs. Durrant, pointing the parasol with which she had rapped on the door at the fine clump of St. John's wort that grew beside it. Mrs. Pascoe looked at the bush deprecatingly.

4. Large sea-bird.
5. Wedding of Lady Cynthia Curzon, daughter of the viceroy of India, to Oswald Mosley (founder of the British Union of Fascists in 1932), at Westminster Abbey in 1920.

"I expect my son in a day or two," said Mrs. Durrant. "Sailing from Falmouth with a friend in a little boat. . . . Any news of Lizzie yet, Mrs. Pascoe?"

Her long-tailed ponies stood twitching their ears on the road twenty yards away. The boy, Curnow, flicked flies off them occasionally. He saw his mistress go into the cottage; come out again; and pass, talking energetically to judge by the movements of her hands, round the vegetable plot in front of the cottage. Mrs. Pascoe was his aunt. Both women surveyed a bush. Mrs. Durrant stooped and picked a sprig from it. Next she pointed (her movements were peremptory; she held herself very upright) at the potatoes. They had the blight. All potatoes that year had the blight. Mrs. Durrant showed Mrs. Pascoe how bad the blight was on her potatoes. Mrs. Durrant talked energetically; Mrs. Pascoe listened submissively. The boy Curnow knew that Mrs. Durrant was saying that it is perfectly simple; you mix the powder in a gallon of water; "I have done it with my own hands in my own garden," Mrs. Durrant was saying.

"You won't have a potato left—you won't have a potato left," Mrs. Durrant was saying in her emphatic voice as they reached the gate. The boy Curnow became as immobile as stone.

Mrs. Durrant took the reins in her hands and settled herself on the driver's seat.

"Take care of that leg, or I shall send the doctor to you," she called back over her shoulder; touched the ponies; and the carriage started forward. The boy Curnow had only just time to swing himself up by the toe of his boot. The boy Curnow, sitting in the middle of the back seat, looked at his aunt.

Mrs. Pascoe stood at the gate looking after them; stood at the gate till the trap was round the corner; stood at the gate, looking now to the right, now to the left; then went back to her cottage.

Soon the ponies attacked the swelling moor road with striving forelegs. Mrs. Durrant let the reins fall slackly, and leant backwards. Her vivacity had left her. Her hawk nose was thin as a bleached bone through which you almost see the light. Her hands, lying on the reins in her lap, were firm even in repose. The upper lip was cut so short that it raised itself almost in a sneer from the front teeth. Her mind skimmed leagues where Mrs. Pascoe's mind adhered to its solitary patch. Her mind skimmed leagues as the ponies climbed the hill road. Forwards and backwards she cast her mind, as if the roofless cottages, mounds of slag, and cottage gardens overgrown with foxglove and bramble cast shade upon her mind. Arrived at the summit, she stopped the carriage. The pale hills were round her, each scattered with ancient stones; beneath was the sea, variable as a southern sea; she herself sat there looking from hill to sea, upright, aquiline, equally poised between gloom and laughter. Suddenly she flicked the ponies so that the boy Curnow had to swing himself up by the toe of his boot.

The rooks settled; the rooks rose. The trees which they touched so capriciously seemed insufficient to lodge their numbers. The tree-tops sang with the breeze in them; the branches creaked audibly and dropped now and then, though the season was midsummer, husks or twigs. Up went the rooks and down again, rising in lesser numbers each time as the sager birds made ready to settle, for the evening was already spent enough to make the air inside the wood almost dark. The moss was soft; the tree-trunks spectral. Beyond them lay a silvery meadow. The pampas grass raised its feathery spears from mounds of green at the end of the meadow. A breadth of water gleamed. Already the convolvulus moth was spinning over the flowers. Orange and purple, nasturtium and cherry pie, were washed into the twilight, but the tobacco plant and the passion flower, over which the great moth spun, were white as china. The rooks creaked their wings together on the tree-tops, and were settling down for sleep when, far off, a familiar sound shook and trembled—increased—fairly dinned in their ears—scared sleepy wings into the air again—the dinner bell at the house.

After six days of salt wind, rain, and sun, Jacob Flanders had put on a dinner jacket.[6] The discreet black object had made its appearance now and then in the boat among tins, pickles, preserved meats, and as the voyage went on had become more and more irrelevant, hardly to be believed in. And now, the world being stable, lit by candle-light, the dinner jacket alone preserved him. He could not be sufficiently thankful. Even so his neck, wrists, and face were exposed without cover, and his whole person, whether exposed or not, tingled and glowed so as to make even black cloth an imperfect screen. He drew back the great red hand that lay on the table-cloth. Surreptitiously it closed upon slim glasses and curved silver forks. The bones of the cutlets were decorated with pink frills—and yesterday he had gnawn ham from the bone! Opposite him were hazy, semi-transparent shapes of yellow and blue. Behind them, again, was the grey-green garden, and among the pear-shaped leaves of the escal-

6. Formal black jacket similar to a tuxedo.

lonia[7] fishing-boats seemed caught and suspended. A sailing ship slowly drew past the women's backs. Two or three figures crossed the terrace hastily in the dusk. The door opened and shut. Nothing settled or stayed unbroken. Like oars rowing now this side, now that, were the sentences that came now here, now there, from either side of the table.

"Oh, Clara, Clara!" exclaimed Mrs. Durrant, and Timothy Durrant adding, "Clara, Clara," Jacob named the shape in yellow gauze Timothy's sister, Clara. The girl sat smiling and flushed. With her brother's dark eyes, she was vaguer and softer than he was. When the laugh died down she said: "But, mother, it was true. He said so, didn't he? Miss Eliot agreed with us. . . ."

But Miss Eliot, tall, grey-headed, was making room beside her for the old man who had come in from the terrace. The dinner would never end, Jacob thought, and he did not wish it to end, though the ship had sailed from one corner of the window-frame to the other, and a light marked the end of the pier. He saw Mrs. Durrant gaze at the light. She turned to him.

"Did you take command, or Timothy?" she said. "Forgive me if I call you Jacob. I've heard so much of you." Then her eyes went back to the sea. Her eyes glazed as she looked at the view.

"A little village once," she said, "and now grown. . . ." She rose, taking her napkin with her, and stood by the window.

"Did you quarrel with Timothy?" Clara asked shyly. "I should have."

Mrs. Durrant came back from the window.

"It gets later and later," she said, sitting upright, and looking down the table. "You ought to be ashamed—all of you. Mr. Clutterbuck, you ought to be ashamed." She raised her voice, for Mr. Clutterbuck was deaf.

"We *are* ashamed," said a girl. But the old man with the beard went on eating plum tart. Mrs. Durrant laughed and leant back in her chair, as if indulging him.

"We put it to you, Mrs. Durrant," said a young man with thick spectacles and a fiery moustache. "I say the conditions were fulfilled. She owes me a sovereign."

"Not *before* the fish—*with* it, Mrs. Durrant," said Charlotte Wilding.

"That was the bet; with the fish," said Clara seriously. "Begonias, mother. To eat them with his fish."

"Oh dear," said Mrs. Durrant.

"Charlotte won't pay you," said Timothy.

"How dare you . . ." said Charlotte.

7. Flowering shrub.

"That privilege will be mine," said the courtly Mr. Wortley, producing a silver case primed with sovereigns and slipping one coin on to the table. Then Mrs. Durrant got up and passed down the room, holding herself very straight, and the girls in yellow and blue and silver gauze followed her, and elderly Miss Eliot in her velvet; and a little rosy woman, hesitating at the door, clean, scrupulous, probably a governess. All passed out at the open door.

"When you are as old as I am, Charlotte," said Mrs. Durrant, drawing the girl's arm within hers as they paced up and down the terrace.

"Why are you so sad?" Charlotte asked impulsively.

"Do I seem to you sad? I hope not," said Mrs. Durrant.

"Well, just now. You're *not* old."

"Old enough to be Timothy's mother." They stopped.

Miss Eliot was looking through Mr. Clutterbuck's telescope at the edge of the terrace. The deaf old man stood beside her, fondling his beard, and reciting the names of the constellations: "Andromeda, Bootes, Sidonia, Cassiopeia. . . ."

"Andromeda," murmured Miss Eliot, shifting the telescope slightly.

Mrs. Durrant and Charlotte looked along the barrel of the instrument pointed at the skies.

"There are *millions* of stars," said Charlotte with conviction. Miss Eliot turned away from the telescope. The young men laughed suddenly in the dining-room.

"Let *me* look," said Charlotte eagerly.

"The stars bore me," said Mrs. Durrant, walking down the terrace with Julia Eliot. "I read a book once about the stars. . . . What are they saying?" She stopped in front of the dining-room window. "Timothy," she noted.

"The silent young man," said Miss Eliot.

"Yes, Jacob Flanders," said Mrs. Durrant.

"Oh, mother! I didn't recognize you!" exclaimed Clara Durrant, coming from the opposite direction with Elsbeth. "How delicious," she breathed, crushing a verbena leaf.[8]

Mrs. Durrant turned and walked away by herself.

"Clara!" she called. Clara went to her.

"How unlike they are!" said Miss Eliot.

Mr. Wortley passed them, smoking a cigar.

"Every day I live I find myself agreeing . . ." he said as he passed them.

"It's so interesting to guess . . ." murmured Julia Eliot.

8. Fragrant plant used in herbal medicine and cosmetics.

"When first we came out we could see the flowers in that bed," said Elsbeth.

"We see very little now," said Miss Eliot.

"She must have been so beautiful, and everybody loved her, of course," said Charlotte. "I suppose Mr. Wortley . . ." she paused.

"Edward's death was a tragedy," said Miss Eliot decidedly.

Here Mr. Erskine joined them.

"There's no such thing as silence," he said positively. "I can hear twenty different sounds on a night like this without counting your voices."

"Make a bet of it?" said Charlotte.

"Done," said Mr. Erskine. "One, the sea; two, the wind; three, a dog; four . . ."

The others passed on.

"Poor Timothy," said Elsbeth.

"A very fine night," shouted Miss Eliot into Mr. Clutterbuck's ear.

"Like to look at the stars?" said the old man, turning the telescope towards Elsbeth.

"Doesn't it make you melancholy—looking at the stars?" shouted Miss Eliot.

"Dear me no, dear me no," Mr. Clutterbuck chuckled when he understood her. "Why should it make me melancholy? Not for a moment—dear me no."

"Thank you, Timothy, but I'm coming in," said Miss Eliot. "Elsbeth, here's a shawl."

"I'm coming in," Elsbeth murmured with her eye to the telescope. "Cassiopeia," she murmured. "Where are you all?" she asked, taking her eye away from the telescope. "How dark it is!"

Mrs. Durrant sat in the drawing-room by a lamp winding a ball of wool. Mr. Clutterbuck read the *Times*. In the distance stood a second lamp, and round it sat the young ladies, flashing scissors over silver-spangled stuff for private theatricals. Mr. Wortley read a book.

"Yes; he is perfectly right," said Mrs. Durrant, drawing herself up and ceasing to wind her wool. And while Mr. Clutterbuck read the rest of Lord Lansdowne's[9] speech she sat upright, without touching her ball.

"Ah, Mr. Flanders," she said, speaking proudly, as if to Lord Lansdowne himself. Then she sighed and began to wind her wool again.

"Sit *there*," she said.

Jacob came out from the dark place by the window where he had

9. British politician (1845–1927), leader of the Conservative opposition after the Liberal victory of 1906; a key figure in negotiations over the removal of the House of Lords' power of veto over parliamentary legislation in 1910.

hovered. The light poured over him, illuminating every cranny of his skin; but not a muscle of his face moved as he sat looking out into the garden.

"I want to hear about your voyage," said Mrs. Durrant.

"Yes," he said.

"Twenty years ago we did the same thing."

"Yes," he said. She looked at him sharply.

"He is extraordinarily awkward," she thought, noticing how he fingered his socks. "Yet so distinguished-looking."

"In those days . . ." she resumed, and told him how they had sailed . . . "my husband, who knew a good deal about sailing, for he kept a yacht before we married" . . . and then how rashly they had defied the fishermen, "almost paid for it with our lives, but so proud of ourselves!" She flung the hand out that held the ball of wool.

"Shall I hold your wool?" Jacob asked stiffly.

"You do that for your mother," said Mrs. Durrant, looking at him again keenly, as she transferred the skein.[1] "Yes, it goes much better."

He smiled; but said nothing.

Elsbeth Siddons hovered behind them with something silver on her arm.

"We want," she said. . . . "I've come . . ." she paused.

"Poor Jacob," said Mrs. Durrant, quietly as if she had known him all his life. "They're going to make you act in their play."

"How I love you!" said Elsbeth, kneeling beside Mrs. Durrant's chair.

"Give me the wool," said Mrs. Durrant.

"He's come—he's come!" cried Charlotte Wilding. "I've won my bet!"

"There's another bunch higher up," murmured Clara Durrant, mounting another step of the ladder. Jacob held the ladder as she stretched out to reach the grapes high up on the vine.

"There!" she said, cutting through the stalk. She looked semi-transparent, pale, wonderfully beautiful up there among the vine leaves and the yellow and purple bunches, the lights swimming over her in coloured islands. Geraniums and begonias stood in pots along planks; tomatoes climbed the walls.

"The leaves really want thinning," she considered, and one green one, spread like the palm of a hand, circled down past Jacob's head.

"I have more than I can eat already," he said, looking up.

1. Coil of wool.

"It does seem absurd . . ." Clara began, "going back to London. . . ."

"Ridiculous," said Jacob, firmly.

"Then . . ." said Clara, "you must come next year, properly," she said, snipping another vine leaf, rather at random.

"If . . . if . . ."

A child ran past the greenhouse shouting. Clara slowly descended the ladder with her basket of grapes.

"One bunch of white, and two of purple," she said, and she placed two great leaves over them where they lay curled warm in the basket.

"I have enjoyed myself," said Jacob, looking down the greenhouse.

"Yes, it's been delightful," she said vaguely.

"Oh, Miss Durrant," he said, taking the basket of grapes; but she walked past him towards the door of the greenhouse.

"You're too good—too good," she thought, thinking of Jacob, thinking that he must not say that he loved her. No, no, no.

The children were whirling past the door, throwing things high into the air.

"Little demons!" she cried. "What have they got?" she asked Jacob.

"Onions, I think," said Jacob. He looked at them without moving.

"Next August, remember, Jacob," said Mrs. Durrant, shaking hands with him on the terrace where the fuchsia hung, like a scarlet ear-ring, behind her head. Mr. Wortley came out of the window in yellow slippers, trailing the *Times* and holding out his hand very cordially.

"Good-bye," said Jacob. "Good-bye," he repeated. "Good-bye," he said once more. Charlotte Wilding flung up her bedroom window and cried out: "Good-bye, Mr. Jacob!"

"Mr. Flanders!" cried Mr. Clutterbuck, trying to extricate himself from his beehive chair.[2] "Jacob Flanders!"

"Too late, Joseph," said Mrs. Durrant.

"Not to sit for me," said Miss Eliot, planting her tripod upon the lawn.

V

"I rather think," said Jacob, taking his pipe from his mouth, "it's in Virgil," and pushing back his chair, he went to the window.

_____

2. Wicker chair with a dome-shaped top.

The rashest drivers in the world are, certainly, the drivers of post-office vans. Swinging down Lamb's Conduit Street,[1] the scarlet van rounded the corner by the pillar box in such a way as to graze the kerb and make the little girl who was standing on tiptoe to post a letter look up, half frightened, half curious. She paused with her hand in the mouth of the box; then dropped her letter and ran away. It is seldom only that we see a child on tiptoe with pity—more often a dim discomfort, a grain of sand in the shoe which it's scarcely worth while to remove—that's our feeling, and so—Jacob turned to the bookcase.

Long ago great people lived here, and coming back from Court past midnight stood, huddling their satin skirts, under the carved door-posts while the footman roused himself from his mattress on the floor, hurriedly fastened the lower buttons of his waistcoat, and let them in. The bitter eighteenth-century rain rushed down the kennel. Southampton Row,[2] however, is chiefly remarkable nowadays for the fact that you will always find a man there trying to sell a tortoise to a tailor. "Showing off the tweed, sir; what the gentry wants is something singular to catch the eye, sir—and clean in their habits, sir!" So they display their tortoises.

At Mudie's corner in Oxford Street[3] all the red and blue beads had run together on the string. The motor omnibuses were locked. Mr. Spalding going to the city looked at Mr. Charles Budgeon bound for Shepherd's Bush.[4] The proximity of the omnibuses gave the outside passengers an opportunity to stare into each other's faces. Yet few took advantage of it. Each had his own business to think of. Each had his past shut in him like the leaves of a book known to him by heart; and his friends could only read the title, James Spalding, or Charles Budgeon, and the passengers going the opposite way could read nothing at all—save "a man with a red moustache," "a young man in grey smoking a pipe." The October sunlight rested upon all these men and women sitting immobile; and little Johnnie Sturgeon took the chance to swing down the staircase, carrying his large mysterious parcel, and so dodging a zigzag course between the wheels he reached the pavement, started to whistle a tune and was soon out of sight—for ever. The omnibuses jerked on, and every single person felt relief at being a little nearer to his journey's end, though some cajoled themselves past the immediate engagement by promise of indulgence beyond—steak and kidney pudding, drink, or a game of

1. In Bloomsbury, London.
2. In Bloomsbury. If Jacob's rooms are on Southampton Row, it would be difficult for him to see a van turning the corner of Lamb's Conduit Street, which is several blocks away.
3. Mudie's circulating library operated out of a grand building, constructed in 1860, on the corner of New Oxford Street (not Oxford Street) and Museum Street.
4. A western suburb; the city: or the City, the financial district of London, in the east.

dominoes in the smoky corner of a city restaurant. Oh yes, human life is very tolerable on the top of an omnibus in Holborn,[5] when the policeman holds up his arm and the sun beats on your back, and if there is such a thing as a shell secreted by man to fit man himself here we find it, on the banks of the Thames, where the great streets join and St. Paul's Cathedral, like the volute[6] on the top of the snail shell, finishes it off. Jacob, getting off his omnibus, loitered up the steps, consulted his watch, and finally made up his mind to go in. . . . Does it need an effort? Yes. These changes of mood wear us out.

Dim it is, haunted by ghosts of white marble, to whom the organ for ever chaunts. If a boot creaks, it's awful; then the order; the discipline. The verger with his rod has life ironed out beneath him. Sweet and holy are the angelic choristers. And for ever round the marble shoulders, in and out of the folded fingers, go the thin high sounds of voice and organ. For ever requiem—repose. Tired with scrubbing the steps of the Prudential Society's office, which she did year in year out, Mrs. Lidgett took her seat beneath the great Duke's tomb,[7] folded her hands, and half closed her eyes. A magnificent place for an old woman to rest in, by the very side of the great Duke's bones, whose victories mean nothing to her, whose name she knows not, though she never fails to greet the little angels opposite, as she passes out, wishing the like on her own tomb, for the leathern curtain of the heart has flapped wide, and out steal on tiptoe thoughts of rest, sweet melodies. . . . Old Spicer, jute merchant, thought nothing of the kind though. Strangely enough he'd never been in St. Paul's these fifty years, though his office windows looked on the church-yard. "So that's all? Well, a gloomy old place . . . Where's Nelson's tomb?[8] No time now—come again—a coin to leave in the box . . . Rain or fine is it? Well, if it would only make up its mind!" Idly the children stray in—the verger[9] dissuades them—and another and another . . . man, woman, man, woman, boy . . . casting their eyes up, pursing their lips, the same shadow brushing the same faces; the leathern curtain of the heart flaps wide.

Nothing could appear more certain from the steps of St. Paul's than that each person is miraculously provided with coat, skirt, and boots; an income; an object. Only Jacob, carrying in his hand Finlay's

---

5. Large commercial street that runs south-east from Bloomsbury.
6. Volute: a spiral twist; Holborn and Aldersgate converge at St. Paul's Cathedral, a splendid Baroque cathedral designed by Sir Christopher Wren and completed in 1710.
7. Monument to the Duke of Wellington, depicting him on horseback, in the North Aisle of the Cathedral, completed in 1912, sixty years after his death; Prudential Society's office: insurance company founded 1848, housed in a magnificent red terracotta and brick Victorian Gothic building designed by Alfred Waterhouse and opened in 1879, situated at Holborn Bars, adjacent to the Holborn Viaduct and a short walk from St. Paul's.
8. Large monument to Admiral Horatio Nelson, who defeated the French and Spanish in 1805 at the Battle of Trafalgar and was killed there, in the South Transept.
9. Church official who acts as assistant to the vicar and caretaker of the church.

Byzantine Empire,[1] which he had bought in Ludgate Hill,[2] looked a little different; for in his hand he carried a book, which book he would at nine-thirty precisely, by his own fireside, open and study, as no one else of all these multitudes would do. They have no houses. The streets belong to them; the shops; the churches; theirs the innumerable desks; the stretched office lights; the vans are theirs, and the railway slung high above the street. If you look closer you will see that three elderly men at a little distance from each other run spiders along the pavement as if the street were their parlour, and here, against the wall, a woman stares at nothing, boot-laces extended, which she does not ask you to buy. The posters are theirs too; and the news on them. A town destroyed; a race won. A homeless people, circling beneath the sky whose blue or white is held off by a ceiling cloth of steel filings and horse dung shredded to dust.

There, under the green shade, with his head bent over white paper, Mr. Sibley transferred figures to folios, and upon each desk you observe, like provender,[3] a bunch of papers, the day's nutriment, slowly consumed by the industrious pen. Innumerable overcoats of the quality prescribed hung empty all day in the corridors, but as the clock struck six each was exactly filled, and the little figures, split apart into trousers or moulded into a single thickness, jerked rapidly with angular forward motion along the pavement; then dropped into darkness. Beneath the pavement, sunk in the earth, hollow drains lined with yellow light for ever conveyed them this way and that, and large letters upon enamel plates represented in the underworld the parks, squares, and circuses of the upper. "Marble Arch—Shepherd's Bush"—to the majority the Arch and the Bush are eternally white letters upon a blue ground. Only at one point—it may be Acton, Holloway, Kensal Rise, Caledonian Road[4]—does the name mean shops where you buy things, and houses, in one of which, down to the right, where the pollard trees grow out of the paving stones, there is a square curtained window, and a bedroom.

Long past sunset an old blind woman sat on a camp-stool with her back to the stone wall of the Union of London and Smith's Bank,[5] clasping a brown mongrel tight in her arms and singing out loud, not for coppers, no, from the depths of her gay wild heart—her sinful, tanned heart—for the child who fetches her is the fruit of sin, and should have been in bed, curtained, asleep, instead of hearing in the lamplight her mother's wild song, where she sits against the Bank,

1. George Finlay's *History of the Byzantine Empire 716–1057* was originally published in 1856, and reprinted in a pocket edition by Everyman in 1906.
2. Street leading to St. Paul's Cathedral.
3. Dry food for livestock.
4. Names of stations on the London Underground.
5. The Union Bank of London, founded 1839, merged with Smith's Bank in 1902 to form the Union of London and Smith's Bank.

singing not for coppers, with her dog against her breast.

Home they went. The grey church spires received them; the hoary city, old, sinful, and majestic. One behind another, round or pointed, piercing the sky or massing themselves, like sailing ships, like granite cliffs, spires and offices, wharves and factories crowd the bank; eternally the pilgrims trudge; barges rest in mid stream heavy laden; as some believe, the city loves her prostitutes.

But few, it seems, are admitted to that degree. Of all the carriages that leave the arch of the Opera House, not one turns eastward,[6] and when the little thief is caught in the empty market-place no one in black-and-white or rose-coloured evening dress blocks the way by pausing with a hand upon the carriage door to help or condemn—though Lady Charles, to do her justice, sighs sadly as she ascends her staircase, takes down Thomas à Kempis,[7] and does not sleep till her mind has lost itself tunnelling into the complexity of things. "Why? Why? Why?" she sighs. On the whole it's best to walk back from the Opera House. Fatigue is the safest sleeping draught.

The autumn season was in full swing. Tristan was twitching his rug up under his armpits twice a week; Isolde[8] waved her scarf in miraculous sympathy with the conductor's baton. In all parts of the house were to be found pink faces and glittering breasts. When a Royal hand attached to an invisible body slipped out and withdrew the red and white bouquet reposing on the scarlet ledge, the Queen of England seemed a name worth dying for. Beauty, in its hothouse variety (which is none of the worst), flowered in box after box; and though nothing was said of profound importance, and though it is generally agreed that wit deserted beautiful lips about the time that Walpole died—at any rate when Victoria in her nightgown descended to meet her ministers,[9] the lips (through an opera glass) remained red, adorable. Bald distinguished men with gold-headed canes strolled down the crimson avenues between the stalls, and only broke from intercourse with the boxes when the lights went down, and the conductor, first bowing to the Queen, next to the bald-headed men, swept round on his feet and raised his wand.

Then two thousand hearts in the semi-darkness remembered, anticipated, travelled dark labyrinths; and Clara Durrant said fare-

---

6. Covent Garden Opera House, built in 1858; the affluent areas of London lie west of it.
7. Christian theologian (1379/80–1471), probable author of *Imitation of Christ*.
8. *Tristan and Isolde*, an opera by Richard Wagner (1813–83), composed 1857–59.
9. Victoria became queen of Great Britain and Ireland in 1837 when her uncle, King William IV, died in the early hours of June 20. Lytton Strachey, a close friend of Virginia Woolf's, wrote in *Queen Victoria* (1921) that the eighteen-year-old Victoria was summoned in the middle of the night to be told of her uncle's death, and that she "got out of bed, put on her dressing-gown, and went, alone, into the room where the messengers were standing"; Sir Robert Walpole, prime minister of Britain from 1721 to 1742, died in 1745.

well to Jacob Flanders, and tasted the sweetness of death in effigy;[1] and Mrs. Durrant, sitting behind her in the dark of the box, sighed her sharp sigh; and Mr. Wortley, shifting his position behind the Italian Ambassador's wife, thought that Brangaena[2] was a trifle hoarse; and suspended in the gallery many feet above their heads, Edward Whittaker surreptitiously held a torch to his miniature score; and . . . and . . .

In short, the observer is choked with observations. Only to prevent us from being submerged by chaos, nature and society between them have arranged a system of classification which is simplicity itself; stalls, boxes, amphitheatre, gallery. The moulds are filled nightly. There is no need to distinguish details. But the difficulty remains— one has to choose. For though I have no wish to be Queen of England—or only for a moment—I would willingly sit beside her; I would hear the Prime Minister's gossip; the countess whisper, and share her memories of halls and gardens; the massive fronts of the respectable conceal after all their secret code; or why so impermeable? And then, doffing one's own headpiece, how strange to assume for a moment some one's—any one's—to be a man of valour who has ruled the Empire; to refer while Brangaena sings to the fragments of Sophocles,[3] or see in a flash, as the shepherd pipes his tune,[4] bridges and aqueducts. But no—we must choose. Never was there a harsher necessity! or one which entails greater pain, more certain disaster; for wherever I seat myself, I die in exile: Whittaker in his lodging-house; Lady Charles at the Manor.

A young man with a Wellington nose,[5] who had occupied a seven-and-sixpenny seat, made his way down the stone stairs when the opera ended, as if he were still set a little apart from his fellows by the influence of the music.

At midnight Jacob Flanders heard a rap on his door.

"By Jove!" he exclaimed. "You're the very man I want!" and without more ado they discovered the lines which he had been seeking all day; only they come not in Virgil, but in Lucretius.[6]

1. At the end of *Tristan and Isolde*, Isolde sings a *Liebestod*—song of love and death—over the body of her dead lover, Tristan, and then dies.
2. Isolde's maid in *Tristan and Isolde*.
3. Ancient Greek tragedian (496–506 B.C.E.), author of *Oedipus Rex* and other works.
4. At the beginning of Act 3 of *Tristan and Isolde*, while Tristan lies dying and waiting for Isolde, a shepherd watches the sea for her ship and pipes a mournful tune until he sees it, when he changes to a joyful melody as a sign to Tristan that Isolde is coming.
5. The Duke of Wellington had a very large, hooked nose.
6. Latin poet and philosopher (first century B.C.E.), author of *De Rerum Natura*.

"Yes; that should make him sit up," said Bonamy, as Jacob stopped reading. Jacob was excited. It was first time he had read his essay aloud.

"Damned swine!" he said, rather too extravagantly; but the praise had gone to his head. Professor Bulteel, of Leeds, had issued an edition of Wycherley[7] without stating that he had left out, disembowelled, or indicated only by asterisks, several indecent words and some indecent phrases. An outrage, Jacob said; a breach of faith; sheer prudery; token of a lewd mind and a disgusting nature. Aristophanes[8] and Shakespeare were cited. Modern life was repudiated. Great play was made with the professorial title, and Leeds as a seat of learning was laughed to scorn. And the extraordinary thing was that these young men were perfectly right—extraordinary, because, even as Jacob copied his pages, he knew that no one would ever print them; and sure enough back they came from the *Fortnightly*, the *Contemporary*, the *Nineteenth Century*[9]—when Jacob threw them into the black wooden box where he kept his mother's letters, his old flannel trousers, and a note or two with the Cornish postmark. The lid shut upon the truth.

This black wooden box, upon which his name was still legible in white paint, stood between the long windows of the sitting-room. The street ran beneath. No doubt the bedroom was behind. The furniture—three wicker chairs and a gate-legged table[1]—came from Cambridge. These houses (Mrs. Garfit's daughter, Mrs. Whitehorn, was the landlady of this one) were built, say, a hundred and fifty years ago. The rooms are shapely, the ceilings high; over the doorway a rose, or a ram's skull, is carved in the wood. The eighteenth century has its distinction. Even the panels, painted in raspberry-coloured paint, have their distinction. . . .

"Distinction"—Mrs. Durrant said that Jacob Flanders was "distinguished-looking." "Extremely awkward," she said, "but so distin-

---

7. William Wycherley (1640–1716), Restoration playwright, author of *The Country-Wife* (1765) and other works. There is no edition by Bulteel.
8. Ancient Greek comic playwright (450–388 B.C.E.), known for the licentiousness of his plays, which include *The Birds* (414 B.C.E.) and *The Frogs* (405 B.C.E.).
9. *Fortnightly Review*, founded in 1865, monthly after 1866, offering sympathetic accounts of working-class and union issues, as well as commentaries by mainstream political economists; *Contemporary Review*, founded in 1866, monthly, advocating moderate social reform; *Nineteenth Century*, founded in 1877, weekly and aimed at a broader readership than either the *Fortnightly* or the *Contemporary*, with a wide range of literary pieces and political discussion. All three were part of the wave of new monthlies and weeklies that started to appear in the second half of the nineteenth century in response to increased literacy and an enlarged middle-class readership.
1. Table with hinged leg or legs that can be swung out to support an extra leaf.

guished-looking." Seeing him for the first time that no doubt is the word for him. Lying back in his chair, taking his pipe from his lips, and saying to Bonamy: "About this opera now" (for they had done with indecency). "This fellow Wagner" . . . distinction was one of the words to use naturally, though, from looking at him, one would have found it difficult to say which seat in the opera house was his, stalls, gallery, or dress circle. A writer? He lacked self-consciousness. A painter? There was something in the shape of his hands (he was descended on his mother's side from a family of the greatest antiquity and deepest obscurity) which indicated taste. Then his mouth—but surely, of all futile occupations this of cataloguing features is the worst. One word is sufficient. But if one cannot find it?

"I like Jacob Flanders," wrote Clara Durrant in her diary. "He is so unworldly. He gives himself no airs, and one can say what one likes to him, though he's frightening because . . ." But Mr. Letts allows little space in his shilling diaries.[2] Clara was not the one to encroach upon Wednesday. Humblest, most candid of women! "No, no, no," she sighed, standing at the greenhouse door, "don't break—don't spoil"—what? Something infinitely wonderful.

But then, this is only a young woman's language, one, too, who loves, or refrains from loving. She wished the moment to continue for ever precisely as it was that July morning. And moments don't. Now, for instance, Jacob was telling a story about some walking tour he'd taken, and the inn was called "The Foaming Pot," which, considering the landlady's name . . . They shouted with laughter. The joke was indecent.

Then Julia Eliot said "the silent young man," and as she dined with Prime Ministers, no doubt she meant: "If he is going to get on in the world, he will have to find his tongue."

Timothy Durrant never made any comment at all.

The housemaid found herself very liberally rewarded.

Mr. Sopwith's opinion was as sentimental as Clara's, though far more skilfully expressed.

Betty Flanders was romantic about Archer and tender about John; she was unreasonably irritated by Jacob's clumsiness in the house.

Captain Barfoot liked him best of the boys; but as for saying why. . . .

It seems then that men and women are equally at fault. It seems that a profound, impartial, and absolutely just opinion of our fellow-

2. John Letts, founder of a stationery business in 1796, produced the world's first commercial diary (datebook) in 1812. Letts diaries still make up 40 percent of the diary market in the United Kingdom.

creatures is utterly unknown. Either we are men, or we are women. Either we are cold, or we are sentimental. Either we are young, or growing old. In any case life is but a procession of shadows, and God knows why it is that we embrace them so eagerly, and see them depart with such anguish, being shadows. And why, if this and much more than this is true, why are we yet surprised in the window corner by a sudden vision that the young man in the chair is of all things in the world the most real, the most solid, the best known to us— why indeed? For the moment after we know nothing about him.

Such is the manner of our seeing. Such the conditions of our love.

("I'm twenty-two. It's nearly the end of October. Life is thoroughly pleasant, although unfortunately there are a great number of fools about. One must apply oneself to something or other—God knows what. Everything is really very jolly—except getting up in the morning and wearing a tail coat.")

"I say, Bonamy, what about Beethoven?"

("Bonamy is an amazing fellow. He knows practically everything— not more about English literature than I do—but then he's read all those Frenchmen.")

"I rather suspect you're talking rot, Bonamy. In spite of what you say, poor old Tennyson. . . ."[3]

("The truth is one ought to have been taught French. Now, I suppose, old Barfoot is talking to my mother. That's an odd affair to be sure. But I can't see Bonamy down there. Damn London!") for the market carts were lumbering down the street.

"What about a walk on Saturday?"

("What's happening on Saturday?")

Then, taking out his pocket-book, he assured himself that the night of the Durrants' party came next week.

But though all this may very well be true—so Jacob thought and spoke—so he crossed his legs—filled his pipe—sipped his whisky, and once looked at his pocket-book, rumpling his hair as he did so, there remains over something which can never be conveyed to a second person save by Jacob himself. Moreover, part of this is not Jacob but Richard Bonamy—the room; the market carts; the hour; the very moment of history. Then consider the effect of sex—how between man and woman it hangs wavy, tremulous, so that here's a valley, there's a peak, when in truth, perhaps, all's as flat as my hand. Even the exact words get the wrong accent on them. But some-

3. Alfred, Lord Tennyson (1809–1892), British poet, author of *In Memoriam* (1850).

thing is always impelling one to hum vibrating, like the hawk moth, at the mouth of the cavern of mystery, endowing Jacob Flanders with all sorts of qualities he had not at all—for though, certainly, he sat talking to Bonamy, half of what he said was too dull to repeat; much unintelligible (about unknown people and Parliament); what remains is mostly a matter of guess work. Yet over him we hang vibrating.

"Yes," said Captain Barfoot, knocking out his pipe on Betty Flanders's hob, and buttoning his coat. "It doubles the work, but I don't mind that."

He was now town councillor. They looked at the night, which was the same as the London night, only a good deal more transparent. Church bells down in the town were striking eleven o'clock. The wind was off the sea. And all the bedroom windows were dark—the Pages were asleep; the Garfits were asleep; the Cranches were asleep—whereas in London at this hour they were burning Guy Fawkes on Parliament Hill.[4]

VI

The flames had fairly caught.

"There's St. Paul's!" some one cried.

As the wood caught the city of London was lit up for a second; on other sides of the fire there were trees. Of the faces which came out fresh and vivid as though painted in yellow and red, the most prominent was a girl's face. By a trick of the firelight she seemed to have no body. The oval of the face and hair hung beside the fire with a dark vacuum for background. As if dazed by the glare, her green-blue eyes stared at the flames. Every muscle of her face was taut. There was something tragic in her thus staring—her age between twenty and twenty-five.

A hand descending from the chequered darkness thrust on her head the conical white hat of a pierrot. Shaking her head, she still stared. A whiskered face appeared above her. They dropped two legs of a table upon the fire and a scattering of twigs and leaves. All this

4. Guy Fawkes Day, November 5, commemorates the foiling of a Catholic plot (the "Gunpowder Plot") to blow up the Houses of Parliament in 1605. Parliament Hill is the high point of Hampstead Heath, so named because Fawkes and his co-conspirators were supposed to have watched from there to see Parliament explode. There is always a large firework display and bonfire, on which an effigy of Guy Fawkes is burned, on Parliament Hill on November 5.

blazed up and showed faces far back, round, pale, smooth, bearded, some with billycock hats[1] on; all intent; showed too St. Paul's floating on the uneven white mist, and two or three narrow, paper-white, extinguisher-shaped spires.

The flames were struggling through the wood and roaring up when, goodness knows where from, pails flung water in beautiful hollow shapes, as of polished tortoiseshell; flung again and again; until the hiss was like a swarm of bees; and all the faces went out.

"Oh Jacob," said the girl, as they pounded up the hill in the dark, "I'm so frightfully unhappy!"

Shouts of laughter came from the others—high, low; some before, others after.

The hotel dining-room was brightly lit. A stag's head in plaster was at one end of the table; at the other some Roman bust blackened and reddened to represent Guy Fawkes, whose night it was. The diners were linked together by lengths of paper roses, so that when it came to singing "Auld Lang Syne"[2] with their hands crossed a pink and yellow line rose and fell the entire length of the table. There was an enormous tapping of green wine-glasses. A young man stood up, and Florinda, taking one of the purplish globes that lay on the table, flung it straight at his head. It crushed to powder.

"I'm so frightfully unhappy!" she said, turning to Jacob, who sat beside her.

The table ran, as if on invisible legs, to the side of the room, and a barrel organ decorated with a red cloth and two pots of paper flowers reeled out waltz music.

Jacob could not dance. He stood against the wall smoking a pipe.

"We think," said two of the dancers, breaking off from the rest, and bowing profoundly before him, "that you are the most beautiful man we have ever seen."

So they wreathed his head with paper flowers. Then somebody brought out a white and gilt chair and made him sit on it. As they passed, people hung glass grapes on his shoulders, until he looked like the figure-head of a wrecked ship. Then Florinda got upon his knee and hid her face in his waistcoat. With one hand he held her; with the other, his pipe.

1. Slang for round, low-crowned, felt hats.
2. Song written by Scottish poet Robert Burns (1759–1796), traditionally sung at the introduction of the New Year and on Burns Night in Scotland.

"Now let us talk," said Jacob, as he walked down Haverstock Hill[3] between four and five o'clock in the morning of November the sixth arm-in-arm with Timmy Durrant, "about something sensible."

The Greeks—yes, that was what they talked about—how when all's said and done, when one's rinsed one's mouth with every literature in the world, including Chinese and Russian (but these Slavs aren't civilized), it's the flavour of Greek that remains. Durrant quoted Aeschylus[4]—Jacob Sophocles. It is true that no Greek could have understood or professor refrained from pointing out—Never mind; what is Greek for if not to be shouted on Haverstock Hill in the dawn? Moreover, Durrant never listened to Sophocles, nor Jacob to Aeschylus. They were boastful, triumphant; it seemed to both that they had read every book in the world; known every sin, passion, and joy. Civilizations stood round them like flowers ready for picking. Ages lapped at their feet like waves fit for sailing. And surveying all this, looming through the fog, the lamplight, the shades of London, the two young men decided in favour of Greece.

"Probably," said Jacob, "we are the only people in the world who know what the Greeks meant."

They drank coffee at a stall where the urns were burnished and little lamps burnt along the counter.

Taking Jacob for a military gentleman, the stall-keeper told him about his boy at Gibraltar,[5] and Jacob cursed the British army and praised the Duke of Wellington. So on again they went down the hill talking about the Greeks.

A strange thing—when you come to think of it—this love of Greek, flourishing in such obscurity, distorted, discouraged, yet leaping out, all of a sudden, especially on leaving crowded rooms, or after a surfeit of print, or when the moon floats among the waves of the hills, or in hollow, sallow, fruitless London days, like a specific;[6] a clean blade; always a miracle. Jacob knew no more Greek than served him to stumble through a play. Of ancient history he knew nothing. However, as he tramped into London it seemed to him that they were making the flagstones ring on the road to the Acropolis, and that if

---

3. Road leading from Hampstead Heath down through Hampstead toward Central London.
4. Ancient Greek tragic playwright (525/524–456/455 B.C.E.), author of the *Oresteia* trilogy.
5. British colony on a small peninsula of Spain's southern Mediterranean coast, and an important British naval base.
6. Drug for a particular disease or condition.

Socrates[7] saw them coming he would bestir himself and say "my fine fellows," for the whole sentiment of Athens was entirely after his heart; free, venturesome, high-spirited. . . . She had called him Jacob without asking his leave. She had sat upon his knee. Thus did all good women in the days of the Greeks.

At this moment there shook out into the air a wavering, quavering, doleful lamentation which seemed to lack strength to unfold itself, and yet flagged on; at the sound of which doors in back streets burst sullenly open; workmen stumped forth.

Florinda was sick.

Mrs. Durrant, sleepless as usual, scored a mark by the side of certain lines in the *Inferno*.[8]

Clara slept buried in her pillows; on her dressing-table dishevelled roses and a pair of long white gloves.

Still wearing the conical white hat of a pierrot, Florinda was sick. The bedroom seemed fit for these catastrophes—cheap, mustard-coloured, half attic, half studio, curiously ornamented with silver paper stars, Welshwomen's hats,[9] and rosaries pendent from the gas brackets. As for Florinda's story, her name had been bestowed upon her by a painter who had wished it to signify that the flower of her maidenhood was still unplucked. Be that as it may, she was without a surname, and for parents had only the photograph of a tombstone beneath which, she said, her father lay buried. Sometimes she would dwell upon the size of it, and rumour had it that Florinda's father had died from the growth of his bones which nothing could stop; just as her mother enjoyed the confidence of a Royal master, and now and again Florinda herself was a Princess, but chiefly when drunk. Thus deserted, pretty into the bargain, with tragic eyes and the lips of a child, she talked more about virginity than women mostly do; and had lost it only the night before, or cherished it beyond the heart in her breast, according to the man she talked to. But did she always talk to men? No, she had her confidante: Mother Stuart. Stu-

---

7. Ancient Greek philosopher (469–399 B.C.E.), who wrote nothing, but whose conversation was recorded by other Greek philosophers such as Plato and Xenophon; the Acropolis: hill in the center of Athens, which used to be the citadel of the ancient city.
8. First part of the long narrative poem *The Divine Comedy* by the Italian poet Dante Alighieri (1265–1321), written 1310–14. *Inferno* describes the poet's visit to Hell.
9. Tall black hats with wide brims, worn over lace caps, traditional dress for women in Wales.

art, as the lady would point out, is the name of a Royal house;[1] but what that signified, and what her business was, no one knew; only that Mrs. Stuart got postal orders every Monday morning, kept a parrot, believed in the transmigration[2] of souls, and could read the future in tea leaves. Dirty lodging-house wall-paper she was behind the chastity of Florinda.

Now Florinda wept, and spent the day wandering the streets; stood at Chelsea watching the river swim past; trailed along the shopping streets; opened her bag and powdered her cheeks in omnibuses; read love letters, propping them against the milk pot in the A.B.C. shop;[3] detected glass in the sugar bowl; accused the waitress of wishing to poison her; declared that young men stared at her; and found herself towards evening slowly sauntering down Jacob's street, when it struck her that she liked that man Jacob better than dirty Jews, and sitting at his table (he was copying his essay upon the Ethics of Indecency), drew off her gloves and told him how Mother Stuart had banged her on the head with the tea-cosy.

Jacob took her word for it that she was chaste. She prattled, sitting by the fireside, of famous painters. The tomb of her father was mentioned. Wild and frail and beautiful she looked, and thus the women of the Greeks were, Jacob thought; and this was life; and himself a man and Florinda chaste.

She left with one of Shelley's[4] poems beneath her arm. Mrs. Stuart, she said, often talked of him.

Marvellous are the innocent. To believe that the girl herself transcends all lies (for Jacob was not such a fool as to believe implicitly), to wonder enviously at the unanchored life—his own seeming petted and even cloistered in comparison—to have at hand as sovereign specifics for all disorders of the soul Adonais[5] and the plays of Shakespeare; to figure out a comradeship all spirited on her side, protective on his, yet equal on both, for women, thought Jacob, are just the same as men—innocence such as this is marvellous enough, and perhaps not so foolish after all.

For when Florinda got home that night she first washed her head; then ate chocolate creams; then opened Shelley. True, she was horribly bored. What on earth was it *about*? She had to wager with herself that she would turn the page before she ate another. In fact

1. Family name of the Scottish monarchs from 1371 to 1714, and of the English monarchs from 1603 to 1714.
2. The passage of the soul into another body at or just before death; postal orders: money orders.
3. Chain of cheap tea shops, run by the Aerated Bread Company, where women could safely eat alone.
4. Percy Bysshe Shelley (1792–1822), British Romantic poet, author of "To a Skylark," "Ode to the West Wind," and other works.
5. Pastoral elegy by Shelley, written in 1821, commemorating the death of Keats.

she slept. But then her day had been a long one, Mother Stuart had thrown the tea-cosy;—there are formidable sights in the streets, and though Florinda was ignorant as an owl, and would never learn to read even her love letters correctly, still she had her feelings, liked some men better than others, and was entirely at the beck and call of life. Whether or not she was a virgin seems a matter of no importance whatever. Unless, indeed, it is the only thing of any importance at all.

Jacob was restless when she left him.

All night men and women seethed up and down the well-known beats.[6] Late home-comers could see shadows against the blinds even in the most respectable suburbs. Not a square in snow or fog lacked its amorous couple. All plays turned on the same subject. Bullets went through heads in hotel bedrooms almost nightly on that account. When the body escaped mutilation, seldom did the heart go to the grave unscarred. Little else was talked of in theatres and popular novels. Yet we say it is a matter of no importance at all.

What with Shakespeare and Adonais, Mozart and Bishop Berkeley[7]—choose whom you like—the fact is concealed and the evenings for most of us pass reputably, or with only the sort of tremor that a snake makes sliding through the grass. But then concealment by itself distracts the mind from the print and the sound. If Florinda had had a mind, she might have read with clearer eyes than we can. She and her sort have solved the question by turning it to a trifle of washing the hands nightly before going to bed, the only difficulty being whether you prefer your water hot or cold, which being settled, the mind can go about its business unassailed.

But it did occur to Jacob, half-way through dinner, to wonder whether she had a mind.

They sat at a little table in the restaurant.

Florinda leant the points of her elbows on the table and held her chin in the cup of her hands. Her cloak had slipped behind her. Gold and white with bright beads on her she emerged, her face flowering from her body, innocent, scarcely tinted, the eyes gazing frankly about her, or slowly settling on Jacob and resting there. She talked:

"You know that big black box the Australian left in my room ever so long ago? . . . I do think furs make a woman look old. . . . That's

6. Usual or regular course.
7. George Berkeley (1685–1753), Scottish bishop and philosopher who argued that all matter, as far as we know, is simply a perception of the human mind; Wolfgang Amadeus Mozart (1756–1791), Austrian composer.

Bechstein come in now. . . . I was wondering what you looked like when you were a little boy, Jacob." She nibbled her roll and looked at him.

"Jacob. You're like one of those statues. . . . I think there are lovely things in the British Museum,[8] don't you? Lots of lovely things . . ." she spoke dreamily. The room was filling; the heat increasing. Talk in a restaurant is dazed sleep-walkers' talk, so many things to look at—so much noise—other people talking. Can one overhear? Oh, but they mustn't overhear *us*.

"That's like Ellen Nagle—that girl . . ." and so on.

"I'm awfully happy since I've known you, Jacob. You're such a *good* man."

The room got fuller and fuller; talk louder; knives more clattering.

"Well, you see what makes her say things like that is . . ."

She stopped. So did every one.

"To-morrow . . . Sunday . . . a beastly . . . you tell me . . . go then!" Crash! And out she swept.

It was at the table next them that the voice spun higher and higher. Suddenly the woman dashed the plates to the floor. The man was left there. Everybody stared. Then—"Well, poor chap, we mustn't sit staring. What a go! Did you hear what she said? By God, he looks a fool! Didn't come up to the scratch, I suppose. All the mustard on the table-cloth. The waiters laughing."

Jacob observed Florinda. In her face there seemed to him something horribly brainless—as she sat staring.

Out she swept, the black woman with the dancing feather in her hat.

Yet she had to go somewhere. The night is not a tumultuous black ocean in which you sink or sail as a star. As a matter of fact it was a wet November night. The lamps of Soho[9] made large greasy spots of light upon the pavement. The by-streets were dark enough to shelter man or woman leaning against the doorways. One detached herself as Jacob and Florinda approached.

"She's dropped her glove," said Florinda.

Jacob, pressing forward, gave it her.

Effusively she thanked him; retraced her steps; dropped her glove again. But why? For whom?

Meanwhile, where had the other woman got to? And the man?

8. National museum founded 1753 in Bloomsbury, London, famous for its ancient statues and archeological displays.
9. Area of central London just southwest of Bloomsbury—the center of London's night life.

The street lamps do not carry far enough to tell us. The voices, angry, lustful, despairing, passionate, were scarcely more than the voices of caged beasts at night. Only they are not caged, nor beasts. Stop a man; ask him the way; he'll tell it you; but one's afraid to ask him the way. What does one fear?—the human eye. At once the pavement narrows, the chasm deepens. There! They've melted into it—both man and woman. Further on, blatantly advertising its meritorious solidity, a boarding-house exhibits behind uncurtained windows its testimony to the soundness of London. There they sit, plainly illuminated, dressed like ladies and gentlemen, in bamboo chairs. The widows of business men prove laboriously that they are related to judges. The wives of coal merchants instantly retort that their fathers kept coachmen. A servant brings coffee, and the crochet basket has to be moved. And so on again into the dark, passing a girl here for sale, or there an old woman with only matches to offer, passing the crowd from the Tube station, the women with veiled hair, passing at length no one but shut doors, carved door-posts, and a solitary policeman, Jacob, with Florinda on his arm, reached his room and, lighting the lamp, said nothing at all.

"I don't like you when you look like that," said Florinda.

The problem is insoluble. The body is harnessed to a brain. Beauty goes hand in hand with stupidity. There she sat staring at the fire as she had stared at the broken mustard-pot. In spite of defending indecency, Jacob doubted whether he liked it in the raw. He had a violent reversion towards male society, cloistered rooms, and the works of the classics; and was ready to turn with wrath upon whoever it was who had fashioned life thus.

Then Florinda laid her hand upon his knee.

After all, it was none of her fault. But the thought saddened him. It's not catastrophes, murders, deaths, diseases, that age and kill us; it's the way people look and laugh, and run up the steps of omnibuses.

Any excuse, though, serves a stupid woman. He told her his head ached.

But when she looked at him, dumbly, half-guessing, half-understanding, apologising perhaps, anyhow saying as he had said, "It's none of my fault," straight and beautiful in body, her face like a shell within its cap, then he knew that cloisters and classics are no use whatever. The problem is insoluble.

VII

About this time a firm of merchants having dealings with the East put on the market little paper flowers which opened on touching water. As it was the custom also to use finger-bowls at the end of dinner, the new discovery was found of excellent service. In these sheltered lakes the little coloured flowers swam and slid; surmounted smooth slippery waves, and sometimes foundered and lay like pebbles on the glass floor. Their fortunes were watched by eyes intent and lovely. It is surely a great discovery that leads to the union of hearts and foundation of homes. The paper flowers did no less.

It must not be thought, though, that they ousted the flowers of nature. Roses, lilies, carnations in particular, looked over the rims of vases and surveyed the bright lives and swift dooms of their artificial relations. Mr. Stuart Ormond made this very observation; and charming it was thought; and Kitty Craster married him on the strength of it six months later. But real flowers can never be dispensed with. If they could, human life would be a different affair altogether. For flowers fade; chrysanthemums are the worst; perfect over night; yellow and jaded next morning—not fit to be seen. On the whole, though the price is sinful, carnations pay best;—it's a question, however, whether it's wise to have them wired.[1] Some shops advise it. Certainly it's the only way to keep them at a dance; but whether it is necessary at dinner parties, unless the rooms are very hot, remains in dispute. Old Mrs. Temple used to recommend an ivy leaf—just one—dropped into the bowl. She said it kept the water pure for days and days. But there is some reason to think that old Mrs. Temple was mistaken.

The little cards, however, with names engraved on them, are a more serious problem than the flowers. More horses' legs have been worn out, more coachmen's lives consumed, more hours of sound afternoon time vainly lavished than served to win us the battle of Waterloo,[2] and pay for it into the bargain. The little demons are the source of as many reprieves, calamities, and anxieties as the battle itself. Sometimes Mrs. Bonham has just gone out; at others she is at home. But, even if the cards should be superseded, which seems unlikely, there are unruly powers blowing life into storms, disordering sedulous[3] mornings, and uprooting the stability of the afternoon—dressmakers, that is to say, and confectioners' shops. Six yards of silk will cover one body; but if you have to devise six hundred shapes for it, and twice as many colours?—in the middle of which

1. Have the stems supported with wire to prevent the flowers from drooping.
2. The Duke of Wellington defeated Napoleon at the Battle of Waterloo in 1815.
3. Hard-working and diligent.

there is the urgent question of the pudding with tufts of green cream and battlements of almond paste. It has not arrived.

The flamingo hours fluttered softly through the sky. But regularly they dipped their wings in pitch black; Notting Hill, for instance, or the purlieus of Clerkenwell.[4] No wonder that Italian remained a hidden art, and the piano always played the same sonata. In order to buy one pair of elastic stockings for Mrs. Page, widow, aged sixty-three, in receipt of five shillings out-door relief,[5] and help from her only son employed in Messrs. Mackie's dye-works, suffering in winter with his chest, letters must be written, columns filled up in the same round, simple hand that wrote in Mr. Letts's diary how the weather was fine, the children demons, and Jacob Flanders unworldly. Clara Durrant procured the stockings, played the sonata, filled the vases, fetched the pudding, left the cards, and when the great invention of paper flowers to swim in finger-bowls was discovered, was one of those who most marvelled at their brief lives.

Nor were there wanting poets to celebrate the theme. Edwin Mallett, for example, wrote his verses ending:

And read their doom in Chloe's eyes,[6]

which caused Clara to blush at the first reading, and to laugh at the second, saying that it was just like him to call her Chloe when her name was Clara. Ridiculous young man! But when, between ten and eleven on a rainy morning, Edwin Mallett laid his life at her feet she ran out of the room and hid herself in her bedroom, and Timothy below could not get on with his work all that morning on account of her sobs.

"Which is the result of enjoying yourself," said Mrs. Durrant severely, surveying the dance programme all scored with the same initials, or rather they were different ones this time—R. B. instead of E. M.; Richard Bonamy it was now, the young man with the Wellington nose.

"But I could never marry a man with a nose like that," said Clara.

"Nonsense," said Mrs. Durrant.

"But I am too severe," she thought to herself. For Clara, losing all vivacity, tore up her dance programme and threw it in the fender.

Such were the very serious consequences of the invention of paper flowers to swim in bowls.

---

4. Notting Hill was a working-class area of north-west London, and Clerkenwell, also working-class, lay just east of Bloomsbury.
5. Welfare payments that did not require the recipient to enter a workhouse.
6. Edwin Mallett is presumably trying to imitate the Greek poem *Daphnis and Chloe*, a pastoral romance written by Longus around 200 C.E.

"Please," said Julia Eliot, taking up her position by the curtain almost opposite the door, "don't introduce me. I like to look on. The amusing thing," she went on, addressing Mr. Salvin, who, owing to his lameness, was accommodated with a chair, "the amusing thing about a party is to watch the people—coming and going, coming and going."

"Last time we met," said Mr. Salvin, "was at the Farquhars. Poor lady! She has much to put up with."

"Doesn't she look charming?" exclaimed Miss Eliot, as Clara Durrant passed them.

"And which of them . . . ? asked Mr. Salvin, dropping his voice and speaking in quizzical tones.

"There are so many . . ." Miss Eliot replied. Three young men stood at the doorway looking about for their hostess.

"You don't remember Elizabeth as I do," said Mr. Salvin, "dancing Highland reels at Banchorie.[7] Clara lacks her mother's spirit. Clara is a little pale."

"What different people one sees here!" said Miss Eliot.

"Happily we are not governed by the evening papers," said Mr. Salvin.

"I never read them," said Miss Eliot. "I know nothing about politics," she added.

"The piano is in tune," said Clara, passing them, "but we may have to ask some one to move it for us."

"Are they going to dance?" asked Mr. Salvin.

"Nobody shall disturb you," said Mrs. Durrant peremptorily as she passed.

"Julia Eliot. It *is* Julia Eliot!" said old Lady Hibbert, holding out both her hands. "And Mr. Salvin. What is going to happen to us, Mr. Salvin? With all my experience of English politics—My dear, I was thinking of your father last night—one of my oldest friends, Mr. Salvin. Never tell me that girls of ten are incapable of love! I had all Shakespeare by heart before I was in my teens, Mr. Salvin!"

"You don't say so," said Mr. Salvin.

"But I do," said Lady Hibbert.

---

7. Misspelling of "Banchory," a resort town on the river Dee in northeastern Scotland, near Aberdeen.

"Oh, Mr. Salvin, I'm so sorry. . . ."

"I will remove myself if you'll kindly lend me a hand," said Mr. Salvin.

"You shall sit by my mother," said Clara. "Everybody seems to come in here. . . . Mr. Calthorp, let me introduce you to Miss Edwards."

"Are you going away for Christmas?" said Mr. Calthorp.

"If my brother gets his leave," said Miss Edwards.

"What regiment is he in?" said Mr. Calthorp.

"The Twentieth Hussars," said Miss Edwards.

"Perhaps he knows my brother?" said Mr. Calthorp.

"I am afraid I did not catch your name," said Miss Edwards.

"Calthorp," said Mr. Calthorp.

"But what proof was there that the marriage service was actually performed?" said Mr. Crosby.

"There is no reason to doubt that Charles James Fox[8] . . ." Mr. Burley began; but here Mrs. Stretton told him that she knew his sister well; had stayed with her not six weeks ago; and thought the house charming, but bleak in winter.

"Going about as girls do nowadays——" said Mrs. Forster.

Mr. Bowley looked round him, and catching sight of Rose Shaw moved towards her, threw out his hands, and exclaimed: "Well!"

"Nothing!" she replied. "Nothing at all—though I left them alone the entire afternoon on purpose."

"Dear me, dear me," said Mr. Bowley. "I will ask Jimmy to breakfast."

"But who could resist her?" cried Rose Shaw. "Dearest Clara—I know we mustn't try to stop you . . ."

---

8. British Whig politician (1749–1806) who in 1795 secretly married Elizabeth Armitstead, with whom he had been living for many years; the marriage was revealed only in 1802.

"You and Mr. Bowley are talking dreadful gossip, I know," said Clara.

"Life is wicked—life is detestable!" cried Rose Shaw.

"There's not much to be said for this sort of thing, is there?" said Timothy Durrant to Jacob.

"Women like it."

"Like what?" said Charlotte Wilding, coming up to them.

"Where have you come from?" said Timothy. "Dining somewhere, I suppose."

"I don't see why not," said Charlotte.

"People must go downstairs," said Clara, passing. "Take Charlotte, Timothy. How d'you do, Mr. Flanders."

"How d'you do, Mr. Flanders," said Julia Eliot, holding out her hand. "What's been happening to you?"

> "Who is Silvia? what is she?
>   That all our swains commend her?"[9]

sang Elsbeth Siddons.

Every one stood where they were, or sat down if a chair was empty.

"Ah," sighed Clara, who stood beside Jacob, half-way through.

> "Then to Silvia let us sing,
>   That Silvia is excelling;
> She excels each mortal thing
>   Upon the dull earth dwelling.
> To her let us garlands bring,"[1]

sang Elsbeth Siddons.

"Ah!" Clara exclaimed out loud, and clapped her gloved hands; and Jacob clapped his bare ones; and then she moved forward and directed people to come in from the doorway.

"You are living in London?" asked Miss Julia Eliot.

"Yes," said Jacob.

"In rooms?"

"Yes."

"There is Mr. Clutterbuck. You always see Mr. Clutterbuck here. He is not very happy at home, I am afraid. They say that Mrs. Clutterbuck . . ." she dropped her voice. "That's why he stays with the Durrants. Were you there when they acted Mr. Wortley's play? Oh,

9. Shakespeare, *The Two Gentlemen of Verona* (1592–93), 4.2.40 ff.; set to music by Austrian composer Franz Schubert (1797–1828) in 1826.
1. Elsbeth is completing the Schubert song.

no, of course not—at the last moment, did you hear—you had to go
to join your mother, I remember, at Harrogate—At the last moment,
as I was saying, just as everything was ready, the clothes finished
and everything—Now Elsbeth is going to sing again. Clara is playing
her accompaniment or turning over for Mr. Carter, I think. No, Mr.
Carter is playing by himself—This is *Bach*,"[2] she whispered, as Mr.
Carter played the first bars.

"Are you fond of music?" said Mrs. Durrant.

"Yes. I like hearing it," said Jacob. "I know nothing about it."

"Very few people do that," said Mrs. Durrant. "I daresay you were
never taught. Why is that, Sir Jasper?—Sir Jasper Bigham—Mr.
Flanders. Why is nobody taught anything that they ought to know,
Sir Jasper?" She left them standing against the wall.

Neither of the gentlemen said anything for three minutes, though
Jacob shifted perhaps five inches to the left, and then as many to the
right. Then Jacob grunted, and suddenly crossed the room.

"Will you come and have something to eat?" he said to Clara Durrant.

"Yes, an ice. Quickly. Now," she said.

Downstairs they went.

But half-way down they met Mr. and Mrs. Gresham, Herbert
Turner, Sylvia Rashleigh, and a friend, whom they had dared to
bring, from America, "knowing that Mrs. Durrant—wishing to show
Mr. Pilcher.—Mr. Pilcher from New York—This is Miss Durrant."

"Whom I have heard so much of," said Mr. Pilcher, bowing low.

So Clara left him.

VIII

About half-past nine Jacob left the house, his door slamming, other
door slamming, buying his paper, mounting his omnibus, or, weather
permitting, walking his road as other people do. Head bent down, a
desk, a telephone, books bound in green leather, electric light. . . .
"Fresh coals, sir?" . . . "Your tea, sir." . . . Talk about football, the
Hotspurs, the Harlequins; six-thirty *Star* brought in by the office boy;
the rooks of Gray's Inn[1] passing overhead; branches in the fog thin

---

2. Johann Sebastian Bach (1685–1750), German Baroque composer, author of the *Bran-
denburg Concertos* (pre-1721) and other works.
1. One of the four Inns of Court, where students train to become barristers, situated just

and brittle; and through the roar of traffic now and again a voice shouting: "Verdict—verdict—winner—winner," while letters accumulate in a basket, Jacob signs them, and each evening finds him, as he takes his coat down, with some muscle of the brain new stretched.

Then, sometimes a game of chess; or pictures in Bond Street,[2] or a long way home to take the air with Bonamy on his arm, meditatively marching, head thrown back, the world a spectacle, the early moon above the steeples coming in for praise, the sea-gulls flying high, Nelson on his column[3] surveying the horizon, and the world our ship.

Meanwhile, poor Betty Flanders's letter, having caught the second post, lay on the hall table—poor Betty Flanders writing her son's name, Jacob Alan Flanders, Esq., as mothers do, and the ink pale, profuse, suggesting how mothers down at Scarborough scribble over the fire with their feet on the fender, when tea's cleared away, and can never, never say, whatever it may be—probably this—Don't go with bad women, do be a good boy; wear your thick shirts; and come back, come back, come back to me.

But she said nothing of the kind. "Do you remember old Miss Wargrave, who used to be so kind when you had the whooping-cough?" she wrote; "she's dead at last, poor thing. They would like it if you wrote. Ellen came over and we spent a nice day shopping. Old Mouse gets very stiff, and we have to walk him up the smallest hill. Rebecca, at last, after I don't know how long, went into Mr. Adamson's. Three teeth, he says, must come out. Such mild weather for the time of year, the little buds actually on the pear trees. And Mrs. Jarvis tells me——" Mrs. Flanders liked Mrs. Jarvis, always said of her that she was too good for such a quiet place, and, though she never listened to her discontent and told her at the end of it (looking up, sucking her thread, or taking off her spectacles) that a little peat wrapped round the iris roots keeps them from the frost, and Parrot's great white sale is Tuesday next, "do remember,"—Mrs. Flanders knew precisely how Mrs. Jarvis felt; and how interesting her letters were, about Mrs. Jarvis, could one read them year in, year out—the unpublished works of women, written by the fireside in pale profu-

---

southeast of Bloomsbury; Tottenham Hotspurs: a premier-league football team based in North London, founded in 1882; the Harlequin Football Club: a rugby union team, founded in 1866 as the Hampstead Football Club, changed its name to the Harlequins in 1870; the *Star*: a radical daily newspaper launched in 1888, with a modern layout and an emphasis on human interest stories.

2. Bond Street runs between Oxford Street and Piccadilly and is famous for its numerous art galleries.

3. Nelson's column in Trafalgar Square, a short walk down Charing Cross Road from Oxford Street, was built 1840–43 to commemorate Sir Horatio Nelson, British naval commander during the Napoleonic Wars. Nelson's forces defeated the French fleet at the Battle of Trafalgar (1805), in which he was killed.

sion, dried by the flame, for the blotting-paper's worn to holes and the nib cleft and clotted. Then Captain Barfoot. Him she called "the Captain," spoke of frankly, yet never without reserve. The Captain was enquiring for her about Garfit's acre; advised chickens; could promise profit; or had the sciatica; or Mrs. Barfoot had been indoors for weeks; or the Captain says things look bad, politics that is, for as Jacob knew, the Captain would sometimes talk, as the evening waned, about Ireland or India; and then Mrs. Flanders would fall musing about Morty, her brother, lost all these years—had the natives got him, was his ship sunk—would the Admiralty tell her?— the Captain knocking his pipe out, as Jacob knew, rising to go, stiffly stretching to pick up Mrs. Flanders's wool which had rolled beneath the chair. Talk of the chicken farm came back and back, the woman, even at fifty, impulsive at heart, sketching on the cloudy future flocks of Leghorns, Cochin Chinas, Orpingtons;[4] like Jacob in the blur of her outline; but powerful as he was; fresh and vigorous, running about the house, scolding Rebecca.

The letter lay upon the hall table; Florinda coming in that night took it up with her, put it on the table as she kissed Jacob, and Jacob seeing the hand, left it there under the lamp, between the biscuit-tin and the tobacco-box. They shut the bedroom door behind them.

The sitting-room neither knew nor cared. The door was shut; and to suppose that wood, when it creaks, transmits anything save that rats are busy and wood dry is childish. These old houses are only brick and wood, soaked in human sweat, grained with human dirt. But if the pale blue envelope lying by the biscuit-box had the feelings of a mother, the heart was torn by the little creak, the sudden stir. Behind the door was the obscene thing, the alarming presence, and terror would come over her as at death, or the birth of a child. Better, perhaps, burst in and face it than sit in the antechamber listening to the little creak, the sudden stir, for her heart was swollen, and pain threaded it. My son, my son—such would be her cry, uttered to hide her vision of him stretched with Florinda, inexcusable, irrational, in a woman with three children living at Scarborough. And the fault lay with Florinda. Indeed, when the door opened and the couple came out, Mrs. Flanders would have flounced upon her— only it was Jacob who came first, in his dressing-gown, amiable, authoritative, beautifully healthy, like a baby after an airing, with an eye clear as running water. Florinda followed, lazily stretching; yawning a little; arranging her hair at the looking-glass—while Jacob read his mother's letter.

4. Breeds of chickens.

Let us consider letters—how they come at breakfast, and at night, with their yellow stamps and their green stamps, immortalized by the postmark—for to see one's own envelope on another's table is to realize how soon deeds sever and become alien. Then at last the power of the mind to quit the body is manifest, and perhaps we fear or hate or wish annihilated this phantom of ourselves, lying on the table. Still, there are letters that merely say how dinner's at seven; others ordering coal; making appointments. The hand in them is scarcely perceptible, let alone the voice or the scowl. Ah, but when the post knocks and the letter comes always the miracle seems repeated—speech attempted. Venerable are letters, infinitely brave, forlorn, and lost.

Life would split asunder without them. "Come to tea, come to dinner, what's the truth of the story? have you heard the news? life in the capital is gay; the Russian dancers. . . ." These are our stays and props. These lace our days together and make of life a perfect globe. And yet, and yet . . . when we go to dinner, when pressing finger-tips we hope to meet somewhere soon, a doubt insinuates itself; is this the way to spend our days? the rare, the limited, so soon dealt out to us—drinking tea? dining out? And the notes accumulate. And the telephones ring. And everywhere we go wires and tubes surround us to carry the voices that try to penetrate before the last card is dealt and the days are over. "Try to penetrate," for as we lift the cup, shake the hand, express the hope, something whispers, Is this all? Can I never know, share, be certain? Am I doomed all my days to write letters, send voices, which fall upon the tea-table, fade upon the passage, making appointments, while life dwindles, to come and dine? Yet letters are venerable; and the telephone valiant, for the journey is a lonely one, and if bound together by notes and telephones we went in company, perhaps—who knows?—we might talk by the way.

Well, people have tried. Byron wrote letters. So did Cowper.[5] For centuries the writing-desk has contained sheets fit precisely for the communications of friends. Masters of language, poets of long ages, have turned from the sheet that endures to the sheet that perishes, pushing aside the tea-tray, drawing close to the fire (for letters are written when the dark presses round a bright red cave), and addressed themselves to the task of reaching, touching, penetrating

---

5. William Cowper (1731–1800), British poet, author of *The Castaway* (1799) and other works, and considered to have been one of the best letter-writers in English.

the individual heart. Were it possible! But words have been used too often; touched and turned, and left exposed to the dust of the street. The words we seek hang close to the tree. We come at dawn and find them sweet beneath the leaf.

Mrs. Flanders wrote letters; Mrs. Jarvis wrote them; Mrs. Durrant too; Mother Stuart actually scented her pages, thereby adding a flavour which the English language fails to provide; Jacob had written in his day long letters about art, morality, and politics to young men at college. Clara Durrant's letters were those of a child. Florinda— the impediment between Florinda and her pen was something impassable. Fancy a butterfly, gnat, or other winged insect, attached to a twig which, clogged with mud, it rolls across a page. Her spelling was abominable. Her sentiments infantile. And for some reason when she wrote she declared her belief in God. Then there were crosses—tear stains; and the hand itself rambling and redeemed only by the fact—which always did redeem Florinda—by the fact that she cared. Yes, whether it was for chocolate creams, hot baths, the shape of her face in the looking-glass, Florinda could no more pretend a feeling than swallow whisky. Incontinent was her rejection. Great men are truthful, and these little prostitutes, staring in the fire, taking out a powder-puff, decorating lips at an inch of looking-glass, have (so Jacob thought) an inviolable fidelity.

Then he saw her turning up Greek Street[6] upon another man's arm.

The light from the arc lamp[7] drenched him from head to toe. He stood for a minute motionless beneath it. Shadows chequered the street. Other figures, single and together, poured out, wavered across, and obliterated Florinda and the man.

The light drenched Jacob from head to toe. You could see the pattern on his trousers; the old thorns on his stick; his shoe laces; bare hands; and face.

It was as if a stone were ground to dust; as if white sparks flew from a livid whetstone,[8] which was his spine; as if the switchback railway, having swooped to the depths, fell, fell, fell. This was in his face.

Whether we know what was in his mind is another question. Granted ten years' seniority and a difference of sex, fear of him comes first; this is swallowed up by a desire to help—overwhelming

6. Street in Soho, running south of Soho Square.
7. Electric street light.
8. Stone for sharpening blades.

sense, reason, and the time of night; anger would follow close on that—with Florinda, with destiny; and then up would bubble an irresponsible optimism. "Surely there's enough light in the street at this moment to drown all our cares in gold!" Ah, what's the use of saying it? Even while you speak and look over your shoulder towards Shaftesbury Avenue,[9] destiny is chipping a dent in him. He has turned to go. As for following him back to his rooms, no—that we won't do.

Yet that, of course, is precisely what one does. He let himself in and shut the door, though it was only striking ten on one of the city clocks. No one can go to bed at ten. Nobody was thinking of going to bed. It was January and dismal, but Mrs. Wagg stood on her doorstep, as if expecting something to happen. A barrel-organ played like an obscene nightingale beneath wet leaves. Children ran across the road. Here and there one could see brown panelling inside the hall door. . . . The march that the mind keeps beneath the windows of others is queer enough. Now distracted by brown panelling; now by a fern in a pot; here improvising a few phrases to dance with the barrel-organ; again snatching a detached gaiety from a drunken man; then altogether absorbed by words the poor shout across the street at each other (so outright, so lusty)—yet all the while having for centre, for magnet, a young man alone in his room.

"Life is wicked—life is detestable," cried Rose Shaw.

The strange thing about life is that though the nature of it must have been apparent to every one for hundreds of years, no one has left any adequate account of it. The streets of London have their map; but our passions are uncharted. What are you going to meet if you turn this corner?

"Holborn straight ahead of you," says the policeman. Ah, but where are you going if instead of brushing past the old man with the white beard, the silver medal, and the cheap violin, you let him go on with his story, which ends in an invitation to step somewhere, to his room, presumably, off Queen's Square,[1] and there he shows you a collection of birds' eggs and a letter from the Prince of Wales's secretary, and this (skipping the intermediate stages) brings you one winter's day to the Essex coast, where the little boat makes off to the ship, and the ship sails and you behold on the skyline the Azores;[2]

9. Greek Street crosses Shaftesbury Avenue, famous for its theaters.
1. Square in Bloomsbury, just east of Russell Square.
2. Group of nine volcanic islands in the Atlantic Ocean, about one thousand miles west of Lisbon, Portugal; a Portuguese colony since 1439.

and the flamingoes rise; and there you sit on the verge of the marsh drinking rum-punch, an outcast from civilization, for you have committed a crime, are infected with yellow fever as likely as not, and—fill in the sketch as you like.

As frequent as street corners in Holborn are these chasms in the continuity of our ways. Yet we keep straight on.

Rose Shaw, talking in rather an emotional manner to Mr. Bowley at Mrs. Durrant's evening party a few nights back, said that life was wicked because a man called Jimmy refused to marry a woman called (if memory serves) Helen Aitken.

Both were beautiful. Both were inanimate. The oval tea-table invariably separated them, and the plate of biscuits was all he ever gave her. He bowed; she inclined her head. They danced. He danced divinely. They sat in the alcove; never a word was said. Her pillow was wet with tears. Kind Mr. Bowley and dear Rose Shaw marvelled and deplored. Bowley had rooms in the Albany.[3] Rose was re-born every evening precisely as the clock struck eight. All four were civilization's triumphs, and if you persist that a command of the English language is part of our inheritance, one can only reply that beauty is almost always dumb. Male beauty in association with female beauty breeds in the onlooker a sense of fear. Often have I seen them—Helen and Jimmy—and likened them to ships adrift, and feared for my own little craft. Or again, have you ever watched fine collie dogs couchant[4] at twenty yards' distance? As she passed him his cup there was that quiver in her flanks. Bowley saw what was up—asked Jimmy to breakfast. Helen must have confided in Rose. For my own part, I find it exceedingly difficult to interpret songs without words. And now Jimmy feeds crows in Flanders and Helen visits hospitals. Oh, life is damnable, life is wicked, as Rose Shaw said.

The lamps of London uphold the dark as upon the points of burning bayonets. The yellow canopy sinks and swells over the great four-poster. Passengers in the mail-coaches running into London in the eighteenth century looked through leafless branches and saw it flar-

3. Originally the town residence of George III's brother, the Albany on Savile Row near
   Piccadilly was converted into exclusive apartments for bachelors in 1803.
4. A term from heraldry, meaning "lying down"; collie dogs: sheepdogs.

ing beneath them. The light burns behind yellow blinds and pink blinds, and above fanlights, and down in basement windows. The street market in Soho is fierce with light. Raw meat, china mugs, and silk stockings blaze in it. Raw voices wrap themselves round the flaring gas-jets. Arms akimbo, they stand on the pavement bawling— Messrs. Kettle and Wilkinson; their wives sit in the shop, furs wrapped round their necks, arms folded, eyes contemptuous. Such faces as one sees. The little man fingering the meat must have squatted before the fire in innumerable lodging-houses, and heard and seen and known so much that it seems to utter itself even volubly from dark eyes, loose lips, as he fingers the meat silently, his face sad as a poet's, and never a song sung. Shawled women carry babies with purple eyelids; boys stand at street corners; girls look across the road—rude illustrations, pictures in a book whose pages we turn over and over as if we should at last find what we look for. Every face, every shop, bedroom window, public-house, and dark square is a picture feverishly turned—in search of what? It is the same with books. What do we seek through millions of pages? Still hopefully turning the pages—oh, here is Jacob's room.

He sat at the table reading the *Globe*.[5] The pinkish sheet was spread flat before him. He propped his face in his hand, so that the skin of his cheek was wrinkled in deep folds. Terribly severe he looked, set, and defiant. (What people go through in half an hour! But nothing could save him. These events are features of our landscape. A foreigner coming to London could scarcely miss seeing St. Paul's.) He judged life. These pinkish and greenish newspapers are thin sheets of gelatine pressed nightly over the brain and heart of the world. They take the impression of the whole. Jacob cast his eye over it. A strike, a murder, football, bodies found; vociferation from all parts of England simultaneously. How miserable it is that the *Globe* newspaper offers nothing better to Jacob Flanders! When a child begins to read history one marvels, sorrowfully, to hear him spell out in his new voice the ancient words.

The Prime Minister's speech was reported in something over five columns. Feeling in his pocket, Jacob took out a pipe and proceeded to fill it. Five minutes, ten minutes, fifteen minutes passed. Jacob took the paper over to the fire. The Prime Minister proposed a measure for giving Home Rule to Ireland.[6] Jacob knocked out his pipe.

5. London evening newspaper with a small circulation, seeking influence over the ruling classes through its editorials; printed on pink paper.
6. The Home Rule movement started in the early nineteenth century. After two Home Rule

He was certainly thinking about Home Rule in Ireland—a very difficult matter. A very cold night.

The snow, which had been falling all night, lay at three o'clock in
the afternoon over the fields and the hill. Clumps of withered grass
stood out upon the hill-top; the furze bushes were black, and now
and then a black shiver crossed the snow as the wind drove flurries
of frozen particles before it. The sound was that of a broom sweeping—sweeping.

The stream crept along by the road unseen by any one. Sticks and
leaves caught in the frozen grass. The sky was sullen grey and the
trees of black iron. Uncompromising was the severity of the country.
At four o'clock the snow was again falling. The day had gone out.

A window tinged yellow about two feet across alone combated the
white fields and the black trees. . . . At six o'clock a man's figure
carrying a lantern crossed the field. . . . A raft of twigs stayed upon
a stone, suddenly detached itself, and floated towards the culvert.[7]
. . . A load of snow slipped and fell from a fir branch. . . . Later there
was a mournful cry. . . . A motor car came along the road shoving
the dark before it. . . . The dark shut down behind it. . . .

Spaces of complete immobility separated each of these movements. The land seemed to lie dead. . . . Then the old shepherd
returned stiffly across the field. Stiffly and painfully the frozen earth
was trodden under and gave beneath pressure like a treadmill. The
worn voices of clocks repeated the fact of the hour all night long.

Jacob, too, heard them, and raked out the fire. He rose. He
stretched himself. He went to bed.

IX

The Countess of Rocksbier sat at the head of the table alone with
Jacob. Fed upon champagne and spices for at least two centuries
(four, if you count the female line), the Countess Lucy looked well
fed. A discriminating nose she had for scents, prolonged, as if in

    bills were defeated in the British parliament in 1886 and 1893, a third bill was introduced
    in 1912 and became law in 1914. The Liberal prime minister supporting the bill was
    Herbert Henry Asquith (1852–1928).
7. Stone or brick tunnel carrying a stream beneath a railway, canal, or road.

quest of them; her underlip protruded a narrow red shelf; her eyes were small, with sandy tufts for eyebrows, and her jowl was heavy. Behind her (the window looked on Grosvenor Square)[1] stood Moll Pratt on the pavement, offering violets for sale; and Mrs. Hilda Thomas, lifting her skirts, preparing to cross the road. One was from Walworth; the other from Putney.[2] Both wore black stockings, but Mrs. Thomas was coiled in furs. The comparison was much in Lady Rocksbier's favour. Moll had more humour, but was violent; stupid too. Hilda Thomas was mealy-mouthed, all her silver frames aslant; egg-cups in the drawing-room; and the windows shrouded. Lady Rocksbier, whatever the deficiencies of her profile, had been a great rider to hounds. She used her knife with authority, tore her chicken bones, asking Jacob's pardon, with her own hands.

"Who is that driving by?" she asked Boxall, the butler.

"Lady Fittlemere's carriage, my lady," which reminded her to send a card to ask after his lordship's health. A rude old lady, Jacob thought. The wine was excellent. She called herself "an old woman"—"so kind to lunch with an old woman"—which flattered him. She talked of Joseph Chamberlain,[3] whom she had known. She said that Jacob must come and meet—one of our celebrities. And the Lady Alice came in with three dogs on a leash, and Jackie, who ran to kiss his grandmother, while Boxall brought in a telegram, and Jacob was given a good cigar.

A few moments before a horse jumps it slows, sidles, gathers itself together, goes up like a monster wave, and pitches down on the further side. Hedges and sky swoop in a semicircle. Then as if your own body ran into the horse's body and it was your own forelegs grown with his that sprang, rushing through the air you go, the ground resilient, bodies a mass of muscles, yet you have command too, upright stillness, eyes accurately judging. Then the curves cease, changing to downright hammer strokes, which jar; and you draw up with a jolt; sitting back a little, sparkling, tingling, glazed with ice over pounding arteries, gasping: "Ah! ho! Hah!" the steam going up from the horses as they jostle together at the cross-roads, where the signpost is, and the woman in the apron stands and stares at the doorway. The man raises himself from the cabbages to stare too.

1. Exclusive address in Mayfair, central London.
2. Lower middle-class suburb of southwest London; Walworth: working-class area of south-east London.
3. Politician and social reformer (1836–1914), known for his imperialist views and his opposition to Irish Home Rule. He was paralyzed by a stroke in 1906.

So Jacob galloped over the fields of Essex, flopped in the mud, lost the hunt, and rode by himself eating sandwiches, looking over the hedges, noticing the colours as if new scraped, cursing his luck.

He had tea at the Inn; and there they all were, slapping, stamping, saying, "After you," clipped, curt, jocose, red as the wattles[4] of turkeys, using free speech until Mrs. Horsefield and her friend Miss Dudding appeared at the doorway with their skirts hitched up, and hair looping down. Then Tom Dudding rapped at the window with his whip. A motor car throbbed in the courtyard. Gentlemen, feeling for matches, moved out, and Jacob went into the bar with Brandy Jones to smoke with the rustics. There was old Jevons with one eye gone, and his clothes the colour of mud, his bag over his back, and his brains laid feet down in earth among the violet roots and the nettle roots; Mary Sanders with her box of wood; and Tom sent for beer, the half-witted son of the sexton—all this within thirty miles of London.

Mrs. Papworth, of Endell Street, Covent Garden, did for Mr. Bonamy in New Square, Lincoln's Inn,[5] and as she washed up the dinner things in the scullery she heard the young gentlemen talking in the room next door. Mr. Sanders was there again; Flanders she meant; and where an inquisitive old woman gets a name wrong, what chance is there that she will faithfully report an argument? As she held the plates under water and then dealt them on the pile beneath the hissing gas, she listened: heard Sanders speaking in a loud rather overbearing tone of voice: "good" he said, and "absolute" and "justice" and "punishment," and "the will of the majority." Then her gentleman piped up; she backed him for argument against Sanders. Yet Sanders was a fine young fellow (here all the scraps went swirling round the sink, scoured after by her purple, almost nailless hands). "Women"—she thought, and wondered what Sanders and her gentleman did in *that* line, one eyelid sinking perceptibly as she mused, for she was the mother of nine—three still-born and one deaf and dumb from birth. Putting the plates in the rack she heard once more Sanders at it again ("He don't give Bonamy a chance," she thought). "Objective something," said Bonamy; and "common ground" and something else—all very long words, she noted. "Book learning does it," she thought to herself, and, as she thrust her arms into her jacket, heard something—might be the little table by the fire—fall; and then

4. Bright fleshy lobes hanging from the neck of a turkey.
5. Law students could rent rooms in Lincoln's Inn, Holborn, where they lived and studied.

stamp, stamp, stamp—as if they were having at each other—round the room, making the plates dance.

"To-morrow's breakfast, sir," she said, opening the door; and there were Sanders and Bonamy like two bulls of Bashan[6] driving each other up and down, making such a racket, and all them chairs in the way. They never noticed her. She felt motherly towards them. "Your breakfast, sir," she said, as they came near. And Bonamy, all his hair touzled and his tie flying, broke off, and pushed Sanders into the arm-chair, and said Mr. Sanders had smashed the coffee-pot and he was teaching Mr. Sanders—

Sure enough, the coffee-pot lay broken on the hearthrug.

"Any day this week except Thursday," wrote Miss Perry, and this was not the first invitation by any means. Were all Miss Perry's weeks blank with the exception of Thursday, and was her only desire to see her old friend's son? Time is issued to spinster ladies of wealth in long white ribbons. These they wind round and round, round and round, assisted by five female servants, a butler, a fine Mexican parrot, regular meals, Mudie's library, and friends dropping in. A little hurt she was already that Jacob had not called.

"Your mother," she said, "is one of my oldest friends."

Miss Rosseter, who was sitting by the fire, holding the *Spectator*[7] between her cheek and the blaze, refused to have a fire screen, but finally accepted one. The weather was then discussed, for in deference to Parkes, who was opening little tables, graver matters were postponed. Miss Rosseter drew Jacob's attention to the beauty of the cabinet.

"So wonderfully clever in picking things up," she said. Miss Perry had found it in Yorkshire. The North of England was discussed. When Jacob spoke they both listened. Miss Perry was bethinking her of something suitable and manly to say when the door opened and Mr. Benson was announced. Now there were four people sitting in that room. Miss Perry aged 66; Miss Rosseter 42; Mr. Benson 38; and Jacob 25.

"My old friend looks as well as ever," said Mr. Benson, tapping the bars of the parrot's cage; Miss Rosseter simultaneously praised the tea; Jacob handed the wrong plates; and Miss Perry signified her desire to approach more closely. "Your brothers," she began vaguely.

"Archer and John," Jacob supplied her. Then to her pleasure she

6. Psalm 22.12: "Many bulls have compassed me: strong bulls of Bashan have beset me round."
7. Weekly magazine, established 1828, publishing educational and cultural articles.

recovered Rebecca's name; and how one day "when you were all little boys, playing in the drawing-room——"

"But Miss Perry has the kettle-holder," said Miss Rosseter, and indeed Miss Perry was clasping it to her breast. (Had she, then, loved Jacob's father?)

"So clever"—"not so good as usual"—"I thought it most unfair," said Mr. Benson and Miss Rosseter, discussing the Saturday *Westminster.* Did they not compete regularly for prizes?[8] Had not Mr. Benson three times won a guinea, and Miss Rosseter once ten and sixpence? Of course Everard Benson had a weak heart, but still, to win prizes, remember parrots, today Miss Perry, despise Miss Rosseter, give tea-parties in his rooms (which were in the style of Whistler,[9] with pretty books on tables), all this, so Jacob felt without knowing him, made him a contemptible ass. As for Miss Rosseter, she had nursed cancer, and now painted water-colours.

"Running away so soon?" said Miss Perry vaguely. "At home every afternoon, if you've nothing better to do—except Thursdays."

"I've never known you desert your old ladies once," Miss Rosseter was saying, and Mr. Benson was stooping over the parrot's cage, and Miss Perry was moving towards the bell. . . .

The fire burnt clear between two pillars of greenish marble, and on the mantelpiece there was a green clock guarded by Britannia[1] leaning on her spear. As for pictures—a maiden in a large hat offered roses over the garden gate to a gentleman in eighteenth-century costume. A mastiff[2] lay extended against a battered door. The lower panes of the windows were of ground glass,[3] and the curtains, accurately looped, were of plush and green too.

Laurette and Jacob sat with their toes in the fender[4] side by side, in two large chairs covered in green plush. Laurette's skirts were

8. The *Saturday Westminster Gazette*, a weekly magazine founded in 1904 and continued as *Weekly Westminster Gazette* from 1922 to 1926, regularly ran a "Problems and Prizes" page that invited readers to send in parodies, essays, poems, epigrams, or stories on a range of topics, including "An Additional Chapter to *Alice Through the Looking Glass*," "Sentences Containing all the Letters of the Alphabet and all the Parts of Speech," "On Other People's Names," and "Story of a Psychical Phenomenon in the Style of Daniel Defoe." Winning entries—sometimes by well-known writers—were published.
9. James McNeill Whistler (1834–1904), painter also famous as a decorative artist of interiors in a style anticipating that of the Aesthetic movement, with its emphasis on color and harmony.
1. Name given by the Romans first to Britain and then to a goddess who personified the country; now a symbol of Britain, usually depicted as a young woman wearing a helmet and Roman robes, carrying the three-pronged trident of Poseidon, Roman god of the sea.
2. Breed of large dog with drooping ears, often used as a watchdog.
3. Opaque glass.
4. Low guard fitted in front of a fireplace to keep ashes, coal, etc., in the hearth.

short, her legs long, thin, and transparently covered. Her fingers stroked her ankles.

"It's not exactly that I don't understand them," she was saying thoughtfully. "I must go and try again."

"What time will you be there?" said Jacob.

She shrugged her shoulders.

"To-morrow?"

No, not to-morrow.

"This weather makes me long for the country," she said, looking over her shoulder at the back view of tall houses through the window.

"I wish you'd been with me on Saturday," said Jacob.

"I used to ride," she said. She got up gracefully, calmly. Jacob got up. She smiled at him. As she shut the door he put so many shillings on the mantelpiece.

Altogether a most reasonable conversation; a most respectable room; an intelligent girl. Only Madame herself seeing Jacob out had about her that leer, that lewdness, that quake of the surface (visible in the eyes chiefly), which threatens to spill the whole bag of ordure,[5] with difficulty held together, over the pavement. In short, something was wrong.

Not so very long ago the workmen had gilt the final "y" in Lord Macaulay's name,[6] and the names stretched in unbroken file round the dome of the British Museum.[7] At a considerable depth beneath, many hundreds of the living sat at the spokes of a cart-wheel copying from printed books into manuscript books; now and then rising to consult the catalogue; regaining their places stealthily, while from time to time a silent man replenished their compartments.

There was a little catastrophe. Miss Marchmont's pile over-balanced and fell into Jacob's compartment. Such things happened to Miss Marchmont. What was she seeking through millions of pages, in her old plush dress, and her wig of claret-coloured hair, with her gems and her chilblains? Sometimes one thing, sometimes another, to confirm her philosophy that colour is sound—or, perhaps, it has something to do with music. She could never quite say, though it was not for lack of trying. And she could not ask you back to her room, for it was "not very clean, I'm afraid," so she must catch

5. Filth.
6. Thomas Macaulay (1800–1859), Baron Macaulay, historian, best known for his *History of England* (1849–61).
7. The famous dome of the circular reading room in the British Museum, originally completed in 1857, was refurbished in 1907 to include the names of a series of British male authors in gilt on the moldings just below its rim.

you in the passage, or take a chair in Hyde Park to explain her philosophy. The rhythm of the soul depends on it—("how rude the little
boys are!" she would say) and Mr. Asquith's Irish policy, and Shakespeare comes in, "and Queen Alexandra[8] most graciously once
acknowledged a copy of my pamphlet," she would say, waving the
little boys magnificently away. But she needs funds to publish her
book, for "publishers are capitalists—publishers are cowards." And
so, digging her elbow into her pile of books it fell over.

Jacob remained quite unmoved.

But Fraser, the atheist, on the other side, detesting plush, more
than once accosted with leaflets, shifted irritably. He abhorred
vagueness—the Christian religion, for example, and old Dean Parker's pronouncements. Dean Parker wrote books and Fraser utterly
destroyed them by force of logic and left his children unbaptized—
his wife did it secretly in the washing basin—but Fraser ignored her,
and went on supporting blasphemers, distributing leaflets, getting
up his facts in the British Museum, always in the same check suit
and fiery tie, but pale, spotted, irritable. Indeed, what a work—to
destroy religion!

Jacob transcribed a whole passage from Marlowe.[9]

Miss Julia Hedge, the feminist, waited for her books. They did not
come. She wetted her pen. She looked about her. Her eye was caught
by the final letters in Lord Macaulay's name. And she read them all
round the dome—the names of great men which remind us——"Oh
damn," said Julia Hedge, "why didn't they leave room for an Eliot or
a Brontë?"[1]

Unfortunate Julia! wetting her pen in bitterness, and leaving her
shoe laces untied. When her books came she applied herself to her
gigantic labours, but perceived through one of the nerves of her exasperated sensibility how composedly, unconcernedly, and with every
consideration the male readers applied themselves to theirs. That
young man for example. What had he got to do except copy out
poetry? And she must study statistics. There are more women than
men. Yes; but if you let women work as men work, they'll die off
much quicker. They'll become extinct. That was her argument.
Death and gall and bitter dust were on her pen-tip; and as the afternoon wore on, red had worked into her cheek-bones and a light was
in her eyes.

But what brought Jacob Flanders to read Marlowe in the British
Museum?

8. Wife of Edward VII, who was king of Britain from 1901 to 1910.
9. Christopher Marlowe (1564–1593), Elizabethan poet and playwright.
1. The three Brontë sisters, Charlotte, Emily, and Anne, all novelists (1816–1855, 1818–
   1848, 1820–1849), authors of *Jane Eyre* (Charlotte), *Wuthering Heights* (Emily), and
   Agnes Grey (Anne); George Eliot: pseudonym of Mary Anne Evans (1819–1880), novelist,
   author of *Middlemarch* and other works.

Youth, youth—something savage—something pedantic. For example there is Mr. Masefield, there is Mr. Bennett.[2] Stuff them into
the flame of Marlowe and burn them to cinders. Let not a shred
remain. Don't palter with the second rate. Detest your own age. Build
a better one. And to set that on foot read incredibly dull essays upon
Marlowe to your friends. For which purpose one must collate editions in the British Museum. One must do the thing oneself. Useless
to trust to the Victorians, who disembowel, or to the living, who are
mere publicists. The flesh and blood of the future depends entirely
upon six young men. And as Jacob was one of them, no doubt he
looked a little regal and pompous as he turned his page, and Julia
Hedge disliked him naturally enough.

But then a pudding-faced man pushed a note towards Jacob, and
Jacob, leaning back in his chair, began an uneasy murmured conversation, and they went off together (Julia Hedge watched them),
and laughed aloud (she thought) directly they were in the hall.

Nobody laughed in the reading-room. There were shiftings, mur-
murings, apologetic sneezes, and sudden unashamed devastating
coughs. The lesson hour was almost over. Ushers were collecting
exercises. Lazy children wanted to stretch. Good ones scribbled
assiduously—ah, another day over and so little done! And now and
then was to be heard from the whole collection of human beings a
heavy sigh, after which the humiliating old man would cough shame-
lessly, and Miss Marchmont hinnied like a horse.

Jacob came back only in time to return his books.

The books were now replaced. A few letters of the alphabet were
sprinkled round the dome. Closely stood together in a ring round
the dome were Plato, Aristotle,[3] Sophocles, and Shakespeare; the
literatures of Rome, Greece, China, India, Persia. One leaf of poetry
was pressed flat against another leaf, one burnished letter laid
smooth against another in a density of meaning, a conglomeration
of loveliness.

"One does want one's tea," said Miss Marchmont, reclaiming her
shabby umbrella.

Miss Marchmont wanted her tea, but could never resist a last look
at the Elgin Marbles.[4] She looked at them sideways, waving her hand
and muttering a word or two of salutation which made Jacob and

2. Arnold Bennett (1867–1931), novelist, author of *The Old Wives' Tale* and other works.
   John Masefield (1876–1967), poet who became poet laureate of Britain in 1930.
3. Ancient Greek philosopher (384–322 B.C.E.), author of *Poetics* and other works; Plato:
   ancient Greek philosopher (c. 428–348 B.C.E.), author of *The Republic* and other works.
4. Collection of ancient Greek sculptures in the British Museum, removed from Athens and
   shipped to England by Thomas Bruce, seventh Lord Elgin, between 1802 and 1812. Own-
   ership of the marbles is still a matter of dispute between Britain and Greece.

the other man turn round. She smiled at them amiably. It all came into her philosophy—that colour is sound, or perhaps it has something to do with music. And having done her service, she hobbled off to tea. It was closing time. The public collected in the hall to receive their umbrellas.

For the most part the students wait their turn very patiently. To stand and wait while some one examines white discs is soothing. The umbrella will certainly be found. But the fact leads you on all day through Macaulay, Hobbes, Gibbon; through octavos, quartos, folios; sinks deeper and deeper through ivory pages and morocco bindings[5] into this density of thought, this conglomeration of knowledge.

Jacob's walking-stick was like all the others; they had muddled the pigeon-holes perhaps.

There is in the British Museum an enormous mind. Consider that Plato is there cheek by jowl with Aristotle; and Shakespeare with Marlowe. This great mind is hoarded beyond the power of any single mind to possess it. Nevertheless (as they take so long finding one's walking-stick) one can't help thinking how one might come with a notebook, sit at a desk, and read it all through. A learned man is the most venerable of all—a man like Huxtable of Trinity, who writes all his letters in Greek, they say, and could have kept his end up with Bentley. And then there is science, pictures, architecture—an enormous mind.

They pushed the walking-stick across the counter. Jacob stood beneath the porch of the British Museum. It was raining. Great Russell Street was glazed and shining—here yellow, here, outside the chemist's, red and pale blue. People scuttled quickly close to the wall; carriages rattled rather helter-skelter down the streets. Well, but a little rain hurts nobody. Jacob walked off much as if he had been in the country; and late that night there he was sitting at his table with his pipe and his book.

The rain poured down. The British Museum stood in one solid immense mound, very pale, very sleek in the rain, not a quarter of a mile from him. The vast mind was sheeted with stone; and each compartment in the depths of it was safe and dry. The night-watchmen, flashing their lanterns over the backs of Plato and Shakespeare, saw that on the twenty-second of February neither flame, rat, nor burglar was going to violate these treasures—poor, highly respectable men, with wives and families at Kentish Town, do their

---

5. Leather made from goatskin often used for bookbinding; Thomas Hobbes; political theorist (1588–1679), author of *Leviathan* and other works; Edward Gibbon: historian (1737–1794), author of *The Decline and Fall of the Roman Empire*; octavos, quartos, folios: printers' designations for different-sized sheets of paper.

best for twenty years to protect Plato and Shakespeare, and then are buried at Highgate.[6]

Stone lies solid over the British Museum, as bone lies cool over the visions and heat of the brain. Only here the brain is Plato's brain and Shakespeare's; the brain has made pots and statues, great bulls and little jewels, and crossed the river of death this way and that incessantly, seeking some landing, now wrapping the body well for its long sleep; now laying a penny piece on the eyes; now turning the toes scrupulously to the East. Meanwhile, Plato continues his dialogue; in spite of the rain; in spite of the cab whistles; in spite of the woman in the mews behind Great Ormond Street who has come home drunk and cries all night long, "Let me in! Let me in!"

In the street below Jacob's room voices were raised.

But he read on. For after all Plato continues imperturbably. And Hamlet utters his soliloquy. And there the Elgin Marbles lie, all night long, old Jones's lantern sometimes recalling Ulysses,[7] or a horse's head; or sometimes a flash of gold, or a mummy's sunk yellow cheek. Plato and Shakespeare continue; and Jacob, who was reading the *Phaedrus*,[8] heard people vociferating round the lamp-post, and the woman battering at the door and crying, "Let me in!" as if a coal had dropped from the fire, or a fly, falling from the ceiling, had lain on its back, too weak to turn over.

The *Phaedrus* is very difficult. And so, when at length one reads straight ahead, falling into step, marching on, becoming (so it seems) momentarily part of this rolling, imperturbable energy, which has driven darkness before it since Plato walked the Acropolis,[9] it is impossible to see to the fire.

The dialogue draws to its close. Plato's argument is done. Plato's argument is stowed away in Jacob's mind, and for five minutes Jacob's mind continues alone, onwards, into the darkness. Then, getting up, he parted the curtains, and saw, with astonishing clearness, how the Springetts opposite had gone to bed; how it rained; how the Jews and the foreign woman, at the end of the street, stood by the pillar-box, arguing.

Every time the door opened and fresh people came in, those already in the room shifted slightly; those who were standing looked

6. Highgate Cemetery: very large burial ground in northwest London. Kentish Town: working-class area of northwest London.
7. Also known as Odysseus: hero of Homer's ancient Greek epic the *Odyssey*.
8. Plato's series of dialogues on aesthetics.
9. Massive rock in the center of Athens on which the Parthenon stands.

over their shoulders; those who were sitting stopped in the middle
of sentences. What with the light, the wine, the strumming of a
guitar, something exciting happened each time the door opened.
Who was coming in?

"That's Gibson."

"The painter?"

"But go on with what you were saying."

They were saying something that was far, far too intimate to be
said outright. But the noise of the voices served like a clapper in little
Mrs. Withers's mind, scaring into the air flocks of small birds, and
then they'd settle, and then she'd feel afraid, put one hand to her
hair, bind both round her knees, and look up at Oliver Skelton nervously, and say:

"Promise, *promise*, you'll tell no one." . . . so considerate he was,
so tender. It was her husband's character that she discussed. He was
cold, she said.

Down upon them came the splendid Magdalen, brown, warm,
voluminous, scarcely brushing the grass with her sandalled feet. Her
hair flew; pins seemed scarcely to attach the flying silks. An actress
of course, a line of light perpetually beneath her. It was only "My
dear" that she said, but her voice went jodelling between Alpine
passes. And down she tumbled on the floor, and sang, since there
was nothing to be said, round ah's and oh's. Mangin, the poet, coming up to her, stood looking down at her, drawing at his pipe. The
dancing began.

Grey-haired Mrs. Keymer asked Dick Graves to tell her who Mangin was, and said that she had seen too much of this sort of thing in
Paris (Magdalen had got upon his knees; now his pipe was in her
mouth) to be shocked. "Who is that?" she said, staying her glasses
when they came to Jacob, for indeed he looked quiet, not indifferent,
but like some one on a beach, watching.

"Oh, my dear, let me lean on you," gasped Helen Askew, hopping
on one foot, for the silver cord round her ankle had worked loose.
Mrs. Keymer turned and looked at the picture on the wall.

"Look at Jacob," said Helen (they were binding his eyes for some
game).

And Dick Graves, being a little drunk, very faithful, and very sim-
ple-minded, told her that he thought Jacob the greatest man he had
ever known. And down they sat cross-legged upon cushions and
talked about Jacob, and Helen's voice trembled, for they both seemed
heroes to her, and the friendship between them so much more beautiful than women's friendships. Anthony Pollett now asked her to
dance, and as she danced she looked at them, over her shoulder,
standing at the table, drinking together.

The magnificent world—the live, sane, vigorous world. . . . These words refer to the stretch of wood pavement between Hammersmith[1] and Holborn in January between two and three in the morning. That was the ground beneath Jacob's feet. It was healthy and magnificent because one room, above a mews, somewhere near the river, contained fifty excited, talkative, friendly people. And then to stride over the pavement (there was scarcely a cab or policeman in sight) is of itself exhilarating. The long loop of Piccadilly, diamond-stitched, shows to best advantage when it is empty. A young man has nothing to fear. On the contrary, though he may not have said anything brilliant, he feels pretty confident he can hold his own. He was pleased to have met Mangin; he admired the young woman on the floor; he liked them all; he liked that sort of thing. In short, all the drums and trumpets were sounding. The street scavengers were the only people about at the moment. It is scarcely necessary to say how well-disposed Jacob felt towards them; how it pleased him to let himself in with his latch-key at his own door; how he seemed to bring back with him into the empty room ten or eleven people whom he had not known when he set out; how he looked about for something to read, and found it, and never read it, and fell asleep.

Indeed, drums and trumpets is no phrase. Indeed, Piccadilly and Holborn, and the empty sitting-room and the sitting-room with fifty people in it are liable at any moment to blow music into the air. Women perhaps are more excitable than men. It is seldom that any one says anything about it, and to see the hordes crossing Waterloo Bridge to catch the non-stop to Surbiton[2] one might think that reason impelled them. No, no. It is the drums and trumpets. Only, should you turn aside into one of those little bays on Waterloo Bridge to think the matter over, it will probably seem to you all a muddle— all a mystery.

They cross the Bridge incessantly. Sometimes in the midst of carts and omnibuses a lorry will appear with great forest trees chained to it. Then, perhaps, a mason's van with newly lettered tombstones

1. In west London, about five miles from Holborn.
2. Commuter town in Surrey, reached by train from Waterloo station, south of the river Thames at the end of Waterloo Bridge.

recording how some one loved some one who is buried at Putney. Then the motor car in front jerks forward, and the tombstones pass too quick for you to read more. All the time the stream of people never ceases passing from the Surrey side to the Strand;[3] from the Strand to the Surrey side. It seems as if the poor had gone raiding the town, and now trapesed back to their own quarters, like beetles scurrying to their holes, for that old woman fairly hobbles towards Waterloo, grasping a shiny bag, as if she had been out into the light and now made off with some scraped chicken bones to her hovel underground. On the other hand, though the wind is rough and blowing in their faces, those girls there, striding hand in hand, shouting out a song, seem to feel neither cold nor shame. They are hatless. They triumph.

The wind has blown up the waves. The river races beneath us, and the men standing on the barges have to lean all their weight on the tiller. A black tarpaulin is tied down over a swelling load of gold. Avalanches of coal glitter blackly. As usual, painters are slung on planks across the great riverside hotels, and the hotel windows have already points of light in them. On the other side the city is white as if with age; St. Paul's swells white above the fretted, pointed, or oblong buildings beside it. The cross alone shines rosy-gilt. But what century have we reached? Has this procession from the Surrey side to the Strand gone on for ever? That old man has been crossing the Bridge these six hundred years, with the rabble of little boys at his heels, for he is drunk, or blind with misery, and tied round with old clouts[4] of clothing such as pilgrims might have worn. He shuffles on. No one stands still. It seems as if we marched to the sound of music; perhaps the wind and the river; perhaps these same drums and trumpets—the ecstasy and hubbub of the soul. Why, even the unhappy laugh, and the policeman, far from judging the drunk man, surveys him humorously, and the little boys scamper back again, and the clerk from Somerset House has nothing but tolerance for him, and the man who is reading half a page of *Lothair*[5] at the bookstall muses charitably, with his eyes off the print, and the girl hesitates at the crossing and turns on him the bright yet vague glance of the young.

Bright yet vague. She is perhaps twenty-two. She is shabby. She crosses the road and looks at the daffodils and the red tulips in the florist's window. She hesitates, and makes off in the direction of

3. Major road running parallel to the river on the north side, connected to Waterloo Bridge.
4. Rags or shreds.
5. Novel by Benjamin Disraeli (1804–1881), prime minister of Britain 1868 and 1874–80, published 1870; Somerset House: a magnificent building at the north end of Waterloo Bridge, completed 1801, which in the years before the First World War housed the Inland Revenue, the Registry of Marriage, Births and Deaths, and the Principal Probate Registry.

Temple Bar.[6] She walks fast, and yet anything distracts her. Now she seems to see, and now to notice nothing.

X

Through the disused graveyard in the parish of St. Pancras,[1] Fanny Elmer strayed between the white tombs which lean against the wall, crossing the grass to read a name, hurrying on when the grave-keeper approached, hurrying into the street, pausing now by a window with blue china, now quickly making up for lost time, abruptly entering a baker's shop, buying rolls, adding cakes, going on again so that any one wishing to follow must fairly trot. She was not drably shabby, though. She wore silk stockings, and silver-buckled shoes, only the red feather in her hat drooped, and the clasp of her bag was weak, for out fell a copy of Madame Tussaud's programme[2] as she walked. She had the ankles of a stag. Her face was hidden. Of course, in this dusk, rapid movements, quick glances, and soaring hopes come naturally enough. She passed right beneath Jacob's window.

The house was flat, dark, and silent. Jacob was at home engaged upon a chess problem, the board being on a stool between his knees. One hand was fingering the hair at the back of his head. He slowly brought it forward and raised the white queen from her square; then put her down again on the same spot. He filled his pipe; ruminated; moved two pawns; advanced the white knight; then ruminated with one finger upon the bishop. Now Fanny Elmer passed beneath the window.

She was on her way to sit to Nick Bramham the painter.

She sat in a flowered Spanish shawl, holding in her hand a yellow novel.

"A little lower, a little looser, so—better, that's right," Bramham mumbled, who was drawing her, and smoking at the same time, and was naturally speechless. His head might have been the work of a sculptor, who had squared the forehead, stretched the mouth, and left marks of his thumbs and streaks from his fingers in the clay. But the eyes had never been shut. They were rather prominent, and rather blood-shot, as if from staring and staring, and when he spoke

6. Memorial built in 1880 marking the official entrance to the City of London (London's financial district); located on Fleet Street between the Royal Courts of Justice and the Temple, east of Waterloo Bridge.
1. Old St. Pancras Churchyard, on Pancras Road behind the station, was an extensive burial ground largely for Roman Catholics. St. Pancras Church moved to a new site further down the Euston Road in 1822, and the last grave in the old churchyard dates from 1854.
2. Madame Tussaud's Wax Museum, established in its present site on Marylebone Road in 1884.

they looked for a second disturbed, but went on staring. An unshaded electric light hung above her head.

As for the beauty of women, it is like the light on the sea, never constant to a single wave. They all have it; they all lose it. Now she is dull and thick as bacon; now transparent as a hanging glass. The fixed faces are the dull ones. Here comes Lady Venice displayed like a monument for admiration, but carved in alabaster, to be set on the mantelpiece and never dusted. A dapper brunette complete from head to foot serves only as an illustration to lie upon the drawing-room table. The women in the streets have the faces of playing cards; the outlines accurately filled in with pink or yellow, and the line drawn tightly round them. Then, at a top-floor window, leaning out, looking down, you see beauty itself; or in the corner of an omnibus; or squatted in a ditch—beauty glowing, suddenly expressive, withdrawn the moment after. No one can count on it or seize it or have it wrapped in paper. Nothing is to be won from the shops, and Heaven knows it would be better to sit at home than haunt the plate-glass windows in the hope of lifting the shining green, the glowing ruby, out of them alive. Sea glass[3] in a saucer loses its lustre no sooner than silks do. Thus if you talk of a beautiful woman you mean only something flying fast which for a second uses the eyes, lips, or cheeks of Fanny Elmer, for example, to glow through.

She was not beautiful, as she sat stiffly; her underlip too prominent; her nose too large; her eyes too near together. She was a thin girl, with brilliant cheeks and dark hair, sulky just now, or stiff with sitting. When Bramham snapped his stick of charcoal she started. Bramham was out of temper. He squatted before the gas fire warming his hands. Meanwhile she looked at his drawing. He grunted. Fanny threw on a dressing-gown and boiled a kettle.

"By God, it's bad," said Bramham.

Fanny dropped on to the floor, clasped her hands round her knees, and looked at him, her beautiful eyes—yes, beauty, flying through the room, shone there for a second. Fanny's eyes seemed to question, to commiserate, to be, for a second, love itself. But she exaggerated. Bramham noticed nothing. And when the kettle boiled, up she scrambled, more like a colt or a puppy than a loving woman.

Now Jacob walked over to the window and stood with his hands in his pockets. Mr. Springett opposite came out, looked at his shop

3. Pieces of glass that have been weathered in the sea and then washed up on the beach; known for their shiny patina and subdued colors.

window, and went in again. The children drifted past, eyeing the pink sticks of sweetstuff. Pickford's van[4] swung down the street. A small boy twirled from a rope. Jacob turned away. Two minutes later he opened the front door, and walked off in the direction of Holborn.

Fanny Elmer took down her cloak from the hook. Nick Bramham unpinned his drawing and rolled it under his arm. They turned out the lights and set off down the street, holding on their way through all the people, motor cars, omnibuses, carts, until they reached Leicester Square,[5] five minutes before Jacob reached it, for his way was slightly longer, and he had been stopped by a block in Holborn waiting to see the King drive by, so that Nick and Fanny were already leaning over the barrier in the promenade at the Empire[6] when Jacob pushed through the swing doors and took his place beside them.

"Hullo, never noticed you," said Nick five minutes later.

"Bloody rot," said Jacob.

"Miss Elmer," said Nick.

Jacob took his pipe out of his mouth very awkwardly.

Very awkward he was. And when they sat upon a plush sofa and let the smoke go up between them and the stage, and heard far off the high-pitched voices and the jolly orchestra breaking in opportunely he was still awkward, only Fanny thought: "What a beautiful voice!" She thought how little he said yet how firm it was. She thought how young men are dignified and aloof, and how unconscious they are, and how quietly one might sit beside Jacob and look at him. And how childlike he would be, come in tired of an evening, she thought, and how majestic; a little overbearing perhaps; "But I wouldn't give way," she thought. He got up and leant over the barrier. The smoke hung about him.

And for ever the beauty of young men seems to be set in smoke, however lustily they chase footballs, or drive cricket balls, dance, run, or stride along roads. Possibly they are soon to lose it. Possibly they look into the eyes of far-away heroes, and take their station among us half contemptuously, she thought (vibrating like a fiddle-string, to be played on and snapped). Anyhow, they love silence, and speak beautifully, each word falling like a disc new cut, not a hubble-bubble of small smooth coins such as girls use; and they move decid-

---

4. Pickford's haulage and moving company, which still exists today, was established in the late seventeenth century.
5. Off Charing Cross Road, just north of Trafalgar Square.
6. The Empire Theatre of Varieties (a music hall) opened in 1884 and was famous for its promenade.

edly, as if they knew how long to stay and when to go—oh, but Mr. Flanders was only gone to get a programme.

"The dancers come right at the end," he said, coming back to them.

And isn't it pleasant, Fanny went on thinking, how young men bring out lots of silver coins from their trouser pockets, and look at them, instead of having just so many in a purse?

Then there she was herself, whirling across the stage in white flounces, and the music was the dance and fling of her own soul, and the whole machinery, rock and gear of the world was spun smoothly into those swift eddies and falls, she felt, as she stood rigid leaning over the barrier two feet from Jacob Flanders.

Her screwed-up black glove dropped to the floor. When Jacob gave it her, she started angrily. For never was there a more irrational passion. And Jacob was afraid of her for a moment—so violent, so dangerous is it when young women stand rigid; grasp the barrier; fall in love.

It was the middle of February. The roofs of Hampstead Garden Suburb[7] lay in a tremulous haze. It was too hot to walk. A dog barked, barked, barked down in the hollow. The liquid shadows went over the plain.

The body after long illness is languid, passive, receptive of sweetness, but too weak to contain it. The tears well and fall as the dog barks in the hollow, the children skim after hoops, the country darkens and brightens. Beyond a veil it seems. Ah, but draw the veil thicker lest I faint with sweetness, Fanny Elmer sighed, as she sat on a bench in Judges Walk[8] looking at Hampstead Garden Suburb. But the dog went on barking. The motor cars hooted on the road. She heard a far-away rush and humming. Agitation was at her heart. Up she got and walked. The grass was freshly green; the sun hot. All round the pond children were stooping to launch little boats; or were drawn back screaming by their nurses.

At mid-day young women walk out into the air. All the men are busy in the town. They stand by the edge of the blue pond. The fresh wind scatters the children's voices all about. *My* children, thought Fanny Elmer. The women stand round the pond, beating off great prancing shaggy dogs. Gently the baby is rocked in the perambulator. The eyes of all the nurses, mothers, and wandering women are a

7. Planned community north of Hampstead Heath, founded in 1907 by Henrietta Barnett.
8. Street running close alongside Hampstead Heath. In fact, it would have been impossible for Fanny to see Hampstead Garden Suburb from there.

little glazed, absorbed. They gently nod instead of answering when the little boys tug at their skirts, begging them to move on.

And Fanny moved, hearing some cry—a workman's whistle perhaps—high in mid air. Now, among the trees, it was the thrush trilling out into the warm air a flutter of jubilation, but fear seemed to spur him, Fanny thought; as if he too were anxious with such joy at his heart—as if he were watched as he sang, and pressed by tumult to sing. There! Restless, he flew to the next tree. She heard his song more faintly. Beyond it was the humming of the wheels and the wind rushing.

She spent tenpence on lunch.

"Dear, miss, she's left her umberella," grumbled the mottled woman in the glass box near the door at the Express Dairy Company's[9] shop.

"Perhaps I'll catch her," answered Milly Edwards, the waitress with the pale plaits of hair; and she dashed through the door.

"No good," she said, coming back a moment later with Fanny's cheap umbrella. She put her hand to her plaits.

"Oh, that door!" grumbled the cashier.

Her hands were cased in black mittens, and the finger-tips that drew in the paper slips were swollen as sausages.

"Pie and greens for one. Large coffee and crumpets. Eggs on toast. Two fruit cakes."

Thus the sharp voices of the waitresses snapped. The lunchers heard their orders repeated with approval; saw the next table served with anticipation. Their own eggs on toast were at last delivered. Their eyes strayed no more.

Damp cubes of pastry fell into mouths opened like triangular bags.

Nelly Jenkinson, the typist, crumbled her cake indifferently enough. Every time the door opened she looked up. What did she expect to see?

The coal merchant read the *Telegraph* without stopping, missed the saucer, and, feeling abstractedly, put the cup down on the table-cloth.

"Did you ever hear the like of that for impertinence?" Mrs. Parsons wound up, brushing the crumbs from her furs.

"Hot milk and scone for one. Pot of tea. Roll and butter," cried the waitresses.

The door opened and shut.

9. Originally a milk delivery company called the Express Country Milk Supply Company, founded in 1864. It also ran teashops, cafés, and bakeries.

Such is the life of the elderly.

It is curious, lying in a boat, to watch the waves. Here are three coming regularly one after another, all much of a size. Then, hurrying after them comes a fourth, very large and menacing; it lifts the boat; on it goes; somehow merges without accomplishing anything; flattens itself out with the rest.

What can be more violent than the fling of boughs in a gale, the tree yielding itself all up the trunk, to the very tip of the branch, streaming and shuddering the way the wind blows, yet never flying in dishevelment away?

The corn squirms and abases itself as if preparing to tug itself free from the roots, and yet is tied down.

Why, from the very windows, even in the dusk, you see a swelling run through the street, an aspiration, as with arms outstretched, eyes desiring, mouths agape. And then we peaceably subside. For if the exaltation lasted we should be blown like foam into the air. The stars would shine through us. We should go down the gale in salt drops— as sometimes happens. For the impetuous spirits will have none of this cradling. Never any swaying or aimlessly lolling for them. Never any making believe, or lying cosily, or genially supposing that one is much like another, fire warm, wine pleasant, extravagance a sin.

"People are so nice, once you know them."

"I couldn't think ill of her. One must remember——" But Nick perhaps, or Fanny Elmer, believing implicitly in the truth of the moment, fling off, sting the cheek, are gone like sharp hail.

"Oh," said Fanny, bursting into the studio three-quarters of an hour late because she had been hanging about the neighbourhood of the Foundling Hospital[1] merely for the chance of seeing Jacob walk down the street, take out his latch-key, and open the door, "I'm afraid I'm late"; upon which Nick said nothing and Fanny grew defiant.

"I'll never come again!" she cried at length.

"Don't, then," Nick replied, and off she ran without so much as good-night.

---

1. Established by Thomas Coram in 1741, the Foundling Hospital was on Guildford Street, which connects with Southampton Row, where Jacob may live, at one end.

How exquisite it was—that dress in Evelina's shop off Shaftesbury Avenue! It was four o'clock on a fine day early in April, and was Fanny the one to spend four o'clock on a fine day indoors? Other girls in that very street sat over ledgers, or drew long threads wearily between silk and gauze; or, festooned with ribbons in Swan and Edgars,[2] rapidly added up pence and farthings on the back of the bill and twisted the yard and three-quarters in tissue paper and asked "Your pleasure?" of the next comer.

In Evelina's shop off Shaftesbury Avenue the parts of a woman were shown separate. In the left hand was her skirt. Twining round a pole in the middle was a feather boa. Ranged like the heads of malefactors on Temple Bar were hats—emerald and white, lightly wreathed or drooping beneath deep-dyed feathers. And on the carpet were her feet—pointed gold, or patent leather slashed with scarlet.

Feasted upon by the eyes of women, the clothes by four o'clock were flyblown like sugar cakes in a baker's window. Fanny eyed them too.

But coming along Gerrard Street was a tall man in a shabby coat. A shadow fell across Evelina's window—Jacob's shadow, though it was not Jacob. And Fanny turned and walked along Gerrard Street[3] and wished that she had read books. Nick never read books, never talked of Ireland, or the House of Lords; and as for his finger-nails! She would learn Latin and read Virgil. She had been a great reader. She had read Scott; she had read Dumas.[4] At the Slade no one read. But no one knew Fanny at the Slade, or guessed how empty it seemed to her; the passion for ear-rings, for dances, for Tonks and Steer[5]— when it was only the French who could paint, Jacob said. For the moderns were futile; painting the least respectable of the arts; and why read anything but Marlowe and Shakespeare, Jacob said, and Fielding[6] if you must read novels?

"Fielding," said Fanny, when the man in Charing Cross Road asked her what book she wanted.

She bought *Tom Jones*.

---

2. Swan and Edgar department store occupied the entire corner of Piccadilly Circus, opposite the end of Shaftesbury Avenue.
3. Runs parallel to Shaftesbury Avenue. Evelina's shop must be on one of the roads that connects Shaftesbury Avenue to Gerrard Street.
4. French novelist and playwright (1802–1870), author of *The Three Musketeers* and other works.
5. Slade School of Fine Art, founded 1871, located on Gower Street, a few blocks north of the British Museum. Virginia Woolf's sister Vanessa Bell was a student there. British painters Henry Tonks (1862–1937) and Philip Wilson Steer (1860–1942) dominated teaching at the Slade in the early years of the twentieth century.
6. Henry Fielding (1707–1754), British novelist, author of *Tom Jones* and other works.

At ten o'clock in the morning, in a room which she shared with a school teacher, Fanny Elmer read *Tom Jones*—that mystic book. For this dull stuff (Fanny thought) about people with odd names is what Jacob likes. Good people like it. Dowdy women who don't mind how they cross their legs read *Tom Jones*—a mystic book; for there is something, Fanny thought, about books which if I had been educated I could have liked—much better than ear-rings and flowers, she sighed, thinking of the corridors at the Slade and the fancy-dress dance next week. She had nothing to wear.

They are real, thought Fanny Elmer, setting her feet on the mantelpiece. Some people are. Nick perhaps, only he was so stupid. And women never—except Miss Sargent, but she went off at lunch-time and gave herself airs. There they sat quietly of a night, reading, she thought. Not going to music-halls; not looking in at shop windows; not wearing each other's clothes, like Robertson who had worn her shawl, and she had worn his waistcoat, which Jacob could only do very awkwardly; for he liked *Tom Jones*.

There it lay on her lap, in double columns, price three and sixpence; the mystic book in which Henry Fielding ever so many years ago rebuked Fanny Elmer for feasting on scarlet,[7] in perfect prose, Jacob said. For he never read modern novels. He liked *Tom Jones*.

"I do like *Tom Jones*," said Fanny at five-thirty that same day early in April when Jacob took out his pipe in the arm-chair opposite.

Alas, women lie! But not Clara Durrant. A flawless mind; a candid nature; a virgin chained to a rock (somewhere off Lowndes Square)[8] eternally pouring out tea for old men in white waistcoats, blue-eyed, looking you straight in the face, playing Bach. Of all women, Jacob honoured her most. But to sit at a table with bread and butter, with dowagers in velvet, and never say more to Clara Durrant than Benson said to the parrot when old Miss Perry poured out tea, was an insufferable outrage upon the liberties and decencies of human nature—or words to that effect. For Jacob said nothing. Only he glared at the fire. Fanny laid down *Tom Jones*.

She stitched or knitted.

"What's that?" asked Jacob.

"For the dance at the Slade."

And she fetched her head-dress; her trousers; her shoes with red tassels. What should she wear?

"I shall be in Paris," said Jacob.

And what is the point of fancy-dress dances? thought Fanny. You

---

7. *Tom Jones*, Book 6, Chapter 1: "To treat of the effects of love to you, must be as absurd as to discourse on colours to a man born blind; since possibly your idea of love may be as absurd as that which we are told such blind man once entertained of the colour scarlet; that colour seemed to him to be very much like the sound of a trumpet: and love probably may, in your opinion, very greatly resemble a dish of soup, or a sirloin of roast-beef."
8. Exclusive address in Knightsbridge, west London.

meet the same people; you wear the same clothes; Mangin gets drunk; Florinda sits on his knee. She flirts outrageously—with Nick Bramham just now.

"In Paris?" said Fanny.

"On my way to Greece," he replied.

For, he said, there is nothing so detestable as London in May.

He would forget her.

A sparrow flew past the window trailing a straw—a straw from a stack stood by a barn in a farmyard. The old brown spaniel snuffs at the base for a rat. Already the upper branches of the elm trees are blotted with nests. The chestnuts have flirted their fans. And the butterflies are flaunting across the rides in the Forest. Perhaps the Purple Emperor[9] is feasting, as Morris says, upon a mass of putrid carrion at the base of an oak tree.

Fanny thought it all came from *Tom Jones*. He could go alone with a book in his pocket and watch the badgers. He would take a train at eight-thirty and walk all night. He saw fire-flies, and brought back glow-worms in pill-boxes. He would hunt with the New Forest Staghounds. It all came from *Tom Jones*; and he would go to Greece with a book in his pocket and forget her.

She fetched her hand-glass. There was her face. And suppose one wreathed Jacob in a turban? There was his face. She lit the lamp. But as the daylight came through the window only half was lit up by the lamp. And though he looked terrible and magnificent and would chuck the Forest, he said, and come to the Slade, and be a Turkish knight or a Roman emperor (and he let her blacken his lips and clenched his teeth and scowled in the glass), still—there lay *Tom Jones*.

XI

"Archer," said Mrs. Flanders with that tenderness which mothers so often display towards their eldest sons, "will be at Gibraltar to-morrow."

The post for which she was waiting (strolling up Dods Hill while the random church bells swung a hymn tune about her head, the clock striking four straight through the circling notes; the grass purpling under a storm-cloud; and the two dozen houses of the village cowering, infinitely humble, in company under a leaf of shadow), the post, with all its variety of messages, envelopes addressed in bold hands, in slanting hands, stamped now with English stamps, again with Colonial stamps, or sometimes hastily dabbed with a yellow bar, the post was about to scatter a myriad messages over the world.

9. Species of butterfly.

Whether we gain or not by this habit of profuse communication it is not for us to say. But that letter-writing is practised mendaciously nowadays, particularly by young men travelling in foreign parts, seems likely enough.

For example, take this scene.

Here was Jacob Flanders gone abroad and staying to break his journey in Paris. (Old Miss Birkbeck, his mother's cousin, had died last June and left him a hundred pounds.)

"You needn't repeat the whole damned thing over again, Cruttendon," said Mallinson, the little bald painter who was sitting at a marble table, splashed with coffee and ringed with wine, talking very fast, and undoubtedly more than a little drunk.

"Well, Flanders, finished writing to your lady?" said Cruttendon, as Jacob came and took his seat beside them, holding in his hand an envelope addressed to Mrs. Flanders, near Scarborough, England.

"Do you uphold Velasquez?"[1] said Cruttendon.

"By God, he does," said Mallinson.

"He always gets like this," said Cruttendon irritably.

Jacob looked at Mallinson with excessive composure.

"I'll tell you the three greatest things that were ever written in the whole of literature," Cruttendon burst out. " 'Hang there like fruit my soul,' "[2] he began. . . .

"Don't listen to a man who don't like Velasquez," said Mallinson.

"Adolphe, don't give Mr. Mallinson any more wine," said Cruttendon.

"Fair play, fair play," said Jacob judicially. "Let a man get drunk if he likes. That's Shakespeare, Cruttendon. I'm with you there. Shakespeare had more guts than all these damned frogs put together. 'Hang there like fruit my soul,' " he began quoting, in a musical rhetorical voice, flourishing his wine-glass. "The devil damn you black, you cream-faced loon!"[3] he exclaimed as the wine washed over the rim.

" 'Hang there like fruit my soul,' " Cruttendon and Jacob both began again at the same moment, and both burst out laughing.

"Curse these flies," said Mallinson, flicking at his bald head. "What do they take me for?"

"Something sweet-smelling," said Cruttendon.

"Shut up, Cruttendon," said Jacob. "The fellow has no manners,"

1. Diego Velázquez (1599–1660), Spanish painter.
2. Shakespeare, *Cymbeline* (1609–10), 5.5.263.
3. Shakespeare, *Macbeth* (1606), 5.3.11 ff.

he explained to Mallinson very politely. "Wants to cut people off their drink. Look here. I want grilled bone. What's the French for grilled bone? Grilled bone, Adolphe. Now you juggins, don't you understand?"

"And I'll tell you, Flanders, the second most beautiful thing in the whole of literature," said Cruttendon, bringing his feet down on to the floor, and leaning right across the table, so that his face almost touched Jacob's face.

" 'Hey diddle diddle, the cat and the fiddle,' "[4] Mallinson interrupted, strumming his fingers on the table. "The most ex-qui-sitely beautiful thing in the whole of literature. . . . Cruttendon is a very good fellow," he remarked confidentially. "But he's a bit of a fool." And he jerked his head forward.

Well, not a word of this was ever told to Mrs. Flanders; nor what happened when they paid the bill and left the restaurant, and walked along the Boulevard Raspaille.[5]

Then here is another scrap of conversation; the time about eleven in the morning; the scene a studio; and the day Sunday.

"I tell you, Flanders," said Cruttendon, "I'd as soon have one of Mallinson's little pictures as a Chardin.[6] And when I say that . . ." he squeezed the tail of an emaciated tube . . . "Chardin was a great swell . . . He sells 'em to pay his dinner now. But wait till the dealers get hold of him. A great swell—oh, a very great swell."

"It's an awfully pleasant life," said Jacob, "messing away up here. Still, it's a stupid art, Cruttendon." He wandered off across the room. "There's this man, Pierre Louÿs now."[7] He took up a book.

"Now my good sir, are you going to settle down?" said Cruttendon.

"That's a solid piece of work," said Jacob, standing a canvas on a chair.

"Oh, that I did ages ago," said Cruttendon, looking over his shoulder.

"You're a pretty competent painter in my opinion," said Jacob after a time.

"Now if you'd like to see what I'm after at the present moment,"

4. Traditional English nursery rhyme.
5. Misspelling for "Raspail," street in the Montparnasse district of Paris.
6. Jean-Baptiste-Siméon Chardin (1699–1779), French painter, famous for painting still lifes and domestic scenes.
7. French novelist and poet (1870–1925), well known in his day for the lesbian poetic sequence *Chansons de Bilitis* (1894).

said Cruttendon, putting a canvas before Jacob. "There. That's it. That's more like it. That's . . ." he squirmed his thumb in a circle round a lamp globe painted white.

"A pretty solid piece of work," said Jacob, straddling his legs in front of it. "But what I wish you'd explain . . ."

Miss Jinny Carslake, pale, freckled, morbid, came into the room.

"Oh Jinny, here's a friend. Flanders. An Englishman. Wealthy. Highly connected. Go on, Flanders. . . ."

Jacob said nothing.

"It's *that*—that's not right," said Jinny Carslake.

"No," said Cruttendon decidedly. "Can't be done."

He took the canvas off the chair and stood it on the floor with its back to them.

"Sit down, ladies and gentlemen. Miss Carslake comes from your part of the world, Flanders. From Devonshire.[8] Oh, I thought you said Devonshire. Very well. She's a daughter of the church too. The black sheep of the family. Her mother writes her such letters. I say—have you one about you? It's generally Sundays they come. Sort of church-bell effect, you know."

"Have you met all the painter men?" said Jinny. "Was Mallinson drunk? If you go to his studio he'll give you one of his pictures. I say, Teddy . . ."

"Half a jiff," said Cruttendon. "What's the season of the year?" He looked out of the window.

"We take a day off on Sundays, Flanders."

"Will he . . ." said Jinny, looking at Jacob. "You . . ."

"Yes, he'll come with us," said Cruttendon.

And then, here is Versailles.[9]

Jinny stood on the stone rim and leant over the pond, clasped by Cruttendon's arms or she would have fallen in. "There! There!" she cried. "Right up to the top!" Some sluggish, sloping-shouldered fish had floated up from the depths to nip her crumbs. "You look," she said, jumping down. And then the dazzling white water, rough and throttled, shot up into the air. The fountain spread itself. Through it came the sound of military music far away. All the water was puckered with drops. A blue air-ball gently bumped the surface. How all the nurses and children and old men and young crowded to the edge,

8. County in southwest England, east of Cornwall.
9. Palace of Versailles, south of Paris, transformed 1661–1710 by Louis XIV into one of the most magnificent royal palaces in Europe.

leant over and waved their sticks! The little girl ran stretching her arms towards her air-ball, but it sank beneath the fountain.

Edward Cruttendon, Jinny Carslake, and Jacob Flanders walked in a row along the yellow gravel path; got on to the grass; so passed under the trees; and came out at the summerhouse where Marie Antoinette used to drink chocolate.[1] In went Edward and Jinny, but Jacob waited outside, sitting on the handle of his walking-stick. Out they came again.

"Well?" said Cruttendon, smiling at Jacob.

Jinny waited; Edward waited; and both looked at Jacob.

"Well?" said Jacob, smiling and pressing both hands on his stick.

"Come along," he decided; and started off. The others followed him, smiling.

And then they went to the little café in the by-street where people sit drinking coffee, watching the soldiers, meditatively knocking ashes into trays.

"But he's quite different," said Jinny, folding her hands over the top of her glass. "I don't suppose you know what Ted means when he says a thing like that," she said, looking at Jacob. "But I do. Sometimes I could kill myself. Sometimes he lies in bed all day long—just lies there. . . . I don't want you right on the table"; she waved her hands. Swollen iridescent pigeons were waddling round their feet.

"Look at that woman's hat," said Cruttendon. "How do they come to think of it? . . . No, Flanders, I don't think I could live like you. When one walks down that street opposite the British Museum—what's it called?—that's what I mean. It's all like that. Those fat women—and the man standing in the middle of the road as if he were going to have a fit . . ."

"Everybody feeds them," said Jinny, waving the pigeons away. "They're stupid old things."

"Well, I don't know," said Jacob, smoking his cigarette. "There's St. Paul's."

"I mean going to an office," said Cruttendon.

1. Marie Antoinette, wife of Louis XVI, was executed in 1793 during the French Revolution; the summerhouse is probably one of the buildings of Le Petit Trianon or Le Hameau, Marie Antoinette's favorite haunts in the gardens of Versailles.

"Hang it all," Jacob expostulated.

"But you don't count," said Jinny, looking at Cruttendon. "You're mad. I mean, you just think of painting."

"Yes, I know. I can't help it. I say, will King George give way about the peers?"[2]

"He'll jolly well have to," said Jacob.

"There!" said Jinny. "He really knows."

"You see, I would if I could," said Cruttendon, "but I simply can't."

"I *think* I could," said Jinny. "Only, it's all the people one dislikes who do it. At home, I mean. They talk of nothing else. Even people like my mother."

"Now if I came and lived here——" said Jacob. "What's my share, Cruttendon? Oh, very well. Have it your own way. Those silly birds, directly one wants them—they've flown away."

And finally under the arc lamps in the Gare des Invalides,[3] with one of those queer movements which are so slight yet so definite, which may wound or pass unnoticed but generally inflict a good deal of discomfort, Jinny and Cruttendon drew together; Jacob stood apart. They had to separate. Something must be said. Nothing was said. A man wheeled a trolley past Jacob's legs so near that he almost grazed them. When Jacob recovered his balance the other two were turning away, though Jinny looked over her shoulder, and Cruttendon, waving his hand, disappeared like the very great genius that he was.

No—Mrs. Flanders was told none of this, though Jacob felt, it is safe to say, that nothing in the world was of greater importance; and as for Cruttendon and Jinny, he thought them the most remarkable people he had ever met—being of course unable to foresee how it fell out in the course of time that Cruttendon took to painting orchards; had therefore to live in Kent; and must, one would think, see through apple blossom by this time, since his wife, for whose sake he did it, eloped with a novelist; but no; Cruttendon still paints orchards, savagely, in solitude. Then Jinny Carslake, after her affair with Lefanu the American painter, frequented Indian philosophers, and now you find her in pensions in Italy cherishing a little jeweller's box containing ordinary pebbles picked off the road. But if you look

2. The Parliament Act of 1911 deprived the House of Lords of their power of veto over proposed legislation; George V, who resisted the Act, was king from 1910 to 1936.
3. Paris metro station for trains to Versailles.

at them steadily, she says, multiplicity becomes unity, which is some-how the secret of life, though it does not prevent her from following the macaroni as it goes round the table, and sometimes, on spring nights, she makes the strangest confidences to shy young English-men.

Jacob had nothing to hide from his mother. It was only that he could make no sense himself of his extraordinary excitement, and as for writing it down——

"Jacob's letters are so like him," said Mrs. Jarvis, folding the sheet.

"Indeed he seems to be having . . ." said Mrs. Flanders, and paused, for she was cutting out a dress and had to straighten the pattern, ". . . a very gay time."

Mrs. Jarvis thought of Paris. At her back the window was open, for it was a mild night; a calm night; when the moon seemed muffled and the apple trees stood perfectly still.

"I never pity the dead," said Mrs. Jarvis, shifting the cushion at her back, and clasping her hands behind her head. Betty Flanders did not hear, for her scissors made so much noise on the table.

"They are at rest," said Mrs. Jarvis. "And we spend our days doing foolish unnecessary things without knowing why."

Mrs. Jarvis was not liked in the village.

"You never walk at this time of night?" she asked Mrs. Flanders.

"It is certainly wonderfully mild," said Mrs. Flanders.

Yet it was years since she had opened the orchard gate and gone out on Dods Hill after dinner.

"It is perfectly dry," said Mrs. Jarvis, as they shut the orchard door and stepped on to the turf.

"I shan't go far," said Betty Flanders. "Yes, Jacob will leave Paris on Wednesday."

"Jacob was always my friend of the three," said Mrs. Jarvis.

"Now, my dear, I am going no further," said Mrs. Flanders. They had climbed the dark hill and reached the Roman camp.

The rampart rose at their feet—the smooth circle surrounding the camp or the grave. How many needles Betty Flanders had lost there! and her garnet brooch.

"It is much clearer than this sometimes," said Mrs. Jarvis, standing upon the ridge. There were no clouds, and yet there was a haze over the sea, and over the moors. The lights of Scarborough flashed, as if a woman wearing a diamond necklace turned her head this way and that.

"How quiet it is!" said Mrs. Jarvis.

Mrs. Flanders rubbed the turf with her toe, thinking of her garnet brooch.

Mrs. Jarvis found it difficult to think of herself to-night. It was so calm. There was no wind; nothing racing, flying, escaping. Black shadows stood still over the silver moors. The furze bushes stood perfectly still. Neither did Mrs. Jarvis think of God. There was a church behind them, of course. The church clock struck ten. Did the strokes reach the furze bush, or did the thorn tree hear them?

Mrs. Flanders was stooping down to pick up a pebble. Sometimes people do find things, Mrs. Jarvis thought, and yet in this hazy moonlight it was impossible to see anything, except bones, and little pieces of chalk.

"Jacob bought it with his own money, and then I brought Mr. Parker up to see the view, and it must have dropped——" Mrs. Flanders murmured.

Did the bones stir, or the rusty swords? Was Mrs. Flanders's two-penny-halfpenny brooch for ever part of the rich accumulation? and if all the ghosts flocked thick and rubbed shoulders with Mrs. Flanders in the circle, would she not have seemed perfectly in her place, a live English matron, growing stout?

The clock struck the quarter.

The frail waves of sound broke among the stiff gorse and the haw-thorn twigs as the church clock divided time into quarters.

Motionless and broad-backed the moors received the statement. "It is fifteen minutes past the hour," but made no answer, unless a bramble stirred.

Yet even in this light the legends on the tombstones could be read, brief voices saying, "I am Bertha Ruck,"[4] "I am Tom Gage." And they say which day of the year they died, and the New Testament says something for them, very proud, very emphatic, or consoling.

The moors accept all that too.

The moonlight falls like a pale page upon the church wall, and illumines the kneeling family in the niche, and the tablet set up in 1780 to the Squire of the parish who relieved the poor, and believed in God—so the measured voice goes on down the marble scroll, as though it could impose itself upon time and the open air.

Now a fox steals out from behind the gorse bushes.

Often, even at night, the church seems full of people. The pews are worn and greasy, and the cassocks in place, and the hymn-books on the ledges. It is a ship with all its crew aboard. The timbers strain to hold the dead and the living, the ploughmen, the carpenters, the fox-hunting gentlemen and the farmers smelling of mud and brandy.

4. The husband of Berta Ruck (1878–1978), popular novelist, felt that the name "Bertha Ruck" was close enough to his wife's that Woolf was implying she was already dead in 1922, and threatened a lawsuit. The matter was settled amicably.

Their tongues join together in syllabling the sharp-cut words, which for ever slice asunder time and the broad-backed moors. Plaint and belief and elegy, despair and triumph, but for the most part good sense and jolly indifference, go trampling out of the windows any time these five hundred years.

Still, as Mrs. Jarvis said, stepping out on to the moors, "How quiet it is!" Quiet at mid-day, except when the hunt scatters across it; quiet in the afternoon, save for the drifting sheep; at night the moor is perfectly quiet.

A garnet brooch has dropped into its grass. A fox pads stealthily. A leaf turns on its edge. Mrs. Jarvis, who is fifty years of age, reposes in the camp in the hazy moonlight.

". . . and," said Mrs. Flanders, straightening her back, "I never cared for Mr. Parker."

"Neither did I," said Mrs. Jarvis. They began to walk home.

But their voices floated for a little above the camp. The moonlight destroyed nothing. The moor accepted everything. Tom Gage cries aloud so long as his tombstone endures. The Roman skeletons are in safe keeping. Betty Flanders's darning needles are safe too and her garnet brooch. And sometimes at mid-day, in the sunshine, the moor seems to hoard these little treasures, like a nurse. But at midnight when no one speaks or gallops, and the thorn tree is perfectly still, it would be foolish to vex the moor with questions—what? and why?

The church clock, however, strikes twelve.

XII

The water fell off a ledge like lead—like a chain with thick white links. The train ran out into a steep green meadow, and Jacob saw striped tulips growing and heard a bird singing, in Italy.

A motor car full of Italian officers ran along the flat road and kept up with the train, raising dust behind it. There were trees laced together with vines—as Virgil said. Here was a station; and a tremendous leave-taking going on, with women in high yellow boots and odd pale boys in ringed socks. Virgil's bees had gone about the plains of Lombardy.[1] It was the custom of the ancients to train vines between elms. Then at Milan[2] there were sharp-winged hawks, of a bright brown, cutting figures over the roofs.

These Italian carriages get damnably hot with the afternoon sun on them, and the chances are that before the engine has pulled to the top of the gorge the clanking chain will have broken. Up, up, up, it goes, like a train on a scenic railway. Every peak is covered with

1. Region of northern Italy.
2. Northern Italian city, capital of the Lombardy region.

sharp trees, and amazing white villages are crowded on ledges. There is always a white tower on the very summit, flat red-frilled roofs, and a sheer drop beneath. It is not a country in which one walks after tea. For one thing there is no grass. A whole hillside will be ruled with olive trees. Already in April the earth is clotted into dry dust between them. And there are neither stiles nor footpaths, nor lanes chequered with the shadows of leaves nor eighteenth-century inns with bow-windows, where one eats ham and eggs. Oh no, Italy is all fierceness, bareness, exposure, and black priests shuffling along the roads. It is strange, too, how you never get away from villas.

Still, to be travelling on one's own with a hundred pounds to spend is a fine affair. And if his money gave out, as it probably would, he would go on foot. He could live on bread and wine—the wine in straw bottles—for after doing Greece he was going to knock off Rome. The Roman civilization was a very inferior affair, no doubt. But Bonamy talked a lot of rot, all the same. "You ought to have been in Athens," he would say to Bonamy when he got back. "Standing on the Parthenon," he would say, or "The ruins of the Coliseum[3] suggest some fairly sublime reflections," which he would write out at length in letters. It might turn to an essay upon civilization. A comparison between the ancients and moderns, with some pretty sharp hits at Mr. Asquith—something in the style of Gibbon.

A stout gentleman laboriously hauled himself in, dusty, baggy, slung with gold chains, and Jacob, regretting that he did not come of the Latin race, looked out of the window.

It is a strange reflection that by travelling two days and nights you are in the heart of Italy. Accidental villas among olive trees appear; and men-servants watering the cactuses. Black victorias[4] drive in between pompous pillars with plaster shields stuck to them. It is at once momentary and astonishingly intimate—to be displayed before the eyes of a foreigner. And there is a lonely hill-top where no one ever comes, and yet it is seen by me who was lately driving down Piccadilly on an omnibus. And what I should like would be to get out among the fields, sit down and hear the grasshoppers, and take up a handful of earth—Italian earth, as this is Italian dust upon my shoes.

Jacob heard them crying strange names at railway stations through the night. The train stopped and he heard frogs croaking close by, and he wrinkled back the blind cautiously and saw a vast strange marsh all white in the moon-light. The carriage was thick with cigar smoke, which floated round the globe with the green shade on it.

---

3. Ancient Roman stadium in Rome, built around 72 C.E. Parthenon: ancient Greek temple to Athena on the Acropolis in Athens, built during the fifth century B.C.E.
4. Light, low, four-wheeled horse-drawn carriages with a hood and seats for two passengers as well as the driver.

The Italian gentleman lay snoring with his boots off and his waistcoat unbuttoned. . . . And all this business of going to Greece seemed to Jacob an intolerable weariness—sitting in hotels by oneself and look- ing at monuments—he'd have done better to go to Cornwall with Timmy Durrant. . . . "O—h," Jacob protested, as the darkness began breaking in front of him and the light showed through, but the man was reaching across him to get something—the fat Italian man in his dicky,[5] unshaven, crumpled, obese, was opening the door and going off to have a wash.

So Jacob sat up, and saw a lean Italian sportsman with a gun walking down the road in the early morning light, and the whole idea of the Parthenon came upon him in a clap.

"By Jove!" he thought, "we must be nearly there!" and he stuck his head out of the window and got the air full in his face.

It is highly exasperating that twenty-five people of your acquain- tance should be able to say straight off something very much to the point about being in Greece, while for yourself there is a stopper upon all emotions whatsoever. For after washing at the hotel at Patras,[6] Jacob had followed the tram lines a mile or so out; and followed them a mile or so back; he had met several droves of turkeys; several strings of donkeys; had got lost in back streets; had read advertisements of corsets and of Maggi's consommé; children had trodden on his toes; the place smelt of bad cheese; and he was glad to find himself suddenly come out opposite his hotel. There was an old copy of the *Daily Mail*[7] lying among coffee-cups; which he read. But what could he do after dinner?

No doubt we should be, on the whole, much worse off than we are without our astonishing gift for illusion. At the age of twelve or so, having given up dolls and broken our steam engines, France, but much more probably Italy, and India almost for a certainty, draws the superfluous imagination. One's aunts have been to Rome; and every one has an uncle who was last heard of—poor man—in Ran- goon.[8] He will never come back any more. But it is the governesses who start the Greek myth. Look at that for a head (they say)—nose, you see, straight as a dart, curls, eyebrows—everything appropriate to manly beauty; while his legs and arms have lines on them which

5. Overalls.
6. Largest port on the Peloponnese peninsula of Greece.
7. Newspaper founded by Lord Northcliffe in 1896—conversational tone, modern layout, short pieces, aimed at women and the lower middle class.
8. Capital city of Myanmar (Burma), a British colony from 1885 to 1948.

indicate a perfect degree of development—the Greeks caring for the body as much as for the face. And the Greeks could paint fruit so that birds pecked at it. First you read Xenophon; then Euripides.[9] One day—that was an occasion, by God—what people have said appears to have sense in it; "the Greek spirit"; the Greek this, that, and the other; though it is absurd, by the way, to say that any Greek comes near Shakespeare. The point is, however, that we have been brought up in an illusion.

Jacob, no doubt, thought something in this fashion, the *Daily Mail* crumpled in his hand; his legs extended; the very picture of boredom.

"But it's the way we're brought up," he went on.

And it all seemed to him very distasteful. Something ought to be done about it. And from being moderately depressed he became like a man about to be executed. Clara Durrant had left him at a party to talk to an American called Pilchard. And he had come all the way to Greece and left her. They wore evening-dresses, and talked nonsense—what damned nonsense—and he put out his hand for the *Globe Trotter,* an international magazine which is supplied free of charge to the proprietors of hotels.

In spite of its ramshackle condition modern Greece is highly advanced in the electric tramway system, so that while Jacob sat in the hotel sitting-room the trams clanked, chimed, rang, rang, rang imperiously to get the donkeys out of the way, and one old woman who refused to budge, beneath the windows. The whole of civilization was being condemned.

The waiter was quite indifferent to that too. Aristotle, a dirty man, carnivorously interested in the body of the only guest now occupying the only arm-chair, came into the room ostentatiously, put something down, put something straight, and saw that Jacob was still there.

"I shall want to be called early to-morrow," said Jacob, over his shoulder. "I am going to Olympia."[1]

This gloom, this surrender to the dark waters which lap us about, is a modern invention. Perhaps, as Cruttendon said, we do not believe enough. Our fathers at any rate had something to demolish. So have we for the matter of that, thought Jacob, crumpling the *Daily Mail* in his hand. He would go into Parliament and make fine speeches—but what use are fine speeches and Parliament, once you surrender an inch to the black waters? Indeed there has never been any explanation of the ebb and flow in our veins—of happiness and unhappiness. That respectability and evening parties where one has

---

9. Ancient Greek tragedian (484?–406 B.C.E.), author of *Medea* and other works; Xenophon: ancient Greek historian (431–350 B.C.E.), author of *Anabasis.*
1. Ruined ancient sanctuary near the west coast of the Peloponnese peninsula, home of the ancient Olympic games.

to dress, and wretched slums at the back of Gray's Inn—something solid, immovable, and grotesque—is at the back of it, Jacob thought probable. But then there was the British Empire which was beginning to puzzle him; nor was he altogether in favour of giving Home Rule to Ireland. What did the *Daily Mail* say about that?

For he had grown to be a man, and was about to be immersed in things—as indeed the chambermaid, emptying his basin upstairs, fingering keys, studs, pencils, and bottles of tabloids[2] strewn on the dressing-table, was aware.

That he had grown to be a man was a fact that Florinda knew, as she knew everything, by instinct.

And Betty Flanders even now suspected it, as she read his letter, posted at Milan, "Telling me," she complained to Mrs. Jarvis, "really nothing that I want to know"; but she brooded over it.

Fanny Elmer felt it to desperation. For he would take his stick and his hat and would walk to the window, and look perfectly absent-minded and very stern too, she thought.

"I am going," he would say, "to cadge a meal off Bonamy."

"Anyhow, I can drown myself in the Thames," Fanny cried, as she hurried past the Foundling Hospital.

"But the *Daily Mail* isn't to be trusted," Jacob said to himself, looking about for something else to read. And he sighed again, being indeed so profoundly gloomy that gloom must have been lodged in him to cloud him at any moment, which was odd in a man who enjoyed things so, was not much given to analysis, but was horribly romantic, of course, Bonamy thought, in his rooms in Lincoln's Inn.

"He will fall in love," thought Bonamy. "Some Greek woman with a straight nose."

It was to Bonamy that Jacob wrote from Patras—to Bonamy who couldn't love a woman and never read a foolish book.

There are very few good books after all, for we can't count profuse histories, travels in mule carts to discover the sources of the Nile, or the volubility of fiction.

I like books whose virtue is all drawn together in a page or two. I

2. Pills.

like sentences that don't budge though armies cross them. I like words to be hard—such were Bonamy's views, and they won him the hostility of those whose taste is all for the fresh growths of the morning, who throw up the window, and find the poppies spread in the sun, and can't forbear a shout of jubilation at the astonishing fertility of English literature. That was not Bonamy's way at all. That his taste in literature affected his friendships, and made him silent, secretive, fastidious, and only quite at his ease with one or two young men of his own way of thinking, was the charge against him.

But then Jacob Flanders was not at all of his own way of thinking— far from it, Bonamy sighed, laying the thin sheets of notepaper on the table and falling into thought about Jacob's character, not for the first time.

The trouble was this romantic vein in him. "But mixed with the stupidity which leads him into these absurd predicaments," thought Bonamy, "there is something—something"—he sighed, for he was fonder of Jacob than of any one in the world.

Jacob went to the window and stood with his hands in his pockets. There he saw three Greeks in kilts; the masts of ships; idle or busy people of the lower classes strolling or stepping out briskly, or falling into groups and gesticulating with their hands. Their lack of concern for him was not the cause of his gloom; but some more profound conviction—it was not that he himself happened to be lonely, but that all people are.

Yet next day, as the train slowly rounded a hill on the way to Olympia, the Greek peasant women were out among the vines; the old Greek men were sitting at the stations, sipping sweet wine. And though Jacob remained gloomy he had never suspected how tremendously pleasant it is to be alone; out of England; on one's own; cut off from the whole thing. There are very sharp bare hills on the way to Olympia; and between them blue sea in triangular spaces. A little like the Cornish coast. Well now, to go walking by oneself all day—to get on to that track and follow it up between the bushes—or are they small trees?—to the top of that mountain from which one can see half the nations of antiquity——

"Yes," said Jacob, for his carriage was empty, "let's look at the map."

Blame it or praise it, there is no denying the wild horse in us. To gallop intemperately; fall on the sand tired out; to feel the earth spin; to have—positively—a rush of friendship for stones and grasses, as if humanity were over, and as for men and women, let them go hang—there is no getting over the fact that this desire seizes us pretty often.

The evening air slightly moved the dirty curtains in the hotel window at Olympia.

"I am full of love for every one," thought Mrs. Wentworth Williams, "—for the poor most of all—for the peasants coming back in the evening with their burdens. And everything is soft and vague and very sad. It is sad, it is sad. But everything has meaning," thought Sandra Wentworth Williams, raising her head a little and looking very beautiful, tragic, and exalted. "One must love everything."

She held in her hand a little book convenient for travelling—stories by Tchekov[3]—as she stood, veiled, in white, in the window of the hotel at Olympia. How beautiful the evening was! and her beauty was its beauty. The tragedy of Greece was the tragedy of all high souls. The inevitable compromise. She seemed to have grasped something. She would write it down. And moving to the table where her husband sat reading she leant her chin in her hands and thought of the peasants, of suffering, of her own beauty, of the inevitable compromise, and of how she would write it down. Nor did Evan Williams say anything brutal, banal, or foolish when he shut his book and put it away to make room for the plates of soup which were now being placed before them. Only his drooping bloodhound eyes and his heavy sallow cheeks expressed his melancholy tolerance, his conviction that though forced to live with circumspection and deliberation he could never possibly achieve any of those objects which, as he knew, are the only ones worth pursuing. His consideration was flawless; his silence unbroken.

"Everything seems to mean so much," said Sandra. But with the sound of her own voice the spell was broken. She forgot the peasants. Only there remained with her a sense of her own beauty, and in front, luckily, there was a looking-glass.

"I am very beautiful," she thought.

She shifted her hat slightly. Her husband saw her looking in the glass; and agreed that beauty is important; it is an inheritance; one cannot ignore it. But it is a barrier; it is in fact rather a bore. So he drank his soup; and kept his eyes fixed upon the window.

"Quails," said Mrs. Wentworth Williams languidly. "And then goat, I suppose; and then . . ."

3. Anton Chekhov (1860–1904), Russian playwright and short-story writer, author of *The Cherry Orchard* and many other works.

"Caramel custard presumably," said her husband in the same cadence, with his toothpick out already.

She laid her spoon upon her plate, and her soup was taken away half finished. Never did she do anything without dignity; for hers was the English type which is so Greek, save that villagers have touched their hats to it, the vicarage reveres it; and upper-gardeners and under-gardeners respectfully straighten their backs as she comes down the broad terrace on Sunday morning, dallying at the stone urns with the Prime Minister to pick a rose—which, perhaps, she was trying to forget, as her eye wandered round the dining-room of the inn at Olympia, seeking the window where her book lay, where a few minutes ago she had discovered something—something very profound it had been, about love and sadness and the peasants.

But it was Evan who sighed; not in despair nor indeed in rebellion. But, being the most ambitious of men and temperamentally the most sluggish, he had accomplished nothing; had the political history of England at his finger-ends, and living much in company with Chatham, Pitt, Burke, and Charles James Fox[4] could not help contrasting himself and his age with them and theirs. "Yet there never was a time when great men are more needed," he was in the habit of saying to himself, with a sigh. Here he was picking his teeth in an inn at Olympia. He had done. But Sandra's eyes wandered.

"Those pink melons are sure to be dangerous," he said gloomily. And as he spoke the door opened and in came a young man in a grey check suit.

"Beautiful but dangerous," said Sandra, immediately talking to her husband in the presence of a third person. ("Ah, an English boy on tour," she thought to herself.)

And Evan knew all that too.

Yes, he knew all that; and he admired her. Very pleasant, he thought, to have affairs. But for himself, what with his height (Napoleon[5] was five feet four, he remembered), his bulk, his inability to impose his own personality (and yet great men are needed more than ever now, he sighed), it was useless. He threw away his cigar, went up to Jacob and asked him, with a simple sort of sincerity which Jacob liked, whether he had come straight out from England.

4. All eighteenth-century politicians: 1st Earl of Chatham, also known as William Pitt, the Elder (1708–1778), British prime minister 1756–61 and 1766–68; William Pitt, the Younger (1759–1806), British prime minister 1783–1801 and 1804–06 during the French Revolutionary and Napoleonic Wars; Edmund Burke (1729–1797), author of *Reflections on the Revolution in France*; Charles James Fox (1749–1806), Britain's first foreign secretary, 1782, 1783, and 1806.
5. French general (1759–1821), emperor of France 1804–14/15.

"How very English!" Sandra laughed when the waiter told them next morning that the young gentleman had left at five to climb the mountain. "I am sure he asked you for a bath?" at which the waiter shook his head, and said that he would ask the manager.

"You do not understand," laughed Sandra. "Never mind."

Stretched on the top of the mountain, quite alone, Jacob enjoyed himself immensely. Probably he had never been so happy in the whole of his life.

But at dinner that night Mr. Williams asked him whether he would like to see the paper; then Mrs. Williams asked him (as they strolled on the terrace smoking—and how could he refuse that man's cigar?) whether he'd seen the theatre by moonlight; whether he knew Everard Sherborn; whether he read Greek and whether (Evan rose silently and went in) if he had to sacrifice one it would be the French literature or the Russian?

"And now," wrote Jacob in his letter to Bonamy, "I shall have to read her cursed book"—her Tchekov, he meant, for she had lent it him.

Though the opinion is unpopular it seems likely enough that bare places, fields too thick with stones to be ploughed, tossing sea-meadows half-way between England and America, suit us better than cities.

There is something absolute in us which despises qualification. It is this which is teased and twisted in society. People come together in a room. "So delighted," says somebody, "to meet you," and that is a lie. And then: "I enjoy the spring more than the autumn now. One does, I think, as one gets older." For women are always, always, always talking about what one feels, and if they say "as one gets older," they mean you to reply with something quite off the point.

Jacob sat himself down in the quarry where the Greeks had cut marble for the theatre. It is hot work walking up Greek hills at mid-day. The wild red cyclamen was out; he had seen the little tortoises hobbling from clump to clump; the air smelt strong and suddenly sweet, and the sun, striking on jagged splinters of marble, was very dazzling to the eyes. Composed, commanding, contemptuous, a little melancholy, and bored with an august kind of boredom, there he sat smoking his pipe.

Bonamy would have said that this was the sort of thing that made him uneasy—when Jacob got into the doldrums, looked like a Margate[6] fisherman out of a job, or a British Admiral. You couldn't make him understand a thing when he was in a mood like that. One had better leave him alone. He was dull. He was apt to be grumpy.

He was up very early, looking at the statues with his Baedeker.[7]

Sandra Wentworth Williams, ranging the world before breakfast in quest of adventure or a point of view, all in white, not so very tall perhaps, but uncommonly upright—Sandra Williams got Jacob's head exactly on a level with the head of the Hermes of Praxiteles.[8] The comparison was all in his favour. But before she could say a single word he had gone out of the Museum and left her.

Still, a lady of fashion travels with more than one dress, and if white suits the morning hour, perhaps sandy yellow with purple spots on it, a black hat, and a volume of Balzac,[9] suit the evening. Thus she was arranged on the terrace when Jacob came in. Very beautiful she looked. With her hands folded she mused, seemed to listen to her husband, seemed to watch the peasants coming down with brushwood on their backs, seemed to notice how the hill changed from blue to black, seemed to discriminate between truth and falsehood, Jacob thought, and crossed his legs suddenly, observing the extreme shabbiness of his trousers.

"But he is very distinguished looking," Sandra decided.

And Evan Williams, lying back in his chair with the paper on his knees, envied them. The best thing he could do would be to publish, with Macmillans,[1] his monograph upon the foreign policy of Chatham. But confound this tumid, queasy feeling—this restlessness, swelling, and heat—it was jealousy ! jealousy ! jealousy ! which he had sworn never to feel again.

"Come with us to Corinth,[2] Flanders," he said with more than his usual energy, stopping by Jacob's chair. He was relieved by Jacob's reply, or rather by the solid, direct, if shy manner in which he said that he would like very much to come with them to Corinth.

"Here is a fellow," thought Evan Williams, "who might do very well in politics."

"I intend to come to Greece every year so long as I live," Jacob wrote to Bonamy. "It is the only chance I can see of protecting oneself from civilization."

6. Seaside resort in Kent.
7. Series of guide-books written by Karl Baedeker (1801–1859).
8. Ancient Greek sculptor (active 370–330 B.C.E.); "Hermes Carrying the Infant Dionysus" is his only surviving sculpture, in the Archeological Museum in Olympia.
9. Honoré de Balzac (1799–1850), French novelist, author of *Le Père Goriot* and many other works.
1. One of the largest publishing firms in the world, founded 1844.
2. City on the narrow strip of land that separates the Peloponnese from northern Greece; the remains of the ancient city are very well preserved.

"Goodness knows what he means by that," Bonamy sighed. For as he never said a clumsy thing himself, these dark sayings of Jacob's made him feel apprehensive, yet somehow impressed, his own turn being all for the definite, the concrete, and the rational.

Nothing could be much simpler than what Sandra said as she descended the Acro-Corinth,[3] keeping to the little path, while Jacob strode over rougher ground by her side. She had been left motherless at the age of four; and the Park was vast.

"One never seemed able to get out of it," she laughed. Of course there was the library, and dear Mr. Jones, and notions about things. "I used to stray into the kitchen and sit upon the butlers' knees," she laughed, sadly though.

Jacob thought that if he had been there he would have saved her; for she had been exposed to great dangers, he felt, and, he thought to himself, "People wouldn't understand a woman talking as she talks."

She made little of the roughness of the hill; and wore breeches, he saw, under her short skirts.

"Women like Fanny Elmer don't," he thought. "What's-her-name Carslake didn't; yet they pretend . . ."

Mrs. Williams said things straight out. He was surprised by his own knowledge of the rules of behaviour; how much more can be said than one thought; how open one can be with a woman; and how little he had known himself before.

Evan joined them on the road; and as they drove along up hill and down hill (for Greece is in a state of effervescence, yet astonishingly clean-cut, a treeless land, where you see the ground between the blades, each hill cut and shaped and outlined as often as not against sparkling deep blue waters, islands white as sand floating on the horizon, occasional groves of palm trees standing in the valleys, which are scattered with black goats, spotted with little olive trees and sometimes have white hollows, rayed and criss-crossed, in their flanks), as they drove up hill and down he scowled in the corner of the carriage, with his paw so tightly closed that the skin was stretched between the knuckles and the little hairs stood upright. Sandra rode opposite, dominant, like a Victory[4] prepared to fling into the air.

"Heartless!" thought Evan (which was untrue).

3. Ancient citadel at Corinth, rising 1,886 feet above sea level.
4. Roman goddess, traditionally depicted with wings.

"Brainless!" he suspected (and that was not true, either). "Still . . . !"
He envied her.

When bedtime came the difficulty was to write to Bonamy, Jacob
found. Yet he had seen Salamis, and Marathon[5] in the distance. Poor
old Bonamy! No; there was something queer about it. He could not
write to Bonamy.

"I shall go to Athens all the same," he resolved, looking very set,
with this hook dragging in his side.

The Williamses had already been to Athens.

Athens is still quite capable of striking a young man as the oddest
combination, the most incongruous assortment. Now it is suburban;
now immortal. Now cheap continental jewellery is laid upon plush
trays. Now the stately woman stands naked, save for a wave of drapery
above the knee. No form can he set on his sensations as he strolls,
one blazing afternoon, along the Parisian boulevard and skips out of
the way of the royal landau[6] which, looking indescribably ramshackle,
rattles along the pitted roadway, saluted by citizens of both sexes
cheaply dressed in bowler hats and continental costumes; though a
shepherd in kilt, cap, and gaiters very nearly drives his herd of goats
between the royal wheels; and all the time the Acropolis surges into
the air, raises itself above the town, like a large immobile wave with
the yellow columns of the Parthenon firmly planted upon it.

The yellow columns of the Parthenon are to be seen at all hours
of the day firmly planted upon the Acropolis; though at sunset, when
the ships in the Piraeus[7] fire their guns, a bell rings, a man in uniform
(the waistcoat unbuttoned) appears; and the women roll up the black
stockings which they are knitting in the shadow of the columns, call
to the children, and troop off down the hill back to their houses.

There they are again, the pillars, the pediment, the Temple of
Victory and the Erechtheum,[8] set on a tawny rock cleft with shadows,

---

5. A plain northeast of Athens; site in 490 B.C.E. of a decisive battle in which the Greeks
repulsed the first Persian invasion of Greece. Salamis: island in the Aegean Sea, west of
Piraeus, site of a famous Greek naval victory over the Persians in 480 B.C.E.
6. Four-wheeled horse-drawn carriage with a soft roof that can be fully or partially folded
back.
7. Port of Athens.
8. Temple on the north side of the Acropolis, with the famous "porch of the maidens," where
six draped female figures serve as pillars; pediment: triangular gable crowning the front of

directly you unlatch your shutters in the morning and, leaning out, hear the clatter, the clamour, the whip cracking in the street below. There they are.

The extreme definiteness with which they stand, now a brilliant white, again yellow, and in some lights red, imposes ideas of durability, of the emergence through the earth of some spiritual energy elsewhere dissipated in elegant trifles. But this durability exists quite independently of our admiration. Although the beauty is sufficiently humane to weaken us, to stir the deep deposit of mud—memories, abandonments, regrets, sentimental devotions—the Parthenon is separate from all that; and if you consider how it has stood out all night, for centuries, you begin to connect the blaze (at midday the glare is dazzling and the frieze almost invisible) with the idea that perhaps it is beauty alone that is immortal.

Added to this, compared with the blistered stucco, the new love songs rasped out to the strum of guitar and gramophone, and the mobile yet insignificant faces of the street, the Parthenon is really astonishing in its silent composure; which is so vigorous that, far from being decayed, the Parthenon appears, on the contrary, likely to outlast the entire world.

"And the Greeks, like sensible men, never bothered to finish the backs of their statues," said Jacob, shading his eyes and observing that the side of the figure which is turned away from view is left in the rough.

He noted the slight irregularity in the line of the steps which "the artistic sense of the Greeks preferred to mathematical accuracy," he read in his guide-book.

He stood on the exact spot where the great statue of Athena[9] used to stand, and identified the more famous landmarks of the scene beneath.

In short he was accurate and diligent; but profoundly morose. Moreover he was pestered by guides. This was on Monday.

But on Wednesday he wrote a telegram to Bonamy, telling him to come at once. And then he crumpled it in his hand and threw it in the gutter.

---

a building above the portico; often recessed and decorated with sculptures in relief; Temple of Victory: tiny temple of Victory, or Athena Nike, completed between 421 and 415 B.C.E., which stands at the main gateway into the Parthenon.

9. Phidias's great ivory and gold statue of Athena, 438 B.C.E., stood in the center of the Parthenon; it was removed in the fifth century C.E., when the Parthenon became a Christian church.

"For one thing he wouldn't come," he thought. "And then I daresay this sort of thing wears off." "This sort of thing" being that uneasy, painful feeling, something like selfishness—one wishes almost that the thing would stop—it is getting more and more beyond what is possible—"If it goes on much longer I shan't be able to cope with it—but if some one else were seeing it at the same time—Bonamy is stuffed in his room in Lincoln's Inn—oh, I say, damn it all, I say,"—the sight of Hymettus, Pentelicus, Lycabettus[1] on one side, and the sea on the other, as one stands in the Parthenon at sunset, the sky pink feathered, the plain all colours, the marble tawny in one's eyes, is thus oppressive. Luckily Jacob had little sense of personal association; he seldom thought of Plato or Socrates in the flesh; on the other hand his feeling for architecture was very strong; he preferred statues to pictures; and he was beginning to think a great deal about the problems of civilization, which were solved, of course, so very remarkably by the ancient Greeks, though their solution is no help to us. Then the hook gave a great tug in his side as he lay in bed on Wednesday night; and he turned over with a desperate sort of tumble, remembering Sandra Wentworth Williams with whom he was in love.

Next day he climbed Pentelicus.

The day after he went up to the Acropolis. The hour was early; the place almost deserted; and possibly there was thunder in the air. But the sun struck full upon the Acropolis.

Jacob's intention was to sit down and read, and, finding a drum of marble conveniently placed, from which Marathon could be seen, and yet it was in the shade, while the Erechtheum blazed white in front of him, there he sat. And after reading a page he put his thumb in his book. Why not rule countries in the way they should be ruled? And he read again.

No doubt his position there overlooking Marathon somehow raised his spirits. Or it may have been that a slow capacious brain has these moments of flowering. Or he had, insensibly, while he was abroad, got into the way of thinking about politics.

And then looking up and seeing the sharp outline, his meditations were given an extraordinary edge; Greece was over; the Parthenon in ruins; yet there he was.

(Ladies with green and white umbrellas passed through the courtyard—French ladies on their way to join their husbands in Constantinople.)[2]

Jacob read on again. And laying the book on the ground he began,

---

1. Mount Hymettus, 3,366 feet high, southeast of Athens; Mount Pentelicus, 3,632 feet high, mountain range northeast of Athens; Mount Lycabettus, 1,100 feet high, northeast of Athens.
2. Founded seventh century B.C.E.; known as Istanbul since the foundation of the Turkish Republic in 1923.

as if inspired by what he had read, to write a note upon the importance of history—upon democracy—one of those scribbles upon which the work of a lifetime may be based; or again, it falls out of a book twenty years later, and one can't remember a word of it. It is a little painful. It had better be burnt.

Jacob wrote; began to draw a straight nose; when all the French ladies opening and shutting their umbrellas just beneath him exclaimed, looking at the sky, that one did not know what to expect—rain or fine weather?

Jacob got up and strolled across to the Erechtheum. There are still several women standing there holding the roof on their heads. Jacob straightened himself slightly; for stability and balance affect the body first. These statues annulled things so! He stared at them, then turned, and there was Madame Lucien Gravé perched on a block of marble with her kodak pointed at his head. Of course she jumped down, in spite of her age, her figure, and her tight boots—having, now that her daughter was married, lapsed with a luxurious abandonment, grand enough in its way, into the fleshy grotesque; she jumped down, but not before Jacob had seen her.

"Damn these women—damn these women!" he thought. And he went to fetch his book which he had left lying on the ground in the Parthenon.

"How they spoil things," he murmured, leaning against one of the pillars, pressing his book tight between his arm and his side. (As for the weather, no doubt the storm would break soon; Athens was under cloud.)

"It is those damned women," said Jacob, without any trace of bitterness, but rather with sadness and disappointment that what might have been should never be.

(This violent disillusionment is generally to be expected in young men in the prime of life, sound of wind and limb, who will soon become fathers of families and directors of banks.)

Then, making sure that the Frenchwomen had gone, and looking cautiously round him, Jacob strolled over to the Erechtheum and looked rather furtively at the goddess on the left-hand side holding the roof on her head. She reminded him of Sandra Wentworth Williams. He looked at her, then looked away. He looked at her, then looked away. He was extraordinarily moved, and with the battered Greek nose in his head, with Sandra in his head, with all sorts of things in his head, off he started to walk right up to the top of Mount Hymettus, alone, in the heat.

That very afternoon Bonamy went expressly to talk about Jacob to tea with Clara Durrant in the square behind Sloane Street[3] where, on hot spring days, there are striped blinds over the front windows, single horses pawing the macadam outside the doors, and elderly gentlemen in yellow waistcoats ringing bells and stepping in very politely when the maid demurely replies that Mrs. Durrant is at home.

Bonamy sat with Clara in the sunny front room with the barrel organ piping sweetly outside; the water-cart going slowly along spraying the pavement;[4] the carriages jingling, and all the silver and chintz, brown and blue rugs and vases filled with green boughs, striped with trembling yellow bars.

The insipidity of what was said needs no illustration—Bonamy kept on gently returning quiet answers and accumulating amazement at an existence squeezed and emasculated within a white satin shoe (Mrs. Durrant meanwhile enunciating strident politics with Sir Somebody in the back room) until the virginity of Clara's soul appeared to him candid; the depths unknown; and he would have brought out Jacob's name had he not begun to feel positively certain that Clara loved him—and could do nothing whatever.

"Nothing whatever!" he exclaimed, as the door shut, and, for a man of his temperament, got a very queer feeling, as he walked through the park, of carriages irresistibly driven; of flower-beds uncompromisingly geometrical; of force rushing round geometrical patterns in the most senseless way in the world. "Was Clara," he thought, pausing to watch the boys bathing in the Serpentine,[5] "the silent woman?—would Jacob marry her?"

But in Athens in the sunshine, in Athens, where it is almost impossible to get afternoon tea, and elderly gentlemen who talk politics talk them all the other way round, in Athens sat Sandra Wentworth Williams, veiled, in white, her legs stretched in front of her, one elbow on the arm of the bamboo chair, blue clouds wavering and drifting from her cigarette.

The orange trees which flourish in the Square of the Constitution,[6] the band, the dragging of feet, the sky, the houses, lemon and

3. Exclusive address in Knightsbridge, west London.
4. Water-carts patrolled the streets of London, spraying the pavements so that they were less dusty.
5. Large bathing pool in Hyde Park, just north of Sloane Street.
6. Also known as "Síntagma," and the center of modern Athens, bordered on one side by the Old Royal Palace (now the home of the Greek parliament) and its gardens.

rose coloured—all this became so significant to Mrs. Wentworth
Williams after her second cup of coffee that she began dramatizing
the story of the noble and impulsive Englishwoman who had offered
a seat in her carriage to the old American lady at Mycenae[7] (Mrs.
Duggan)—not altogether a false story, though it said nothing of
Evan, standing first on one foot, then on the other, waiting for the
women to stop chattering.

"I am putting the life of Father Damien into verse," Mrs. Duggan
had said, for she had lost everything—everything in the world, husband and child and everything, but faith remained.

Sandra, floating from the particular to the universal, lay back in a
trance.

The flight of time which hurries us so tragically along; the eternal
drudge and drone, now bursting into fiery flame like those brief balls
of yellow among green leaves (she was looking at orange trees); kisses
on lips that are to die; the world turning, turning in mazes of heat
and sound—though to be sure there is the quiet evening with its
lovely pallor, "For I am sensitive to every side of it," Sandra thought,
"and Mrs. Duggan will write to me for ever, and I shall answer her
letters." Now the royal band marching by with the national flag
stirred wider rings of emotion, and life became something that the
courageous mount and ride out to sea on—the hair blown back (so
she envisaged it, and the breeze stirred slightly among the orange
trees) and she herself was emerging from silver spray—when she saw
Jacob. He was standing in the Square with a book under his arm
looking vacantly about him. That he was heavily built and might
become stout in time was a fact.

But she suspected him of being a mere bumpkin.

"There is that young man," she said, peevishly, throwing away her
cigarette, "that Mr. Flanders."

"Where?" said Evan. "I don't see him."

"Oh, walking away—behind the trees now. No, you can't see him.
But we are sure to run into him," which, of course, they did.

But how far was he a mere bumpkin? How far was Jacob Flanders
at the age of twenty-six a stupid fellow? It is no use trying to sum
people up. One must follow hints, not exactly what is said, nor yet
entirely what is done. Some, it is true, take ineffaceable impressions
of character at once. Others dally, loiter, and get blown this way and

7. Ancient Greek city in the Peloponnese, site of Agamemnon's palace.

that. Kind old ladies assure us that cats are often the best judges of
character. A cat will always go to a good man, they say; but then,
Mrs. Whitehorn, Jacob's landlady, loathed cats.

There is also the highly respectable opinion that character-
mongering is much overdone nowadays. After all, what does it matter—that Fanny Elmer was all sentiment and sensation, and Mrs.
Durrant hard as iron? that Clara, owing (so the character-mongers
said) largely to her mother's influence, never yet had the chance to
do anything off her own bat, and only to very observant eyes displayed deeps of feeling which were positively alarming; and would
certainly throw herself away upon some one unworthy of her one of
these days unless, so the character-mongers said, she had a spark of
her mother's spirit in her—was somehow heroic. But what a term to
apply to Clara Durrant! Simple to a degree, others thought her. And
that is the very reason, so they said, why she attracts Dick Bonamy—
the young man with the Wellington nose. Now *he's* a dark horse if
you like. And there these gossips would suddenly pause. Obviously
they meant to hint at his peculiar disposition—long rumoured
among them.

"But sometimes it is precisely a woman like Clara that men of that
temperament need . . ." Miss Julia Eliot would hint.

"Well," Mr. Bowley would reply, "it may be so."

For however long these gossips sit, and however they stuff out
their victims' characters till they are swollen and tender as the livers
of geese exposed to a hot fire, they never come to a decision.

"That young man, Jacob Flanders," they would say, "so distinguished looking—and yet so awkward." Then they would apply themselves to Jacob and vacillate eternally between the two extremes. He
rode to hounds—after a fashion, for he hadn't a penny.

"Did you ever hear who his father was?" asked Julia Eliot.

"His mother, they say, is somehow connected with the Rocks-
biers," replied Mr. Bowley.

"He doesn't overwork himself anyhow."

"His friends are very fond of him."

"Dick Bonamy, you mean?"

"No, I didn't mean that. It's evidently the other way with Jacob.
He is precisely the young man to fall headlong in love and repent it
for the rest of his life."

"Oh, Mr. Bowley," said Mrs. Durrant, sweeping down upon them
in her imperious manner, "you remember Mrs. Adams? Well, that is
her niece." And Mr. Bowley, getting up, bowed politely and fetched
strawberries.

So we are driven back to see what the other side means—the men
in clubs and Cabinets—when they say that character-drawing is a

frivolous fireside art, a matter of pins and needles, exquisite outlines enclosing vacancy, flourishes, and mere scrawls.

The battleships ray out over the North Sea, keeping their stations accurately apart.[8] At a given signal all the guns are trained on a target which (the master gunner counts the seconds, watch in hand—at the sixth he looks up) flames into splinters. With equal nonchalance a dozen young men in the prime of life descend with composed faces into the depths of the sea; and there impassively (though with perfect mastery of machinery) suffocate uncomplainingly together. Like blocks of tin soldiers the army covers the cornfield, moves up the hillside, stops, reels slightly this way and that, and falls flat, save that, through field-glasses, it can be seen that one or two pieces still agitate up and down like fragments of broken match-stick.

These actions, together with the incessant commerce of banks, laboratories, chancellories, and houses of business, are the strokes which oar the world forward, they say. And they are dealt by men as smoothly sculptured as the impassive policeman at Ludgate Circus.[9] But you will observe that far from being padded to rotundity his face is stiff from force of will, and lean from the effort of keeping it so. When his right arm rises, all the force in his veins flows straight from shoulder to finger-tips; not an ounce is diverted into sudden impulses, sentimental regrets, wire-drawn distinctions. The buses punctually stop.

It is thus that we live, they say, driven by an unseizable force. They say that the novelists never catch it; that it goes hurtling through their nets and leaves them torn to ribbons. This, they say, is what we live by—this unseizable force.

"Where are the men?" said old General Gibbons, looking round the drawing-room, full as usual on Sunday afternoons of well-dressed people. "Where are the guns?"

Mrs. Durrant looked too.

Clara, thinking that her mother wanted her, came in; then went out again.

They were talking about Germany at the Durrants, and Jacob (driven by this unseizable force) walked rapidly down Hermes Street[1] and ran straight into the Williamses.

---

8. World War I began in August 1914, and eventually involved the Allied Powers (France, Great Britain, Russia, the United States, and other smaller countries) against the Central Powers (Germany, Austria-Hungary, Turkey/Ottoman Empire, and other smaller countries). Woolf does not seem to have any particular battle or skirmish in mind in this paragraph.
9. Busy intersection at the end of Fleet Street, not far from St. Paul's.
1. Main shopping street in Athens, running between Monastiraki and Síntagma Squares.

"Oh!" cried Sandra, with a cordiality which she suddenly felt. And Evan added, "What luck!"

The dinner which they gave him in the hotel which looks on to the Square of the Constitution was excellent. Plated baskets contained fresh rolls. There was real butter. And the meat scarcely needed the disguise of innumerable little red and green vegetables glazed in sauce.

It was strange, though. There were the little tables set out at intervals on the scarlet floor with the Greek King's monogram wrought in yellow. Sandra dined in her hat, veiled as usual. Evan looked this way and that over his shoulder; imperturbable yet supple; and sometimes sighed. It was strange. For they were English people come together in Athens on a May evening. Jacob, helping himself to this and that, answered intelligently, yet with a ring in his voice.

The Williamses were going to Constantinople early next morning, they said.

"Before you are up," said Sandra.

They would leave Jacob alone, then. Turning very slightly, Evan ordered something—a bottle of wine—from which he helped Jacob, with a kind of solicitude, with a kind of paternal solicitude, if that were possible. To be left alone—that was good for a young fellow. Never was there a time when the country had more need of men. He sighed.

"And you have been to the Acropolis?" asked Sandra.

"Yes," said Jacob. And they moved off to the window together, while Evan spoke to the head waiter about calling them early.

"It is astonishing," said Jacob, in a gruff voice.

Sandra opened her eyes very slightly. Possibly her nostrils expanded a little too.

"At half-past six then," said Evan, coming towards them, looking as if he faced something in facing his wife and Jacob standing with their backs to the window.

Sandra smiled at him.

And, as he went to the window and had nothing to say she added, in broken half-sentences:

"Well, but how lovely—wouldn't it be? The Acropolis, Evan—or are you too tired?"

At that Evan looked at them, or, since Jacob was staring ahead of him, at his wife, surlily, sullenly, yet with a kind of distress—not that she would pity him. Nor would the implacable spirit of love, for anything he could do, cease its tortures.

They left him and he sat in the smoking-room, which looks out on to the Square of the Constitution.

"Evan is happier alone," said Sandra. "We have been separated from the newspapers. Well, it is better that people should have what they want. . . . You have seen all these wonderful things since we met. . . . What impression . . . I think that you are changed."

"You want to go to the Acropolis," said Jacob. "Up here then."

"One will remember it all one's life," said Sandra.

"Yes," said Jacob. "I wish you could have come in the day-time."

"This is more wonderful," said Sandra, waving her hand.

Jacob looked vaguely.

"But you should see the Parthenon in the day-time," he said. "You couldn't come tomorrow—it would be too early?"

"You have sat there for hours and hours by yourself?"

"There were some awful women this morning," said Jacob.

"Awful women?" Sandra echoed.

"Frenchwomen."

"But something very wonderful has happened," said Sandra. Ten minutes, fifteen minutes, half an hour—that was all the time before her.

"Yes," he said.

"When one is your age—when one is young. What will you do? You will fall in love—oh yes! But don't be in too great a hurry. I am so much older."

She was brushed off the pavement by parading men.

"Shall we go on?" Jacob asked.

"Let us go on," she insisted.

For she could not stop until she had told him—or heard him say—or was it some action on his part that she required? Far away on the horizon she discerned it and could not rest.

"You'd never get English people to sit out like this," he said.

"Never—no. When you get back to England you won't forget this—or come with us to Constantinople!" she cried suddenly.

"But then . . ."

Sandra sighed.

"You must go to Delphi,[2] of course," she said. "But," she asked herself, "what do I want from him? Perhaps it is something that I have missed. . . ."

2. Ancient Greek temple to Apollo on the slopes of Mount Parnassus, site of the Pythian oracle.

"You will get there about six in the evening," she said. "You will see the eagles."[3]

Jacob looked set and even desperate by the light at the street corner; and yet composed. He was suffering perhaps. He was credulous. Yet there was something caustic about him. He had in him the seeds of extreme disillusionment, which would come to him from women in middle life. Perhaps if one strove hard enough to reach the top of the hill it need not come to him—this disillusionment from women in middle life.

"The hotel is awful," she said. "The last visitors had left their basins full of dirty water. There is always that," she laughed.

"The people one meets *are* beastly," Jacob said.

His excitement was clear enough.

"Write and tell me about it," she said. "And tell me what you feel and what you think. Tell me everything."

The night was dark. The Acropolis was a jagged mound.

"I should like to, awfully," he said.

"When we get back to London, we shall meet . . ."

"Yes."

"I suppose they leave the gates open?" he asked.

"We could climb them!" she answered wildly.

Obscuring the moon and altogether darkening the Acropolis the clouds passed from east to west. The clouds solidified; the vapours thickened; the trailing veils stayed and accumulated.

It was dark now over Athens, except for gauzy red streaks where the streets ran; and the front of the Palace[4] was cadaverous from electric light. At sea the piers stood out, marked by separate dots; the waves being invisible, and promontories and islands were dark humps with a few lights.

"I'd love to bring my brother, if I may," Jacob murmured.

"And then when your mother comes to London——," said Sandra.

The mainland of Greece was dark; and somewhere off Euboea[5] a cloud must have touched the waves and spattered them—the dolphins circling deeper and deeper into the sea. Violent was the wind now rushing down the Sea of Marmara between Greece and the plains of Troy.[6]

In Greece and the uplands of Albania[7] and Turkey, the wind

3. According to Greek mythology, Zeus released two eagles, one from the east, the other from the west, and caused them to fly toward the center of the earth; they met at the future site of Delphi, and eagles can still be seen there in the sky.
4. Old Royal Palace at Síntagma.
5. Large island hugging the coastline north of Athens.
6. The Sea of Marmara divides Turkey from east to west, with Istanbul at its eastern end and Troy south of its western end; under the Treaty of Sèvres (1920), the Greeks gained control of the land north of the Sea of Marmara, but after violent Turkish resistance led by Mustafa Kemal, it was restored to Turkey in the Treaty of Lausanne in 1923.
7. Country bordered to the south by Greece; became independent in 1912.

scours the sand and the dust, and sows itself thick with dry particles.
And then it pelts the smooth domes of the mosques, and makes the
cypresses, standing stiff by the turbaned tombstones of Mohammed-
ans, creak and bristle.

Sandra's veils were swirled about her.

"I will give you my copy," said Jacob. "Here. Will you keep it?"

(The book was the poems of Donne.)[8]

Now the agitation of the air uncovered a racing star. Now it was
dark. Now one after another lights were extinguished. Now great
towns—Paris—Constantinople—London—were black as strewn
rocks. Waterways might be distinguished. In England the trees were
heavy in leaf. Here perhaps in some southern wood an old man lit
dry ferns and the birds were startled. The sheep coughed; one flower
bent slightly towards another. The English sky is softer, milkier than
the Eastern. Something gentle has passed into it from the grass-
rounded hills, something damp. The salt gale blew in at Betty Flanders's bedroom window, and the widow lady, raising herself slightly
on her elbow, sighed like one who realizes, but would fain ward off
a little longer—oh, a little longer!—the oppression of eternity.

But to return to Jacob and Sandra.

They had vanished. There was the Acropolis; but had they reached
it? The columns and the Temple remain; the emotion of the living
breaks fresh on them year after year; and of that what remains?

As for reaching the Acropolis who shall say that we ever do it, or
that when Jacob woke next morning he found anything hard and
durable to keep for ever? Still, he went with them to Constantinople.

Sandra Wentworth Williams certainly woke to find a copy of
Donne's poems upon her dressing-table. And the book would be
stood on the shelf in the English country house where Sally Duggan's
Life of Father Damien in verse would join it one of these days. There
were ten or twelve little volumes already. Strolling in at dusk, Sandra
would open the books and her eyes would brighten (but not at the
print), and subsiding into the arm-chair she would suck back again
the soul of the moment; or, for sometimes she was restless, would
pull out book after book and swing across the whole space of her life
like an acrobat from bar to bar. She had had her moments. Meanwhile, the great clock on the landing ticked and Sandra would hear
time accumulating, and ask herself, "What for? What for?"

"What for? What for?" Sandra would say, putting the book back,
and strolling to the looking-glass and pressing her hair. And Miss
Edwards would be startled at dinner, as she opened her mouth to
admit roast mutton, by Sandra's sudden solicitude: "Are you happy,

---

8. John Donne (1572–1631), British poet known for both his love poems and his religious
lyrics.

Miss Edwards?"—a thing Cissy Edwards hadn't thought of for years.

"What for? What for?" Jacob never asked himself any such question, to judge by the way he laced his boots; shaved himself; to judge
by the depth of his sleep that night, with the wind fidgeting at the
shutters, and half-a-dozen mosquitoes singing in his ears. He was
young—a man. And then Sandra was right when she judged him to
be credulous as yet. At forty it might be a different matter. Already
he had marked the things he liked in Donne, and they were savage
enough. However, you might place beside them passages of the pur-
est poetry in Shakespeare.

But the wind was rolling the darkness through the streets of Athens, rolling it, one might suppose, with a sort of trampling energy of
mood which forbids too close an analysis of the feelings of any single
person, or inspection of features. All faces—Greek, Levantine,[9]
Turkish, English—would have looked much the same in that darkness. At length the columns and the Temples whiten, yellow, turn
rose; and the Pyramids and St. Peter's[1] arise, and at last sluggish St.
Paul's looms up.

The Christians have the right to rouse most cities with their interpretation of the day's meaning. Then, less melodiously, dissenters of
different sects issue a cantankerous emendation.[2] The steamers,
resounding like gigantic tuning-forks, state the old old fact—how
there is a sea coldly, greenly, swaying outside. But nowadays it is the
thin voice of duty, piping in a white thread from the top of a funnel,
that collects the largest multitudes, and night is nothing but a long-
drawn sigh between hammer-strokes, a deep breath—you can hear
it from an open window even in the heart of London.

But who, save the nerve-worn and sleepless, or thinkers standing
with hands to the eyes on some crag above the multitude, see things
thus in skeleton outline, bare of flesh? In Surbiton the skeleton is
wrapped in flesh.

"The kettle never boils so well on a sunny morning," says Mrs.
Grandage, glancing at the clock on the mantelpiece. Then the grey
Persian cat stretches itself on the window-seat, and buffets a moth
with soft round paws. And before breakfast is half over (they were
late to-day) a baby is deposited in her lap, and she must guard the
sugar basin while Tom Grandage reads the golfing article in the
Times, sips his coffee, wipes his moustaches, and is off to the office,
where he is the greatest authority upon the foreign exchanges and
marked for promotion.

The skeleton is well wrapped in flesh. Even this dark night when

9. From the islands or countries of the Eastern Mediterranean.
1. The Pyramids of Giza, near Cairo in Egypt, built c. 2575–c. 2465 B.C.E.; St. Peter's Basil-
ica, in Rome, completed 1615, one of the largest Christian churches in the world.
2. Correction.

the wind rolls the darkness through Lombard Street and Fetter Lane and Bedford Square it stirs (since it is summer-time and the height of the season) plane trees spangled with electric light, and curtains still preserving the room from the dawn. People still murmur over the last word said on the staircase, or strain, all through their dreams, for the voice of the alarum clock. So when the wind roams through a forest innumerable twigs stir; hives are brushed; insects sway on grass blades; the spider runs rapidly up a crease in the bark; and the whole air is tremulous with breathing; elastic with filaments.

Only here—in Lombard Street and Fetter Lane and Bedford Square[3]—each insect carries a globe of the world in his head, and the webs of the forest are schemes evolved for the smooth conduct of business; and honey is treasure of one sort and another; and the stir in the air is the indescribable agitation of life.

But colour returns; runs up the stalks of the grass; blows out into tulips and crocuses; solidly stripes the tree trunks; and fills the gauze of the air and the grasses and pools.

The Bank of England emerges; and the Monument with its bristling head of golden hair; the dray horses[4] crossing London Bridge show grey and strawberry and iron-coloured. There is a whir of wings as the suburban trains rush into the terminus. And the light mounts over the faces of all the tall blind houses, slides through a chink and paints the lustrous bellying crimson curtains; the green wine-glasses; the coffee-cups; and the chairs standing askew.

Sunlight strikes in upon shaving-glasses; and gleaming brass cans; upon all the jolly trappings of the day; the bright, inquisitive, armoured, resplendent, summer's day, which has long since vanquished chaos; which has dried the melancholy mediaeval mists; drained the swamp and stood glass and stone upon it; and equipped our brains and bodies with such an armoury of weapons that merely to see the flash and thrust of limbs engaged in the conduct of daily life is better than the old pageant of armies drawn out in battle array upon the plain.

XIII

"The height of the season," said Bonamy.

The sun had already blistered the paint on the backs of the green chairs in Hyde Park; peeled the bark off the plane trees; and turned

3. Streets in London: Lombard Street, in the City east of St. Paul's; Fetter Lane, between Holborn and Fleet Street; Bedford Square, in Bloomsbury.
4. Large, powerful horses used for pulling a dray, a low cart designed for heavy loads; the Bank of England: on Threadneedle Street in the City; the Monument: a column standing 202 feet high, just north of London Bridge in the City, erected in the 1670s to commemorate the Great Fire of London in 1666, surmounted by a gilt "Vase of Flames" with golden flames protruding from it.

the earth to powder and to smooth yellow pebbles. Hyde Park was circled, incessantly, by turning wheels.

"The height of the season," said Bonamy sarcastically.

He was sarcastic because of Clara Durrant; because Jacob had come back from Greece very brown and lean, with his pockets full of Greek notes, which he pulled out when the chair man came for pence; because Jacob was silent.

"He has not said a word to show that he is glad to see me," thought Bonamy bitterly.

The motor-cars passed incessantly over the bridge of the Serpentine; the upper classes walked upright, or bent themselves gracefully over the palings; the lower classes lay with their knees cocked up, flat on their backs; the sheep grazed on pointed wooden legs;[1] small children ran down the sloping grass, stretched their arms, and fell.

"Very urbane," Jacob brought out.

"Urbane" on the lips of Jacob had mysteriously all the shapeliness of a character which Bonamy thought daily more sublime, devastating, terrific than ever, though he was still, and perhaps would be for ever, barbaric, obscure.

What superlatives! What adjectives! How acquit Bonamy of sentimentality of the grossest sort; of being tossed like a cork on the waves; of having no steady insight into character; of being unsupported by reason, and of drawing no comfort whatever from the works of the classics?

"The height of civilization," said Jacob.

He was fond of using Latin words.

Magnanimity, virtue—such words when Jacob used them in talk with Bonamy meant that he took control of the situation; that Bonamy would play round him like an affectionate spaniel; and that (as likely as not) they would end by rolling on the floor.

"And Greece?" said Bonamy. "The Parthenon and all that?"

"There's none of this European mysticism," said Jacob.

"It's the atmosphere, I suppose," said Bonamy. "And you went to Constantinople?"

"Yes," said Jacob.

Bonamy paused, moved a pebble; then darted in with the rapidity and certainty of a lizard's tongue.

"You are in love!" he exclaimed.

Jacob blushed.

The sharpest of knives never cut so deep.

As for responding, or taking the least account of it, Jacob stared straight ahead of him, fixed, monolithic—oh, very beautiful!—like a British Admiral, exclaimed Bonamy in a rage, rising from his seat

1. Sheep used to graze in Hyde Park.

and walking off; waiting for some sound; none came; too proud to look back; walking quicker and quicker until he found himself gazing into motor cars and cursing women. Where was the pretty woman's face? Clara's—Fanny's—Florinda's? Who was the pretty little creature?

Not Clara Durrant.

The Aberdeen[2] terrier must be exercised, and as Mr. Bowley was going that very moment—would like nothing better than a walk—they went together, Clara and kind little Bowley—Bowley who had rooms in the Albany, Bowley who wrote letters to the *Times* in a jocular vein about foreign hotels and the Aurora Borealis[3]—Bowley who liked young people and walked down Piccadilly with his right arm resting on the boss of his back.

"Little demon!" cried Clara, and attached Troy to his chain.

Bowley anticipated—hoped for—a confidence. Devoted to her mother, Clara sometimes felt her a little, well, her mother was so sure of herself that she could not understand other people being—being—"as ludicrous as I am," Clara jerked out (the dog tugging her forwards). And Bowley thought she looked like a huntress and turned over in his mind which it should be—some pale virgin with a slip of the moon in her hair, which was a flight for Bowley.

The colour was in her cheeks. To have spoken outright about her mother—still, it was only to Mr. Bowley, who loved her, as everybody must; but to speak was unnatural to her, yet it was awful to feel, as she had done all day, that she *must* tell some one.

"Wait till we cross the road," she said to the dog, bending down.

Happily she had recovered by that time.

"She thinks so much about England," she said. "She is so anxious——"

Bowley was defrauded as usual. Clara never confided in any one.

"Why don't the young people settle it, eh?" he wanted to ask. "What's all this about England?"—a question poor Clara could not have answered, since, as Mrs. Durrant discussed with Sir Edgar the policy of Sir Edward Grey,[4] Clara only wondered why the cabinet looked dusty, and Jacob had never come. Oh, here was Mrs. Cowley Johnson . . .

2. Small, lively dog, now known as "Scottish terrier."
3. Display of colored light in the night sky, also known as the "Northern Lights."
4. British politician (1862–1933), foreign secretary 1905–16; in the weeks leading up to World War I, until the last few days before the war began on August 4, 1914, Grey favored mediation over a declaration of war on Germany.

And Clara would hand the pretty china tea-cups, and smile at the compliment—that no one in London made tea so well as she did.

"We get it at Brocklebank's," she said, "in Cursitor Street."[5]

Ought she not to be grateful? Ought she not to be happy? Especially since her mother looked so well and enjoyed so much talking to Sir Edgar about Morocco, Venezuela, or some such place.

"Jacob! Jacob!" thought Clara; and kind Mr. Bowley, who was ever so good with old ladies, looked; stopped; wondered whether Elizabeth wasn't too harsh with her daughter; wondered about Bonamy, Jacob—which young fellow was it?—and jumped up directly Clara said she must exercise Troy.

They had reached the site of the old Exhibition.[6] They looked at the tulips.[7] Stiff and curled, the little rods of waxy smoothness rose from the earth, nourished yet contained, suffused with scarlet and coral pink. Each had its shadow; each grew trimly in the diamond-shaped wedge as the gardener had planned it.

"Barnes never gets them to grow like that," Clara mused; she sighed.

"You are neglecting your friends," said Bowley, as some one, going the other way, lifted his hat. She started; acknowledged Mr. Lionel Parry's bow; wasted on him what had sprung for Jacob.

("Jacob! Jacob!" she thought.)

"But you'll get run over if I let you go," she said to the dog.

"England seems all right," said Mr. Bowley.

The loop of the railing beneath the statue of Achilles[8] was full of parasols and waistcoats; chains and bangles; of ladies and gentlemen, lounging elegantly, lightly observant.

" 'This statue was erected by the women of England . . . ' " Clara read out with a foolish little laugh. "Oh, Mr. Bowley! Oh!" Gallop—gallop—gallop—a horse galloped past without a rider. The stirrups swung; the pebbles spurted.

5. In Holborn, off Fetter Lane.
6. The Great Exhibition of 1851 took place in Hyde Park in a huge, specially designed, glass building (the "Crystal Palace"), which was moved to Sydenham in 1852 and destroyed by fire in 1936.
7. As Woolf acknowledged in her letter to C. P. Sanger (p. 171), tulips do not in fact bloom in August, the month in which this scene is set.
8. The Wellington Monument, a nude statue of Achilles, cast by Richard Westmacott in 1822, is in the southwest corner of Hyde Park. The inscription reads: "To Arthur, Duke of Wellington, and his brave companions in arms, this statue of Achilles cast from cannons won at the victories of Salmanaca, Vittoria, Toulouse and Waterloo is inscribed by their countrywomen. Placed on this spot on the XVIII day of June MDCXXII by command of His Majesty George III."

"Oh, stop! Stop it, Mr. Bowley!" she cried, white, trembling, gripping his arm, utterly unconscious, the tears coming.

"Tut-tut!" said Mr. Bowley in his dressing-room an hour later. "Tut-tut!"—a comment that was profound enough, though inarticulately expressed, since his valet was handing his shirt studs.

Julia Eliot, too, had seen the horse run away, and had risen from her seat to watch the end of the incident, which, since she came of a sporting family, seemed to her slightly ridiculous. Sure enough the little man came pounding behind with his breeches dusty; looked thoroughly annoyed; and was being helped to mount by a policeman when Julia Eliot, with a sardonic smile, turned towards the Marble Arch[9] on her errand of mercy. It was only to visit a sick old lady who had known her mother and perhaps the Duke of Wellington; for Julia shared the love of her sex for the distressed; liked to visit death-beds; threw slippers at weddings; received confidences by the dozen; knew more pedigrees than a scholar knows dates, and was one of the kindliest, most generous, least continent of women.

Yet five minutes after she had passed the statue of Achilles she had the rapt look of one brushing through crowds on a summer's afternoon, when the trees are rustling, the wheels churning yellow, and the tumult of the present seems like an elegy for past youth and past summers, and there rose in her mind a curious sadness, as if time and eternity showed through skirts and waistcoats, and she saw people passing tragically to destruction. Yet, Heaven knows, Julia was no fool. A sharper woman at a bargain did not exist. She was always punctual. The watch on her wrist gave her twelve minutes and a half in which to reach Bruton Street.[1] Lady Congreve expected her at five.

9. Ceremonial arch designed by John Nash in 1828, originally the chief entrance to Buckingham Palace, moved to the northeast corner of Hyde Park in 1851.
1. A short walk from Marble Arch, Bruton Street runs between Berkeley Square and New Bond Street in exclusive Mayfair.

The gilt clock at Verrey's[2] was striking five.

Florinda looked at it with a dull expression, like an animal. She looked at the clock; looked at the door; looked at the long glass opposite; disposed her cloak; drew closer to the table, for she was pregnant—no doubt about it, Mother Stuart said, recommending remedies, consulting friends; sunk, caught by the heel, as she tripped so lightly over the surface.

Her tumbler of pinkish sweet stuff was set down by the waiter; and she sucked, through a straw, her eyes on the looking-glass, on the door, now soothed by the sweet taste. When Nick Bramham came in it was plain, even to the young Swiss waiter, that there was a bargain between them. Nick hitched his clothes together clumsily; ran his fingers through his hair; sat down, to an ordeal, nervously. She looked at him; and set off laughing; laughed—laughed— laughed. The young Swiss waiter, standing with crossed legs by the pillar, laughed too.

The door opened; in came the roar of Regent Street, the roar of traffic, impersonal, unpitying; and sunshine grained with dirt. The Swiss waiter must see to the newcomers. Bramham lifted his glass.

"He's like Jacob," said Florinda, looking at the newcomer.

"The way he stares." She stopped laughing.

Jacob, leaning forward, drew a plan of the Parthenon in the dust in Hyde Park, a network of strokes at least, which may have been the Parthenon, or again a mathematical diagram. And why was the pebble so emphatically ground in at the corner? It was not to count his notes that he took out a wad of papers and read a long flowing letter which Sandra had written two days ago at Milton Dower House with his book before her and in her mind the memory of something said or attempted, some moment in the dark on the road to the Acropolis which (such was her creed) mattered for ever.

"He is," she mused, "like that man in Molière."

She meant Alceste.[3] She meant that he was severe. She meant that she could deceive him.

"Or could I not?" she thought, putting the poems of Donne back in the bookcase. "Jacob," she went on, going to the window and looking over the spotted flower-beds across the grass where the pie-

2. French restaurant and café on the corner of Hanover Street and Regent Street, near Oxford Circus.
3. *Le Misanthrope*, a play by Molière (1622–1673), first produced in 1666, tells the story of Alceste, who withdraws from society in disgust at the hypocrisy and superficiality of the world in which he lives.

bald cows grazed under beech trees, "Jacob would be shocked."

The perambulator was going through the little gate in the railing. She kissed her hand; directed by the nurse, Jimmy waved his.

"*He's* a small boy," she said, thinking of Jacob.

And yet—Alceste?

"What a nuisance you are!" Jacob grumbled, stretching out first one leg and then the other and feeling in each trouser-pocket for his chair ticket.[4]

"I expect the sheep have eaten it," he said. "Why do you keep sheep?"

"Sorry to disturb you, sir," said the ticket-collector, his hand deep in the enormous pouch of pence.

"Well, I hope they pay you for it," said Jacob. "There you are. No. You stick to it. Go and get drunk."

He had parted with half-a-crown, tolerantly, compassionately, with considerable contempt for his species.

Even now poor Fanny Elmer was dealing, as she walked along the Strand, in her incompetent way with this very careless, indifferent, sublime manner he had of talking to railway guards or porters; or Mrs. Whitehorn, when she consulted him about her little boy who was beaten by the schoolmaster.

Sustained entirely upon picture post cards for the past two months, Fanny's idea of Jacob was more statuesque, noble, and eyeless than ever. To reinforce her vision she had taken to visiting the British Museum, where, keeping her eyes downcast until she was alongside of the battered Ulysses, she opened them and got a fresh shock of Jacob's presence, enough to last her half a day. But this was wearing thin. And she wrote now—poems, letters that were never posted, saw his face in advertisements on hoardings, and would cross the road to let the barrel-organ turn her musings to rhapsody. But at breakfast (she shared rooms with a teacher), when the butter was smeared about the plate, and the prongs of the forks were clotted with old egg yolk, she revised these visions violently; was, in truth, very cross; was losing her complexion, as Margery Jackson told her, bringing the whole thing down (as she laced her stout boots) to a

4. To show that Jacob has paid for his rented deck-chair.

level of mother-wit, vulgarity, and sentiment, for she had loved too;
and been a fool.

"One's godmothers ought to have told one," said Fanny, looking
in at the window of Bacon, the mapseller,[5] in the Strand—told one
that it is no use making a fuss; this is life, they should have said, as
Fanny said it now, looking at the large yellow globe marked with
steamship lines.

"This is life. This is life," said Fanny.

"A very hard face," thought Miss Barrett, on the other side of the
glass, buying maps of the Syrian desert and waiting impatiently to
be served. "Girls look old so soon nowadays."

The equator swam behind tears.

"Piccadilly?" Fanny asked the conductor of the omnibus, and
climbed to the top. After all, he would, he must, come back to her.

But Jacob might have been thinking of Rome; of architecture; of
jurisprudence; as he sat under the plane tree in Hyde Park.

The omnibus stopped outside Charing Cross;[6] and behind it were
clogged omnibuses, vans, motor-cars, for a procession with banners
was passing down Whitehall,[7] and elderly people were stiffly descending from between the paws of the slippery lions,[8] where they had
been testifying to their faith, singing lustily, raising their eyes from
their music to look into the sky, and still their eyes were on the sky
as they marched behind the gold letters of their creed.

The traffic stopped, and the sun, no longer sprayed out by the
breeze, became almost too hot. But the procession passed; the banners glittered far away down Whitehall; the traffic was released;
lurched on; spun to a smooth continuous uproar; swerving round the
curve of Cockspur Streets;[9] and sweeping past Government offices
and equestrian statues down Whitehall to the prickly spires, the tethered grey fleet of masonry, and the large white clock of Westminster.[1]

5. George W. Bacon, Ltd., at 127 Strand, on the corner of Savoy Street near Waterloo Bridge;
   one of the main publishers and distributors of maps in the late nineteenth and early
   twentieth centuries.
6. At the west end of the Strand, just below Trafalgar Square.
7. This paragraph appears to be a reconstruction of August 4, 1914, the day Britain declared
   war on Germany; the procession is a pro-war demonstration; Whitehall leads from Trafalgar Square to the Houses of Parliament, past Downing Street, the residence of the
   British prime minister.
8. At the foot of Nelson's Column on Trafalgar Square are four giant bronze lions sculpted
   in 1868 by Edwin Landseer, using metal from enemy cannons captured at the Battle of
   Trafalgar.
9. Bordering Trafalgar Square on the south, leading into Whitehall.
1. The Houses of Parliament, built on the banks of the Thames, 1837–60, by Charles Barry

Five strokes Big Ben intoned; Nelson received the salute. The wires of the Admiralty[2] shivered with some far-away communication. A voice kept remarking that Prime Ministers and Viceroys spoke in the Reichstag; entered Lahore; said that the Emperor travelled; in Milan they rioted; said there were rumours in Vienna; said that the Ambassador at Constantinople had audience with the Sultan; the fleet was at Gibraltar.[3] The voice continued, imprinting on the faces of the clerks in Whitehall (Timothy Durrant was one of them) something of its own inexorable gravity, as they listened, deciphered, wrote down. Papers accumulated, inscribed with the utterances of Kaisers, the statistics of rice-fields, the growling of hundreds of work-people, plotting sedition in back streets, or gathering in the Calcutta bazaars,[4] or mustering their forces in the uplands of Albania,[5] where the hills are sand-coloured, and bones lie unburied.

The voice spoke plainly in the square quiet room with heavy tables, where one elderly man[6] made notes on the margin of type-written sheets, his silver-topped umbrella leaning against the bookcase.

His head—bald, red-veined, hollow-looking—represented all the heads in the building. His head, with the amiable pale eyes, carried the burden of knowledge across the street; laid it before his colleagues,[7] who came equally burdened; and then the sixteen gentlemen, lifting their pens or turning perhaps rather wearily in their chairs, decreed that the course of history should shape itself this way or that way, being manfully determined, as their faces showed, to

---

and Augustus Pugin, have many Gothic spires; the large white clock houses Big Ben, first rung in 1859.

2. Until 1964, the government department that managed naval affairs, housed in a large building on Whitehall built in 1900.

3. A British naval base; the voice: presumably a continuous radio communication of the latest developments overseas; the Reichstag (German parliament) convened on August 4, 1914, for speeches from Kaiser Wilhelm II and the German chancellor Theobald von Bethmann-Hollweg, and to express support for the previous day's declaration of war on France and the German invasion of Belgium that morning; the Lahore Infantry Division of the Indian Army (then under British control) was mobilized to France shortly after the beginning of the war; Franz-Josef, the emperor of Austro-Hungary, declared war on Serbia on July 28, 1914; rioting broke out when Italy declared its neutrality on August 3, 1914; Vienna was the capital of the Austro-Hungarian Empire; the Sultan, leader of the Ottoman Empire, at first adopted a policy of ambivalent neutrality in the war (a position from which the British ambassador is here trying to dissuade him), but at the beginning of November 1914 he declared a military jihad (holy war) against France, Russia, and Great Britain, and joined the war on the German side.

4. Resistance to the war increased after the Ottoman Empire became involved in November 1914 because India was now fighting against a Muslim country; there was also anger in India against the regional quota system for enlistment, which came close to conscription.

5. At the beginning of the war Albania split along religious and tribal lines, and was occupied by a succession of powers on both sides until by the end of 1914 two-thirds of the country was controlled by Austro-Hungary and Bulgaria.

6. Prime Minister Asquith, in Downing Street.

7. Asquith crosses Whitehall to chair a meeting of the British cabinet at 11 A.M., at which an ultimatum was crafted demanding Germany's immediate withdrawal from neutral Belgium.

impose some coherency upon Rajahs and Kaisers and the muttering in bazaars, the secret gatherings, plainly visible in Whitehall, of kilted peasants in Albanian uplands; to control the course of events.

Pitt and Chatham, Burke and Gladstone[8] looked from side to side with fixed marble eyes and an air of immortal quiescence which perhaps the living may have envied, the air being full of whistling and concussions, as the procession with its banners passed down Whitehall. Moreover, some were troubled with dyspepsia; one had at that very moment cracked the glass of his spectacles; another spoke in Glasgow to-morrow; altogether they looked too red, fat, pale or lean, to be dealing, as the marble heads had dealt, with the course of history.

Timmy Durrant in his little room in the Admiralty, going to consult a Blue book,[9] stopped for a moment by the window, and observed the placard tied round the lamp-post.

Miss Thomas, one of the typists, said to her friend that if the Cabinet was going to sit much longer she should miss her boy outside the Gaiety.[1]

Timmy Durrant, returning with his Blue book under his arm, noticed a little knot of people at the street corner; conglomerated as though one of them knew something; and the others, pressing round him, looked up, looked down, looked along the street. What was it that he knew?

Timothy, placing the Blue book before him, studied a paper sent round by the Treasury for information. Mr. Crawley, his fellow-clerk, impaled a letter on a skewer.

Jacob rose from his chair in Hyde Park, tore his ticket to pieces, and walked away.

"Such a sunset," wrote Mrs. Flanders in her letter to Archer at Singapore.[2] "One couldn't make up one's mind to come indoors," she wrote. "It seemed wicked to waste even a moment."

The long windows of Kensington Palace[3] flushed fiery rose as Jacob walked away; a flock of wild duck flew over the Serpentine; and the trees were stood against the sky, blackly, magnificently.

8. William Gladstone (1809–1898), British politician, prime minister from 1868 to 1874, 1880 to 1885, 1886, and 1892 to 1894.
9. Official Parliamentary report, traditionally issued in a dark blue cover.
1. Gaiety Theater, established 1864, on the western corner of Aldwych and the Strand.
2. Anachronistic: the British did not establish a naval base in Singapore, a British colony, until 1921.
3. Royal palace at the west end of Kensington Gardens, which lie adjacent to Hyde Park on its west side.

"Jacob," wrote Mrs. Flanders, with the red light on her page, "is hard at work after his delightful journey . . ."

"The Kaiser," the far-away voice remarked in Whitehall, "received me in audience."[4]

"Now I know that face—" said the Reverend Andrew Floyd, coming out of Carter's[5] shop in Piccadilly, "but who the dickens—?" and he watched Jacob, turned round to look at him, but could not be sure——

"Oh, Jacob Flanders!" he remembered in a flash.

But he was so tall; so unconscious; such a fine young fellow.

"I gave him Byron's works," Andrew Floyd mused, and started forward, as Jacob crossed the road; but hesitated, and let the moment pass, and lost the opportunity.

Another procession, without banners, was blocking Long Acre.[6] Carriages, with dowagers in amethyst and gentlemen spotted with carnations, intercepted cabs and motor-cars turned in the opposite direction, in which jaded men in white waistcoats lolled, on their way home to shrubberies and billiard-rooms in Putney and Wimbledon.[7]

Two barrel-organs played by the kerb, and horses coming out of Aldridge's[8] with white labels on their buttocks straddled across the road and were smartly jerked back.

Mrs. Durrant, sitting with Mr. Wortley in a motor-car, was impatient lest they should miss the overture.

But Mr. Wortley, always urbane, always in time for the overture, buttoned his gloves, and admired Miss Clara.

"A shame to spend such a night in the theatre!" said Mrs. Durrant, seeing all the windows of the coachmakers in Long Acre ablaze.

"Think of your moors!" said Mr. Wortley to Clara.

"Ah! but Clara likes this better," Mrs. Durrant laughed.

"I don't know—really," said Clara, looking at the blazing windows. She started.

She saw Jacob.

"Who?" asked Mrs. Durrant sharply, leaning forward.

4. At 7 P.M. on August 4, 1914, the British ambassador to Germany, Edward Goschen, met the German chancellor von Bethmann-Hollweg (not the Kaiser, as Woolf says) to present him with the British ultimatum regarding Belgian neutrality; a state of war between Britain and Germany was declared at 11 P.M.
5. Restaurant in Piccadilly.
6. Runs east from Charing Cross Road, through Covent Garden.
7. Middle-class suburb in southwest London.
8. Aldridge's Repository, horse-seller's yard on St. Martin's Lane.

But she saw no one.

Under the arch of the Opera House large faces and lean ones, the powdered and the hairy, all alike were red in the sunset; and, quickened by the great hanging lamps with their repressed primrose lights, by the tramp, and the scarlet, and the pompous ceremony, some ladies looked for a moment into steaming bedrooms near by, where women with loose hair leaned out of windows, where girls—where children—(the long mirrors held the ladies suspended) but one must follow; one must not block the way.

Clara's moors were fine enough. The Phoenicians slept under their piled grey rocks; the chimneys of the old mines pointed starkly;[9] early moths blurred the heather-bells; cart-wheels could be heard grinding on the road far beneath; and the suck and sighing of the waves sounded gently, persistently, for ever.

Shading her eyes with her hand Mrs. Pascoe stood in her cabbage-garden looking out to sea. Two steamers and a sailing-ship crossed each other; passed each other; and in the bay the gulls kept alighting on a log, rising high, returning again to the log, while some rode in upon the waves and stood on the rim of the water until the moon blanched all to whiteness.

Mrs. Pascoe had gone indoors long ago.

But the red light was on the columns of the Parthenon, and the Greek women who were knitting their stockings and sometimes crying to a child to come and have the insects picked from its head were as jolly as sand-martins in the heat, quarrelling, scolding, suckling their babies, until the ships in the Piraeus fired their guns.[1]

The sound spread itself flat, and then went tunnelling its way with fitful explosions among the channels of the islands.

Darkness drops like a knife over Greece.

"The guns?"[2] said Betty Flanders, half asleep, getting out of bed and going to the window, which was decorated with a fringe of dark leaves.

9. A seafaring people, living in what is now Lebanon about 1000 B.C.E., who came to Britain in search of tin, abundant in Cornwall where "Clara's moors" are situated; the "old mines" are Cornish tin mines.
1. Greece did not officially enter the war until 1917, on the side of Germany.
2. Scarborough, believed by the Germans to be fortified, was attacked by German battle cruisers in December 1914, the first attack on Britain since 1778; 124 were killed and 500 injured.

"Not at this distance," she thought. "It is the sea."

Again, far away, she heard the dull sound, as if nocturnal women were beating great carpets. There was Morty lost, and Seabrook dead; her sons fighting for their country. But were the chickens safe? Was that some one moving downstairs? Rebecca with the toothache? No. The nocturnal women were beating great carpets. Her hens shifted slightly on their perches.

XIV

"He left everything just as it was," Bonamy marvelled. "Nothing arranged. All his letters strewn about for any one to read. What did he expect? Did he think he would come back?" he mused, standing in the middle of Jacob's room.

The eighteenth century has its distinction. These houses were built, say, a hundred and fifty years ago. The rooms are shapely, the ceilings high; over the doorways a rose or a ram's skull is carved in the wood. Even the panels, painted in raspberry-coloured paint, have their distinction.

Bonamy took up a bill for a hunting-crop.

"That seems to be paid," he said.

There were Sandra's letters.

Mrs. Durrant was taking a party to Greenwich.

Lady Rocksbier hoped for the pleasure . . .

Listless is the air in an empty room, just swelling the curtain; the flowers in the jar shift. One fibre in the wicker arm-chair creaks, though no one sits there.

Bonamy crossed to the window. Pickford's van swung down the street. The omnibuses were locked together at Mudie's corner. Engines throbbed, and carters, jamming the brakes down, pulled their horses sharp up. A harsh and unhappy voice cried something unintelligible. And then suddenly all the leaves seemed to raise themselves.

"Jacob! Jacob!" cried Bonamy, standing by the window. The leaves sank down again.

"Such confusion everywhere!" exclaimed Betty Flanders, bursting open the bedroom door.

Bonamy turned away from the window.

"What am I to do with these, Mr. Bonamy?"

She held out a pair of Jacob's old shoes.

THE END

Extracts from the Holograph Draft[†]

A number of fairly substantial passages were deleted from the holograph draft before the novel was published, and some shed light on Woolf's evolving plans for the novel and on her efforts to establish a new fictional voice. Some of the most important of those passages are reprinted here, from *Virginia Woolf's "Jacob's Room": The Holograph Draft*, transcribed and edited by Edward L. Bishop (New York: Pace University Press, 1998). The three notebooks in which the manuscript of *Jacob's Room* appears are housed in the Henry W. and Albert A. Berg Collection of English and American Literature at the New York Public Library. The notebooks have been numbered one to three, and the Berg Collection has added page numbers on both sides of each page. I give both the Berg Collection notebook and page number, and the numbers of the pages on which the extracts are reprinted in Bishop's edition of the holograph.

1. The section at the beginning of Chapter 4, where Jacob and Timmy Durrant are boating round the Scilly Isles (pp. 35–39), does not appear in the manuscript. Instead, the chapter begins with a lengthy description of Mrs Pascoe, which appears, in a much shorter version, on pp. 40–41 of this volume. In the manuscript, the following passage is inserted after the sentence "A peacock butterfly now spread himself upon the teasle, fresh and newly emerged, as the blue and chocolate down on his wings testified" (p. 41):

Yet no butterfly does much more than

stain a patch on ~~one's~~ the retina; or ~~. . . . M^{rs.} M^{rs.}~~
                                                        was
~~There is the Gurnard Head, too, 'I love to see the look'~~

~~in words. The poet wrote something about 'cased in~~
                            As for
~~the unfeeling armour~~ of   The black rocks in the sea

testified. to the ~~way in which~~ endurance of this solitary

crag of human life, fronting its waves -   .Meanwhile

† From *Virginia Woolf's "Jacob's Room": The Holograph Text*, transcribed and edited by Edward L. Bishop (New York: Pace University Press, 1988). Reprinted by permission of The Society of Authors on behalf of the Estate of Virginia Woolf and Pace University Press.

145

M^rs. Pascoe had taken down the gaudy box placed
askew upon her mantelpiece had made the tea, &
was about to sip her first cup.   w

What with ~~the~~ buzzing of a blue bottle & the ticking of the
clock the little room was noisy; & ~~a rich~~ geranium
in the window gave forth a rich musty smell.
She drank deeply & comfortably, cut herself a piece of
bread, spread the butter thick, & in doing so ~~revealed~~
showed hands knobbed with labour & grimed with dirt.
                    perhaps   small size
~~The Perhap Perhaps~~ owing / to the ~~heat~~ of the room, &
the rich musty smell of the geranium in the window,
                           emphatic
the presence of   the body became very ~~important. Two bodies would~~
M^rs. Pascoe   She wore a dirty white ~~k~~ cloth of some kind round her
neck, & the creases ~~of~~ in her skin were marked by black
grains.   ~~w When her husband came in, the~~ Two
bodies together would ~~create an intolerable sense of~~
~~be~~ make it impossible to think of anything except the
body.   One might go into the scullery; the other
stumble up the stairs to the bedroom; but ~~in this~~
~~four roomed cottage an~~ there would be no escaping
the body.   ~~Its functions are detestable~~.   An earth
closet out in the rain - sickness - a woman's period - ~~copul~~
copulation upstairs in the double bed, ~~or here before the fire~~
               childbirth
~~perhaps - the~~ birth - ~~all all that veils & places in the shadow~~
~~these natural functions of the body are all bodies~~
as the room filled with bodies, ~~these functions & desires~~
~~would assert themselves. all these functions and desires would~~
~~press~~ become prominent, it would be impossible not to
think solely of these functions & desires. ~~& Whether The~~
~~small room is altogether filled with the body~~.
Yet the room was scrupulously clean. Her face ~~showed~~
~~no~~ was assuredly not soft, sensual, or lecherous; but
hard, wise, wholesome rather, ~~sn~~..signifying in a room
full of sophisticated people, ~~the a sav~~ the flesh & blood of
life; yet wistfully, for she too ~~might could h~~ would have
liked to ~~a~~ ride in a carriage with springs. ~~& &~~ The soft

swift syllables of educated speech often shamed her, few

rude one.

~~plain ones.~~ A^nd then all night to hear the grinding of the

Atlantic upon the rocks, instead of hansom cabs & footmen

whistling for ~~mo~~ motor cars. So she may have dreamed,

in her
wedding
dress

holding the picture paper close to her eyes; though in what

guise

~~shape~~ Lady Cynthia ~~Mosley~~ appeared ~~to~~ against seventy

years of sea, sky, & cliff side, ~~none~~ none can tell.   ~~A~~

Awkward to both would have been the encounter; for

undoubtedly old cottage women say disconcerting things at

weddings.

From Berg Collection Notebook 1, Berg p. 99; reprinted in Bishop, ed., pp. 57–58.

2. Near the beginning of Chapter 6, the holograph draft inserts the following sentences after Florinda says, for the first time: "I'm so frightfully unhappy!" (p. 58):

do

Jacob's
~~r~~ Christian
~~he~~ is it -

You're not a Jew, are you? she said.   "I hate Jews" . . . . .

And she told him how a Jew had played her a dirty

trick, leaving ~~all~~ his dirty clothes scattered over the room, &

she having to pawn her mothers watch to pay the rent.

From Berg Collection Notebook 1, Berg p. 155; reprinted in Bishop, ed., p. 87.

3. In the holograph, the following passage describing Jacob's boat trip with Timothy Durrant is inserted after the end of Chapter 7 and the sentence "So Clara left him" (p. 70):

After toiling up the hill side, there   ~~filling~~ filling up the gap between

the hills on the horizon is ~~the~~ undoubtedly, the sea.

        The Sea! the Sea!

what

But ~~why~~ that cry ~~should~~ signifies, it ~~w~~ is hard to say.

~~Perhaps~~ - a certain ~~amount of~~ relief; a sense of freedom;

licence to indulge dreams.

    Then the little boat sidles up to the pier,

standing up

John Stephens in ~~his~~ oilskins ~~sp~~ throws a rope

which Mathew Paynter finally catches & secures.

You jump a little too much to the right. Directly

afterwards the land is seen from the sea. The ~~spiri~~

As a face composed in sleep it looks, quiet, spiritual.

In particular the smoke from the houses is visible.
                    the shore
There hang over it the atmosphere of something left

behind, to which one has said farewell. But in

the boat itself ~~the~~ boots, hands, jerseys, are ~~lifesize~~
                    & near
~~as~~ large as life; the oars creak upon the rowlocks,

which are now spat upon, now moistened with sea water.

The sea about midday, is dull enough. For out at sea,

where the waves are not breaking but swelling &

sinking - ~~swelling & sinking~~ there is nothing to

expect; everywhere is the same material, agitated by the same

movement.

And that perhaps is a disillusionment.

Lying full length in his little cabin on deck, Jacob

~~came~~ concluded that ~~there is little~~ to be out of sight of

land is nothing in particular. ~~Inf Indeed, about~~

~~midday, it seemed to him that to catch sight of England~~

again ~~would be in was desirable~~. ~~The   Now was the~~

However, he would prove the matter, - he would read

Shakespeare. ~~He had~~ provided ~~Shakespeare to read out~~

~~of sight of land, & had for in order to~~

Only, if the sea is merely brown-purple water, there is

                    *   *   *

                                will
no reason to suppose that any miracle ~~would~~ happen.

He looked for ~~the~~ signs of the court of Devonshire; saw none;

& opened King Lear.

   ~~B~~ The management of the Primus stoves had been

entrusted to him. Happily ~~Jimmy Durrant~~ it was

time to attend to them; for he could make nothing of

King Lear. Yet everything had been propitious. Silence,

sea, sky; dinner to get ready with one's own hands; & a

Cornish sailor, chewing tobacco, ~~with~~ rings in his ears -

Finding an old number of Punch Jacob fiercely stayed

his mind with that. Didactically he had primed his

box with this paper edition of all the great writers.

It is a very serious thing on the second day of a voyage to

~~find no sign~~ to disbelieve in so much.

From Berg Collection Notebook 1, Berg pp. 207, 209; reprinted in
Bishop, ed., pp. 115, 117.

4. The following passage is inserted in Chapter 8 in the holograph,
   after the description of Betty Flanders's letters to Jacob and the
   sentence that ends: "running about the house, scolding Rebecca"
   (p. 72):

Poor Betty Flanders! ~~Hard~~ Poor mothers - poor women - poor

anyone indeed who lives in ignorance, & must ~~hide their~~

hint what they want to ask instead of asking it. This question

                                     then say
she cd not   of her son's chastity, - ~~& then, are you hiding anything,~~
w ask
             ~~the sense that ignorance of.~~ how it mattered, ~~to her,~~

                                        ed
as if   someone, or something interven~~ing~~, he becoming strange - indeed

             she never knew him as she knew the others, ~~his~~ something

came between ~~estranging~~ them, the way he lounged or ~~smoked~~, though
                                        of her lads, ...
             she knew him for the finest, the most powerful - for

most like his
ather too,   which very reason, as she sat over the fire, she turned to him,

             tried to figure him in London, planned to visit him,

             thought of shops in Oxford Street, where she used to deal,

             went back to old days, simple ~~pieties~~ children, tea at

             Burzard's after the dentist, & then returned to Jacob, now
                                        Could she question him? No, she ~~tried~~
             grown a man with passions; ~~so she sighed & wrote on~~

             ~~tried to make him~~

From Berg Collection Notebook 2, Berg p. 3; reprinted in Bishop,
ed., p. 122.

5. Woolf wrote two versions of the passage that opens Chapter 10, in
   which Fanny Elmer walks through the disused graveyard in St Pancras. The second draft is very close to the published version, but
   the first draft is substantially different:

There is a deserted graveyard in the parish of St Pancras,
                                  strayed
& there Fanny Filmer often ~~stopp~~ strolled, ~~reading the names~~

~~on the stones~~, & & notice read the names on the weather-beaten

stone, & noticed the bent yellow crocuses. Once a

catalogue of Madame Tussaud's show dropped from her

~~bag.~~ hand. And once, when no one was looking,

                         turf

she stepped across the ~~bi grass~~ & pushed aside the

grass & read ~~the name which~~ a date ~~that~~ which had been

overgrown. She started when the grave keeper in his

laced hat appeared. ~~She hurried through the gate.~~

She flushed & passed him with her eyes cast down.

At the gate she hesitated, & was for running back &

telling him that she meant to bring bulbs & plant

them; but she wavered.

                                         &

    Fanny Filmer was thus courageous ~~& sudden~~: thus

cast down. She was ~~at an~~ now violent & now as soft

as water. She had one hundred pounds a year & had come

to London to make her way upon the stage -

From Berg Collection Notebook 2, Berg p. 73; reprinted in Bishop, ed., p. 158.

6.   In Chapter 10, instead of the passage beginning "Such is the life of the elderly" and ending "off she ran without so much as good-night" (p. 96), the holograph draft inserts a lengthy description of Fanny's journey to Nick Bramham's studio and of Nick's misery when Fanny is late and his jealousy over her relationship with Jacob. The last few paragraphs of Chapter 10 in the published version, after "off she ran without so much as good-night," do not appear in the holograph. The deleted text in the holograph is as follows:

A great broom had swept the streets, Fanny thought. as she leant

                                          - so clean

a little forward in the front seat of the motor omnibus.   they were

A broom had swept the sky—so clear the air was ,   & yet ~~so~~ so

                                                   bare

It was the ~~milk~~ milky air of early spring.   ~~Brilliantly~~

Crystal clear were the shop windows; with all their

                   & yellows

greens & reds   displayed for a moment as the omnibus

swung ~~to~~ down the hill.   ~~Very few people were~~   ~~The~~

~~tramlines gleamed silver.~~   ~~Very few people were on~~

~~the pavement.~~   Single figures flitted along the pavement.

                   pale yellow

~~The lamps~~ Points of light ~~wer~~ ~~sprung here - there -~~

~~were high & low & then were all the ground~~

pierced ~~through here~~ the fading ~~of~~ afternoon -

~~And~~ She thought the world transparent, spiritual.

She thought that men & women had stars in their with

breasts.

"I've lost my umbrella" she said to the conductor.

Friendly the
world was.
~~She~~ smiling at him. He smiled back at her. - so ~~He had~~

~~sad honest eyes, & beautiful white teeth~~. He

pressed
~~held~~ her arm, as she stepped onto the pavement.

~~And~~ A little boy was spinning his top ~~against~~ by

the wall of school[bread?] shop; & he crooked his

arm to protect it from the passers by, & hissed, as

the ~~top spun~~, like a groom, ~~in~~ with engrossed.

~~The~~ in watching it. ~~He~~ Carefully / she stepped ~~round him;~~ the out

~~watched him tenderly~~. to avoid his top.

~~Lover are charitable; they~~ So charitable

o plainly they
erceive what
eeps us
are lovers. So tenderly they respect the private

flames of others. So.

Down Jacob's street she passed. His windows

were dark. She passed on. She came back. Now

they were ~~alight~~ illuminated. Her heart crowded

~~the~~ its beats. ~~But~~ Hhow could she go in? How

woman selling
olets pressed her
speak to him? And who was with him?

~~Now passion washed out all tenderness for others.~~

But ~~She was cruel as a balked horse~~ what now had

* * *

she of violets? She hated women.

Poor Nick Bramham was mixing blue & white on his

palate. On a chair stood a blue pot, & a bunch of &

bananas, ~~she~~ Quickly, decidedly, he ~~glan~~ looked from

his palate to the chair & back again. He looked at

the window. ~~He lit the gas~~. He lit the gas.

Nothing could be done. He opened a large book of

Michael Angelo's drawings which lay, stuffed with

old envelopes & ~~sht~~ sheets of ~~paper~~, upon the drawing table.   He had lunched there off sardines, olives

and bread.   He ~~p~~ shuffled through the pages:

the plates were all loose. ~~He ran his fingers~~

~~through his hair.~~   ~~And then His tears began to fall~~

~~one by one on the page.~~   ~~He pushed it away.~~

            He   a tumbler

~~The tumbler fell &~~ was knocked over, ~~& rolled on the~~

~~floor~~. which rolled upon the floor. He stooped -

     Poor Nick Bramham! - & Utterly unable to

                 or

master tumblers,   ~~clear a~~ clear a way for himself;

                         only

depending on Fanny Elmer, wishing   to paint - but

easily down cast; lost like a child, now that

Fanny loved another; hurt; discontented; waiting

for Fanny to come -   "but she's with Jacob

Flandèrs ;   Somehow the tumbler **t** rolled

beneath his foot & he kicked it; ~~Then~~ So that it

wobbled foolishly away.   And then he burst

out crying.

~~He~~ The papers slid out of the book & fluttered to the floor.

Suddenly ~~rolling~~ throwing himself over he pressed his face

            ~~in a cushion & burst into tears.~~ There he sobbed.

in the sofa

corner

His thick soled boots kicked out—~~he~~ pawed the pages, the

old letters -

~~And then, when the~~

                              tree

[~~Like some uneasy sea; like some storm tossed forest,~~]

[like sharp waves, **v** violent branches; ~~The the~~

like the thongs of whips, ~~or~~ the lashing of tails, -

~~like always like something jerked~~, flung out &

                        passions

jerked back, - that is what ~~feelings are here in~~

~~London.~~ ~~goes on down in the street~~   life is like, in

London, for the young.

     ~~Waves. The waves~~ It is curious, ~~to watch,~~ ~~lie~~

lying in a boat to watch the waves. Here are three

            regularly

coming/one after another, ~~regularly~~, all much of a

size; Then hurrying after them comes a fourth,

very large, ~~as if to~~ menacing; it **s** lifts the boat; as

it goes; & somehow merges, without accomplishing
anything, in the others.

What can be more violent, more desperate than the
fling of boughs in a gale - ~~yielding themself~~
the tree yielding itself all the way up the trunk &
to the very tip of the branch - streaming, &
shuddering the way the wind blows - yet broken off
sharp? never flying in dishevelment away.

The corn ~~even bows~~ ^{squirms} & abases itself as if it

prepared to ~~fly~~ ^{tug out} from from its roots: yet is tied.

down.

* * * -

Now it is Fanny Elmer, & next year some fair round eyed
girl from the provinces, come to learn anatomy at
University college hospital & lunching off buns ~~at~~ in
an A.B.C. shop. Now it is life itself - the days of the week,
that are blown into transparent crests over which
~~we one sails. the~~ we are lifted; up, down: up, down.
Why, from the very windows, even in the dusk, you
~~seem to~~ see a ~~wave in~~ swelling run through
the street, an aspiration, a sizing up, as with
arms out stretched, ~~mouths~~ ^{eyes} desiring, mouths
agape - Down, down again - ~~For to the~~ For if
the exultation lasted, we should be blown like ~~the~~
~~soft foam~~ foam right into the air. The stars
would shine through us. We should go down the
gale in ~~slt~~ salt drops. As sometimes happens.
For the impetuous spirits ~~have done with life &~~
~~leapt the bridge, or snatched the razor~~ - have stepped
~~off the~~ ^{trifled} are not to be tampered with.
will have none of this cradling. Off they fly, from
the waves' crest; ~~never again to be sucked back;~~
~~lulled, soothed, aimlessly swaying, straight at the~~
Never any swaying, or aimlessly lolling for them.

~~One person is different from another, always;~~
Never any making believe, or lying cosy, or genially
supposing that one ~~man~~ is much like another,
& fire warm, & wine pleasant, & extravagance a sin:
~~mistake.~~ "People are so nice, once you know them."
    "Oh but ~~I couldn't speak~~ you ~~must~~
~~make allowances for her.~~" I couldn't speak ill of her."
    So the waves croon to us. Safe we lie.
~~The next. No, for them a leap from a Bridge or~~
~~a razor.~~ But they ~~believe that.~~ – Nick, perhaps,
or Fanny Elmer ~~for~~ ridiculously supposing that
this is the worst, the last, the end; ~~that as the other~~
leap, snatch knives, take drugs, or, prevented,
drift like wreckage across the track.

riding the crest,   fling off, ~~down the wind, Heaven knows where,~~
sting the cheek on a
with sharp hail, & are seen no more, &

    Perhaps - perhaps. For life, this dark-eyed mother,
    with all her violence, spurning us, bidding us fly,
    vanish, never learn to grow old, yet if you press
close   ~~cling~~ to her murmurs; ~~as a~~ some secret.
    What?   Only one word. Listen. Another.
    No sense to it.   No.   But lean closer.   Follow
    after.   ~~The The darkness gathers. A great hall;~~
    ~~dimly lit, with resonant, sounding.~~   ~~The light~~
    down the great hall, dimly lit, with the curved
150
280   ceiling, - ~~noise resounding~~ Resonant with echoes;
1200   alarming; tapers blown out; g cold gusts
300
    from what sea?   Life, life, booming: ~~her~~
42,00
    ~~secret,~~ & the lightning; & ~~Terror~~ I say, how
    vast it is! How musical! ~~Oh she sings~~ She draws
ground into
    ~~on top of the growling, what melody! like a~~   us on.
    ~~There he sat, sobbing; He sat~~ A question breathed
                                      by the sea
40,000   ~~Something laughing.~~
40 . . .
8. . . .   There he sat with his hands on his knees ~~looking into~~
    ~~the fire &~~ while the tears ran down his cheeks.

150
280
———
1200
300
———
42000

"~~Oh said~~ Fanny, bursting ~~into the room~~, into the room.

They hated each other. All that evening they

quarrelled - ~~infinitely unhappy both of them.~~

shall

"I ~~will~~ never come again" she said.

From Berg Collection Notebook 2, Berg pp. 99–107; reprinted in
Bishop, ed., pp. 173–79.

7. In the holograph, Chapter 11, which in the published version
begins with four paragraphs mostly focused on Betty Flanders, has
a much longer introduction that explores Betty's life and feelings
in much more detail, before shifting the scene to Jacob in Paris:

Betty Flanders stood on a chair at the top of the house,
stirring the   water tank
~~banging the side of~~ the ~~cistern~~ with a broom handle.

~~The hollow sound~~ Curious ringed stockings she wore,

for, bending over ~~the tank~~, her legs were visible.

From the kitchen came at regular ~~sucking sound~~,

intervals a creak followed by a suck.
in the water.
Water chuckled, & pipes groaned, but ~~nothing~~

perhaps there was some obstruction in the tank -

~~curt~~   Betty Flanders went on banging. The

tank resounded. hollow. "~~It~~ oh" she cried. "Stop" - "There" -
was   ing
This happene~~d~~ precisely at three fortyfive on Wednesday

~~February March~~ the 23rd. of March.
people
Strange indeed are the uses to which ~~men & women~~

put these few moments of ~~i~~ daylight; ~~for certainly~~

~~a space of this particular texture, daylight~~, this fabric

~~issued~~ of peculiar texture; which, so long as we live, we

call ~~week~~ Wednesday, Thursday or Friday -
was
And Rebecca ~~in the kitchen had been~~ pumping in the

~~kitchen.~~   She waited to hear Betty Flanders call out

~~from~~ her chair at the top of the house -

Indeed when the ~~fish~~ man with the fish barrow came

round & knocked at the front door, neither of them heard

him.   He came round to the back.

~~And~~ Betty Flanders got down off her chair, & descended

carrying her broom, which she held in her hands as

, is strictly
ted
r all
igh somebody
ways
g it up.
g it—

she examined the cod, the hake, the herring, & the
bloater.   Somehow, by taking the fish in her hand, by

made up her mind

inclining her nose very slightly towards it, she ~~knew its value~~. what to buy.

   Something was wrong with the sucker of the pump.
Something was wrong with the oil stove.   Mr.
Humphrey Piper scraping his boots went into the
kitchen to have a look.   Whereupon Betty
Flanders seemed to bethink her that it was high time -
~~considering the hour~~, rather late in the day indeed -
the ~~weat~~ clouds brewing up perhaps - She put on
her galoshes, & standing the broom against the
store cupboard, ~~seems says b bustled,~~ *went out* ~~out~~ along the
~~garden path~~ garden path —

The handsome chickens were parading in the orchard. Like a
general in ~~cock~~ cocked hat the rooster walked in front.
Driven on some unknown quest the troop swept through the
long grass. Mrs. Flanders knelt by the brown earth at the

foot *root*

~~base~~ of the great pear tree, & ~~drove a~~ pressed ~~a twig~~ her fingers
here & there into the soft earth.   ~~Into each hole she dropped~~
~~a tiny green seed~~. The brown lumps stuck to her finger.
Her flesh grazed the pinkish glistening coils of worms.
~~The~~ Into each hole she dropped a tiny grey seed; & that done
~~pressed~~ filled each hole with earth, *&* ~~pressed it firmly~~
                                                in a circle
& pressed it lightly on top. until ~~in a circle~~ round the pear
                        a ring
tree lay sleeping ~~a the a~~ ~~a circle of the seeds~~ of
soft blue flowers. She raised herself, with difficulty
for she was growing stout; & ~~proceeded to~~   Now she
~~p pinched the buds~~ gently felt the buds, on the apple trees; a
fetched a pruning hook & began ~~snipped~~ snipping
among the bushes here & there, ~~& her~~ the hook
squeaking ~~as she~~ each time ~~she cut a with it~~, it
opened & shut.   Already the ~~blossom~~ blossom was
                    showed
swollen & / pinkish ~~through the~~ white.   And each time

she looked up into the boughs she saw ~~the mild bluish~~
~~sky~~ them held like a pattern against the mild grey-blue
~~bluish~~ sky.   Suddenly, ~~yet~~ with a thudding fulness the
~~bells~~ church bells began rumbling over the
beating out   muffled & blows
scale, ~~sounding~~ with irregular ~~force~~, a fragment from a
hymn.   She opened the orchard door & went out
over Garfits field ~~up~~ a little way up Dodds Hill.
The tears came to Betty Flanders eyes as she stood ~~in the~~
~~orchard~~ beneath the apple tree. All the past ~~seemed to~~
~~quiver which stood in her deep & tranquil was stirred into~~
~~eddies by the~~ seemed to quiver in her. She felt
scarcely able to contain fifty five years of life; ~~her~~
~~three sons; memories; the present moment. Then~~ [the
~~cock led his troop on their voyage through the long grass.~~]
                                eddies in the
for the random bells made the ~~waters eddy~~ deep pool.
~~Eddy~~   Indeed she was very happy. One hundred
chickens ~~were~~ . . . the potatoes had kept all the year round . . .
          fruit
the ~~blossom~~ was ~~p~~ promising . . . nice, kind, good

ear
Captain
Barfoot

people in ~~the village~~. . .   She opened the orchard gate, &
                              towards
walked a little way up Garfits acre ~~to~~ ~~up~~ Dodd's Hill
                    her share of
The mother of three sons embraced / the ~~whole~~ globe.
          to
She stood (~~she was~~ drew breath) like a rooted tree;
                                     veins
sustenance coming to her ~~throu~~ from ~~veins veins~~

ickling

running through the deep earth.
~~that ran through deep springs deep in the earth.~~
"Archer" she thought, will be at Gibraltar to morrow"
She had heard that it was a great rock, much ~~inf.~~
infested with apes. She figured him dancing in a
blue jacket with stiff gold scrolls. ~~upon it~~   And Jacob in
Paris on his way to Greece. And dear little Johnnie . . .
All the time the random ~~old~~ bells kept swinging
                              about
~~out~~ & the ~~hym~~ hymn tune curled round her head.
"Mr. Jarvis practising" she thought;   ~~The Up~~ a
~~little further she walked. A few steps further on~~
                                      a
The purple in the air ~~promised thunder; rain shower~~ -
~~For it was~~ became suddenly deeper. ~~A rain~~

~~hill above~~ She looked back ^{at the sky} ~~above the village~~ ~~at the village, lying slightly beneath her.~~
~~& saw that the~~ & saw the village ^{laid under a leaf} ~~washed~~ ~~shaped a~~ with shadow.

Indeed it was half past four. The church ~~struck~~ clock
^{the half hour} ~~was~~ striking through the hymn tune.   From all this

Was there something queer in the sounds, queer in the
^{light} purple,- a little ominous?   ~~The~~
^{downstairs} she returned. All the lamps were / in the living rooms.
The loaves were on the table. Mrs. Cranch, Mrs. Gage,
Mrs. Woolman, Mrs Garfit were all taking ~~h~~ hold of the
kettles. And from the chimneys smoke went up. regularly.
The bells enclosed the village. It seemed as if somehow,
~~could you hear it~~ a clock ticked - a heart beat - up & down
went the breast - & ~~dow~~ all the men sat ~~down~~ at the tables -
save that old Cranch was upstairs with the
bronchitis - & it was ~~half twent~~ half past four in the village,
& the village, ~~t~~ lay against the earth, trusting to it,
^{two dozen lights} shining out ~~very mildly~~ against the storm cloud; ~~which~~
infinitely ~~quiet~~ humble - a little community, all in
time, ~~with each other, knowing each other~~,- yes, but
~~to~~ this evening, somehow strange to Betty Flanders, as she
returned; ~~as~~   No one survives. The little company is
~~afloat on a~~ voyaging,   We who have been bound together
for so many years ~~are bound to be overwhelmed at
last;~~ will be scattered. Grafit drinks, she thought.
Betty Page is in the agony of childbirth. The ~~bells~~ bells
~~throbbed painfully~~. thudded as if it hurt them.
However there was the postman on his red bicycle
swinging off to deliver letters at the Rectory. Her door
turn - she hurried forward, ~~desiring more than~~
fearing ill news, took the little packet, shuffled through -

>———————————<

My dearest Mother,

   Jacob wrote, having withdrawn to a side
table away from the others; & feeling ~~a little~~ it
romantic to ~~st~~ sit in a cafe & write ~~on paper~~

~~supplied free~~ with a pointed nib, in violet ink,

while everyone talked French.

      Your loving Jacob, he

signed himself.

From Berg Collection Notebook 2, Berg pp. 109–15; reprinted in Bishop, ed., pp. 180–83.

8. In the holograph, the account of Jacob's visit to Versailles with Edward Cruttendon and Jinny Carslake is significantly longer than in the published version, including several versions of a number of passages, and a long section describing an argument the three have just before they leave Versailles. This passage occurs between the paragraph that ends " 'Those silly birds, directly one wants them— they've flown away' " and the one that begins "And finally under the arc lamps in the Gare des Invalides" (p. 104).

esday
April 1921   The great argument, which is always the same, has been discussed since

the very earliest times ~~of all~~, is never settled, & is handed down to

                     a
the next generation, ~~as the most priceless part of their inheritance~~.

a priceless part of their inheritance, since the hours spent pacing

gravel paths, are the best of all.   ~~True, I am am pacing a~~

~~gravel path; but are these my Are these legs?~~   Pacing gravel

paths, yes; but soon the legs disappear; & the body;

& the mind ~~vaults~~ floats into the blue.   What are we? &

whence do we come? Those insoluble questions ~~provide~~ spread

         their
~~an soft blue immense~~ background - ~~a a~~ & against it

              reality
truth is questioned & ~~reality? Whether objects exist; that~~

      is scored
the apple tree; hyacinths appear momentous; the kingdom of

France fades to a green veil. & [The lozenge shaped bed, the

yew hedge, the tapering white God, Priapus or another]

   The great argument ploughs its way, & people voyage together,

doing their best to find foothold, yet valiantly determined

not to ~~allow anyone~~ to ~~make~~ landing on a false shore.

~~Such are the dangers of the enterprise that~~ The enterprise is

full of danger, maybe of temper.   To hear their voices

~~raised~~ as they turned right about under the grin of the

God Priapus, one would have fancied a quarrel - but

where people possess no bodies ~~how can they quarrel?-~~

~~th~~ only their minds can graze each other in the void.

Jinny's check skirt flowed across their legs; Cruttendon

held his hat pressed between his arm & his side; His

fair pale face, pale hair, ~~& green eyes; I~~ he was

dressed in a light tweed - made him the most

conspicuous of the three.

"Well, I dont know what I'm talking about" he said; exclaimed

ruffling his hand through his hair. & then he & they stopped

Jinny both exclaimed simultaneously that the

colour of pink hyacinths in the shadow is bright violet -

Jacob had vanquished.

You could see t so much in the way he smiled, rather

queerly, & then looked at ~~the~~ France lying beneath him,

for after an argument the landscape must rearrange itself,

& people have been known to feel abashed & discomposed ~~at~~ by

the existence of good arable land, flights of rooks, steam

ploughs, ~~good~~ trains & the rest of it after this ~~excursion into~~ morning

effort to arrive at the truth. However, one may easily put too

fine a point on it. ~~Jacob was inclined for~~ a & the

~~difficulty is not~~   Our flights from solid earth are strictly

tethered. A thousand strings attach us to this & that &

~~forbid~~ the other, & only once in a hundred years does

some poet or thinker cut free. The ordinary person has

an advantage over the extraordinary in being ~~thus~~ all in a

muddle, at the mercy of instincts, responsive to hunger -

thirst & vanity & desire & kindliness, ~~& convention~~ &

~~though~~   so long as he is not smoothed over ~~in an~~

~~effort to by the plough, or~~ the steam roller, & brought into

conformity with the rest. ~~And this has been the~~

~~fate~~   And this has been the fate of ~~w~~ painters rather

than of writers; explain it how you will.   It was probably it is

the existence of patrons, so Cruttendon, said: ~~that had~~

~~ruined many fine fellows~~. For art had been servile

all through the eighteenth century; & was only now

asserting itself   ~~Then~~ they ~~talked about~~ religion, & how But what wanted was

in the days ~~when it was possible to hold a~~ everything Cruttendon was impossible without faith, & there was none; or

worse than none; & ~~Cruttendon~~ ^{he} thought that men of

university training ought to see to it - ~~& Jinny~~

~~all of which~~ ^{Then} & Jinny getting up from ~~the chair~~ ^{her} chair

(they had settled round a marble table on the terrace)

went up to the kiosk, speared a plate full of

tle cakes   ~~pastries, with which she returned.~~ & ~~nutmeats~~

"Which d'you like?" she asked Jacob.

And ~~later~~ later they went back to the station.

There is a wedge ~~shaped strip~~ of pavement between tramlines

outside the Gare St Lazare.

     Oh hang it all —

  ^{fellow}

~~My good Sir,~~ What rot you talk - Jacob broke in.

From Berg Collection Notebook 2, Berg pp. 139–43; reprinted in
Bishop, ed., pp. 199–201.

9. In the holograph, there is an extended passage in Chapter 12 that
explores Bonamy's feelings about Jacob as Jacob mopes about the
hotel in Patras. The holograph at this point becomes very disjointed
and choppy, but this passage appears to have been intended to
follow the paragraph ending "he was fonder of Jacob than of any
one in the world" (p. 112):

"He will fall in love," thought Bonamy.

"Some Greek woman with a straight nose" he thought. ~~bitterly~~.

It was this kind of bitterness which frequently led him to

read Chaucer. - if not Chaucer some other of the

ancients ~~who~~ - Donne perhaps or Ben Jonson -

for though a number of people write well enough nowadays,

what we have lost entirely is vigour of language.

There is a scene for example in Bartholomew Fair of a

fat woman scolding which could not be pieced together

by twenty of our young men writing in concert; & then

~~this~~ when this torrent of language gets its way,

    ^{that}

the chances are it sweeps down with it something

~~lovely - somethin - as & phrase like a flash of lightning~~.

astonishing. Bonamy turned the pages.

~~"He will fall in love" he thought again.~~

"It would be just like Jacob" he thought, "to
marry a woman with a straight nose - & ~~then~~
~~they'd have children with even straight noses -~~
~~He was t~~hinking of a peasant woman, someone
strapping & ~~inarticulate,~~ who would sit on the
other side of the fire place smok~~ing~~ & saying
nothing, & ~~Jacob would say nothing.~~ Jacob
~~would be lost for ever~~.

But after all it takes a week for a letter ~~to~~
from Greece to reach England - the gulf is one of those
which blurs ever feature in ~~the~~ a friends face.
And then, however we may disguise it, can we deny
the deep chasm which separates us? On this side of it -
that is within Bonamy's room, all is acute even to
distraction - the boys shouting in the mews - the tick of the
clock - & the ~~silence~~ quality of the silence - ~~on the~~
~~other~~, but Jacob ~~is far away on the other side~~, a ghost
at the end of a thread of memory which falters before it
reaches him -

Those who complained that Bonamy could find comfort in
books were quite right - He could read & he could stop &
he could read again -

There is a consolation in literature, after all.
The ~~emotional readers take up a book &~~ serious readers
brush everything else aside, & ~~set themselves sternly to~~
read a play at a time, without stopping, or
stopping only to make ~~sure that they their~~ note, ~~so that~~
of the ~~the to~~ line, say, ~~which~~ was influenced by Marlowe -
the emotional readers on the other hand, like Sandra
Wentworth Williams are for ever running ~~ove~~
off the page ~~"saying to themselves"~~ onto the
landscape thus -
"I

Bonamy would have said, ~~with some truth~~, that
this was the sort of thing that made him uneasy -

when Jacob got in to ~~his grumpy~~ the doldrums - looked

like a mogul boatman out of a job - or ~~Dr Johnson~~

~~after~~ aristocr or a British peer - ~~or~~ quite uncivilized - ~~very fine of~~

course; but you couldn't make him understand a word

when he was in a mood like this - One had better

leave him. He was dull - imposing

From Berg Collection Notebook 2, Berg pp. 233–37; reprinted in Bishop, ed., pp. 249–51.

10. In Chapter 12, just before the passage in which Sandra Wentworth Williams catches sight of Jacob in the Square of the Constitution, a passage appears in the holograph that describes the temporary waning of Jacob's feelings for Sandra. It occurs just before the paragraph beginning "But in Athens in the sunshine, in Athens" (p. 122):

Long before Jacob descended Hymettus his romance had faded & left

him glum; yet happy enough too, & - ~~I mean~~ quite able to carry on

with life, - It is useless to attempt to give a name to

that sort of mood. - Presumably his was coloured a little by

the emotions of the morning; & those who can't help

feeling themselves part of ~~every~~ the landscape would

have been aware of the ~~great hills, the~~ & ~~Athens~~ new of the craggy

~~Athens on the plain;~~ but how far Jacob was ~~at the~~

in influenced by such things ~~it is impossible~~ one cannot to say -

Mrs. Wentworth Williams was romantic in the

sense that ~~a~~ walz music, a cup of coffee, a private

view of an evening party stimulated the tips of her

nerves to such an extent that she improvised

~~views~~ emotions of the most sweeping character, on the

gust of which she said some very foolish things &

some charming ones; & astounded comparative

strangers by the intimacy of her confidences &

~~But~~ Her romance ~~faded & left h~~ lingered & left her peevish.

(margin, left:) he average nood, ~~the~~ he weather wh. is neither wet nor fine nears hill ~~with the~~ above the white scattered homes

(margin insertion:) of the [Harpies?]

From Berg Collection Notebook 2, Berg p. 243; reprinted in Bishop, ed., p. 254.

VIRGINIA WOOLF AND THE NOVEL

Notebooks

Canceled Epigraph†

Atque in perpetuum, frater, ave atque vale.

Julian Thoby Stephen

(1881–1906)

Atque in perpetuum, frater, ave atque vale.

Plans for the Novel‡

Reflections upon beginning a work of fiction to be called, perhaps, Jacob's Room: Thursday, April. 15th 1920.

I think the main point is that it should be free.
Yet what about form?
Let us suppose that the Room will hold it together.
Intensity of life compared with immobility.
Experiences.
To change style at will.

---

† Possible epigraph for *Jacob's Room*, from notebook in Monk's House Papers/B.2q. (Sussex), reverse of p. 17, 1 p., not numbered, heading only, all lines canceled, June/July 1922. From Catullus, *Carmina* no. 101: "And so forever, brother, hail and farewell." Thoby Stephen was Virginia Woolf's brother; he died in 1906 at the age of twenty-six. From Brenda Silver, ed., *Virginia Woolf's Reading Notebooks* (Princeton: Princeton University Press, 1983), pp. 237–318.
‡ From *Jacob's Room: The Holograph Notebooks*, 3 vols., I, MS 1, containing the manuscript version of *Jacob's Room*, Berg Collection, New York Public Library. Reprinted from Edward L. Bishop, ed., *Virginia Woolf's "Jacob's Room": The Holograph Draft* (New York: Pace University Press, 1998), p. 1.

Diaries

January 26, 1920[†]

The day after my birthday; in fact I'm 38. Well, I've no doubt I'm a great deal happier than I was at 28; & happier today than I was yesterday having this afternoon arrived at some idea of a new form for a new novel. Suppose one thing should open out of another—as in An Unwritten Novel—only not for 10 pages but 200 or so— doesn't that give the looseness & lightness I want: doesnt that get closer & yet keep form & speed, & enclose everything, everything?[1] My doubt is how far it will (include) enclose the human heart—Am I sufficiently mistress of my dialogue to net it there? For I figure that the approach will be entirely different this time: no scaffolding; scarcely a brick to be seen; all crepuscular, but the heart, the passion, humour, everything as bright as fire in the mist. Then I'll find room for so much—a gaiety—an inconsequence—a light spirited stepping at my sweet will. Whether I'm sufficiently mistress of things—thats the doubt; but conceive mark on the wall, K[ew]. G[ardens]. & unwritten novel taking hands & dancing in unity.[2] What the unity shall be I have yet to discover: the theme is a blank to me; but I see immense possibilities in the form I hit upon more or less by chance 2 weeks ago. I suppose the danger is the damned egotistical self; which ruins Joyce & [Dorothy] Richardson to my mind: is one pliant & rich enough to provide a wall for the book from oneself without its becoming, as in Joyce & Richardson,[3] narrowing & restricting? My hope is that I've learnt my business sufficiently now to provide all sorts of entertainments. Anyhow, there's no doubt the way lies

---

† From *The Diary of Virginia Woolf*, 5 vols., ed. Anne Olivier Bell and Andrew McNeillie (New York: Harcourt Brace, 1977–84), II: 13–14. Copyright © 1978 by Quentin Bell and Angelica Garnett. Reprinted by permission of Harcourt, Inc. Editorial notes copyright © 1978 by Anne Olivier Bell and Andrew McNeillie. Reprinted by permission of Harcourt, Inc.

1. *An Unwritten Novel* was published in the *London Mercury* of July 1920 (Kp C203), and reprinted by the Hogarth Press in the collection *Monday or Tuesday* (1921).
2. VW's *The Mark on the Wall* was published by the Hogarth Press in 1917 and *Kew Gardens* in 1919.
3. Dorothy Richardson (1821–1880), British novelist, author of the multivolume *Pilgrimage* (1915–67); James Joyce (1882–1941), Irish novelist and short-story writer, author of *Ulysses* (1922) [*Editor*].

somewhere in that direction; I must still grope & experiment but this afternoon I had a gleam of light. Indeed, I think from the ease with which I'm developing the unwritten novel there must be a path for me there.

*   *   *

September 20, 1920†

To go on with Eliot,[1] as if one were making out a scientific observation—he left last night directly after dinner. He improved as the day went on; laughed more openly; became nicer. L[eonard] whose opinion on this matter I respect, found him disappointing in brain—less powerful than he expected, & with little play of mind. I kept myself successfully from being submerged, though feeling the waters rise once or twice. I mean by this that he completely neglected my claims to be a writer, & had I been meek, I suppose I should have gone under—felt him & his views dominant & subversive.* * * Now he wants to describe externals. Joyce gives internals. His novel Ulysses, presents the life of man in 16 incidents, all taking place (I think) in one day. This, so far as he has seen it, is extremely brilliant, he says. Perhaps we shall try to publish it. Ulysses, according to Joyce, is the greatest character in history[.] Joyce himself is an insignificant man, wearing very thick eyeglasses,* * * self-centered, & perfectly self assured. There is much to be said about Eliot from different aspects—for instance, the difficulty of getting into touch with clever people.—& so forth—anaemia, self-consciousness; but also, his mind is not yet blunted or blurred. He wishes to write precise English; but catches himself out in slips; & if anyone asked him whether he meant what he said, he would have to say no, very often. Now in all this L[eonard] showed up much better than I did; but I didn't much mind.

† From *The Diary of Virginia Woolf*, 5 vols., ed. Anne Olivier Bell and Andrew McNeillie (New York: Harcourt Brace, 1977–84), II: 67–68. Copyright © 1978 by Quentin Bell and Angelica Garnett. Reprinted by permission of Harcourt, Inc. Editorial notes copyright © 1978 by Anne Olivier Bell and Andrew McNeillie. Reprinted by permission of Harcourt, Inc.
1. T. S. Eliot (1888–1965), poet, friend of Virginia Woolf, author of *The Waste Land* (1922) and other works [*Editor*].

September 26, 1920†

But I think I minded more than I let on; for somehow Jacob has come to a stop, in the middle of that party too, which I enjoyed so much. Eliot coming on the heel of a long stretch of writing fiction (2 months without a break) made me listless; cast shade upon me; & the mind when engaged upon fiction wants all its boldness & self-confidence. He said nothing—but I reflected how what I'm doing is probably being better done by Mr Joyce. Then I began to wonder what it is that I am doing: to suspect, as is usual in such cases, that I have not thought my plan out plainly enough—so to dwindle, niggle, hesitate—which means that one's lost. But I think my 2 months of work are the cause of it, seeing that I now find myself veering round to [John] Evelyn, & even making up a paper upon Women, as a counterblast to Mr Bennett's adverse views reported in the papers.[1] Two weeks ago I made up Jacob incessantly on my walks. An odd thing the human mind! so capricious, faithless, infinitely shying at shadows. Perhaps at the bottom of my mind, I feel that I'm distanced by L. in every respect.

July 26, 1922‡

On Sunday L. read through Jacob's Room. He thinks it my best work. But his first remark was that it was amazingly well written. We argued about it. He calls it a work of genius; he thinks it unlike any other novel; he says that the people are ghosts; he says it is very strange. I have no philosophy of life he says; my people are puppets, moved hither & thither by fate. He doesn't agree that fate works in this way. Thinks I should use my 'method', on one or two characters next time; & he found it very interesting, & beautiful, & without lapse (save perhaps the party) & quite intelligible.* * * I am on the whole pleased. Neither of us knows what the public will think.

† From *The Diary of Virginia Woolf*, 5 vols., ed. Anne Olivier Bell and Andrew McNeillie (New York: Harcourt Brace, 1977–84), II: 68–69. Copyright © 1978 by Quentin Bell and Angelica Garnett. Reprinted by permission of Harcourt, Inc. Editorial notes copyright © 1978 by Anne Olivier Bell and Andrew McNeillie. Reprinted by permission of Harcourt, Inc.

1. Arnold Bennett's collection of essays dealing with contemporary society and in particular with 'women of the top class and of those classes which . . . imitate the top . . . class' was published as *Our Women* in September 1920, and attracted a good deal of attention in the popular press. His general argument was that 'intellectually and creatively man is the superior of woman'.

‡ From *The Diary of Virginia Woolf*, 5 vols., ed. Anne Olivier Bell and Andrew McNeillie (New York: Harcourt Brace, 1977–84), II: 186. Copyright © 1978 by Quentin Bell and Angelica Garnett. Reprinted by permission of Harcourt, Inc. Editorial notes copyright © 1978 by Anne Olivier Bell and Andrew McNeillie. Reprinted by permission of Harcourt, Inc.

There's no doubt in my mind that I have found out how to begin (at 40) to say something in my own voice; & that interests me so that I feel I can go ahead without praise.

October 29, 1922†

* * *I mean I'm too riddled with talk & harassed with the usual worry of people who like & people who don't like J.R. to concentrate. There was the Times review on Thursday—long, a little tepid, I think; saying that one can't make characters in this way; flattering enough.[1] Of course, I had a letter from Morgan in the opposite sense—the letter I've liked best of all.[2] We have sold 650, I think; & have ordered a second edition. My sensations?—as usual—mixed. I shall never write a book that is an entire success. This time the reviews are against me, & the private people enthusiastic. Either I am a great writer or a nincompoop. "An elderly sensualist" the Daily News calls me. Pall Mall passes me over as negligible.[3] I expect to be neglected & sneered at. And what will be the fate of our second thousand then? So far of course, the success is much more than we expected. I think I am better pleased so far than I have ever been.* * * But I want to be quit of all this. It hangs about me like Mary Butts' scent.[4] I dont want to be totting up compliments, & comparing reviews. I want to think out Mrs Dalloway.[5] I want to foresee this book better than the others, & get the utmost out of it. I expect I could have screwed Jacob up tighter if I had foreseen; but I had to make my path as I went.

* * *

November 7, 1922‡

I am, probably, through the splash, & must really try to settle in again. It has not been, publicly, much of a splash. The reviews have

† From *The Diary of Virginia Woolf*, 5 vols., ed. Anne Olivier Bell and Andrew McNeillie (New York: Harcourt Brace, 1977–84), II: 209–10. Copyright © 1978 by Quentin Bell and Angelica Garnett. Reprinted by permission of Harcourt, Inc. Notes are by the Editor.
1. Reprinted in this volume, p. 211.
2. Reprinted in this volume, p. 210.
3. *Daily News* review reprinted in this volume, p. 213; *Pall Mall Gazette* review reprinted in this volume, p. 214.
4. Novelist and short-story writer (1893–1937), known for her bohemian lifestyle; Woolf thought her cheap.
5. *Mrs Dalloway*, Woolf's next novel, published 1924.
‡ From *The Diary of Virginia Woolf*, 5 vols., ed. Anne Olivier Bell and Andrew McNeillie (New York: Harcourt Brace, 1977–84), II: 210–11. Copyright © 1978 by Quentin Bell and Angelica Garnett. Reprinted by permission of Harcourt, Inc. Editorial notes copyright © 1978 by Anne Olivier Bell and Andrew McNeillie. Reprinted by permission of Harcourt, Inc.

said more against me than for me—on the whole. Its so odd how little I mind—& odd how little I care much that Clive [Bell][1] thinks it a masterpiece. Yet the private praise has been the most whole hearted I've yet had. They seem to agree that I have accomplished what in the other books I only got near accomplishing. But we scarcely sell, though it has been out 10 days.* * *

* * *

1. Art critic and journalist (1881–1964), married to Virginia Woolf's sister Vanessa [*Editor*].

Letters

Virginia Woolf to C. P. Sanger, October 30, 1922†

Hogarth House, Paradise Road,
Richmond

30th Oct. 1922

My dear Charlie,

I think a close study of Jacob's Room, should you ever wish to approach the book again, will reveal many passages which a trained mind would have pinched much closer together: and others where the mistakes are glaring. What about lilacs in April, fountains in Neville's Court, tulips in August etc etc etc. I am not going to pick them all out for your benefit. What I do feel is that education helps one to be drastic with oneself, instead of sloppy, and as age increases I do more and more believe in thought as an element of fiction. You are quite right, I am sure, in having grave doubts about the form of Jacob's Room. So have I. It would take too long to explain why I had this time to use it, and what I hope next time to do with it. I am getting the most contradictory opinions daily, and feel quite at sea as to the success or failure of the whole. But as you ought to know, I have a humble respect, not to say veneration, for your judgment, and so if you found good in it, I am immensely encouraged.

* * *

Ever so many thanks for writing.

Yours ever,
Virginia Woolf

† From *The Letters of Virginia Woolf*, 6 vols., ed. Nigel Nicolson and Joanne Trautmann (New York: Harcourt Brace Jovanovich, 1977–82), II: 577–78. Copyright © 1976 by Quentin Bell and Angelica Garnett. Reprinted by permission of Harcourt, Inc. Editorial notes copyright © 1976 by Joanne Trautmann and Nigel Nicolson. Reprinted by permission of Harcourt, Inc.
  C. P. Sanger: Charles Perry Sanger (1871–1930), lawyer and critic.

Virginia Woolf to Clive Bell, November 7, 1922†

Hogarth House, Paradise Road,
Richmond, Surrey

Tuesday [7 November 1922]

Dearest Clive,

I assure you with my hand on my heart that the talk about J's Room did nothing but intrigue and interest me.

* * *

J. is nothing but an experiment, as I've always said; an interesting experiment; and nothing more: unless indeed, being stirred up by a little discussion and criticism, which is the blood of life, I can push on further next time. The direction of that however must wait till I can somehow nail you to the wall, and then proceed to pour out endlessly.* * *

* * *

Yr V. W.

† From *The Letters of Virginia Woolf,* 6 vols., ed. Nigel Nicolson and Joanne Trautmann (New York: Harcourt Brace Jovanovich, 1977–82), II: 580–81. Copyright © 1976 by Quentin Bell and Angelica Garnett. Reprinted by permission of Harcourt, Inc. Editorial notes copyright © 1976 by Joanne Trautmann and Nigel Nicolson. Reprinted by permission of Harcourt, Inc.
   Clive Bell: art critic and journalist (1881–1964), married to Virginia Woolf's sister Vanessa.

Essays

Modern Novels†

In making any survey, even the freest and loosest, of modern fiction it is difficult not to take it for granted that the modern practice of the art is somehow an improvement upon the old. With their simple tools and primitive materials, it might be said, Fielding did well and Jane Austen[1] even better, but compare their opportunities with ours! Their masterpieces certainly have a strange air of simplicity. And yet the analogy between literature and the process, to choose an example, of making bicycles scarcely holds good beyond the first glance. It is doubtful whether in the course of the centuries, though we have learnt much about making machines; we have learnt anything about making literature. We do not come to write better; all that we can be said to do is to keep moving, now a little in this direction, now in that, but with a circular tendency should the whole course of the track be viewed from a sufficiently lofty pinnacle. It need scarcely be said that we make no claim to stand even momentarily upon that vantage ground; we seem to see ourselves on the flat, in the crowd, half blind with dust, and looking back with a sort of envy at those happy warriors whose battle is won and whose achievements wear so serene an air of accomplishment that in our envy we can scarcely refrain from whispering that the prize was not so rare, nor the battle so fierce, as our own. Let the historian of literature decide. It is for him, too, to ascertain whether we are now at the beginning, or middle, or end, of a great period of prose fiction; all that we ourselves can know is that, whatever stage we have reached, we are still in the thick of the battle. This very sense of heights reached by others and unassailable by us, this envious belief that Fielding, Thackeray,[2] or Jane Austen were set an easier problem, however triumphantly they may have solved it, is a proof, not that we have improved upon them,

† Originally published in the *Times Literary Supplement,* April 10, 1919; reprinted from *The Essays of Virginia Woolf,* ed. Andrew McNeillie, 4 vols. (New York: Harcourt Brace Jovanovich, 1989–91), III: 30–37. Copyright © 1988 by Quentin Bell and Angelica Garnett, editorial notes copyright © 1988 by Andrew McNeillie. Reprinted by permission of Harcourt, Inc.
1. Henry Fielding (1707–1754); Jane Austen (1775–1817).
2. W. M. Thackeray (1811–1863).

still less that we have given up the game and left them the victors, but only that we still strive and press on.

Our quarrel, then, is not with the classics, and if we speak of quarrelling with Mr Wells, Mr Bennett and Mr Galsworthy[3] it is partly that by the mere fact of their existence in the flesh their work has a living, breathing, everyday imperfection which bids us take what liberties with it we choose. But it is also true that, while we thank them for a thousand gifts, we reserve our unconditional gratitude for Mr Hardy, for Mr Conrad, and in a much lesser degree for the Mr Hudson of *The Purple Land, Green Mansions,* and *Far Away and Long Ago.*[4] The former, differently and in different measures, have excited so many hopes and disappointed them so persistently that our gratitude largely takes the form of thanking them for having shown us what it is that we certainly could not do, but as certainly, perhaps, do not wish to do. No single phrase will sum up the charge or grievance which we have to bring against a mass of work so large in its volume and embodying so many qualities, both admirable and the reverse. If we tried to formulate our meaning in one word we should say that these three writers are materialists, and for that reason have disappointed us and left us with the feeling that the sooner English fiction turns its back upon them, as politely as may be, and marches, if only into the desert, the better for its soul. Of course, no single word reaches the centre of three separate targets. In the case of Mr Wells it falls notably wide of the mark. And yet even in his case it indicates to our thinking the fatal alloy in his genius, the great clod of clay that has got itself mixed up with the purity of his inspiration. But Mr Bennett is perhaps the worst culprit of the three, inasmuch as he is by far the best workman. He can make a book so well constructed and solid in its craftsmanship that it is difficult for the most exacting of critics to see through what chink or crevice decay can creep in. There is not so much as a draught between the frames of the windows, or a crack in the boards. And yet—if life should refuse to live there? That is a risk which the creator of *The Old Wives' Tale,* George Cannon, Edwin Clayhanger,[5] and hosts of other figures, may well claim to have surmounted. His characters live abundantly, even unexpectedly, but it still remains to ask how do they live, and what do they live for? More and more they seem to us, deserting even the well-built villa in the Five Towns, to spend their time in some softly padded first-class railway carriage, fitted with bells and buttons innumerable; and the destiny to which they

3. H. G. Wells (1866–1946);* * * Arnold Bennett (1867–1931); John Galsworthy (1867–1933)* * *
4. Thomas Hardy (1840–1928); Joseph Conrad (1857–1924); W. H. Hudson (1841–1922), *The Purple Land* (1885), *Green Mansions* (1904), and *Far Away and Long Ago* (1918)* * *
5. *The Old Wives' Tale* (1908); George Cannon appears in the 'Clayhanger' trilogy (*Clayhanger*, 1910, *Hilda Lessways,* 1911, *These Twain,* 1916).

travel so luxuriously becomes more and more unquestionably an eternity of bliss spent in the very best hotel in Brighton. It can scarcely be said of Mr Wells that he is a materialist in the sense that he takes too much delight in the solidity of his fabric. His mind is too generous in its sympathies to allow him to spend much time in making things shipshape and substantial. He is a materialist from sheer goodness of heart, taking upon his shoulders the work that ought to have been discharged by Government officials, and in the plethora of his ideas and facts scarcely having leisure to realise, or forgetting to think important, the crudity and coarseness of his human beings. Yet what more damaging criticism can there be both of his earth and of his Heaven than that they are to be inhabited here and hereafter by his Joans and Peters? Does not the inferiority of their natures tarnish whatever institutions and ideals may be provided for them by the generosity of their Creator? Nor, profoundly though we respect the integrity and humanity of Mr Galsworthy, shall we find what we seek in his pages.

We have to admit that we are exacting, and further, that we find it difficult to justify this, the essential thing, has moved off, or on, and refuses to be contained any longer in such ill-fitting vestments as we provide. Nevertheless we go on perseveringly, conscientiously, constructing our thirty-two chapters after a design which more and more ceases to resemble the vision in our minds. So much of the enormous labour of proving the solidity, the likeness to life, of the story is not merely labour thrown away but labour misplaced to the extent of obscuring and blotting out the light of the conception. The mediocrity of most novels seems to arise from a conviction on the part of the writer that unless his plot provides scenes of tragedy, comedy, and excitement, an air of probability so impeccable that if all his figures were to come to life they would find themselves dressed down to the last button in the fashion of the hour, he has failed in his duty to the public. If this, roughly as we have stated it, represents his vision, his mediocrity may be said to be natural rather than imposed; but as often as not we may suspect some moment of hesitation in which the question suggests itself whether life is like this after all? Is it not possible that the accent falls a little differently, that the moment of importance came before or after, that, if one were free and could set down what one chose, there would be no plot, little probability, and a vague general confusion in which the clear-cut features of the tragic, the comic, the passionate, and the lyrical were dissolved beyond the possibility of separate recognition? The mind, exposed to the ordinary course of life, receives upon its surface a myriad impressions—trivial, fantastic, evanescent, or engraved with the sharpness of steel. From all sides they come, an incessant shower of innumerable atoms, composing in their sum what we might venture to call life itself; and to figure further as the semi-transparent envelope, or luminous halo, surrounding us from the beginning of consciousness to the end. Is it not perhaps the chief task of the novelist to convey this incessantly varying spirit with whatever stress or sudden deviation it may display, and as little admixture of the alien and external as possible? We are not pleading merely for courage and sincerity; but suggesting that the proper stuff for fiction is a little other than custom would have us believe it.

In some such fashion as this do we seek to define the element which distinguishes the work of several young writers, among whom Mr James Joyce[6] is the most notable, from that of their predecessors. It attempts to come closer to life, and to preserve more sincerely and exactly what interests and moves them by discarding most of the conventions which are commonly observed by the novelists. Let us record the atoms as they fall upon the mind in the order in which they fall, let us trace the pattern, however disconnected and incoherent in appearance, which each sight or incident scores upon the consciousness. Let us not take it for granted that life exists more in what is commonly thought big than in what is commonly thought small. Any one who has read *The Portrait of the Artist as a Young Man* or what promises to be a far more interesting work, *Ulysses,* now appearing in the *Little Review,* will have hazarded some theory of this nature as to Mr Joyce's intention.[7] On our part it is hazarded rather than affirmed; but whatever the exact intention there can be no question but that it is of the utmost sincerity and that the result, difficult or unpleasant as we may judge it, is undeniably distinct. In contrast to those whom we have called materialists Mr Joyce is spiritual; concerned at all costs to reveal the flickerings of that innermost flame which flashes its myriad messages through the brain, he disregards with complete courage whatever seems to him adventitious, though it be probability or coherence or any other of the handrails to which we cling for support when we set our imaginations free. Faced, as in the Cemetery scene, by so much that, in its restless scintillations, in its irrelevance, its flashes of deep significance succeeded by incoherent inanities, seems to be life itself, we have to fumble rather awkwardly if we want to say what else we wish; and for what reason a work of such originality yet fails to compare, for

6. James Joyce (1882–1941).
7. *Portrait of the Artist as a Young Man* (1916–17), *Ulysses* (1922). As early as April 1918 Harriet Weaver had approached the Woolfs in the hope that The Hogarth Press might publish the whole of *Ulysses* (of which the first thirteen episodes, and a part of the fourteenth, had started appearing in the *Little Review* the previous month, continuing until December 1920), but for several reasons, legal and practical, this proved impossible. However, VW made reading notes on those episodes that appeared in the *Little Review* March–October 1918.* * *

we must take high examples, with 'Youth' or *Jude the Obscure*.[8] It fails, one might say simply, because of the comparative poverty of the writer's mind. But it is possible to press a little further and wonder whether we may not refer our sense of being in a bright and yet somehow strictly confined apartment rather than at large beneath the sky to some limitation imposed by the method as well as by the mind. Is it due to the method that we feel neither jovial nor magnanimous, but centred in a self which in spite of its tremor of susceptibility never reaches out or embraces or comprehends what is outside and beyond? Does the emphasis laid perhaps didactically upon indecency contribute to this effect of the angular and isolated? Or is it merely that in any effort of such courage the faults as well as the virtues are left naked to the view? In any case we need not attribute too much importance to the method. Any method is right, every method is right, that expresses what we wish to express. This one has the merit of giving closer shape to what we were prepared to call life itself; did not the reading of *Ulysses* suggest how much of life is excluded and ignored, and did it not come with a shock to open *Tristram Shandy* and even *Pendennis*,[9] and be by them convinced that there are other aspects of life, and larger ones into the bargain?

However this may be, the problem before the novelist at present, as we suppose it to have been in the past, is to contrive a means of being free to set down what he chooses. He has to have the courage to say that what interests him is no longer this, but that; out of 'that' alone must he construct his work. The tendency of the moderns and part of their perplexity is no doubt that they find their interest more and more in [the] dark region of psychology. At once therefore the accent falls a little differently; it becomes apparent that the emphasis is upon something hitherto ignored or unstressed in that relation, a feeling, a point of view suggesting a different and obscure outline of form, incomprehensible to our predecessors. No one but a modern, perhaps no one but a Russian, would have felt the interest of the situation which Tchehov has made into the short story which he calls 'Gusev'.[1] Some Russian soldiers are lying ill in the hospital of a ship which is taking them back to Russia. We are given scraps of their talk; a few of their thoughts; then one of the soldiers dies, and is taken away; the talk goes on among the others for a time; until Gusev himself dies and, looking 'like a carrot or a radish',[2] is thrown over-

---

8. 'Youth' (1902)* * * Thomas Hardy's *Jude the Obscure* (1896).
9. *The Life and Opinions of Tristram Shandy* (1759–67) by Laurence Sterne and *The History of Pendennis* (1848–50) by W. M. Thackeray.
1. For this story see *The Witch and Other Stories* by Anton Tchehov (1860–1904), trans. Constance Garnett (Chatto & Windus, 1918)* * *
2. *The Witch and Other Stories*, 'Gusev', p. 166: 'Sewn up in the sail cloth he looked like a carrot or a radish: broad at the head and narrow at the feet . . .'

board. The emphasis is laid upon such unexpected places that at first
it seems as if there were no emphasis at all; and then, as the eyes
accustom themselves to twilight and discern the shapes of things in
a room, we see how complete the story is, how profound, and how
truly in obedience to his vision Tchehov has chosen this, that, and
the other, and placed them together to compose something new. But
it is impossible to say that this is humorous or that tragic, or even
that it is proper to call the whole a short story, since the writer seems
careless of brevity and intensity, and leaves us with the suggestion
that the strange chords he has struck sound on and on. There is,
perhaps, no need that a short story should be brief and intense, as
there is perhaps no answer to the questions which it raises.

The most inconclusive remarks upon modern English fiction can
hardly avoid some mention of the Russian influence, and if the Russians are mentioned one runs the risk of feeling that to write of any
fiction save theirs is a waste of time. If we want understanding of
the soul and heart where else shall we find it of comparable profun-
dity? If we are sick of our own materialism the least considerable of
their novelists has by right of birth a natural reverence for the human
spirit. 'Learn to make yourself akin to people . . . but let this sympathy be not with the mind—for it is easy with the mind—but with
the heart, with love towards them.'[3] In every great Russian writer we
seem to discern the features of a saint, if sympathy for the sufferings
of others, love towards them, endeavour to reach some goal worthy
of the most exacting demands of the spirit constitute saintliness. It
is the saint in them which confounds us with a feeling of our own
irreligious triviality, and turns so many of our famous novels to tinsel
and trickery. The conclusions of the Russian mind, thus comprehensive and compassionate, are inevitably perhaps of the utmost sadness. It might indeed be more true to speak of the inconclusiveness
of the Russian mind. It is the sense that there is no answer, that if
honestly examined life presents question after question which must
be left to sound on and on after the story is over in hopeless interrogation that fills us with a deep, and finally it may be with a resent-
ful, despair. They are right perhaps; unquestionably they see further
than we do and without our gross impediments of vision. But perhaps
we see something that escapes them, or why should this voice of
protest mix itself with our gloom? The voice of protest is the voice
of another and an ancient civilisation which seems to have bred in
us the instinct to enjoy and fight rather than to suffer and under-

3. *The Village Priest, and Other Stories* by Elena Militsina and Mikhail Saltikov, trans. from
   the Russian by Beatrix L. Tollemache, with an intro. by C. Hagberg Wright (T. Fisher
   Unwin, 1918), the title story, by Militsina, p. 34; the ellipsis marks the omission of: 'I
   would even like to add: make yourself indispensable to them'.* * *

stand. English fiction from Sterne to Meredith[4] bears witness to our natural delight in humour and comedy, in the beauty of earth, in the activities of the intellect, and in the splendour of the body. But any deductions that we may draw from the comparison of one fiction with another are futile, save as they flood us with a view of infinite possibilities, assure us that there is no bound to the horizon, and nothing forbidden but falsity and pretence. 'The proper stuff of fiction' does not exist; everything is the proper stuff of fiction; whatever one honestly thinks, whatever one honestly feels. No perception comes amiss; every good quality whether of the mind or spirit is drawn upon and used and turned by the magic of art to something little or large, but endlessly different, everlastingly new. All that fiction asks of us is that we should break her and bully her, honour and love her, till she yields to our bidding, for so her youth is perpetually renewed and her sovereignty assured.

4. Laurence Sterne (1713–1768); George Meredith (1828–1909).

Short Stories

The Mark on the Wall†

Perhaps it was the middle of January in the present year that I first looked up and saw the mark on the wall. In order to fix a date it is necessary to remember what one saw. So now I think of the fire; the steady film of yellow light upon the page of my book; the three chrysanthemums in the round glass bowl on the mantelpiece. Yes, it must have been the winter time, and we had just finished our tea, for I remember that I was smoking a cigarette when I looked up and saw the mark on the wall for the first time. I looked up through the smoke of my cigarette and my eye lodged for a moment upon the burning coals, and that old fancy of the crimson flag flapping from the castle tower came into my mind, and I thought of the cavalcade of red knights riding up the side of the black rock. Rather to my relief the sight of the mark interrupted the fancy, for it is an old fancy, an automatic fancy, made as a child perhaps. The mark was a small round mark, black upon the white wall, about six or seven inches above the mantelpiece.

How readily our thoughts swarm upon a new object, lifting it a little way, as ants carry a blade of straw so feverishly, and then leave it . . . If that mark was made by a nail, it can't have been for a picture, it must have been for a miniature—the miniature of a lady with white powdered curls, powder-dusted cheeks, and lips like red carnations. A fraud of course, for the people who had this house before us would have chosen pictures in that way—an old picture for an old room. That is the sort of people they were—very interesting people, and I think of them so often, in such queer places, because one will never see them again, never know what happened next. They wanted to leave this house because they wanted to change their style of furniture, so he said, and he was in process of saying that in his opinion art should have ideas behind it when we were torn asunder, as one is torn from the old lady about to pour out tea and the young man

† Originally published in *Two Stories* (London: Hogarth, 1917); reprinted from Susan Dick, ed., *The Complete Shorter Fiction of Virginia Woolf*, 2nd ed. (New York: Harcourt Brace, 1989), pp. 83–89. Copyright © 1944 and renewed 1972 by Harcourt, Inc. Reprinted by permission of the publisher.

about to hit the tennis ball in the back garden of the suburban villa as one rushes past in the train.

But as for that mark, I'm not sure about it; I don't believe it was made by a nail after all; it's too big, too round, for that. I might get up, but if I got up and looked at it, ten to one I shouldn't be able to say for certain; because once a thing's done, no one ever knows how it happened. Oh! dear me, the mystery of life! The inaccuracy of thought! The ignorance of humanity! To show how very little control of our possessions we have—what an accidental affair this living is after all our civilisation—let me just count over a few of the things lost in our lifetime, beginning, for that seems always the most mysterious of losses—what cat would gnaw, what rat would nibble— three pale blue canisters of book-binding tools? Then there were the bird cages, the iron hoops, the steel skates, the Queen Anne coal-scuttle, the bagatelle board, the hand organ—all gone, and jewels too. Opals and emeralds, they lie about the roots of turnips. What a scraping paring affair it is to be sure! The wonder is that I've any clothes on my back, that I sit surrounded by solid furniture at this moment. Why, if one wants to compare life to anything, one must liken it to being blown through the Tube at fifty miles an hour— landing at the other end without a single hairpin in one's hair! Shot out at the feet of God entirely naked! Tumbling head over heels in the asphodel meadows like brown paper parcels pitched down a shoot in the post office! With one's hair flying back like the tail of a racehorse. Yes, that seems to express the rapidity of life, the perpetual waste and repair; all so casual, all so haphazard. . . .

But after life. The slow pulling down of thick green stalks so that the cup of the flower, as it turns over, deluges one with purple and red light. Why, after all, should one not be born there as one is born here, helpless, speechless, unable to focus one's eyesight, groping at the roots of the grass, at the toes of the Giants? As for saying which are trees, and which are men and women, or whether there are such things, that one won't be in a condition to do for fifty years or so. There will be nothing but spaces of light and dark, intersected by thick stalks, and rather higher up perhaps, rose-shaped blots of an indistinct colour—dim pinks and blues—which will, as time goes on, become more definite, become—I don't know what. . . .

And yet the mark on the wall is not a hole at all. It may even be caused by some round black substance, such as a small rose leaf, left over from the summer, and I, not being a very vigilant housekeeper— look at the dust on the mantelpiece, for example, the dust which, so they say, buried Troy three times over, only fragments of pots utterly refusing annihilation, as one can believe.

The tree outside the window taps very gently on the pane. . . . I want to think quietly, calmly, spaciously, never to be interrupted,

never to have to rise from my chair, to slip easily from one thing to
another, without any sense of hostility, or obstacle. I want to sink
deeper and deeper, away from the surface, with its hard separate
facts. To steady myself, let me catch hold of the first idea that passes.
. . . Shakespeare. . . . Well, he will do as well as another. A man who
sat himself solidly in an arm-chair, and looked into the fire, so—A
shower of ideas fell perpetually from some very high Heaven down
through his mind. He leant his forehead on his hand, and people,
looking in through the open door—for this scene is supposed to take
place on a summer's evening—But how dull this is, this historical
fiction! It doesn't interest me at all. I wish I could hit upon a pleasant
track of thought, a track indirectly reflecting credit upon myself, for
those are the pleasantest thoughts, and very frequent even in the
minds of modest mouse-coloured people, who believe genuinely that
they dislike to hear their own praises. They are not thoughts directly
praising oneself; that is the beauty of them; they are thoughts like
this:

  'And then I came into the room. They were discussing botany. I
said how I'd seen a flower growing on a dust heap on the site of an
old house in Kingsway. The seed, I said, must have been sown in the
reign of Charles the First. What flowers grew in the reign of Charles
the First?' I asked—(but I don't remember the answer). Tall flowers
with purple tassels to them perhaps. And so it goes on. All the time
I'm dressing up the figure of myself in my own mind, lovingly,
stealthily, not openly adoring it, for if I did that, I should catch myself
out, and stretch my hand at once for a book in self-protection.
Indeed, it is curious how instinctively one protects the image of oneself from idolatry or any other handling that could make it ridiculous,
or too unlike the original to be believed in any longer. Or is it not so
very curious after all? It is a matter of great importance. Suppose the
looking-glass smashes, the image disappears, and the romantic figure
with the green of forest depths all about it is there no longer, but
only that shell of a person which is seen by other people—what an
airless, shallow, bald, prominent world it becomes! A world not to
be lived in. As we face each other in omnibuses and underground
railways we are looking into the mirror; that accounts for the vagueness, the gleam of glassiness, in our eyes. And the novelists in future
will realise more and more the importance of these reflections, for
of course there is not one reflection but an almost infinite number;
those are the depths they will explore, those the phantoms they will
pursue, leaving the description of reality more and more out of their
stories, taking a knowledge of it for granted, as the Greeks did and
Shakespeare perhaps—but these generalisations are very worthless.
The military sound of the word is enough. It recalls leading articles,
cabinet ministers—a whole class of things indeed which as a child

one thought the thing itself, the standard thing, the real thing, from which one could not depart save at the risk of nameless damnation. Generalisations bring back somehow Sunday in London, Sunday afternoon walks, Sunday luncheons, and also ways of speaking of the dead, clothes, and habits—like the habit of sitting all together in one room until a certain hour, although nobody liked it. There was a rule for everything. The rule for tablecloths at that particular period was that they should be made of tapestry with little yellow compartments marked upon them, such as you may see in photographs of the carpets in the corridors of the royal palaces. Tablecloths of a different kind were not real tablecloths. How shocking, and yet how wonderful it was to discover that these real things, Sunday luncheons, Sunday walks, country houses, and tablecloths were not entirely real, were indeed half phantoms, and the damnation which visited the disbeliever in them was only a sense of illegitimate freedom. What now takes the place of those things I wonder, those real standard things? Men perhaps, should you be a woman; the masculine point of view which governs our lives, which sets the standard, which establishes Whitaker's Table of Precedency,[1] which has become, I suppose, since the war half a phantom to many men and women, which soon, one may hope, will be laughed into the dustbin where the phantoms go, the mahogany sideboards and the Landseer prints,[2] Gods and Devils, Hell and so forth, leaving us all with an intoxicating sense of illegitimate freedom—if freedom exists. . . .

In certain lights that mark on the wall seems actually to project from the wall. Nor is it entirely circular. I cannot be sure, but it seems to cast a perceptible shadow, suggesting that if I ran my finger down that strip of the wall it would, at a certain point, mount and descend a small tumulus, a smooth tumulus like those barrows on the South Downs which are, they say, either tombs or camps. Of the two I should prefer them to be tombs, desiring melancholy like most English people, and finding it natural at the end of a walk to think of the bones stretched beneath the turf. . . . There must be some book about it. Some antiquary must have dug up those bones and given them a name. . . . What sort of a man is an antiquary, I wonder? Retired Colonels for the most part, I daresay, leading parties of aged labourers to the top here, examining clods of earth and stone, and getting into correspondence with the neighbouring clergy, which, being opened at breakfast time, gives them a feeling of importance, and the comparison of arrowheads necessitates cross-country journeys to the country towns, an agreeable necessity both to them

1. This is probably a reference to 'The Peerage of the United Kingdom', which is included in Whitaker's *Almanack*.
2. Many of the popular paintings of Sir Edwin Henry Landseer (1802–1873) were reproduced in steel engravings by his brother Thomas (1795–1880).

and to their elderly wives, who wish to make plum jam or to clean out the study, and have every reason for keeping that great question of the camp or the tomb in perpetual suspension, while the Colonel himself feels agreeably philosophic in accumulating evidence on both sides of the question. It is true that he does finally incline to believe in the camp; and, being opposed, indites a pamphlet which he is about to read at the quarterly meeting of the local society when a stroke lays him low, and his last conscious thoughts are not of wife or child, but of the camp and that arrowhead there, which is now in the case at the local museum, together with the foot of a Chinese murderess, a handful of Elizabethan nails, a great many Tudor clay pipes, a piece of Roman pottery, and the wine-glass that Nelson drank out of—proving I really don't know what.

No, no, nothing is proved, nothing is known. And if I were to get up at this very moment and ascertain that the mark on the wall is really—what shall I say?—the head of a gigantic old nail, driven in two hundred years ago, which has now, owing to the patient attrition of many generations of housemaids, revealed its head above the coat of paint, and is taking its first view of modern life in the sight of a white-walled fire-lit room, what should I gain? Knowledge? Matter for further speculation? I can think sitting still as well as standing up. And what is knowledge? What are our learned men save the descendants of witches and hermits who crouched in caves and in woods brewing herbs, interrogating shrew-mice and writing down the language of the stars? And the less we honour them as our superstitions dwindle and our respect for beauty and health of mind increases . . . Yes, one could imagine a very pleasant world. A quiet spacious world, with the flowers so red and blue in the open fields. A world without professors or specialists or house-keepers with the profiles of policemen, a world which one could slice with one's thought as a fish slices the water with his fin, grazing the stems of the water-lilies, hanging suspended over nests of white sea eggs. . . . How peaceful it is down here, rooted in the centre of the world and gazing up through the grey waters, with their sudden gleams of light, and their reflections—if it were not for Whitaker's Almanack—if it were not for the Table of Precedency!

I must jump up and see for myself what that mark on the wall really is—a nail, a rose-leaf, a crack in the wood?

Here is Nature once more at her old game of self-preservation. This train of thought, she perceives, is threatening mere waste of energy, even some collision with reality, for who will ever be able to lift a finger against Whitaker's Table of Precedency? The Archbishop of Canterbury is followed by the Lord High Chancellor; the Lord High Chancellor is followed by the Archbishop of York. Everybody follows somebody, such is the philosophy of Whitaker; and the great thing is to know who follows whom. Whitaker knows, and let that, so Nature counsels, comfort you, instead of enraging you; and if you can't be comforted, if you must shatter this hour of peace, think of the mark on the wall.

I understand Nature's game—her prompting to take action as a way of ending any thought that threatens to excite or to pain. Hence, I suppose, comes our slight contempt for men of action—men, we assume, who don't think. Still, there's no harm in putting a full stop to one's disagreeable thoughts by looking at a mark on the wall.

Indeed, now that I have fixed my eyes upon it, I feel that I have grasped a plank in the sea; I feel a satisfying sense of reality which at once turns the two Archbishops and the Lord High Chancellor to the shadows of shades. Here is something definite, something real. Thus, waking from a midnight dream of horror, one hastily turns on the light and lies quiescent, worshipping the chest of drawers, worshipping solidity, worshipping reality, worshipping the impersonal world which is proof of some existence other than ours. That is what one wants to be sure of. . . . Wood is a pleasant thing to think about. It comes from a tree; and trees grow, and we don't know how they grow. For years and years they grow, without paying any attention to us, in meadows, in forests, and by the side of rivers—all things one likes to think about. The cows swish their tails beneath them on hot afternoons; they paint rivers so green that when a moorhen dives one expects to see its feathers all green when it comes up again. I like to think of the fish balanced against the stream like flags blown out; and of water-beetles slowly raising domes of mud upon the bed of the river. I like to think of the tree itself: first the close dry sensation of being wood; then the grinding of the storm; then the slow, delicious ooze of sap. I like to think of it, too, on winter's nights standing in the empty field with all leaves close-furled, nothing tender exposed to the iron bullets of the moon, a naked mast upon an earth that goes tumbling, tumbling all night long. The song of birds must sound very loud and strange in June; and how cold the feet of insects must feel upon it, as they make laborious progresses up the creases of the bark, or sun themselves upon the thin green awning of the leaves, and look straight in front of them with diamond-cut red eyes. . . . One by one the fibres snap beneath the immense cold pressure of the earth, then the last storm comes and, falling, the highest branches drive deep into the ground again. Even so, life isn't done with; there are a million patient, watchful lives still for a tree, all over the world, in bedrooms, in ships, on the pavement, lining rooms, where men and women sit after tea, smoking cigarettes. It is full of peaceful thoughts, happy thoughts, this tree. I should like to take each one separately—but something is getting in the way. . . . Where was I? What has it all been about? A tree? A river? The

Downs? Whitaker's Almanack? The fields of asphodel? I can't
remember a thing. Everything's moving, falling, slipping, vanishing.
. . . There is a vast upheaval of matter. Someone is standing over me
and saying—
   'I'm going out to buy a newspaper.'
   'Yes?'
   'Though it's no good buying newspapers. . . . Nothing ever hap-
pens. Curse this war; God damn this war! . . . All the same, I don't
see why we should have a snail on our wall.'
   Ah, the mark on the wall! It was a snail.

Kew Gardens†

From the oval-shaped flower-bed there rose perhaps a hundred stalks
spreading into heart-shaped or tongue-shaped leaves half way up and
unfurling at the tip red or blue or yellow petals marked with spots
of colour raised upon the surface; and from the red, blue or yellow
gloom of the throat emerged a straight bar, rough with gold dust and
slightly clubbed at the end. The petals were voluminous enough to
be stirred by the summer breeze, and when they moved, the red, blue
and yellow lights passed one over the other, staining an inch of the
brown earth beneath with a spot of the most intricate colour. The
light fell either upon the smooth grey back of a pebble, or the shell
of a snail with its brown circular veins, or, falling into a raindrop, it
expanded with such intensity of red, blue and yellow the thin walls
of water that one expected them to burst and disappear. Instead, the
drop was left in a second silver grey once more, and the light now
settled upon the flesh of a leaf, revealing the branching thread of
fibre beneath the surface, and again it moved on and spread its illumination in the vast green spaces beneath the dome of the heart-
shaped and tongue-shaped leaves. Then the breeze stirred rather
more briskly overhead and the colour was flashed into the air above,
into the eyes of the men and women who walk in Kew Gardens in
July.
   The figures of these men and women straggled past the flower-
bed with a curiously irregular movement not unlike that of the white
and blue butterflies who crossed the turf in zig-zag flights from bed
to bed. The man was about six inches in front of the woman, strolling
carelessly, while she bore on with greater purpose, only turning her
head now and then to see that the children were not too far behind.

† Originally published by the Hogarth Press in May 1919; reprinted from Susan Dick, ed.,
 The Complete Shorter Fiction of Virginia Woolf, 2nd ed. (New York: Harcourt Brace,
 1989), pp. 90–95. Copyright © 1944 and renewed 1972 by Harcourt, Inc. Reprinted by
 permission of the publisher.

The man kept this distance in front of the woman purposely, though perhaps unconsciously, for he wanted to go on with his thoughts.

'Fifteen years ago I came here with Lily,' he thought. 'We sat somewhere over there by a lake, and I begged her to marry me all through the hot afternoon. How the dragon-fly kept circling round us: how clearly I see the dragon-fly and her shoe with the square silver buckle at the toe. All the time I spoke I saw her shoe and when it moved impatiently I knew without looking up what she was going to say: the whole of her seemed to be in her shoe. And my love, my desire, were in the dragon-fly; for some reason I thought that if it settled there, on that leaf, the broad one with the red flower in the middle of it, if the dragon-fly settled on the leaf she would say "Yes" at once. But the dragon-fly went round and round: it never settled anywhere—of course not, happily not, or I shouldn't be walking here with Eleanor and the children—Tell me, Eleanor, d'you ever think of the past?'

'Why do you ask, Simon?'

'Because I've been thinking of the past. I've been thinking of Lily, the woman I might have married . . . Well, why are you silent? Do you mind my thinking of the past?'

'Why should I mind, Simon? Doesn't one always think of the past, in a garden with men and women lying under the trees? Aren't they one's past, all that remains of it, those men and women, those ghosts lying under the trees, . . . one's happiness, one's reality?'

'For me, a square silver shoe-buckle and a dragon-fly—'

'For me, a kiss. Imagine six little girls sitting before their easels twenty years ago, down by the side of a lake, painting the water-lilies, the first red water-lilies I'd ever seen. And suddenly a kiss, there on the back of my neck. And my hand shook all the afternoon so that I couldn't paint. I took out my watch and marked the hour when I would allow myself to think of the kiss for five minutes only—it was so precious—the kiss of an old grey-haired woman with a wart on her nose, the mother of all my kisses all my life. Come Caroline, come Hubert.'

They walked on past the flower-bed, now walking four abreast, and soon diminished in size among the trees and looked half transparent as the sunlight and shade swam over their backs in large trembling irregular patches.

In the oval flower-bed the snail, whose shell had been stained red, blue and yellow for the space of two minutes or so, now appeared to be moving very slightly in its shell, and next began to labour over the crumbs of loose earth which broke away and rolled down as it passed over them. It appeared to have a definite goal in front of it, differing in this respect from the singular high-stepping angular green insect who attempted to cross in front of it, and waited for a second with its antennae trembling as if in deliberation, and then stepped off as rapidly and strangely in the opposite direction. Brown cliffs with deep green lakes in the hollows, flat blade-like trees that waved from root to tip, round boulders of grey stone, vast crumpled surfaces of a thin crackling texture—all these objects lay across the snail's progress between one stalk and another to his goal. Before he had decided whether to circumvent the arched tent of a dead leaf or to breast it there came past the bed the feet of other human beings.

This time they were both men. The younger of the two wore an expression of perhaps unnatural calm; he raised his eyes and fixed them very steadily in front of him while his companion spoke, and directly his companion had done speaking he looked on the ground again and sometimes opened his lips only after a long pause and sometimes did not open them at all. The elder man had a curiously uneven and shaky method of walking, jerking his hand forward and throwing up his head abruptly, rather in the manner of an impatient carriage horse tired of waiting outside a house; but in the man these gestures were irresolute and pointless. He talked almost incessantly; he smiled to himself and again began to talk, as if the smile had been an answer. He was talking about spirits—the spirits of the dead, who, according to him, were even now telling him all sorts of odd things about their experiences in Heaven.

'Heaven was known to the ancients as Thessaly, William, and now, with this war, the spirit matter is rolling between the hills like thunder.' He paused, seemed to listen, smiled, jerked his head and continued:—

'You have a small electric battery and a piece of rubber to insulate the wire—isolate?—insulate?—well, we'll skip the details, no good going into details that wouldn't be understood—and in short the little machine stands in any convenient position by the head of the bed, we will say, on a neat mahogany stand. All arrangements being properly fixed by workmen under my direction, the widow applies her ear and summons the spirit by sign as agreed. Women! Widows! Women in black—'

Here he seemed to have caught sight of a woman's dress in the distance, which in the shade looked a purple black. He took off his hat, placed his hand upon his heart, and hurried towards her muttering and gesticulating feverishly. But William caught him by the sleeve and touched a flower with the tip of his walking-stick in order to divert the old man's attention. After looking at it for a moment in some confusion the old man bent his ear to it and seemed to answer a voice speaking from it, for he began talking about the forests of Uruguay which he had visited hundreds of years ago in company with the most beautiful young woman in Europe. He could be heard murmuring about forests of Uruguay blanketed with the wax petals of tropical roses, nightingales, sea beaches, mermaids and women drowned at sea, as he suffered himself to be moved on by William, upon whose face the look of stoical patience grew slowly deeper and deeper.

Following his steps so closely as to be slightly puzzled by his gestures came two elderly women of the lower middle class, one stout and ponderous, the other rosy-cheeked and nimble. Like most people of their station they were frankly fascinated by any signs of eccentricity betokening a disordered brain, especially in the well-to-do; but they were too far off to be certain whether the gestures were merely eccentric or genuinely mad. After they had scrutinised the old man's back in silence for a moment and given each other a queer, sly look, they went on energetically piecing together their very complicated dialogue:

'Nell, Bert, Lot, Cess, Phil, Pa, he says, I says, she says, I says, I says, I says—'

'My Bert, Sis, Bill, Grandad, the old man, sugar,
    Sugar, flour, kippers, greens
    Sugar, sugar, sugar.'

The ponderous woman looked through the pattern of falling words at the flowers standing cool, firm and upright in the earth, with a curious expression. She saw them as a sleeper waking from a heavy sleep sees a brass candlestick reflecting the light in an unfamiliar way, and closes his eyes and opens them, and seeing the brass candlestick again, finally starts broad awake and stares at the candlestick with all his powers. So the heavy woman came to a standstill opposite the oval shaped flower-bed, and ceased even to pretend to listen to what the other woman was saying. She stood there letting the words fall over her, swaying the top part of her body slowly backwards and forwards, looking at the flowers. Then she suggested that they should find a seat and have their tea.

The snail had now considered every possible method of reaching his goal without going round the dead leaf or climbing over it. Let alone the effort needed for climbing a leaf, he was doubtful whether the thin texture which vibrated with such an alarming crackle when touched even by the tip of his horns would bear his weight; and this determined him finally to creep beneath it, for there was a point where the leaf curved high enough from the ground to admit him. He had just inserted his head in the opening and was taking stock of the high brown roof and was getting used to the cool brown light when two other people came past outside on the turf. This time they were both young, a young man and a young woman. They were both in the prime of youth, or even in that season which precedes the prime of youth, the season before the smooth pink folds of the flower have burst their gummy case, when the wings of the butterfly, though fully grown, are motionless in the sun.

'Lucky it isn't Friday,' he observed.

'Why? D'you believe in luck?'

'They make you pay sixpence on Friday.'

'What's sixpence anyway? Isn't it worth sixpence?'

'What's "it"—what do you mean by "it"?'

'O anything—I mean—you know what I mean.'

Long pauses came between each of these remarks: they were uttered in toneless and monotonous voices. The couple stood still on the edge of the flower-bed, and together pressed the end of her parasol deep down into the soft earth. The action and the fact that his hand rested on the top of hers expressed their feelings in a strange way, as these short insignificant words also expressed something, words with short wings for their heavy body of meaning, inadequate to carry them far and thus alighting awkwardly upon the very common objects that surrounded them and were to their inexperienced touch so massive: but who knows (so they thought as they pressed the parasol into the earth) what precipices aren't concealed in them, or what slopes of ice don't shine in the sun on the other side? Who knows? Who has ever seen this before? Even when she wondered what sort of tea they gave you at Kew, he felt that something loomed up behind her words, and stood vast and solid behind them; and the mist very slowly rose and uncovered—O Heavens,—what were those shapes?—little white tables, and waitresses who looked first at her and then at him; and there was a bill that he would pay with a real two shilling piece, and it was real, all real, he assured himself, fingering the coin in his pocket, real to everyone except to him and to her; even to him it began to seem real; and then—but it was too exciting to stand and think any longer, and he pulled the parasol out of the earth with a jerk and was impatient to find the place where one had tea with other people, like other people.

'Come along, Trissie; it's time we had our tea.'

'Wherever *does* one have one's tea?' she asked with the oddest thrill of excitement in her voice, looking vaguely round and letting herself be drawn on down the grass path, trailing her parasol, turning her head this way and that way, forgetting her tea, wishing to go down there and then down there, remembering orchids and cranes among wild flowers, a Chinese pagoda and a crimson-crested bird; but he bore her on.

Thus one couple after another with much the same irregular and aimless movement passed the flower-bed and were enveloped in layer after layer of green-blue vapour, in which at first their bodies had substance and a dash of colour, but later both substance and colour dissolved in the green-blue atmosphere. How hot it was! So hot that even the thrush chose to hop, like a mechanical bird, in the shadow of the flowers, with long pauses between one movement and the next; instead of rambling vaguely the white butterflies danced once above another, making with their white shifting flakes the outline of a shattered marble column above the tallest flowers; the glass roofs of the palm house shone as if a whole market full of shiny green umbrellas had opened in the sun; and in the drone of the aeroplane the voice of the summer sky murmured its fierce soul. Yellow and black, pink and snow white, shapes of all these colours, men, women and children, were spotted for a second upon the horizon, and then, seeing the breadth of yellow that lay upon the grass, they wavered and sought shade beneath the trees, dissolving like drops of water in the yellow and green atmosphere, staining it faintly with red and blue. It seemed as if all gross and heavy bodies had sunk down in the heat motionless and lay huddled upon the ground, but their voices went wavering from them as if they were flames lolling from the thick waxen bodies of candles. Voices, yes, voices, wordless voices, breaking the silence suddenly with such depth of contentment, such passion of desire, or, in the voices of children, such freshness of surprise; breaking the silence? But there was no silence; all the time the motor omnibuses were turning their wheels and changing their gear; like a vast nest of Chinese boxes all of wrought steel turning ceaselessly one within another the city murmured; on the top of which the voices cried aloud and the petals of myriads of flowers flashed their colours into the air.

An Unwritten Novel†

Such an expression of unhappiness was enough by itself to make one's eyes slide above the paper's edge to the poor woman's face—insignificant without that look, almost a symbol of human destiny with it. Life's what you see in people's eyes; life's what they learn, and, having learnt it, never, though they seek to hide it, cease to be aware of—what? That life's like that, it seems. Five faces opposite—five mature faces—and the knowledge in each face. Strange though, how people

---

† Originally published in *London Mercury* (July 1920); reprinted from Susan Dick, ed., *The Complete Shorter Fiction of Virginia Woolf*, 2nd ed. (New York: Harcourt Brace, 1989), pp. 112–21. Copyright © 1944 and renewed 1972 by Harcourt, Inc. Reprinted by permission of the publisher. Editorial notes copyright © 1985 by Susan Dick. Reprinted by permission of Harcourt, Inc.
  VW's reference to 'An Unwritten Novel' in a diary entry for 26 January 1920 suggests that it was written around that time.° ° ° The brackets within the text are VW's.
  VW's revisions consisted of the deletion of three brief passages which are given in notes 3, 4, and 5 below. The deleted passage appears between the asterisks.

want to conceal it! Marks of reticence are on all those faces: lips shut, eyes shaded, each one of the five doing something to hide or stultify his knowledge. One smokes; another reads; a third checks entries in a pocket-book; a fourth stares at the map of the line framed opposite and the fifth—the terrible thing about the fifth is that she does nothing at all. She looks at life. Ah, but my poor, unfortunate woman, do play the game—do, for all our sakes, conceal it!

As if she heard me, she looked up, shifted slightly in her seat and sighed. She seemed to apologise and at the same time to say to me, 'If only you knew!' Then she looked at life again. 'But I do know,' I answered silently, glancing at *The Times* for manners' sake: 'I know the whole business. "Peace between Germany and the Allied Powers was yesterday officially ushered in at Paris[1]—Signor Nitti, the Italian Prime Minister—a passenger train at Doncaster was in collision with a goods train . . ." We all know—*The Times* knows—but we pretend we don't.' My eyes had once more crept over the paper's rim. She shuddered, twitched her arm queerly to the middle of her back and shook her head. Again I dipped into my great reservoir of life. 'Take what you like,' I continued, 'births, deaths, marriages, Court Circular, the habits of birds, Leonardo da Vinci, the Sandhills murder, high wages and the cost of living—oh, take what you like,' I repeated, 'it's all in *The Times*!' Again with infinite weariness she moved her head from side to side until, like a top exhausted with spinning, it settled on her neck.

The Times was no protection against such sorrow as hers. But other human beings forbade intercourse. The best thing to do against life was to fold the paper so that it made a perfect square, crisp, thick, impervious even to life. This done, I glanced up quickly, armed with a shield of my own. She pierced through my shield; she gazed into my eyes as if searching any sediment of courage at the depths of them and damping it to clay. Her twitch alone denied all hope, discounted all illusion.

So we rattled through Surrey and across the border into Sussex. But with my eyes upon life I did not see that the other travellers had left, one by one, till, save for the man who read, we were alone together. Here was Three Bridges station. We drew slowly down the platform and stopped. Was he going to leave us? I prayed both ways—I prayed last that he might stay. At that instant he roused himself, crumpled his paper contemptuously, like a thing done with, burst open the door and left us alone.

The unhappy woman, leaning a little forward, palely and colourlessly addressed me—talked of stations and holidays, of brothers at

1. The Treaty of Versailles, signed in Paris on 28 June 1919, went into effect on 10 January 1920.

Eastbourne, and the time of year, which was, I forget now, early or late. But at last looking from the window and seeing, I knew, only life, she breathed. 'Staying away—that's the drawback of it—' Ah, now we approached the catastrophe, 'My sister-in-law'—the bitterness of her tone was like lemon on cold steel, and speaking, not to me, but to herself, she muttered, 'Nonsense, she would say—that's what they all say,' and while she spoke she fidgeted as though the skin on her back were as a plucked fowl's in a poulterer's shopwindow.

'Oh, that cow!' she broke off nervously, as though the great wooden cow in the meadow had shocked her and saved her from some indiscretion. Then she shuddered, and then she made the awkward angular movement that I had seen before, as if, after the spasm, some spot between the shoulders burnt or itched. Then again she looked the most unhappy woman in the world, and I once more reproached her, though not with the same conviction, for if there were a reason, and if I knew the reason, the stigma was removed from life.

'Sisters-in-law,' I said—

Her lips pursed as if to spit venom at the word; pursed they remained. All she did was to take her glove and rub hard at a spot on the window-pane. She rubbed as if she would rub something out for ever—some stain, some indelible contamination. Indeed, the spot remained for all her rubbing, and back she sank with the shudder and the clutch of the arm I had come to expect. Something impelled me to take my glove and rub my window. There, too, was a little speck on the glass. For all my rubbing it remained. And then the spasm went through me; I crooked my arm and plucked at the middle of my back. My skin, too, felt like the damp chicken's skin in the poulterer's shop window; one spot between the shoulders itched and irritated, felt clammy, felt raw. Could I reach it? Surreptitiously I tried. She saw me. A smile of infinite irony, infinite sorrow, flitted and faded from her face. But she had communicated, shared her secret, passed her poison; she would speak no more. Leaning back in my corner, shielding my eyes from her eyes, seeing only the slopes and hollows, greys and purples, of the winter's landscape, I read her message, deciphered her secret, reading it beneath her gaze.

Hilda's the sister-in-law. Hilda? Hilda? Hilda Marsh—Hilda the blooming, the full bosomed, the matronly. Hilda stands at the door as the cab draws up, holding a coin. 'Poor Minnie, more of a grasshopper than ever—old cloak she had last year. Well, well, with two children these days one can't do more. No, Minnie. I've got it; here you are, cabby—none of your ways with me. Come in Minnie. Oh, I could carry *you*, let alone your basket!' So they go into the dining-room. 'Aunt Minnie, children.'

Slowly the knives and forks sink from the upright. Down they get (Bob and Barbara), hold out hands stiffly; back again to their chairs, staring between the resumed mouthfuls. [But this we'll skip; ornaments, curtains, trefoil china plate, yellow oblongs of cheese, white squares of biscuit—skip—oh, but wait! Half-way through luncheon one of those shivers; Bob stares at her, spoon in mouth. 'Get on with your pudding, Bob;' but Hilda disapproves. 'Why *should* she twitch?' Skip, skip, till we reach the landing on the upper floor; stairs brass–bound; linoleum worn; oh, yes! little bedroom looking out over the roofs of Eastbourne—zigzagging roofs like the spines of caterpillars this way, that way, striped red and yellow, with blue-black slating. Now, Minnie, the door's shut; Hilda heavily descends to the basement, you unstrap the straps of your basket, lay on the bed a meagre nightgown, stand side by side furred felt slippers. The looking-glass—no, you avoid the looking-glass. Some methodical disposition of hairpins. Perhaps the shell box has something in it? You shake it; it's the pearly stud there was last year—that's all. And then the sniff, the sigh, the sitting by the window. Three o'clock on a December afternoon; the rain drizzling; one light low in the skylight of a drapery emporium, another high in a servant's bedroom—this one goes out. That gives her nothing to look at. A moment's blankness—then, what are you thinking? (Let me peep across at her opposite; she's asleep or pretending it; so what would she think about sitting at the window at three o'clock in the afternoon? Health, money, bills, her God?) Yes, sitting on the very edge of the chair looking over the roofs of Eastbourne, Minnie Marsh prays to God. That's all very well; and she may rub the pane too, as though to see God better; but what God does she see? Who's the God of Minnie Marsh, the God of the back streets of Eastbourne, the God of three o'clock in the afternoon? I, too, see roofs, I see sky; but, oh, dear—this seeing of Gods! More like President Kruger than Prince Albert[2]—that's the best I can do for him; and I see him on a chair, in a black frock-coat, not so very high up either; I can manage a cloud or two for him to sit on; and then his hand trailing in the cloud holds a rod, a truncheon is it?—black, thick, thorned—a brutal old bully—Minnie's God! Did he send the itch and the patch and the twitch? Is that why she prays? What she rubs on the window is the stain of sin. Oh, she committed some crime!

I have my choice of crimes. The woods flit and fly—in summer there are bluebells; in the opening there, when Spring comes, primroses. A parting, was it, twenty years ago? Vows broken? Not Min-

2. Paulus Kruger (1825–1904), leader of the Boers in their 1880 rebellion against Britain and subsequently president of the Transvaal, contrasts sharply with Queen Victoria's beloved Prince Albert (1819–1861) whose earnest Christianity took a far less aggressive form.

nie's! . . . She was faithful. How she nursed her mother! All her savings on the tombstones—wreaths under glass—daffodils in jars. But I'm off the track. A crime . . . They would say she kept her sorrow, suppressed her secret—her sex, they'd say—the scientific people. But what flummery to saddle *her* with sex! No—more like this. Passing down the streets of Croydon twenty years ago, the violet loops of ribbon in the draper's window spangled in the electric light catch her eye. She lingers—past six. Still by running she can reach home. She pushes through the glass swing door. It's sale-time. Shallow trays brim with ribbons.[3] She pauses, pulls this, fingers that with the raised roses on it—no need to choose, no need to buy, and each tray with its surprises. 'We don't shut till seven', and then it *is* seven. She runs, she rushes, home she reaches, but too late. Neighbours— the doctor—baby brother—the kettle—scalded—hospital—dead— or only the shock of it, the blame? Ah, but the detail matters nothing! It's what she carries with her; the spot, the crime, the thing to expiate, always there between her shoulders. 'Yes,' she seems to nod to me, 'it's the thing I did.'

Whether you did, or what you did, I don't mind; it's not the thing I want. The draper's window looped with violet—that'll do; a little cheap perhaps, a little commonplace—since one has a choice of crimes, but then so many (let me peep across again—still sleeping, or pretending sleep! white, worn, the mouth closed—a touch of obstinacy, more than one would think—no hint of sex)—so many crimes aren't *your* crime; your crime was cheap; only the retribution solemn; for now the church door opens, the hard wooden pew receives her; on the brown tiles she kneels; every day, winter, summer, dusk, dawn (here she's at it) prays. All her sins fall, fall, for ever fall. The spot receives them. It's raised, it's red, it's burning. Next she twitches. Small boys point. 'Bob at lunch today'—But elderly women are the worst.

Indeed now you can't sit praying any longer. Kruger's sunk beneath the clouds—washed over as with a painter's brush of liquid grey, to which he adds a tinge of black—even the tip of the truncheon gone now. That's what always happens! Just as you've seen him, felt him, someone interrupts. It's Hilda now.

How you hate her! She'll even lock the bathroom door overnight, too, though it's only cold water you want, and sometimes when the night's been bad it seems as if washing helped.[4] And John at breakfast—the children—meals are worst, and sometimes there are friends—ferns, don't altogether hide 'em—they guess too; so out you

---

3. brim with ribbons *all along the counters.*
4. as if washing helped. *You take the sponge, the pumice-stone, you scrape and scrub, you squirm and sluice; it can't be done—let *me* try; I can't reach it either—the spot between the shoulders—cold water only—why should she grudge that?*

go along the front, where the waves are grey, and the papers blow, and the glass shelters green and draughty, and the chairs cost tuppence—too much—for there must be preachers along the sands. Ah, that's a nigger—that's a funny man—that's a man with parakeets—poor little creatures! Is there no one here who thinks of God?—just up there, over the pier, with his rod—but no—there's nothing but grey in the sky or if it's blue the white clouds hide him, and the music—it's military music—and what are they fishing for? Do they catch them? How the children stare! Well, then home a back way—'Home a back way!' The words have meaning; might have been spoken by the old man with whiskers—no, no, he didn't really speak; but everything has meaning—placards leaning against doorways—names above shop-windows—red fruit in baskets—women's heads in the hairdresser's—all say 'Minnie Marsh!' But here's a jerk. 'Eggs are cheaper!' That's what always happens! I was heading her over the waterfall, straight for madness, when, like a flock of dream sheep, she turns t'other way and runs between my fingers. Eggs are cheaper. Tethered to the shores of the world, none of the crimes, sorrows, rhapsodies, or insanities for poor Minnie Marsh; never late for luncheon; never caught in a storm without a mackintosh; never utterly unconscious of the cheapness of eggs. So she reaches home—scrapes her boots.

Have I read you right? But the human face—the human face at the top of the fullest sheet of print holds more, withholds more. Now, eyes open, she looks out; and in the human eye—how d'you define it?—there's a break—a division—so that when you've grasped the stem the butterfly's off—the moth that hangs in the evening over the yellow flower—move, raise your hand, off, high, away. I won't raise my hand. Hang still, then, quiver, life, soul, spirit, whatever you are of Minnie Marsh—I, too, on my flower—the hawk over the down—alone, or what were the worth of life? To rise; hang still in the evening, in the midday; hang still over the down. The flicker of a hand—off, up! then poised again. Alone, unseen; seeing all so still down there, all so lovely. None seeing, none caring. The eyes of others our prisons; their thoughts our cages. Air above, air below. And the moon and immortality . . . Oh, but I drop to the turf! Are you down too, you in the corner, what's your name—woman—Minnie Marsh; some such name as that? There she is, tight to her blossom; opening her hand-bag, from which she takes a hollow shell—an egg—who was saying that eggs were cheaper? You or I? Oh, it was you who said it on the way home, you remember, when the old gentleman, suddenly opening his umbrella—or sneezing was it? Anyhow, Kruger went, and you came 'home a back way', and scraped your boots. Yes. And now you lay across your knees a pocket-handkerchief into which drop little angular fragments of eggshell—fragments of a map—a puzzle. I wish I could piece them together! If you would only sit still. She's moved her knees—the map's in bits again. Down the slopes of the Andes the white blocks of marble go bounding and hurtling, crushing to death a whole troop of Spanish muleteers, with their convoy—Drake's booty, gold and silver. But to return—

To what, to where? She opened the door, and, putting her umbrella in the stand—that goes without saying: so, too, the whiff of beef from the basement; dot, dot, dot. But what I cannot thus eliminate, what I must, head down, eyes shut, with the courage of a battalion and the blindness of a bull, charge and disperse are, indubitably, the figures behind the ferns, commercial travellers. There I've hidden them all this time in the hope that somehow they'd disappear, or better still emerge, as indeed they must, if the story's to go on gathering richness and rotundity, destiny and tragedy, as stories should, rolling along with it two, if not three, commercial travellers and a whole grove of aspidistra. 'The fronds of the aspidistra only partly concealed the commercial travellers—' Rhododendrons would conceal him utterly, and into the bargain give me my fling of red and white, for which I starve and strive; but rhododendrons in Eastbourne—in December—on the Marshes' table—no, no, I dare not; it's all a matter of crusts and cruets, frills and ferns. Perhaps there'll be a moment later by the sea. Moreover, I feel, pleasantly pricking through the green fretwork and over the glacis of cut glass, a desire to peer and peep at the man opposite—one's as much as I can manage. James Moggridge is it, whom the Marshes call Jimmy? [Minnie you must promise not to twitch till I've got this straight.] James Moggridge travels in—shall we say buttons?—but the time's not come for bringing *them* in—the big and the little on the long cards, some peacock-eyed, others dull gold; cairngorms some, and others coral sprays—but I say the time's not come. He travels, and on Thursday, his Eastbourne day, takes his meals with the Marshes. His red face, his little steady eyes—by no means altogether commonplace—his enormous appetite (that's safe; he won't look at Minnie till the bread's swamped the gravy dry), napkin tucked diamond-wise—but this is primitive, and whatever it may do the reader, don't take me in. Let's dodge to the Moggridge household, set that in motion. Well, the family boots are mended on Sundays by James himself. He reads *Truth*. But his passion? Roses—and his wife a retired hospital nurse—interesting—for God's sake let me have one woman with a name I like! But no; she's of the unborn children of the mind, illicit, none the less loved, like my rhododendrons. How many die in every novel that's written—the best, the dearest, while Moggridge lives. It's life's fault. Here's Minnie eating her egg at the moment opposite[5] and at t'other end of the line—are we past Lewes?—there must be Jimmy—or what's her twitch for?

There must be Moggridge—life's fault. Life imposes her laws; life blocks the way; life's behind the fern; life's the tyrant; oh, but not the bully! No, for I assure you I come willingly; I come wooed by Heaven knows what compulsion across ferns and cruets, table splashed and bottles smeared. I come irresistibly to lodge myself somewhere on the firm flesh, in the robust spine, wherever I can penetrate or find foothold on the person, in the soul, of Moggridge the man. The enormous stability of the fabric; the spine tough as whalebone, straight as oak-tree; the ribs radiating branches; the flesh taut tarpaulin; the red hollows; the suck and regurgitation of the heart; while from above meat falls in brown cubes and beer gushes to be churned to blood again and so we reach the eyes. Behind the aspidistra they see something: black, white, dismal; now the plate again; behind the aspidistra they see an elderly woman; 'Marsh's sister. Hilda's more my sort'; the tablecloth now. 'Marsh would know what's wrong with Morrises . . . ' talk that over; cheese has come; the plate again; turn it round—the enormous fingers; now the woman opposite. 'Marsh's sister—not a bit like Marsh; wretched, elderly female . . . You should feed your hens. . . . God's truth, what's set her twitching? Not what *I* said? Dear, dear, dear! these elderly women. Dear, dear!'

[Yes, Minnie; I know you've twitched, but one moment—James Moggridge.]

'Dear, dear, dear!' How beautiful the sound is! like the knock of a mallet on seasoned timber, like the throb of the heart of an ancient whaler when the seas press thick and the green is clouded. 'Dear, dear!' what a passing bell for the souls of the fretful to soothe them and solace them, lap them in linen, saying, 'So long. Good luck to you!' and then, 'What's your pleasure?' for though Moggridge would pluck his rose for her, that's done, that's over. Now what's the next thing? 'Madam, you'll miss your train,' for they don't linger.

That's the man's way; that's the sound that reverberates; that's St Paul's and the motor-omnibuses. But we're brushing the crumbs off. Oh, Moggridge, you won't stay? You must be off? Are you driving through Eastbourne this afternoon in one of those little carriages? Are you the man who's walled up in green cardboard boxes, and sometimes has the blinds down, and sometimes sits so solemn staring like a sphinx, and always there's a look of the sepulchral, something of the undertaker, the coffin, and the dusk about horse and driver? Do tell me—but the doors slammed. We shall never meet again. Moggridge, farewell!

---

5. opposite *(I can't bear to watch her!)*

Yes, yes, I'm coming. Right up to the top of the house. One moment I'll linger. How the mud goes round in the mind—what a swirl these monsters leave, the waters rocking, the weeds waving and green here, black there, striking to the sand, till by degrees the atoms reassemble, the deposit sifts itself, and again through the eyes one sees clear and still, and there comes to the lips some prayer for the departed, some obsequy for the souls of those one nods to, the people one never meets again.

James Moggridge is dead now, gone for ever. Well, Minnie—'I can face it no longer.' If she said that—(Let me look at her. She is brushing the eggshell into deep declivities). She said it certainly, leaning against the wall of the bedroom, and plucking at the little balls which edge the claret-coloured curtain. But when the self speaks to the self, who is speaking?—the entombed soul, the spirit driven in, in, in to the central catacomb; the self that took the veil and left the world—a coward perhaps, yet somehow beautiful, as it flits with its lantern restlessly up and down the dark corridors. 'I can bear it no longer,' her spirit says. 'That man at lunch—Hilda—the children.' Oh, heavens, her sob! It's the spirit wailing its destiny, the spirit driven hither, thither, lodging on the diminishing carpets—meagre footholds—shrunken shreds of all the vanishing universe—love, life, faith, husband, children, I know not what splendours and pageantries glimpsed in girlhood. 'Not for me—not for me.'

But then—the muffins, the bald elderly dog? Bead mats I should fancy and the consolation of underlinen. If Minnie Marsh were run over and taken to hospital, nurses and doctors themselves would exclaim. . . . There's the vista and the vision—there's the distance— the blue blot at the end of the avenue, while, after all, the tea is rich, the muffin hot, and the dog—'Benny, to your basket, sir, and see what mother's brought you!' So, taking the glove with the worn thumb, defying once more the encroaching demon of what's called going in holes, you renew the fortifications, threading the grey wool, running it in and out.

Running it in and out, across and over, spinning a web through which God himself—hush, don't think of God! How firm the stitches are! You must be proud of your darning. Let nothing disturb her. Let the light fall gently, and the clouds show an inner vest of the first green leaf. Let the sparrow perch on the twig and shake the raindrop hanging to the twig's elbow . . . Why look up? Was it a sound, a thought? Oh, heavens! Back again to the thing you did, the plate glass with the violet loops? But Hilda will come. Ignominies, humiliations, oh! Close the breach.

Having mended her glove, Minnie Marsh lays it in the drawer. She shuts the drawer with decision. I catch sight of her face in the glass. Lips are pursed. Chin held high. Next she laces her shoes. Then she touches her throat. What's your brooch? Mistletoe or merrythought? And what is happening? Unless I'm much mistaken, the pulse's quickened, the moment's coming, the threads are racing, Niagara's ahead. Here's the crisis! Heaven be with you! Down she goes. Courage, courage! Face it, be it! For God's sake don't wait on the mat now! There's the door! I'm on your side. Speak! Confront her, confound her soul!

'Oh, I beg your pardon! Yes, this is Eastbourne. I'll reach it down for you. Let me try the handle.' [But, Minnie, though we keep up pretences, I've read you right—I'm with you now.]

'That's all your luggage?'

'Much obliged, I'm sure.'

(But why do you look about you? Hilda won't come to the station, nor John; and Moggridge is driving at the far side of Eastbourne.)

'I'll wait by my bag, ma'am, that's safest. He said he'd meet me . . . Oh, there he is! That's my son.'

So they walk off together.

Well, but I'm confounded. . . . Surely Minnie, you know better! A strange young man. . . . Stop! I'll tell him—Minnie!—Miss Marsh!—I don't know though. There's something queer in her cloak as it blows. Oh, but it's untrue, it's indecent. . . . Look how he bends as they reach the gateway. She finds her ticket. What's the joke? Off they go, down the road, side by side. . . . Well, my world's done for! What do I stand on? What do I know? That's not Minnie. There never was Moggridge. Who am I? Life's bare as bone.

And yet the last look of them—he stepping from the kerb and she following him round the edge of the big building brims me with wonder—floods me anew. Mysterious figures! Mother and son. Who are you? Why do you walk down the street? Where tonight will you sleep, and then, tomorrow? Oh, how it whirls and surges—floats me afresh! I start after them. People drive this way and that. The white light splutters and pours. Plate-glass windows. Carnations; chrysanthemums. Ivy in dark gardens. Milk carts at the door. Wherever I go, mysterious figures, I see you, turning the corner, mothers and sons; you, you, you. I hasten, I follow. This, I fancy, must be the sea. Grey is the landscape; dim as ashes; the water murmurs and moves. If I fall on my knees, if I go through the ritual, the ancient antics, it's you, unknown figures, you I adore; if I open my arms, it's you I embrace, you I draw to me—adorable world!

A Woman's College from Outside†

The feathery-white moon never let the sky grow dark; all night the chestnut blossoms were white in the green, and dim was the cow-parsley in the meadows. Neither to Tartary nor to Arabia went the wind of the Cambridge courts, but lapsed dreamily in the midst of grey-blue clouds over the roofs of Newnham. There, in the garden, if she needed space to wander, she might find it among the trees; and as none but women's faces could meet her face, she might unveil it blank, featureless, and gaze into rooms where at that hour, blank, featureless, eyelids white over eyes, ringless hands extended upon sheets, slept innumerable women. But here and there a light still burned.

A double light one might figure in Angela's room, seeing how bright Angela herself was, and how bright came back the reflection of herself from the square glass. The whole of her was perfectly delineated—perhaps the soul. For the glass held up an untrembling image—white and gold, red slippers, pale hair with blue stones in it, and never a ripple or shadow to break the smooth kiss of Angela and her reflection in the glass, as if she were glad to be Angela. Anyhow the moment was glad—the bright picture hung in the heart of night, the shrine hollowed in the nocturnal blackness. Strange indeed to have this visible proof of the rightness of things; this lily floating flawless upon Time's pool, fearless, as if this were sufficient—this reflection. Which meditation she betrayed by turning, and the mirror held nothing at all, or only the brass bedstead, and she, running here and there, patting, and darting, became like a woman in a house, and changed again, pursing her lips over a black book and marking with her finger what surely could not be a firm grasp of the science of economics. Only Angela Williams was at Newnham for the purpose of earning her living, and could not forget even in moments of impassioned adoration the cheques of her father at Swansea; her mother washing in the scullery: pink frocks out to dry on the line; tokens that even the lily no longer floats flawless upon the pool, but has a name on a card like another.

A. Williams—one may read it in the moonlight; and next to it some Mary or Eleanor, Mildred, Sarah, Phoebe upon square cards on their doors. All names, nothing but names. The cool white light withered

---

† Originally intended as Chapter X of *Jacob's Room* (*Holograph Notebooks*, I, Berg Collection, pp. 85–91), first published in *Atalanta's Garland: Being the Book of the Edinburgh University Women's Union* (1926); reprinted from Susan Dick, ed., *The Complete Shorter Fiction of Virginia Woolf*, 2nd ed. (New York: Harcourt Brace, 1989), pp. 144–48. Copyright © 1985 by Quentin Bell and Angelica Garnett. Reprinted by permission of Harcourt, Inc. Editorial notes copyright © 1985 by Susan Dick. Reprinted by permission of Harcourt, Inc.

them and starched them until it seemed as if the only purpose of all these names was to rise martially in order should there be a call on them to extinguish a fire, suppress an insurrection, or pass an examination. Such is the power of names written upon cards pinned upon doors. Such too the resemblance, what with tiles, corridors, and bedroom doors, to dairy or nunnery, a place of seclusion or discipline, where the bowl of milk stands cool and pure and there's a great washing of linen.

At that very moment soft laughter came from behind a door. A prim-voiced clock struck the hour—one, two. Now if the clock were issuing his commands, they were disregarded. Fire, insurrection, examination, were all snowed under by laughter, or softly uprooted, the sound seeming to bubble up from the depths and gently waft away the hour, rules, discipline. The bed was strewn with cards. Sally was on the floor. Helena in the chair. Good Bertha clasping her hands by the fire-place. A. Williams came in yawning.

'Because it's utterly and intolerably damnable,' said Helena.

'Damnable,' echoed Bertha. Then yawned.

'We're not eunuchs.'

'I saw her slipping in by the back gate with that old hat on. They don't want us to know.'

'They?' said Angela. 'She.'

Then the laughter.

The cards were spread, falling with their red and yellow faces on the table, and hands were dabbled in the cards. Good Bertha, leaning with her head against the chair, sighed profoundly. For she would willingly have slept, but since night is free pasturage, a limitless field, since night is unmoulded richness, one must tunnel into its darkness. One must hang it with jewels. Night was shared in secret, day browsed on by the whole flock. The blinds were up. A mist was on the garden. Sitting on the floor by the window (while the others played), body, mind, both together, seemed blown through the air, to trail across the bushes. Ah, but she desired to stretch out in bed and to sleep! She believed that no one felt her desire for sleep; she believed humbly—sleepily—with sudden nods and lurchings, that other people were wide awake. When they laughed all together a bird chirped in its sleep out in the garden, as if the laughter—

Yes, as if the laughter (for she dozed now) floated out much like mist and attached itself by soft elastic shreds to plants and bushes, so that the garden was vaporous and clouded. And then, swept by the wind, the bushes would bow themselves and the white vapour blow off across the world.

From all the rooms where women slept this vapour issued, attaching itself to shrubs, like mist, and then blew freely out into the open. Elderly women slept, who would on waking immediately clasp the ivory rod of office. Now smooth and colourless, reposing deeply, they lay surrounded, lay supported, by the bodies of youth recumbent or grouped at the window; pouring forth into the garden this bubbling laughter, this irresponsible laughter: this laughter of mind and body floating away rules, hours, discipline: immensely fertilising, yet formless, chaotic, trailing and straying and tufting the rose-bushes with shreds of vapour.

'Ah,' breathed Angela, standing at the window in her night-gown. Pain was in her voice. She leant her head out. The mist was cleft as if her voice parted it. She had been talking, while the others played, to Alice Avery, about Bamborough Castle; the colour of the sands at evening; upon which Alice said she would write and settle the day, in August, and stooping, kissed her, at least touched her head with her hand, and Angela, positively unable to sit still, like one possessed of a wind-lashed sea in her heart, roamed up and down the room (the witness of such a scene) throwing her arms out to relieve this excitement, this astonishment at the incredible stooping of the miraculous tree with the golden fruit at its summit—hadn't it dropped into her arms? She held it glowing to her breast, a thing not to be touched, thought of, or spoken about, but left to glow there. And then, slowly putting there her stockings, there her slippers, folding her petticoat neatly on top, Angela, her other name being Williams, realised—how could she express it?—that after the dark churning of myriad ages here was light at the end of the tunnel; life; the world. Beneath her it lay—all good; all lovable. Such was her discovery.

Indeed, how could one then feel surprise if, lying in bed, she could not close her eyes?—something irresistibly unclosed them—if in the shallow darkness chair and chest of drawers looked stately, and the looking-glass precious with its ashen hint of day? Sucking her thumb like a child (her age nineteen last November), she lay in this good world, this new world, this world at the end of the tunnel, until a desire to see it or forestall it drove her, tossing her blankets, to guide herself to the window, and there, looking out upon the garden, where the mist lay, all the windows open, one fiery-bluish, something murmuring in the distance, the world of course, and the morning coming, 'Oh,' she cried, as if in pain.

CRITICISM

Contemporary Reception
and Reviews

Lytton Strachey to Virginia Woolf,
October 9, 1922†

I finished Jacob last night—a most wonderful achievement—more like poetry, it seems to me, than anything else, and as such I prophesy immortal. The technique of the narrative is astonishing—how you manage to leave out everything that's dreary, and yet retain enough string for your pearls I can hardly understand. I occasionally almost screamed with joy at the writing. Of course you're very romantic—which alarms me slightly—I am such a Bonamy. Once or twice I thought you were in danger of becoming George-Meredithian[1] in style–or was that a delusion? Something of the sort certainly seems to me *the* danger for your genre. But so far you're safe. You're a romantic in Sirius,[2] I fancy—which after all is a good way off from Box Hill.[3] The impression left on one as a whole is glorious. And then, as one remembers detail after detail—the pier at Scarborough, the rooks and the dinner-bell, the clergyman's wife on the moors, St. Paul's, the British Museum at night, the Parthenon—one's head whirls round and round. Jacob himself I think is very successful—in a most remarkable and original way. Of course I see something of Thoby in him, as I suppose was intended.

† From Robin Majumdar and Allen McLaurin, eds., *Virginia Woolf: The Critical Heritage* (London: Routledge, 1975), pp. 93–94. Notes are by the Editor.

   Lytton Strachey: biographer and critic (1880–1932), friend of Virginia Woolf, author of *Eminent Victorians* (1918).
1. British novelist (1828–1909), author of *The Egoist* (1879) and *Diana of the Crossways* (1884), known for his experiments with narrative.
2. Brightest star in the night sky.
3. Setting of a famous scene in Jane Austen's novel *Emma* (1815).

Virginia Woolf to Lytton Strachey, October 9 [10?], 1922†

I breathe more freely now that I have your letter though I think your praise is extravagant—I can't believe you really like a work so utterly devoid of so many virtues; but it gives me immense pleasure to dream that you do. Of course you put your infallible finger upon the spot—romanticism. How do I catch it? Not from my father. I think it must have been my Great Aunts. But some of it, I think, comes from the effort of breaking with complete representation. One flies into the air. Next time, I mean to stick closer to facts. There are millions of things I want to get your opinion on—This is merely to heave a sigh of relief that you don't cast me off, for nobody else's praise ever gives me quite as much pleasure as yours.

Thursday lunch.

Your loving
Virginia

E. M. Forster to Virginia Woolf, October 24, 1922‡

Dear Virginia,

I like *Jacob's Room* and am sure it is good. You have clean cut away the difficulties that so bother me and that I feared in *Night & Day* were gaining on you—all those Blue Books[1] of the interior and exterior life of the various characters—their spiritual development, income, social positions, etc. etc. The danger is that when cut away these detach with them something that ought to remain—at least according to my notion of a novel, namely the reader's interest in at least one of the characters as a character—if that goes we merely swing about among blobs of amusement or pathos. You keep this interest in Jacob. This I find a tremendous achievement—the greatest in the book and

---

†   From *The Letters of Virginia Woolf*, ed. Nigel Nicolson and Joanne Trautmann (London: Hogarth, 1976), II, *The Question of Things Happening*: 568–69. Copyright © 1976 by Quentin Bell and Angelica Garnett. Reprinted by permission of Harcourt, Inc.

‡   From *Selected Letters of E. M. Forster*, ed. Mary Lago and P. N. Furbank (Cambridge: The Belknap Press of Harvard University Press, 1985), II:32. Copyright © 1985 by The Provost and Scholars of King's College, Cambridge. Selection copyright © 1985 by Mary Lago and P. N. Furbank.

    E. M. Forster: Edward Morgan Forster (1879–1970), novelist and friend of Virginia Woolf, author of *A Room with a View* (1908) and *Passage to India* (1924), among many others.

1. Parliamentary reports; *Night and Day*: Woolf's most recent novel, 1919 [*Editor*].

the making of the book. I don't yet understand how, with your method, you managed it, but of course am reading the book again. Have only just finished it; and am confused by wondering what developments, both of style and form, might come out of it, which is of course outside the present point. The book was quite long enough—! this means not what it looks, but that some of your odd new instruments gave hints of scratches and grinds towards the end. e.g. the Proper Nomenclature. Having once taken such an instrument up you couldn't possibly lay it down, its occasional application to the surface was imperative. This is a minor point though, for the damage done by the scratches is too little to count. They disappear in the general liberation.—One very important thing is that most of the book is seen through happiness; you have got quite clear from the sensitive sorrower whom novelists cadge up to as the easiest medium for observations.

* * *

Thank you very much for giving me the book. I do think it an amazing success, and it's full of beauty, indeed is beautiful.

Morgan

A. S. McDOWALL

The Enchantment of a Mirror†

One might describe Mrs Woolf's new novel as the opposite of *Night and Day*,[1] her last; or one might say that it is rather like the method of *Monday or Tuesday*[2] applied to a continuous story. But this novel is limpid and definite. It would be truer to say that it is different from any other—Mrs Woolf's or anyone else's—though the remark sounds both vague and sweeping. At first you may be drawn by resemblances. This bright and endless race of things and thoughts, small acts, incongruous sensations, impressions so brief and yet pervasive that you hardly separate the mental from the external, what is it but the new vision of life as practised by So-and-so or So-and-so? The vision may be as old, indeed, as Heracleitus[3]; but could he,

† Originally published in *Times Literary Supplement* (October 26, 1922); reprinted from Robin Majumdar and Allen McLaurin, eds., *Virginia Woolf: The Critical Heritage* (London: Routledge, 1975), pp. 95–97. Notes are by the Editor.
1. *Night and Day*, 1919.
2. Woolf, *Monday or Tuesday*, a collection of short stories, 1921.
3. Greek philosopher (540–480 B.C.E.).

or Pater[4] even, have guessed how far artists would carry the process of weaving and unweaving? Mrs Woolf, you will say, is in this movement. Possibly; but her fabric is woven with threads so entirely of her own that it becomes quite different.

First, however, for its unlikeness to the normal. Jacob Flanders, absorbed with the half-savage, half-winning absorption of youth, and lovable since his friends and several women love him, is in the brief career which we follow by glimpses the mutest of all heroes. He is a 'silent young man'; Mrs Woolf's method increases his silence. But there is his room, his behaviour, his impressions; there are the scenes, the numerous people who float into the story for a moment or eddy round its centre. There is Mrs Jarvis, for example:

[Quotes pp. 25–6 'short, dark, with kindling eyes' to 'give it her.'] [19]

Is Mrs Jarvis, then, a vivid little excrescence? When we ask what she and others are doing to the story, and find possible but not very obvious, answers, we are getting nearer to the real interest of Mrs Woolf's novel. It is not Jacob's history simply, nor anyone else's, but the queer simultaneousness of life, with all those incongruous threads which now run parallel, now intersect, and then part as unaccountably. Jacob is in the middle like a waif or a little marching soldier. And these odd conjunctions and sequences of life, which are much too delicate to be called slices, have been brought to a focus in Mrs Woolf's mirror.

It is an amusingly clear and yet enchanted glass which she holds up to things; that is her quality. This stream of incidents, persons, and their momentary thoughts and feelings, which would be intolerable if it were just allowed to flow, is arrested and decanted, as it were, into little phials of crystal vividness. Mrs Woolf has the art of dividing the continuous and yet making one feel that the stream flows remorselessly. The definite Mrs Durrant, the romantic little light-of-love Florinda, shy and charming Clara, the people in the streets, the moors and the sea, London and Athens—they all rise into delicious moments of reality and light before they melt back into the shadow. And each of those moments has caught a gleam of wit from the surface of the mirror, or a musing thought from the reflective depths in it. Ought we to complain, then, because Mrs Woolf can make beauty and significance out of what we generally find insignificant, or because her own musings tinge those of her personages

---

4. Walter Pater (1839–1894), art critic and writer: "It is with this movement, with the passage and dissolution of impressions, images, sensations, that analysis leaves off—that continual vanishing away, that strange, perpetual, weaving and unweaving of ourselves" ("Conclusion" to *The Renaissance*, 1872).

sometimes? We know the stream of life at first-hand already; what this novel adds, with the lightest strokes, and all the coolness of restraint, is a knowledge of the vision of the author.

And it is much to be taken as far as we are here into that subtle, slyly mocking, and yet poignant vision; for Mrs Woolf has seldom expressed it more beguilingly than she does in this novel. It will even make us forget to treat the novel as a story. If, however, we come back to that, we should have to say that it does not create persons and characters as we secretly desire to know them. We do not know Jacob as an individual, though we promptly seize his type; perhaps we do not know anyone in the book otherwise than as a really intuitive person knows his acquaintances, filling in the blanks, if he is imaginative, by his imagination. And that, Mrs Woolf might say, is all we can know in life, or need to know in a book, if we forgo the psychology which she spares us. But it might still be questioned whether her beings, while they intersect, really act upon each other, or whether her method does not condemn them to be external. It is an ungrateful suspicion to have about a book which has embodied their passing thoughts so vividly. But what she has undoubtedly done is to give a quickened sense of the promise and pity in a single destiny, seen against those wilful, intersecting lines of chance and nature. And, with the pity of it, there is the delicious humour which infects every page, the charm of writing that seems as simple as talking but is always exquisite. It is a great deal to have brought back from an adventure; yet, after all, what we relish as much as anything in Mrs. Woolf's method is its adventurousness.

LEWIS BETTANY

From Middle Aged Sensualists†

In many of his stories of the 'Five Towns', Mr Bennett[1] used to bore his greatest admirers by his tiresome trick of presenting a girl's naive interest in boarding a bus or taking a railway journey as a passion for romance. This sense of wonder, a wonder very different from that expressed by Browne[2] and Traherne,[3] is an irritating feature of Mrs Woolf's new story, which is so full of parentheses and suppressions,

---

† Originally published in *Daily News* (October 27, 1922); reprinted from Robin Majumdar and Allen McLaurin, eds., *Virginia Woolf: The Critical Heritage* (London: Routledge, 1975), p. 98. Notes are by the Editor.
1. Arnold Bennett (1867–1931), author of a series of realistic novels about the fictitious "Five Towns," an industrial region in the north of England.
2. Thomas Browne (1605–1682), physician and author of *Religio Medici* (1635).
3. Thomas Traherne (1636?–1674), one of the metaphysical poets.

so tedious in its rediscoveries of the obvious, and so marred by its
occasional lapses into indelicacy, that I found great difficulty in discovering what it was all about. Those who care to read about the
adolescent ardours of a half-baked young Cambridge man in literature, love and travel, will find what they like in *Jacob's Room*. I
thought most of the book very pretentious and very cheap; but some
of the observations and impressions seemed to me quite happy.

UNSIGNED

An Impressionist†

Mrs Woolf is a very clever writer, whose originality expends itself in
ways that are only doubtfully worth while. She attempts in prose
what so many have attempted in verse—the achievement of art while
evading the problems of form—and we can see little sign of the product becoming of more than technical interest. Most deftly does she
catch and convey the impression of a scene, an incident, a passing
figure, or a relationship, but no true novel can be built out of a mere
accumulation of these notebook entries. In *Jacob's Room* there is not
only no story, but there is no perceptible development of any kind.
We get an outline of the kind of young man that Jacob was and of
the kind of woman that his mother was, and very subtly and admirably are some of the features touched in.

REBECCA WEST

Untitled Review‡

There is an expression, one of those unused phrases that nest in the
tall tree-top of the idiom book, 'I would rather have his room than
his company.' One learned its French equivalent, which was not less
excluded from common speech (strange and beautiful it is, like one
of Swinburne's[1] nature poems, this mating of unuttered phrases with
their alien fellow-outcast over frontier seas and mountains, through

† Originally published in *Pall Mall Gazette* (October 27, 1922); reprinted from Robin
  Majumdar and Allen McLaurin, eds., *Virginia Woolf: The Critical Heritage* (London: Routledge, 1975), p. 99.
‡ Originally published in *New Statesman* (November 4, 1922); reprinted from Robin Majumdar and Allen McLaurin, eds., *Virginia Woolf: The Critical Heritage* (London: Routledge,
  1975) pp. 100–102. Notes are by the Editor.
    Rebecca West: feminist novelist and journalist (1892–1983), author of *The Return of
  the Soldier* (1918).
1. Algernon Charles Swinburne (1837–1909), poet.

the kind ponderous idiom-book), and it was forgotten, till it should be recalled by Mrs Woolf's last book. Very strongly has Mrs Woolf preferred Jacob's room to his company. Jacob lives, but that is hearsay. Jacob dies; there could be nothing more negative than the death of one who never (that we could learn for certain) lived, reported by a mouth that makes every human event she speaks of seem as if it had not happened. But his room we know. 'The eighteenth century has its distinction. These houses were built, say, a hundred and fifty years ago. The rooms are shapely, the ceilings high; over the doorways a rose or a ram's skull is carved in wood. Even the panels, painted in raspberry-coloured paint, have their distinction.' We know so much about it; how his mother's letter, in its pale blue envelope, lay waiting for him by the biscuit-box; how the *Globe*[2] looked pinkish under the lamplight and was stared at, but not read, one cold night; how the room heard, at hours when the elderly lie abed, young men disputing on whether this or that line came in Virgil or Lucretius;[3] and how, Jacob dead in the war, it felt his absence. 'Listless is the air in an empty room, just swelling the curtain; the flowers in the jar shift. One fibre in the wicker armchair creaks, though no one sits there . . .'

Mrs Woolf has again provided us with a demonstration that she is at once a negligible novelist and a supremely important writer. The novel may be exactly what it likes. It may be fifteen thousand words, or five hundred thousand; it may be written as simply as a melody in one part or as elaborately as a symphony. But it must, surely, submit to one limitation. It must primarily concern itself with humanity. Only the long drive of the human will can be fitly commemorated in the long drive of the novel form. Now from that point of view *Jacob's Room* is a failure. The fault of it is not that it is about commonplace people—that, indeed, is never a fault—but that it is not about individuals at all but about types as seen through the refractions of commonplace observers' eyes. Jacob's mother, Betty Flanders, is based on the conventional exclamations that such a figure of bluff maternity would evoke from a commonplace observer; so, too, Florinda the whore, so, too, Mother Stuart, her *entrepreneuse*;[4] so, too, Clara Durrant, the nice girl; and Sandra Wentworth Williams, humorous but wholly a reported thing, dredged up from the talk of some cosmopolitan tea-party.

But take the book not as a novel but as a portfolio, and it is indubitably precious. A portfolio is indeed an appropriate image, for

2. London evening newspaper with a small circulation, seeking influence over the upper and middle classes through its editorials; printed on pink paper.
3. Roman poet and philosopher (c. 99–c. 55 B.C.E.), author of *De Rerum Naturae*; Virgil: Roman poet (70–19 B.C.E.), author of *The Aeneid*.
4. Female businesswoman; here, madam.

not only are Mrs Woolf's contributions to her age loose leaves, but they are also connected closely with the pictorial arts. Though she may have read Jane Austen and the Russians and James Joyce[5] with more than common delight and intelligence, it is nothing in literature that has made her. She can write supremely well only of what can be painted; best of all, perhaps, of what has been painted. Take, for example, one of the rare occasions when the people in the book evoke emotion, the short and subtle and extremely funny conversation between Miss Edwards and Mr Calthorp at the Durrants' party. The temptation is to ascribe it (since it plainly hardly came of itself) to the influence of Jane Austen. But if that had been the source the conversation would have had some high lights of verbal amusingness on it instead of being simply a success in suggestion, in the evocation of a prim social atmosphere. The derivation is surely a drawing in *Punch*,[6] a pre-Du Maurier[7] drawing of discreet ladies in spread skirts and young men with peg-top trousers and curling beards, sitting at parties glorious with the innocent pretentiousness of hired pineapples and *ad hoc* waiters from the pastrycook's.

There is dull stuff near the beginning about the Scilly Isles;[8] none of the old people whose hints Mrs Woolf can take, painted those parts. There is a good outing with the foxhounds in Essex, to which Morland[9] and the old hunting prints have given their jollity. But best of all are Mrs Woolf's London series.* * *

* * *She tells how Rotten Row[1] looks on a sweet afternoon; how the leather curtain flaps at the door of St Paul's; how the morning army looks pouring over Waterloo Bridge. She is less successful with her considered characters than with her odd vignettes, less successful with Jacob than with Mrs Grandage. Yet this is no brick-counting, no extension of the careful cataloguing 'Nature Notes' method to the phenomena of town. It is authentic poetry, cognisant of the soul.

5. Irish novelist and short-story writer (1882–1941), author of *Ulysses* (1922); Jane Austen: English novelist (1775–1817), author of *Pride and Prejudice*; the Russians: in "Modern Novels" (1919) Woolf mentions short-story writer Anton Tchehov (1860–1904) as an example of a Russian writer she admired.
6. British satirical magazine, founded 1841.
7. George Du Maurier (1834–1896), novelist and artist, author of *Trilby* (1894), joined the staff of *Punch* as an illustrator in 1864.
8. Archipelago of islands about thirty miles off the coast of Cornwall.
9. George Morland (1763–1804), English genre painter who specialized in animal portraits and landscapes.
1. Bridle path through Hyde Park in London.

W. L. COURTNEY

Untitled Review†

In estimating the tendencies of a particular era in literature it is well to take extreme cases. We recognise that there are certain distinctive peculiarities about modern novels. But in order to make sure of the fact we need only take up a book like *Jacob's Room*, by Mrs Virginia Woolf. Even so, we shall be a little perplexed, for sometimes—perhaps oftener than not—we do not quite understand what the authoress is driving at, nor are we in a position to feel certain that she achieves the results at which she aims. One thing is clear. Instead of a straightforward narrative dealing with certain characters, with the interactions of those characters on one another, and with the destiny which carries them to their appointed end, we have a perfectly different art form. There is no particular story to tell, unless, indeed, you can gather some kind of story out of the piecemeal references to personages and things. But what does emerge is the constant activity, the perpetual reaction of a sensitive mind upon the impressions which come through the senses—so that an event or a character is not viewed as it is, but only as steeped in the consciousness of the author. That is the great and decisive difference between an older art-method and a later, and sometimes the contrast is a little embarrassing. The old craving for a plot still remains in our unregenerate breasts, and when all that we receive in compensation for what we have lost is the attitude of Mrs Virginia Woolf towards her creations—or rather, perhaps, a theory of life as interpreted by a clever observer—there must inevitably be some confusion and a mixture of mere narration with the intrusions and philosophisings of a superior mind. Anything like an objective creation becomes impossible. By an objective creation I mean the portrayal of a particular thing, person, or incident as it exists in itself. Flaubert[1] thought that that was the only right way of writing a novel, and hence his theory—driven hard by a man who consciously lived his life apart from others—was the absolute exclusion of the author's personality from the written page. Mrs Woolf confidently chatters as though she were seated in an armchair playing with her puppets. It is she who gives them life. It is she who imparts to them such character as they are allowed to possess. They talk well because the author of their being talks well. They say clever things, not as from their own mouths, but

† Originally published in *Daily Telegraph* (November 10, 1922); reprinted from Robin Majumdar and Allen McLaurin, eds., *Virginia Woolf: The Critical Heritage* (London: Routledge, 1975), pp. 103–05. Notes are by the Editor.
1. Gustave Flaubert (1821–1880), French novelist, author of *Madame Bovary* (1856).

as prompted by their creator. And if their creator appears to be a clever and original woman, her creations have the stamp of real life. But does she really care for them? Is she enamoured of her puppets? I wonder.

We begin merrily enough with something that looks as if it might be interesting narrative. Here is Mrs Flanders, anxious about her children, of whom Jacob is the prominent one, and Archer and John are allowed to fall into the background. Jacob is obviously to be the hero. He has his own definite views, young as he is. He is not made for obedience. He clearly determines to live his life in his own way. And he is very handsome. Most women admire him, though they concede that he is very shy and awkward, a youth who often prefers silence to speech. Mrs Flanders has her own little romance to think of, but that does not interfere with her duty towards her children. And so, somehow or other, money is got together to send Jacob to college, and to enable him to make his big plunge into life. Then, of course, the usual incidents happen. We pass through a number of scenes of revelry and boredom, and such names are tossed up on the surface of the story as Florinda—who is not much better than she should be—Clara Durrant, Sandra, and others. His male friends also flit hither and thither—Timothy Durrant, Clara's brother, and Bonamy, and Mr Benson. But the way in which these personages are treated is, of course, the chief point in *Jacob's Room*. Although Mrs Woolf abjures realism, yet she is realistic enough when it comes to the treatment of ordinary episodes. No one is more happily inspired than she when it comes to dialogue and conversation. She will give us the impression of a conversation by making several people talk, as it were, at once, each with his or her own particular interest, so that you get voices coming from left and right, voices up by the window or by the fireplace, voices bidding farewell or saying goodday—all the mixture of different interests which a crowded drawing room can contain. The result to an old-fashioned reader is sufficiently curious.* * *

In similar fashion Mrs Woolf achieves her backgrounds with a great deal of skill. Whether we find ourselves at Cambridge or on Hampstead Heath, in the suburbs of London or on board a yacht, or in Athens, we find the same graphic and picturesque touch, and the picture is drawn, arresting, vivid, intriguing, just as this point or that point in the mise en scène is brought out for a moment in high light. She gets atmosphere in her own fashion without aiming at any special exercise of cleverness; she uses similes and strange locutions, often bizarre, but undoubtedly adding to the effect.* * * Yes, the author knows how to give us atmosphere, and perhaps that is a sufficient justification of her method. She is very unlike other writers, except that now and again she reminds us of Dorothy Richardson.[2] But in her instinct for the nuances of character, in the keen discernment of those small, unessential things which go to the making of life, she scores again and again. Her theory of art ought, I suppose, to be called 'impressionist'. She does not describe; she merely indicates; throughout there is always the pervasive character and spirit of Virginia Woolf. It is she who makes the vital difference. Without her names are merely names, and do not represent anything alive. For some readers it is a drawback, though others will perhaps consider it a fortunate circumstance, that there is so little sense of unity, so striking a want of connection and harmony between the different stages of her history. To be impressionist is often to be incoherent, inconsequent, lacking all design and construction. But if you want to know what a modern novel is like, you have only to read *Jacob's Room*, by Virginia Woolf. In its tense, syncopated movements, its staccato impulsiveness, do you not discern the influence of Jazz?

UNSIGNED

Dissolving Views†

Those who, like the present writer, thought, after reading *Night and Day*,[1] that Mrs Woolf's next novel would be something of an event, must be prepared to find that *Jacob's Room* bears hardly any resemblance to its predecessor. Mrs Woolf has, indeed, discovered a somewhat new way of writing a novel—a way that is just a little like that developed by Mr James Joyce,[2] but far more detached and far more selective. The method, briefly, is snapshot photography, with a highly sensitive, perfected camera handled by an artist. The result is a crowded album of little pictures—of Jacob as a boy; of Jacob's mother and home at Scarborough; of Jacob at Cambridge (an admirable one, this, full of compressed but very significant and satisfying detail); of Jacob in London, and the women who fall in love with him there; of Jacob travelling in Greece, half in love himself now with the vaguely emotional Mrs Sandra Wentworth Williams; of

2. Dorothy Richardson (1821–1880), British novelist, author of the multivolume *Pilgrimage* (1915–67).
† Originally published in *Yorkshire Post* (November 29, 1922); reprinted from Robin Majumdar and Allen McLaurin, eds., *Virginia Woolf: The Critical Heritage* (London: Routledge, 1975), pp. 107–08. Notes are by the Editor.
1. 1919.
2. Irish novelist and short-story writer (1882–1941), author of *Ulysses* (1922).

Jacob's room, empty, being tidied by his friend Bonamy, after Jacob (we gather) has been killed in the war.

No one could question Mrs Woolf's great abilities as a writer. There are passages in this book, such as that describing Jacob and a Cambridge friend approaching the Scilly Isles[3] in a little sailing yacht, which contain nothing resembling a 'purple patch', and yet achieve a remarkably pure, lyrical beauty; there are many passages in which some impression—of London in summer, of a drawing-room conversation, of a character or a landscape—is seized and presented with admirable economy and truth. But all this seems to us no more than the material for a novel, and Mrs Woolf has done hardly anything to put it together. *Jacob's Room* has no narrative, no design, above all, no perspective: its dissolving views come before us one by one, each taking the full light for a moment, then vanishing completely. One remembers with regret the strong, harmonious structure of *Night and Day*; beside that *Jacob's Room*, beautiful as much of it is, seems flickering, impermanent. Nevertheless, if, as we think probable, Mrs Woolf has experienced a strong impulse to adopt this form, and no other, for her new novel, she is certainly doing right to obey: for she is, unlike most of her contemporaries, a genuine artist.

JOHN MIDDLETON MURRY

From Romance†

* * *

The most original minds among those of the younger generation who have chosen prose-fiction for their medium have seemed to care less and less for plot. Not even a desultory story attracts them. Character, atmosphere, an attitude to life, a quality of perception—these things have interested a D. H. Lawrence, a Katherine Mansfield,[1] a Virginia Woolf; but the old mechanism of story not at all. They represent a logical and necessary development of the realism of twenty years ago. Not one of them has solved the problem of the *novel*; neither did

---

3. Archipelago of islands about thirty miles off the coast of Cornwall.
† Originally published in *Nation and Athenaeum* (March 10, 1923); reprinted from Robin Majumdar and Allen McLaurin, eds., *Virginia Woolf: The Critical Heritage* (London: Routledge, 1975), pp. 109. Notes are by the Editor.
  John Middleton Murry: editor and critic (1889–1957), married to writer Katherine Mansfield.
1. British short-story writer (1888–1923), born in New Zealand; D. H. Lawrence: British novelist (1885–1930), author of *Women in Love* (1921).

Marcel Proust, nor has Mr Joyce or Miss Richardson[2] solved it. None
of them has really any use for a story. It is a kind of nursery-game
for them—at the best a trick; and they have more important things
to do than waste time playing tricks or learning how to play them.

The consequence is that the novel has reached a kind of *impasse*.
The artists have, to a very large extent, outrun their audience. Perhaps they have outrun themselves a little, too. At any rate, it seems
to be true that they have as yet achieved creative perfection only in
the short story. 'Prelude', 'Wintry Peacock', 'The Daughters of the
Late Colonel',[3] are things which will pass to immortality entire; of
the novels, probably no more than scraps. They lack constructive
solidity, they are fluid and fragmentary, brilliant and incoherent. And
the public still likes a story.

T. S. Eliot to Virginia Woolf, December 4, 1922†

The Criterion,
9 Clarence Gate Gardens,
London N.W.I

Dear Virginia,

*   *   *

I started to read *Jacob's Room* * * * and am now starting again
and I hope that I shall have time to read it thoroughly.* * *It
will not be a surprise to you to be told that it is a book which
requires very careful reading—I should say compels very careful
reading because there is a great deal of excitement in reading
it. I can only say so far it seems to me that you have really
accomplished what you set out to do in this book, and that you
have freed yourself from any compromise between the traditional novel and your original gift. It seems to me that you have
bridged a certain gap which existed between your other novels
and the experimental prose of *Monday or Tuesday* and that you
have made a remarkable success. But I hope that I shall have

2. Dorothy Richardson (1821–1880), British novelist, author of the multivolume *Pilgrimage*
   (1915–67); Marcel Proust: French novelist (1871–1922), author of *Á la recherche du
   temps perdu* (*In Search of Lost Time*) (1913–27); Mr. Joyce: James Joyce (1882–1941),
   Irish novelist and short-story writer, author of *Ulysses* (1922).
3. "Prelude" and "The Daughters of the Late Colonel" are short stories by Katherine Mansfield; "Wintry Peacock" is a short story by D. H. Lawrence.
† From *The Letters of T. S. Eliot*, ed. Valerie Eliot (New York: Harcourt Brace, 1988), I:
   606–07.
   T. S. Eliot: Thomas Stearns Eliot (1888–1965), poet and friend of Virginia Woolf,
   author of *The Waste Land* (1922).

more interesting and more detailed observations to make after
I consider that I have really mastered the book.

*   *   *

Yours always,
Tom.

MAXWELL BODENHEIM

Underneath the Paint in *Jacob's Room*†

The art of painting, on the whole, seems to be animated by a swifter
boldness than that of literature, and is less inclined to consolidate
its victories and to remain timidly within the conquered realm of
blended content and expression. The impressionists, headed by
Monet,[1] flourished in painting many decades ago, but the impressionists in English literature have only arrived during the past four
or five years. The recent revolts in literature—the Dadaists and
expressionists[2]—have attained more intensity and publicity than
numbers and influence, and have, after all, dominated only one-
hundredth of the output in contemporary literature, while the rebel-
lions in painting have gained a larger and more commanding
position. In addition, the work of cubist[3] painters has been far more
important than that of the literary Dadaists and has attained a greater
precision and sureness. On the whole, the art of painting has been
sturdier and less uncertain than its rival, the belated impressionist
school in literature.

Ironically enough, the founder of this method, Dorothy Richardson,[4] has been practically ignored, while her lesser imitators are rev-
eling in the praise of myopic critics, and among these imitators
Virginia Woolf flourishes. Her novel, *Jacob's Room*, is a rambling,
redundant affair, in which the commonplace details and motives of
ordinary people are divided and subdivided until they form a series

---

† Originally published in *Nation* (New York: March 28, 1923); reprinted from Robin Majumdar and Allen McLaurin, eds., *Virginia Woolf: The Critical Heritage* (London: Routledge,
  1975), pp. 110–11. Notes are by the Editor.
1. Claude Monet (1840–1926), French landscape painter, founder of impressionism.
2. Participants in an early twentieth-century movement in art and literature in which realism
   and naturalism are rejected to communicate a psychological or spiritual reality; Dadaists:
   proponents of "Dada" or "Dadaism," a nihilistic movement among European artists and
   writers that lasted from 1916 to 1922. Most Dadaist literature deliberately made no sense.
3. Participants in an early twentieth-century movement in art among painters such as Pablo
   Picasso and Georges Braque, in which the three-dimensional subject was fragmented and
   redefined within a shallow plane or within several interlocking planes.
4. British novelist (1821–1880), author of the multivolume *Pilgrimage* (1915–67).

of atoms, and the author's speculations upon these atoms have the volubility of conversation in a drawing-room. Mrs Woolf does not seem to believe that anything should be omitted, and lingers over the little, everyday motives and waking impulses of her undistinguished people, and the significance held by the hosts of inanimate objects which these people touch and see. The result is frequently an endless parade of details that grow more and more uninteresting, proceeding in an impulsive fashion and darting here and there with indefatigable minuteness.* * *

* * *'This is just like life', as one critic wrote in praise of *Jacob's Room*, but I do not approach the novel for a verbatim account of life and I am more intrigued by a condensation that displays only the salient items. There are too many moderately subtle stenographers in literature at present. *Jacob's Room* revolves jerkily around the figure of Jacob Flanders, from his boyhood to his death in the late World War, while still a young man. His groping for thoughts, emotions, and prejudices, and his occasional affairs with blithely shallow women, reveal him as an average young man, half pathetic and half ludicrous, but he is advanced with such a microscopical effusiveness and with so many irrelevant details that one is tempted to mutter: 'I see and meet at least fifty Jacob Flanders every month of my life, and if the introduction must be repeated it should hold a brevity and suggestiveness which these actual men do not possess.'

*   *   *

ARNOLD BENNETT

Is the Novel Decaying?†

If I have heard it once, I have heard fifty times during the past year the complaint that no young novelists with promise of first-rate importance are rising up to take the place of the important middle-aged. Upon this matter I have two lines of thought.

What makes a novel important enough to impress itself upon both the discriminating few and the less discriminating many? (For first-class prestige is not obtained unless both sorts of readers are in the end impressed.) The first thing is that the novel should seem to be true. It cannot seem true if the characters do not seem to be real.

† Originally published in *Cassell's Weekly* (March 28, 1923); reprinted from Robin Majumdar and Allen McLaurin, eds., *Virginia Woolf: The Critical Heritage* (London: Routledge, 1975), pp. 112–13.
    Arnold Bennett: author (1867–1931) of a series of realistic novels about the fictitious "Five Towns," an industrial region in the north of England.

Style counts; plot counts; invention counts; originality of outlook counts; wide information counts; wide sympathy counts. But none of these counts anything like so much as the convincingness of the characters. If the characters are real the novel will have a chance; if they are not oblivion will be its portion.

*   *   *

The foundation of good fiction is character creating, and nothing else. The characters must be so fully true that they possess even their own creator. Every deviation from truth, every omission of truth, necessarily impairs the emotional power and therefore weakens the interest.

I think that we have to-day a number of young novelists who display all manner of good qualities—originality of view, ingenuity of presentment, sound common sense, and even style. But they appear to me to be interested more in details than in the full creation of their individual characters. They are so busy with states of society as to half forget that any society consists of individuals, and they attach too much weight to cleverness, which is perhaps the lowest of all artistic qualities.

I have seldom read a cleverer book than Virginia Woolf's *Jacob's Room*, a novel which has made a great stir in a small world. It is packed and bursting with originality, and it is exquisitely written. But the characters do not vitally survive in the mind because the author has been obsessed by details of originality and cleverness. I regard this book as characteristic of the new novelists who have recently gained the attention of the alert and the curious, and I admit that for myself I cannot yet descry any coming big novelists.

*   *   *

CLIVE BELL

From Virginia Woolf†

For most of those even who had followed her career from the time when she first found editors not unwilling to give a chance to a girl who happened to be the daughter of Leslie Stephen,[1] most, I say,

---

† Originally published in *Dial* (December 1924); reprinted from Robin Majumdar and Allen McLaurin, eds., *Virginia Woolf: The Critical Heritage* (London: Routledge, 1975), pp. 138, 142–44, 146–47. Notes are by the Editor.

Clive Bell: art critic and journalist (1881–1964), married to Virginia Woolf's sister Vanessa.

1. Critic and man of letters (1832–1904), first editor of the *Dictionary of National Biography*, Virginia Woolf's father.

felt that, till the publication of *Jacob's Room*, she had never publicly proved what they had never doubted—that she possessed genius of a high order.* * *

*   *   *

Follow several short stories and sketches, brought together and published in 1921, under the title of *Monday or Tuesday*. This is Virginia Woolf practicing. Apparently, she herself was dissatisfied with *Night and Day* and felt the need of discovering an appropriate form. Hence, I presume, these experiments: of which one, 'A Society', is quite beneath her genius; and another, 'A Haunted House', in style at any rate, seems to me unfortunately redolent of contemporary influences.* * * She is in search of a form in which to express a vision—a vision of which she is now perfectly sure. That is the problem of which *Jacob's Room* is the brilliantly successful solution; but before attempting to analyse the solution I had better try to formulate, what so far I seem only to have fumbled, my notion, that is, of the vision to be expressed.

What makes Virginia Woolf's books read queerly is that they have at once the air of high fantasticality and blazing realism. And the explanation of this is, unless I mistake, that, though she is externalizing a vision and not making a map of life, the vision is anything but visionary in the vulgar sense of the word. Her world is not a dream world; she sees, and sees acutely, what the reviewer in a hurry calls 'the real world'.* * * It is a perfectly comprehensible world in which no one has the least difficulty in believing; only she sees it through coloured, or I had rather say oddly cut, glasses. Or is it we who see it through stained glass—glass stained with our ruling passions? That is a question I shall not attempt to decide. Only let me give one example of the difference between her vision and ours. When we—most of us I should say—see a pair of lovers sitting on a seat we feel—if we feel anything worth writing about—not purely the romance of the scene, or of the situation even: to some extent we share the feelings of the lovers. Our emotion, I mean, is not purely aesthetic; it is sympathetic in the strictest sense of the term. And it is because we to some extent share the excitement of the actors that, more often than not, we miss the full aesthetic import of the drama. We fail to feel some things because we feel others too much. Now Mrs Woolf sees more purely or, if you will, less passionately. At all events her emotion is not in the least self-regarding. She watches life, as it were through a cool sheet of glass: let those who dare, call the glass distorting. She knows what the lovers are saying; she knows (not feels) what they are feeling; she misses not one subtle, betraying, gesture. Assuredly, she feels the romance of the situation, but she does not share the romantic feelings of the actors.

No one could be more conscious of the romance of life. Open a book of hers almost anywhere and catch her expressing a vision of the country or, better still, of the town: not Flaubert, in that famous scene in *L'Education Sentimentale*,[2] gives a stronger sense of the romance and excitingness of a great city than Mrs Woolf has given in half a dozen descriptions of London. But when Jacob and Florinda are together in the bedroom, and when Jacob walks out 'in his dressing-gown, amiable, authoritative, beautifully healthy, like a baby after an airing,' and Florinda follows 'lazily stretching, yawning a little, arranging her hair in the looking-glass,' we have not had the thrill we couldn't help expecting: we have not been given a love scene as we understand it. Nothing of much consequence, we feel, has been going on behind that door; or rather, something of consequence only in relation to Mrs Flanders' letter which is lying on the table. Nor is this surprising when we reflect that it was not the love affair, but the effect of the love affair, which really interested Mrs Woolf. What was going on in the bedroom caught her imagination not as an end, but as a means. And though it is a particular Jacob and a particular Florinda that she sees, acutely, beautifully, through her wall of glass, it is in relation to a comic, poignant, familiar little tragedy, which beginning in Scarborough spreads round the world, that she sees them.

Take two other love-scenes from *Jacob's Room*—one happy, the other pathetic: Clara Durrant picking grapes and dimly realizing that she is in love with Jacob; Clara Durrant walking in the park with kind Mr Bowley and realizing that Jacob is not in love with her. Each is all over in a page or so—large print too: in the first there is more lyricism than a nineteenth century poet would have got into a hundred stanzas; and an eighteenth century novelist would have allowed himself half a volume at least to give a less devastating picture of a broken heart. Both are scenes of affecting beauty—I use these two grave words as seriously as it is possible for a notoriously frivolous person to use them: neither is passionate. Both are seen with unsurpassable precision; both are rendered by means of touch and elimination attainable only by an artist of genius; both give a vision—I use the word again and advisedly—of someone feeling intensely; but the feeling which the artist has observed and expressed she has not shared. Also, if I understand her art aright, she does not intend us to share it: she intends us to appreciate, to admire. Her emotion comes from her sense of the scene, and ours from reacting to that sense. This pure, this almost painterlike vision is Virginia Woolf's peculiarity: it is what distinguishes her from all her contemporaries.

2. Novel published in 1870 by French writer Gustave Flaubert (1821–1880), author of *Madame Bovary* (1856). A number of detailed Paris street scenes are scattered throughout the novel.

* * *

It is not quite true to say that the form Mrs Woolf discovered for herself and employed in *Jacob's Room* was a development of 'The Mark on the Wall'. That form contained admirably well a single vision, complete in itself; what she now needed was a form to match that series of visions, glimpses and glances, stunning crashes and faint echoes, fainter perfumes and pungent stinks, which we, God forgive us, are pleased to call life. . . . 'Who saw life steadily, and saw it whole.'

Well, Mrs Woolf is not Sophocles, nor Matthew Arnold[3] either; so she wanted something to hold together in a unity her series of fragmentary revelations, glimpses, glances, and scraps of glances: she wanted a thread that could be cut and knotted at both ends. Obviously, the only principle of unity in her kaleidoscopic experience was her own personality, and no great wizardry is needed to see that an equivalent for this in a work of imagination would be an imagined personality—a hero in fact. The question was, how to establish an equivalence between the various and disinterested aesthetic experience of a contemplative artist and the early life and adventures of a kinetic, not to say strapping, young gentleman. Her solution is charming and ingenious. The hero is gradually to be built up out of other people's reactions to him: other people's reactions and, I must be allowed to add the reactions—if reactions are what they have— of places. We are gradually to infer the character of the cause from the nature of its effects on persons, places, and things. Here is impressionism with a vengeance: if the technique consisted in 'little touches', the composition is a matter of 'frank oppositions' and the whole will dawn on us only when the last harmony is established.

Jacob's character, Jacob's temperament, Jacob's way, Jacob's personal appearance, Jacob in fact, must always be present to hold together the bright fragments which are the author's sense of life— not of Jacob's life, but of the life in which Jacob moves. We shall find him first an active ingredient in his mother's world, then conditioning a scene or two at Cambridge, a source of feeling and speculation in a country house, in what the Sunday papers call 'Bohemia', in the hearts of men and women, in London, Paris, and Athens. And all the while Jacob is not merely affecting, he is being affected: reverse the engines, the principle of unity works just as well. Jacob is growing up, Jacob is being revealed: the men and women who love or are loved play their parts; Cambridge, Cornwall, London, Paris, and Athens play theirs; the trains, the taxicabs, the omnibuses, the changes of season, St Paul's Cathedral, jute-merchants, charwomen,

---

3. British poet and critic (1822–1888), author of *Culture and Anarchy* (1869); Sophocles: ancient Greek tragedian (496–406 B.C.E.), author of *Oedipus Rex* and other works.

the crowds crossing Waterloo Bridge, all add their quota to that vision of the young man who for one second stands revealed before he vanishes in the war for ever. Down he goes; leaving a pair of shoes to wring the hearts of a man and woman as they rummage in the characteristic disorder of Jacob's room.

The form which Mrs Woolf evolved in *Jacob's Room* gave her a freedom she had not enjoyed in either of her preceding novels. The coherence of the work is assured by the fact that the author cannot leave go of the thread without losing interest in her theme. Jacob is the sole theme; and since Jacob is to be built up gradually and so revealed, however discursive she may be in giving her sense of his surroundings she dare not cease to be for ever looking to the beginning and the end. And the reader too feels that he must keep tight hold; for in the pieces given he knows that he must see the whole, and the pieces will not be given twice. Yet, for the author, compared with the difficulties of such a novel as *Night and Day* (the difficulty of keeping each thread on a separate finger and weaving all together at the appointed moment) the difficulty of grasping this one thread firmly is child's play. For there is but one thread; and since she has no fear of losing it, she can venture to explore every corner of her vision. Anywhere, on anything, Jacob can leave his mark and so relate it to the whole. Best of all, so pervasive is the hero's temperament, so wide the sphere of his influence, and so easily can he be kept moving towards his goal—which is our enlightenment—that Mrs Woolf cannot only fly to the ends of her vision and back again, but, without stepping outside the charmed circle of an artistic unity, can, from time to time, hush the instruments of her orchestra to make, in her own voice, her own cool, humorous comment. She has found a form in which to be completely herself.

Literary Criticism

JUDY LITTLE

Jacob's Room as Comedy:
Woolf's Parodic *Bildungsroman*†

Early readers of *Jacob's Room* responded to the book's comic elements as well as to its pathos; modern critics, on the other hand, concentrate on the form, and usually comment also on the sad absurdity of Jacob's life, a life cut off prematurely by the First World War. The comedy is of primary importance, however, and it is closely linked to the book's form and to Jacob's 'character', sketchy as his character may seem to be. The novel is in some ways a parody, and many of its peculiarities in form, point of view and characterisation are linked to the parodic impulse. The comedy and the 'form' of *Jacob's Room* derive partly from a strategy of literary attack. The form shows very clearly the marks of its being a playful yet serious rebellion; it is held together by the shadowy structure of the very thing it is against: the *Bildungsroman*.

The parodic mocking of the form generates some mocking of subject as well. The *Bildungsroman*, when it concerns a capable Edwardian male, must deal in part with the hero's experience of British institutions of higher learning, for instance. In *Jacob's Room* the traditional male growth-pattern, full of great expectation, falls like a tattered mantle around the shoulders of the indecisive hero, heir of the ages. The musing and amused narrator mocks the structure of her story; she mocks the conventions of the hero's progress; and, by implication, she mocks the values behind those conventions. In this way, a very mild, even cheerful, feminism often coincides with the narrator's playful wrenching of traditional patterns.

Certainly Virginia Woolf wanted no more than the shadow of a structure in her third novel; she aimed for a 'looseness and lightness', a form with no 'scaffolding': 'Scarcely a brick to be seen; all crepuscular, but the heart, the passion, humour, everything as bright as

† From *New Feminist Essays on Virginia Woolf*, ed. Jane Marcus (Lincoln: University of Nebraska Press, 1981), pp. 105–24. Reprinted by permission of the publisher.

fire in the mist. Then I'll find room for so much—a gaiety—an inconsequence—a light spirited stepping at my sweet will.'¹ If the form is
right, she will find room for everything she wants to put in, including
humour, gaiety, inconsequence. Among those who have criticised
the result, however, is Virginia Woolf herself. In October 1922, after
the publication of *Jacob's Room*, she wrote, 'I expect I could have
screwed *Jacob* up tighter, if I had foreseen; but I had to make my
path as I went.'² The book's peculiarities of characterisation and its
patchwork design have often come in for criticism.³ The greatest
artistic liability, according to most critics, is the inconsistency on the
part of the narrator; she sometimes disclaims omniscience, especially
with regard to Jacob, and at other times readily assumes it, even
giving us Jacob's feelings and thoughts on occasion.⁴ Awkward and
arbitrary as this shifting in and out of omniscience may seem, it
contributes considerably to the 'humour' and 'gaiety' which the
author hoped to incorporate into the work. Clive Bell was perhaps
responding to these qualities when he praised the narrator's 'cool,
humorous comment'. Likewise an early reviewer admired the narrator's 'subtle, slyly mocking, and yet poignant vision'. This reviewer
wrote also of 'the delicious humour which infects every page'.⁵ The
'humorous comment', and especially the 'mocking, and yet poignant
vision', often hinge on a radically unconventional switch in perspective, an omniscient narrator suddenly telling us the ironic truth after
another narrator—or the same one—has been merely guessing at
Jacob's words or thoughts. At other times the movement seems to
be in the opposite direction; the narrator pretends to be the omniscient author of a *Bildungsroman*, and then teases the reader—and
the form—by asserting that 'it is no use trying to sum people up'.⁶

The *Bildungsroman* was an extremely popular form in the nineteenth and early twentieth centuries,⁷ and parody was overdue; actu-

1. Virginia Woolf, *A Writer's Diary*, ed. Leonard Woolf (London: Hogarth Press, 1975) p. 23.
2. Ibid., p. 54.
3. An early reviewer calls *Jacob's Room* a 'rag-bag of impressions' (*New Age*, 21 Dec 1922,
   p. 123); see in *Virginia Woolf: The Critical Heritage*, ed. Robin Majumdar and Allen
   McLaurin (London and Boston, Mass.: Routledge & Kegan Paul, 1975) p. 108. The rapid
   transitions, according to James Hafley, often contribute to a sense of structural incoher-
   ence; see *The Glass Roof: Virginia Woolf as Novelist* (New York: Russell and Russell, 1963)
   pp. 58–9. J. K. Johnstone criticises the lack of inevitable links among the episodes; see
   The Bloomsbury Group (London: Secker & Warburg, 1954) p. 328.
4. See esp. Hafley, *The Glass Roof*, pp. 52, 53, 55; and Nancy Topping Bazin, *Virginia Woolf
   and the Androgynous Vision* (New Brunswick, NJ: Rutgers University Press, 1973) p. 98.
5. Clive Bell, 'Virginia Woolf' (*Dial*, Dec 1924, pp. 451–65) in *Virginia Woolf: The Critical
   Heritage*, p. 147; A. S. McDowall (unsigned review, *Times Literary Supplement*, 26 Oct
   1922, p. 683) in *Virginia Woolf: The Critical Heritage*, pp. 96–7. Winifred Holtby also
   praises the comedy in *Jacob's Room*, especially the portraits of eccentric scholars; see
   Virginia Woolf (1932; repr. Folcroft, Penn.: Folcroft Press, 1969) pp. 123–4.
6. Virginia Woolf, *Jacob's Room* (London: Hogarth Press, 1971) p. 153 [123]. Page references in the text are to this edition. [Bracketed page numbers refer to this Norton Critical
   Edition.]
7. For a discussion of the form and its rise in popularity, see J. H. Buckley, *Season of Youth:*

ally, there had been a few parodies, or semi-parodies, and Woolf had
read them, among many other specimens of this genre. Meredith, for
instance, was one of her favourite writers;[8] his *Bildungsromane* tend
to be comic, certain elements of the convention often being violated
or mocked. His *Evan Harrington* and *Harry Richmond* are comic *Bildungsromane*. In *Richard Feveral*, Richard's father, Sir Austin, keeps
a notebook in which he plans the phases of his son's life, labelling
them 'The Blooming Season', 'The Magnetic Age', and so on. Sir Austin's notebook reads like the chapter titles of a *Bildungsroman*, as
J. H. Buckley points out.[9] Austin Feveral's plans backfire, and his
effort to write the script for his son's life—to 'sum him up', as Woolf
might say—represents a cruel parody of what could have been a real
life; Richard becomes confused and hardened by his father's rigid
expectations, and manages a rebellion that wrecks his own life.

In 1918 and 1919 Virginia Woolf reviewed *Bildungsromane* of
Compton Mackenzie, H. G. Wells and Dorothy Richardson. Particularly interesting are her remarks about the satirically drawn characters in Wells's novel *Joan and Peter*. Peter's father, an aunt, a
schoolmistress, are characters whose motives and actions are too pat
and mechanical to be quite believable; they are 'burlesques' rather
than characters, and Woolf finds them contributing to the 'crudeness
of the satire', which yet by its crudeness convinces the reader of the
author's honest anger.[1] Woolf's review is largely devoted to an analysis of these peculiar characters and to the attitude of social criticism
which made the author create them.

In a review of *Limbo*, an early collection of Aldous Huxley's short
stories, Woolf again gives special attention to the opportunities and
to the dangers of satire. She censures Huxley for being too obviously
clever, and she feels that his range is limited; if asked to talk about
something he believes in, she asserts, he could only stammer. And
yet she likes his 'Farcical History of Richard Greenow' well enough

---

The Bildungsroman from Dickens to Golding (Cambridge, Mass.: Harvard University Press,
1974) pp. 1–22; and William C. Frierson, *The English Novel in Transition, 1885–1940*
(Norman: University of Oklahoma Press, 1942) pp. 193–210.

8. Quentin Bell sees Meredith as primarily an early influence in *Virginia Woolf: A Biography*
(New York: Harcourt, Brace, Jovanovich, 1972) vol. I, p. 138. Woolf discusses Meredith
in several essays. In 'Hours in a Library' (1916), she lists the books that a person would
have read by the age of twenty; the list includes 'the whole of Meredith'. See *Collected
Essays* (London: Hogarth Press, 1972) vol. II, p. 35.

9. Buckley, *Season of Youth*, p. 64.

1. Virginia Woolf, 'The Rights of Youth', a review of H. G. Wells, *Joan and Peter* (*Times
Literary Supplement*, 19 Sep 1918), in Woolf, *Contemporary Writers* (London: Hogarth
Press, 1965) pp. 90–3. See also her reviews of Mackenzie's books *The Early Life and
Adventures of Sylvia Scarlett* (*Times Literary Supplement*, 29 Aug 1918) and *Sylvia and
Michael* (*Times Literary Supplement*, 20 Mar 1919) in *Contemporary Writers*, pp. 82–6.
She finds Mackenzie's Sylvia too thinly characterised and the action too swift. Woolf
stands by Richardson's refusal to use realism, but does not feel that Richardson has mas-
tered her method yet; see Woolf, 'The Tunnel', a review of Dorothy Richardson *The Tunnel*
(*Times Literary Supplement*, 13 Feb 1919) in *Contemporary Writers*, pp. 120–2.

to quote it at some length. This story is a raucously parodic *Bildungsroman*, giving us the early life, education and grotesque failure of Richard. His great discovery is that he is a 'hermaphrodite', and his true vocation—writing novels—is carried on by his second self, 'Pearl Bellairs'. He conscientiously objects to the World War, and he dies in an insane asylum. Woolf is especially amused by Huxley's portrait of a 'fellow of Canteloup', Canteloup being a college of Oxford. She quotes a passage in which Huxley juxtaposes the scholar's 'dazzling academic career' with his furrowed face, sloppy eating habits ('his clothes were disgusting with the spilth of many years of dirty feeding') and incessant talking.[2] Huxley's portrait of the Oxford scholar is more sordid than Woolf's satiric sketches of dons in *Jacob's Room*, but the purpose in each case is the same: the educators of the young are seen as ludicrously inadequate. Woolf gives us 'poor old Huxtable', who cannot walk straight, who changes clothes as mechanically as clockwork, who is miserly and priestly. Sopwith, also priestly, is an incessant talker; he is respected, but with growing ambiguity by his one-time undergraduates as they reach a more mature judgement. And Cowan, Virgil's image, or the nearest Cambridge can come to this, is gluttonous and self-indulgent (pp. 37–40) [29–31].

After quoting Huxley's portrait of a scholar, Woolf continues her discussion:

> There is an equally amusing description of a dinner with the Headmaster of Aesop and Mrs Crawister, a lady of 'swelling port' and unexpected utterance, who talks to the bewildered boys now about eschatology, now about Manx cats ('No tails, no tails, like men. How symbolical everything is!'), now about the unhappy fate of the carrion crow, who mates for life.[3]

Jacob, like Richard Greenow, must sit through a painful meal given by a scholar, Mr Plumer; his wife, like Richard's hostess, is a lady of 'unexpected utterance', her conversation calling a halt to social intercourse rather than facilitating it. Groaning, Jacob leaves the house after this introduction to the suffocating banalities which the world seeks to impose on him (pp. 31–4) [24–26].

Jacob, however, is 'obstinate'; at least, this is his mother's interpretation of the fact that he does not conform to her notion of obedience (pp. 9, 21) [6, 16]. Jacob and the world do not fit each other; he cannot conform to expectations. This basic quality of his mysterious personality is symbolised in the form of the novel—the

---

2. Virginia Woolf, 'Cleverness and Youth', a review of Aldous Huxley, *Limbo* (*Times Literary Supplement*, 5 Feb 1920) in *Contemporary Writers*, p. 150; and see Huxley, 'Farcical History of Richard Greenow', in *Limbo* (London: Chatto & Windus, 1946) pp. 40–1.
3. Woolf, review of *Limbo*, in *Contemporary Writers*, p. 150. See in *Limbo*, pp. 13–22.

pat elements of the *Bildungsroman* structure are one by one introduced, and one by one tossed away as irrelevant. Avrom Fleishman
has said that *Jacob's Room* extends 'the *Bildungsroman* form into a
fitful sequence of unachieved experiences rather than a coherent
process', and J. H. Buckley suggests that *Jacob's Room* may be 'potentially a Bildungsroman'.[4] But Woolf's novel is not an effort to extend
the *Bildungsroman*; it is, among other things, an attack on this form.
It attacks the notion that a conventionalised fictional 'summing up'
can fit a real life, or that a young Englishman's storybook socialisa-
tion is anything but a burlesque of his real stumblings toward self-
discovery. Rather than being a potential *Bildungsroman*, *Jacob's
Room* is a light-heartedly decadent one. It seems almost as though
Virginia Woolf deliberately chose the traditions of the *Bildungsroman* in order to play havoc with them.

All of the traditional elements are in the novel, but Jacob walks
through his story as though he does not see the traditions. He is an
orphan, or partly an orphan, because his father has died; but nothing
Dickensian is ever made of this, Jacob being neither better nor worse
for the fact. He moves, as a young man, from the provinces to London, but the narrator mines no moral riches out of this circumstance.
Tom Jones and Pip would have gone badly to seed, and would have
emerged with a greater knowledge of humanity and of themselves.
But Jacob is not corrupted, and his move to the city is not made into
one of the signposts of the novel. Jacob's education is something that
barely happens to him, yet all the scenery is there—all the scenery
for the awakening of his mind and for his rebelling against stodgy
traditions. Finally, Jacob, unlike the typical *Bildungsroman* hero,
receives no revelation, no 'epiphany'. Yet opportunity after opportunity is supplied by the author; she deliberately makes Jacob look
the other way, or she mocks the offered moment. Virginia Woolf
drags in all the *Bildungsroman* scenery; then she lets Jacob walk
aimlessly about, as though the stage were bare. The effect is a
remarkable tension that gives fictional embodiment to the pathos,
and comedy, of Jacob's life—a life which becomes emblematic of all
lives to the extent that they do not fit expected patterns, and instead
obstinately resist a 'summing up'.

No one takes charge of Jacob's education. There is no Helen
Ambrose in this story, as there was in Woolf's first, and more or less
conventional, *Bildungsroman*. There is no Uncle Oswald, as there is
in Wells's novel, back from Africa just in time to salvage from other
relatives the education of Joan and Peter. Certainly no one goes to
the lengths that Austin Feveral goes, keeping a notebook, and giving

4. Avrom Fleishman, *Virginia Woolf: A Critical Reading* (Baltimore: Johns Hopkins University Press, 1975) p. 46; Buckley, *Season of Youth*, p. 263.

labels to the stages of his son's growth. No one cares enough about
Jacob's development either to help or to hinder him. There is, however, Mr Floyd, whose proposal of marriage Mrs Flanders rejects,
and who teaches Latin to her boys. When he leaves the village he
lets the boys choose a gift from him, and Jacob chooses the works
of Byron (p. 19) [14]. In any other *Bildungsroman*, and indeed in
any of Woolf's other novels, such a gesture would cast ripples over
the hero's future. And Byron is mentioned again; Byron, the sea, the
lighthouse, the sheep's jaw, are mentioned by the narrator as belonging to the 'obstinate irrepressible conviction' which gives youth its
sense of identity (p. 34) [26]. Late in the novel Mr Floyd sees Jacob
in London, and at first does not recognise him; Mr Floyd recalls, as
though the recollection proves irrelevant to his present observation
of Jacob, that the young man had once accepted the works of Byron
from him (pp. 173–4) [141]. But is Jacob Byronic? Is there even any
irony in his lack of Byronism? He has many love affairs, he travels
in Europe; he tries to write, but his essay is rejected. He seems to
respond to nature, and yet, it is really the narrator whom a landscape
moves to lyrical utterance. Jacob is generally happier than Byron,
and Jacob's passions and his travels do not issue into imaginative
responses to doges and bridges. When Jacob meets Sandra Wentworth Williams, he suffers from his desire, but he suffers pitifully
and simply; he writes no impassioned poems.

Jacob's selection of a book from among his early tutor's volumes
proves to be no special signal to his character. Nor does his university
experience assume the importance of a solemn milestone. Moved on
some occasions to a fleeting appreciation of the atmosphere of Cambridge, Jacob must also tolerate caricature dons and oppressive
luncheons. The comedy of some of the Cambridge episodes may
indeed be, as Aileen Pippett suggested, Woolf's 'mocking revenge
upon the ancient institutions where she was never able to study'.[5] A
few years later, in *A Room of One's Own*, Woolf does certainly build
some uncomfortable comedy out of the alarmed gentleman in the
fluttering black gown who denies a woman entrance to the library at
'Oxbridge'. Women are 'locked out', denied access not only to the
library, but to the entire centuries-old tradition of knowledge and of
intellectual training. And yet, Woolf goes on to observe, this circumstance may not be as dangerous as being 'locked in' to the same
tradition.[6] The narrator of *Jacob's Room* is similarly outside the male
institutions through which she moves the hero. Even the hero,
though sometimes stirred by his college experience, is oddly untrans-

---

5. Aileen Pippett, *The Moth and the Star: A Biography of Virginia Woolf* (Boston, Mass.:
   Little, Brown, 1953) pp. 150–1.
6. Virginia Woolf, *A Room of One's Own* (New York: Harcourt, Brace and World, 1957)
   pp. 7–8, 24.

formed by it. He too is somewhat on the outside. The narrator refuses
to let him be quite 'locked in'—either by the institution or by the
fiction pattern to which a well-brought-up male character usually
conforms. Jacob's education neither crushes him nor ennobles him;
it perhaps has not very much to do with him. Unlike Stephen Dedalus, Jacob apparently develops no potent and complex theory of art
or philosophy. Nor does he meet a G. E. Moore.

   To Jacob, Cambridge offers Huxtable, Sopwith and Cowan, who
are figures of inadequacy—inadequacy rather than destructiveness.
These scholars do not display the thin-lipped, rigidly restrained asce-
ticism of the priests in *A Portrait of the Artist as a Young Man*, for
instance. We are not made to feel that Jacob must escape from the
Huxtables and Sopwiths or risk injury to his soul. Jacob's orientation
is not religious, so there is no solemn moment during which someone
approaches him about a possible vocation; yet the narrator points to
the possibility, perhaps the necessity, of Jacob's making some kind
of life choice. Just after the painful luncheon given by Mr Plumer,
the narrator speaks of the shock, to a person of about twenty, which
the world makes as it begins to oppose 'the obstinate irrepressible
conviction which makes youth so intolerably disagreeable—"I am
what I am, and intend to be it", for which there will be no form in
the world unless Jacob makes one for himself. The Plumers will try
to prevent him from making it' (p. 34) [26]. There will be no form
for his life—no shape for the irrepressible conviction of identity—
unless Jacob makes the form. But does Jacob choose at all? In his
passivity and lack of initiative he resembles another Jacob, the hero
of Beresford's novel *The Early History of Jacob Stahl* (1911). His
relatives want Jacob Stahl to choose a profession, and they particularly suggest the taking of Holy Orders. Jacob resists, because 'he
had a full share of obstinacy if he lacked determination—his powers
of resistance were greater than his capacity for initiative'.[7] Similarly
Jacob Flanders, although he too is obstinate, lacks 'determination'.
He neither embraces, nor rebels strenuously against, any aspect of
his education.

   Both the narrator and Jacob have a casual though sensuous attitude towards intellectual endeavour; both seem to take lightly the
notion of Jacob's being the heir of the ages. Beresford, on the other
hand, fluffs his prose into a brief rhapsody while he contemplates

---

7. J. D. Beresford, *The Early History of Jacob Stahl* (Boston, Mass.: Little, Brown, 1911) p. 55.
    In a review of Beresford's later novel *Revolution* (*Times Literary Supplement*, 27 Jan 1921),
    Woolf mentions his trilogy dealing with Jacob Stahl; she praises Beresford's earlier novels,
    including *Jacob Stahl*, as 'very memorable'. See Woolf, *Contemporary Writers*, pp. 155–6.
    The two Jacobs are alike in their passivity, their obstinacy, their reluctance to take a
    definite course of action, and their painful love relationships. In other respects Woolf's
    Jacob shows little resemblance to Beresford's. Another namesake is the biblical Jacob, as
    Manly Johnson argues in *Virginia Woolf* (New York: R. Ungar, 1973) pp. 44–5.

Jacob Stahl as the 'heir of the ages!' He describes the stars cooling
and contracting, until at last their energy becomes Jacob.[8] With
somewhat more energy H. G. Wells, writing of the war's effect on
young people, loads with irony the idea of inheritance. After Peter
is badly wounded, his guardian Oswald reflects bitterly on the way
the world has treated its 'heir'.[9] Wells's Peter and Woolf's Jacob are
brutally deceived heirs, but the narrator in Wells's novel provides
voluminous hortatory comment on the failures of British education
and on the need for the young heirs to rebuild their world. In *Jacob's
Room*, however, neither Jacob nor the narrator reaps any edification
out of the notion of inherited responsibilities or opportunities. As
Jacob comes to the window of his friend Simeon's room, the narrator
observes his face; he looks satisfied,

> indeed masterly; which expression changed slightly as he stood
> there, the sound of the clock conveying to him (it may be) a
> sense of old buildings and time; and himself the inheritor; and
> then to-morrow; and friends; at the thought of whom, in sheer
> confidence and pleasure, it seemed, he yawned and stretched
> himself. (p. 43) [34]

The narrator offers only tentative interpretations here, but Jacob's
actions are described without ambiguity. He looked satisfied, masterly; he yawned and stretched. The notion of his being 'an inheritor'
is very much underplayed; here there is none of the earnestness of
Wells or Beresford behind the idea. For this heir the notion does not
carry with it any Victorian moral urgency, or even the mildly reform-
ist moral energy of the Edwardian era.[1]

The two undergraduates continue their discussion, and one of
them mentions 'Julian the Apostate'. The narrator is more interested
in the lyric atmosphere of midnight and wind than she is in observing
which man spoke the phrase. Nevertheless, she definitely asserts that
Simeon is the one who says, 'Somehow it seems to matter.' Of the
two, he is evidently the more interested in the philosophical ramifi-
cations of the emperor's backsliding. Jacob says, 'Well, you seem to
have studied the subject.' Then something in both Jacob's consciousness and that of the narrator experiences the pleasure and intimacy
which pervade the room following this intellectual discussion:

> He appeared extraordinarily happy, as if his pleasure would brim
> and spill down the sides if Simeon spoke.

8. Beresford, *Jacob Stahl*, pp. 321–3.
9. H. G. Wells, *Joan and Peter: The Story of an Education* (New York: Macmillan, 1918)
   pp. 19, 549.
1. Prewar reformers urged society to make minor adjustments but to maintain essentially the
   same structure; as George Dangerfield phrased it, 'reform' at this time meant 'a passionate
   desire to preserve, by improvement, the shape of things as they were'; quoted by Frierson
   in *The English Novel in Transition*, pp. 143–4.

Simeon said nothing. Jacob remained standing. But intimacy—the room was full of it, still, deep, like a pool. Without
need of movement or speech it rose softly and washed over
everything, mollifying, kindling, and coating the mind with the
lustre of pearl, so that if you talk of a light, of Cambridge burning, it's not languages only. It's Julian the Apostate. (p. 44) [35]

A discussion that might have been the springboard for Jacob's *non
serviam*, or for his defining of a 'form' for his life, is instead enjoyed
as a sensuous event—by Jacob and by the narrator. Jacob arrives at
no great sense of purpose and identity, as Stephen Dedalus does in
his lengthy deliberations with Cranly. Jacob *enjoys* his mind and the
ideas that he 'inherits' from the past; he does not do anything so
practical as tie together his own ego with them.

A later image suggests that the heritage of the ages is to Jacob a
neutral pleasure, something to be enjoyed rather than shouldered
and carried onward as part of the white man's burden. After leaving
Florinda at the Guy Fawkes party, Jacob and Timmy are in high
spirits, quoting Greek and feeling generally exuberant: 'They were
boastful, triumphant; it seemed to both that they had read every book
in the world; known every sin, passion, and joy. Civilizations stood
round them like flowers ready for picking. Ages lapped at their feet
like waves fit for sailing' (p. 74) [59]. For Jacob, intellectual conversation is valuable because it creates intimacy between friends. Ages
lap at his feet, beckoning this Cambridge sportsman to a pleasant
pastime of sailing. His sense of being an heir is linked, in his own
mind, to the fact that Florinda called him by his first name, and sat
on his knee. 'Thus did all good women in the days of the Greeks'
(p. 75) [60]. Jacob here stereotypes both Greece and Florinda. Like
the female statues of the Erechtheum, Florinda is pedestalled, a feminine prop for the structure of ancient civilisation as envisioned by
Jacob Flanders. This recent Cambridge graduate, unlike the narrator, is only too ready to sum people up—especially women, and especially 'the Greeks'. The comedy of this section is so generously
sympathetic that it is hardly even ironic. The hilarity is carried further some time later when Jacob sees Florinda 'turning up Greek
Street upon another man's arm' (p. 93) [74].

This does not mean that Jacob never has a serious thought. He
and his Cambridge friends do engage in cerebral manoeuvres, but
the hint of youthful discovery or youthful rebellion is immediately
ploughed under by a context of shared laughter and sensuous enjoy-
ment. The narrator's frequent shifts of distance contribute much to
the short duration of any philosophical or rebellious musings. Moving back a little, she suggests that the story may be following a typical
Bildungsroman pattern; she hints that Bonamy or Jacob may be
resenting the fact of Keats's early death—perhaps her characters are

about to raise clenched fists against God or the nature of things. But no, she moves in closer, and without any hedging tells us that Jacob, 'who sat astride a chair and ate dates from a long box, burst out laughing' (p. 42) [33].

True, this method of narration, this inconsistency with regard to distance, is perhaps confusing. I am not sure that it is necessarily an ineffective approach, however. Hafley is right when he says that, while one narrator insists on the impossibility of knowing Jacob, another narrator does a good job of disproving this by moving easily into the minds of other characters.[2] There are in a sense two narrators, or one narrator who insists on giving us a twofold vision of Jacob, a vision that shows the conventional pattern which he 'should' follow, and almost simultaneously points out that he is not following the pattern. This method is an extended version of what Woolf does in 'An Unwritten Novel'. There, a 'narrator' within the narrator's head invents an elaborate story about a woman who happens to ride opposite in a train; the narrator calls her 'Minnie Marsh'. But, when the unknown woman leaves the train, the frame narrator must admit that the supposed 'Minnie' really seems happier and more at ease in the world than the storymaking imagination had envisioned. The frame narrator has to admit the mystery which results from the discrepancy between the two portraits—the imaginary one and the one revealed briefly and incompletely by the facts. A similar double narrator prevails in *Jacob's Room*. She is continually sketching the novelistic pattern that growing youths are 'supposed' to follow; then she suddenly provides a close-up of Jacob eating dates or finding in the cheap Florinda the emblem of all things Greek. The effect is comic, and serves often as a parodic gesture in which novels, and other conventional 'plots' in people's minds, are shown to be false.

Even Jacob's mildly rebellious gestures are mocked. He drafts an essay against the prudery of an editor's bowdlerised Wycherly, and Bonamy praises it. But, although Jacob goes through all the *Bildungsroman* motions on this occasion, the event becomes a parodic rather than a real instance of rebellion:

> An outrage, Jacob said; a breach of faith; sheer prudery; token of a lewd mind and a disgusting nature. Aristophanes and Shakespeare were cited. Modern life was repudiated. Great play was made with the professional title, and Leeds as a seat of learning was laughed to scorn. And the extraordinary thing was that these young men were perfectly right—extraordinary, because, even as Jacob copied his pages, he knew that no one would ever print them. . . . (p. 68) [54]

2. Hafley, *The Glass Roof*, p. 52.

The style here completely demolishes any moral significance which the scene might have had if it had been approached in a more realistic manner, one that used dialogue and allowed us to overhear Jacob's thoughts in this moment of ethical triumph. Instead the passage reads like a list of items which every good novelist should include while narrating the hero's discovery of his own ethic—repudiate 'modern life', make 'great play' with the 'professional title', laugh at the 'seat of learning'. The distance, and the generalities which contribute to the distance, make the scene a parody of a moment of insight and self-assertion.

When the essay is returned from several journals, Jacob throws it in a special box. 'The lid shut upon the truth' (p. 69) [54]. In one sense, the closed lid represents Jacob's refusal to face the evidently mediocre statement which he made of his idea; he passively accepts the failure. In another sense the 'truth' is in the essay and in the perception of these young men, as the narrator suggests. Society closes the lid on Jacob's protest, but he did not protest really vigorously. Jacob does not pursue further this minor challenge to things as they are; it does not become an important event on which his development hinges.

Nor does Jacob's development hinge upon love or sex. This conventional item of a *Bildungsroman* makes its appearance in *Jacob's Room*, but the women Jacob meets neither build nor destroy his character. He meets the 'good' girl (Clara), and several versions of the 'bad' girl. He meets a more mature, and experienced woman, Sandra Wentworth Williams, who is already married; perhaps she will do for him what Lawrence's Clara does for Paul Morel in *Sons and Lovers*. Jacob, however, does not arrive at a more complete knowledge of himself as a result of the relationship with Sandra. Instead, he just falls painfully in love, and suffers terribly from this 'hook dragging in his side' (pp. 146, 149) [118, 120].

His affair with Florinda had been one of 'innocence' and simplicity; he accepted in the beginning her assertion of virginity. His relationship with Sandra seems to complement the Florinda relationship, because Jacob now assumes he really knows himself and knows women. As he and Sandra descend the Acro-Corinth, Sandra indulges herself and Jacob in some snippets of her sentimentally melancholy childhood: she was orphaned at four, wandered in the huge library and in the kitchen, and she sat on the butler's knee. Responding, 'Jacob thought that if he had been there he would have saved her; for she had been exposed to great dangers, he felt' (p. 145) [117]. Great dangers? Wandering through a library and sitting on a butler's knee? Jacob's imaginings here have no basis in the very slim data he has about Sandra. He is simply playing, safely and momentarily, with the notion of some vague heroism. A few seconds later, he is thinking of 'how little he had known himself before' (p. 146) [117]—before meeting Sandra. But there has been no great change; his seeming growth is ironic, mere imaginary play on his part. Jacob's transformation from 'innocence' to 'knowledge' is parodic, not real. His only 'knowledge' is the uncomfortable sensation of a hook dragging in his side.

It might be argued that the slender sketch of Jacob's growth is an accident or flaw in the construction of the novel, a failure on the part of an author who was trying out a new method. I don't think so. Woolf can give a heavy, substantial representation to a character's consciousness, thoughts, growth and important moments; she did so in *The Voyage Out* and *Night and Day*, and she does so in *Jacob's Room*, but in this third novel she reserves for the narrator a fuller representation of consciousness. Furthermore, other occasions support the sense of Jacob's tenuous, ironic 'growth', and of his parodic, half-hearted travelling through typical *Bildungsroman* territory. Jacob goes to the Acropolis, for instance, and sits down to read:

> And laying the book on the ground he began, as if inspired by what he had read, to write a note upon the importance of history—upon democracy—one of those scribbles upon which the work of a lifetime may be based; or again, it falls out of a book twenty years later, and one can't remember a word of it. It is a little painful. It had better be burnt.
>
> Jacob wrote; began to draw a straight nose. . . . (pp. 149–50) [120–21]

At this point democracy and the straight nose are interrupted by women on tour. The comedy is doubled and tripled. First Jacob interrupts himself by turning from democracy to a straight nose; then the sightseeing women interrupt the drawing of the nose. To be fair to Jacob, we would have to point out that the narrator may be responsible for the comic thoughts about juvenilia on democracy; she does not say definitely that Jacob himself writes such a 'painful' note. She moves in closer, however, and we do see Jacob drawing a straight nose. His meditations on history are probably not those of a future Gibbon or a Clive Bell. Jacob curses the women for interrupting him, but the comedy of the scene began earlier; he had interrupted himself.

The narrator continues the parodic portrait of a British youth's disillusionment with Athens:

> 'It is those damned women', said Jacob, without any trace of bitterness, but rather with sadness and disappointment that what might have been should never be.
>
> (This violent disillusionment is generally to be expected in

young men in the prime of life, sound of wind and limb, who
will soon become fathers of families and directors of banks.)
(p. 150) [121]

Jacob's disillusionment here hardly deserves the adjective 'violent'
which the narrator ironically applies, looking ahead to the prosaic
destiny which—except for the war—ordinarily awaits young men
such as Jacob; they become 'fathers of families and directors of
banks', not great historians and thinkers. Jacob's 'disappointment
that what might have been should never be' approaches cliché in its
phrasing; it is parodic, just as his supposed realisation—'how little
he had known himself before'—was parodic.

The narrator puts the cap on this comic scene by letting us see
Jacob as he looks at the sculptures of the Erechtheum:

> Jacob strolled over to the Erechtheum and looked rather fur-
> tively at the goddess on the left-hand side holding the roof on
> her head. She reminded him of Sandra Wentworth Williams.
> He looked at her, then looked away. He looked at her, then
> looked away. He was extraordinarily moved, and with the bat-
> tered Greek nose in his head, with Sandra in his head, with all
> sorts of things in his head, off he started to walk right up to the
> top of Mount Hymettus, alone, in the heat. (p. 151) [121]

This is farcical ('He looked at her, then looked away. He looked at
her, then looked away'). Jacob's stagey double-take lets all the air out
of the potentially epiphanic balloon. And, instead of the idealised
'straight' nose he had been drawing, his head is full of the 'battered
Greek nose' which he somehow associates with Sandra. What a
descent from Bonamy's prediction that Jacob would fall in love with
'some Greek woman with a straight nose' (p. 139) [111]! For Jacob,
no bird-girl stands symbolically on a beach; if she did, he would
probably notice her crooked nose instead of rising to the occasion
with a lyrical definition of his identity and his vocation.

Jacob's apparently climactic opportunity for love and insight is his
night-time visit to the Acropolis with Sandra. Woolf does not
describe it. The narrator's own reflections indicate that she has deliberately turned away from this event. As Jacob and Sandra climb, the
narrator's perspective widens, giving us Paris, Constantinople, London and Betty Flanders, who sighs 'like one who realizes, but would
fain ward off a little longer—oh, a little longer!—the oppression of
eternity' (p. 160) [129]. Meanwhile Jacob and Sandra have vanished
from the narrator's view. 'There was the Acropolis; but had they
reached it?' The answer to the narrator's question may be 'Yes', in
the sense that Jacob may have literally reached the Acropolis with
Sandra. From what we know of Jacob, however, 'No' would be the

answer to the more symbolic aspect of the narrator's question. 'As for reaching the Acropolis who shall say that we ever do it, or that when Jacob woke next morning he found anything hard and durable to keep for ever?' (ibid.). It is doubtful that he carried away anything durable from this event—doubtful that he reached the 'Acropolis' of symbolic insight. Later, back in London, he is essentially unchanged, and still suffering from his unmanageable passions. He draws a sketch of the Parthenon in the dust in Hyde Park, and reads a letter from Sandra about her memory 'of something said or attempted, some moment in the dark on the road to the Acropolis which (such was her creed) mattered for ever' (p. 169) [136]. Moments belong to Sandra's creed, not to Jacob's. He overlooks them, or distorts them; she, on the other hand, makes moments, contrives them.

Some sort of 'moment' of insight is present even in Woolf's early novels. The newly engaged Katharine Hilbery, for instance, 'held in her hands for one brief moment the globe which we spend our lives in trying to shape, round, whole, and entire from the confusion of chaos'.[3] In *Jacob's Room*, however, the narrator goes out of her way to undercut such occasions. Clara Durrant, writing about Jacob in her diary, wishes that the moment of Jacob's July visit could continue for ever. 'And moments don't', the narrator offers as a transitional comment, going on to describe Jacob in London laughing at an obscene joke (p. 70) [55]. Sandra's moments—part of a self-conscious 'creed'—come in for downright ridicule. The narrator troubles to point out the 'dirty curtains' of the hotel window in Olympia where Sandra stands, contemplating the burdened peasants as they return for the evening:

> She seemed to have grasped something. She would write it down. And moving to the table where her husband sat reading she leant her chin in her hands and thought of the peasants, of suffering, of her own beauty, of the inevitable compromise, and of how she would write it down. (pp. 140–1) [113]

Her sentimental musings self-consciously place her own beauty in the middle of the picture. She says, 'Everything seems to mean so much'; then she notices her own reflection in a mirror, and she thinks, 'I am very beautiful' (p. 141) [113]. After the big occasion of her visit to the Acropolis with Jacob, she reflects on their relationship, sucking back again 'the soul of the moment': ' "What for? What for?" Sandra would say, putting the book back, and strolling to the looking-glass and pressing her hair' (pp. 160–1) [129]. Neither Clara nor Sandra looks very deeply into herself; neither makes any real discovery about her life. Sandra, indeed, can look only *at* herself.

3. Virginia Woolf, *Night and Day* (London: Hogarth Press, 1971) p. 533.

Nor is Jacob really the sort of meditative, introspective character by which an author can make the most of the usual *Bildungsroman* format; his obstinately non-reflective personality is, however, fine material for a parody of this traditional form. The narrator does allow that Jacob's personality may change with age:

> 'What for? What for?' Jacob never asked himself any such questions, to judge by the way he laced his boots; shaved himself; to judge by the depth of his sleep that night, with the wind fidgeting at the shutters, and half-a-dozen mosquitoes singing in his ears. He was young—a man. And then Sandra was right when she judged him to be credulous as yet. At forty it might be a different matter. (p. 161) [130]

Sandra asks 'What for?' in a self-conscious manner that makes a mockery of the question. Jacob never even asks. Probably. The narrator in this passage is once again giving us a tentative view; we must try 'to judge' on the basis of the evidence. Other evidence suggests that Jacob does not ask such questions; except for occasions when he is in love, he enjoys life, and is 'not much given to analysis' (pp. 138–9) [111]. Like all young people in a *Bildungsroman*, he is supposed to ask 'What for?' But he maintains his own obstinate mystery, and neither asks for revelation nor receives any.[4]

The narrator, not Jacob or Clara or Sandra, has the imaginative and lyrical responses to Greece and to the English landscape. She gives us the spectacular and melancholy beauty of the Cornish coast as Timmy and Jacob sail close to it (pp. 47–8) [35–6]. She gives us the illuminating meditation on the 'exaltation' of young people such as Fanny Elmer and Nick Bramham whose restless energy, if it were any more intense, would blow them 'like foam into the air'; if we had such continual ecstasy, 'the stars would shine through us' (pp. 119–20) [96]. And the narrator, not Jacob, gives us the longest meditation on the immortal beauty of the Parthenon (pp. 146–8) [118–19]. In this book, the narrator has the moments of insight; she is, in her own right, a distinct and important 'character', as recent critics have observed.[5]

Part of her insight emerges in the very 'looseness' and 'gaiety' of the novel's structure, in the sketchy, continually qualified account

4. With regard to Jacob's passivity and his lack of intellectual exertion, it is important to distinguish him from Woolf's brother, Thoby Stephen. It is true that the absurd brevity of Jacob's life suggests parallels with Thoby and with Rupert Brooke. Jane Novak argues for caution, however, in making such parallels. Thoby had a sense of humour; he had more self-confidence and a greater intellect than Jacob has. See Novak, *The Razor Edge of Balance: A Study of Virginia Woolf* (Coral Gables, Fla: University of Miami Press, 1975) pp. 101–3.

5. See especially Barry S. Morgenstern, 'The Self-conscious Narrator in *Jacob's Room*', *Modern Fiction Studies*, Autumn 1972, pp. 351–61. Others who comment briefly on the narrator as a character are Hafley, *The Glass Roof*, pp. 49–50; and Novak, *The Razor Edge of Balance*, pp. 87–8.

of Jacob's development. The narrator needs this very flexible perspective, one which allows her to assume omniscience on occasion, and at other times to speak in her own voice, a woman who is older than Jacob and who finds him difficult to know. The flexible perspective allows the *Bildungsroman* elements to be introduced, almost as though they were hypotheses about behaviour; then, with a shift of perspective, the narrator can 'correct' the conventional assumption, and show us how far from the convention the mysterious Jacob is. The parodic approach to his character, his growing up, his love affairs, and his travels, yields both comedy and a solid conviction of his 'obstinate' reality. Jacob is not 'characterised' in a traditional way. Instead, he is teased into a tentative existence, and he walks around, somewhat at a loss, in his own parodic *Bildungsroman*.

The resulting humour is directed not only at a highly conventional literary form, but at the male hero whom the form so often featured. The sympathetic laughter of the narrator is subtly feminist, but she rescues Jacob—by her very refusal to sum him up—from any severe censure. After all, he does not always fit the mocked pattern. His very deviation from the *Bildungsroman* parodies the pattern, and at the same time asserts his own mysterious reality and his specialness as a human being.

ALEX ZWERDLING

Jacob's Room: Woolf's Satiric Elegy†

Virginia Woolf's *Jacob's Room* appeared in 1922, the *annus mirabilis* of modern literature that also produced *Ulysses* and *The Waste Land*. Perhaps for that reason, and because the novel was the first of Woolf's longer fictions to break with conventional narrative technique, it is often interpreted as a paradigmatic modernist text rather than as a unique work. Its peculiarities are treated as illustrative of the revolution in twentieth-century literature, though in fact some of them are idiosyncratic. The book was certainly Woolf's first consciously experimental novel; and it has remained her most baffling one: its narrative techniques are so innovative that they call attention to themselves; its central character, Jacob Flanders, seems to be a classic instance of psychological inscrutability in fiction; and its rapidly shifting tone, now somber, now mocking, deprives Woolf's audience of a stable sense of her own attitude toward the world she

† From *English Literary History* 48 (1981): 894–913. Copyright © The Johns Hopkins University Press. Reprinted by permission of The Johns Hopkins University Press.

describes. These problems of narrative method, characterization, and tone are interrelated, as I hope to show, but they can be illuminated only by an attempt to understand Woolf's fundamental aims in writing the particular novel *Jacob's Room*, rather than by assuming she was interested in fictional innovation for its own sake.

Jacob's Room is often taken to be simply a technical exercise. David Daiches, for example, suggests that it was written "one might say, for the sake of style."[1] And indeed Woolf's first thoughts about the book in her diary are concerned with method rather than matter: "Suppose one thing should open out of another—as in *An Unwritten Novel*—only not for 10 pages but 200 or so—doesn't that give the looseness and lightness I want; doesn't that get closer and yet keep form and speed, and enclose everything, everything?"[2] Her diary entries as she works on the book continue to deal more with narrative strategy than with defining the "everything, everything" the novel is designed to present. Essentially, Woolf was trying to work free of the conventions of realism she attacked with such devastating wit in her essay "Mr. Bennett and Mrs. Brown," that style of fiction in which the character is kept waiting in the wings until his entire environment and life history have been exhaustively described. She thought the machinery too ponderous for the quick-witted reader and was determined to perfect a vehicle that would move faster.

The style of *Jacob's Room* is that of the sketchbook artist rather than the academic painter. Scenes are swiftly and allusively outlined, not filled in, the essential relationships between characters intimated in brief but typical vignettes chosen seemingly at random from their daily lives: a don's luncheon party at Cambridge, a day spent reading in the British Museum, a walk with a friend. No incident is decisive or fully developed. Nothing is explained or given special significance. The narrative unit is generally two or three pages long and not obviously connected to the one before or after. The effect is extremely economical and suggestive but at the same time frustrating for an audience trained to read in larger units and look for meaning and coherence. All of this was clearly innovative, as Woolf's first readers saw. Lytton Strachey writes her: "The technique of the narrative is astonishing—how you manage to leave out everything that's dreary, and yet retain enough string for your pearls I can hardly understand."[3] And E. M. Forster is similarly baffled; he wonders how Woolf keeps the reader interested in Jacob when almost everything that would have defined his character has been eliminated: "I don't

1. David Daiches, *Virginia Woolf* (New York: New Directions, 1963), p. 61.
2. Virginia Woolf, *A Writer's Diary*, ed. Leonard Woolf (London: Hogarth, 1972), p. 23; hereafter cited as *AWD*.
3. Virginia Woolf and Lytton Strachey, *Letters*, ed. Leonard Woolf and James Strachey (London: Hogarth Press and Chatto and Windus, 1969), p. 103.

yet understand how, with your method, you managed it," he writes, but he is certain that this is the book's greatest achievement.[4] Not all of Woolf's readers have been convinced that the narrative technique, interesting as it is, *was* successful, however. The book is often attacked on the grounds that it has no unity and that Jacob himself remains unknowable. Joan Bennett, for example, insists that the novel's vividly realized episodes "build up no whole that can be held in the mind" and that "Jacob remains a nebulous young man, indeed almost any young man."[5] J. K. Johnstone complains that the very vividness of the incidents "detracts from the unity of the novel," while "the character who might unite all its various scenes, is—not there; his effects upon others are there; but he himself is absent."[6] Such dismissive judgments seem to me based on an unwillingness to think about Woolf's technique in relation to purpose. Both the obvious fragmentation of the novel and the inscrutability of its central character are, I think, deliberate. But in order to understand why Woolf chose to write a novel that can be characterized in these ways, one has to move beyond speculation about narrative technique as such to an understanding of why she needed these particular techniques in the particular book she was writing. For despite her obvious interest in technical experiment, she always thought of narrative style as purposive—a means to an end. Since the ends of her individual novels were never the same, her technical choices ought to be looked at not as attempts to "revolutionize modern fiction" but as individual solutions to the problem at hand. And the problem at hand can not be intelligently discussed without considering the book's subject matter.[7]

4. E. M. Forster, letter to Virginia Woolf, 24 October 1922, Berg Collection, New York Public Library. Quotations from the materials in the Henry W. and Albert A. Berg Collection of English and American Literature (Astor, Lenox, and Tilden Foundations) are published with the permission of the Collection and of the relevant copyright holders. I am grateful to King's College, Cambridge and The Society of Authors for allowing me to quote Forster's letter.

5. Joan Bennett, *Virginia Woolf: Her Art as a Novelist* (Cambridge: Cambridge University Press, 1964), pp. 95, 96.

6. J. K. Johnstone, *The Bloomsbury Group: A Study of E. M. Forster, Lytton Strachey, Virginia Woolf, and Their Circle* (London: Secker and Warburg, 1954), pp. 332, 334.

7. Woolf's most interesting comment on her own experimental methods in fiction was a direct response to critics who treated her next novel, *Mrs. Dalloway*, as a conscious methodological experiment. Her insistence on the inaccuracy of this view is equally pertinent to an understanding of *Jacob's Room* and is worth quoting at some length: "The book, it was said, was the deliberate offspring of a method. The author, it was said, dissatisfied with the form of fiction then in vogue, was determined to beg, borrow, steal or even create another of her own. But, as far as it is possible to be honest about the mysterious process of the mind, the facts are otherwise. Dissatisfied the writer may have been; but her dissatisfaction was primarily with nature for giving an idea, without providing a house for it to live in. . . . The novel was the obvious lodging, but the novel it seemed was built on the wrong plan. Thus rebuked the idea started as the oyster starts or the snail to secrete a house for itself. And this it did without any conscious direction. . . . It was necessary to write the book first and to invent a theory afterwards" (Virginia Woolf, "Introduction" to her *Mrs. Dalloway* [New York: Modern Library, 1928], pp. vii–viii). It is evident from this description that Woolf begins with a subject rather than with a method; and that the

Jacob's Room is about a young man who is killed in the First World War. By naming her hero Jacob Flanders, Woolf immediately predicts his fate. As her first readers in 1922 would certainly have known, Flanders was a synonym for death in battle. The words of John McCrae's "In Flanders Fields"—"the most popular poem of the war"[8]—were common property:

> In Flanders fields, the poppies blow
> Between the crosses, row on row. . . .
> We are the Dead. Short days ago
> We lived, felt dawn, saw sunset glow,
>   Loved and were loved, and now we lie
>   In Flanders fields.[9]

According to official sources, nearly a third of the million British soldiers killed in World War I lost their lives in the Flanders mud. And the heaviest losses were among the young officers of Jacob's class. In the words of A. J. P. Taylor, "The roll of honour in every school and college bore witness to the talents which had perished—the men of promise born during the eighteen-nineties whose promise was not fulfilled."[1]

Although *Jacob's Room* is not in any direct sense a war novel, the references to the coming conflict are carefully embedded in the narrative, so that Woolf's first readers would have been constantly reminded of the imminent catastrophe. Jacob goes up to Cambridge in 1906. His growth from adolescence to young manhood takes place against the relentless ticking of a time bomb. We may be reading about his intellectual and amorous adventures, but we are also witnessing the preparation of cannon fodder. Woolf keeps us aware of Jacob's impending fate by moving back and forth in time, for example when she rounds off the story of a young couple in Jacob's set with the words "And now Jimmy feeds crows in Flanders and Helen visits hospitals."[2] Her novel alludes to certain well-known public events of the years just before the war—the Irish Home Rule Bill (p. 97) [77], the transformation of the House of Lords (p. 129) [104]—in a way that indirectly would have reminded her original audience of dates—1911, 1912, 1913.[3] Toward the end of the book, the preparations

subject seems to have a will of its own rather than allowing the novelist to shape it according to a preconceived theory of narration or a pre-existing form.

8. Paul Fussell, *The Great War and Modern Memory* (New York: Oxford University Press, 1975), p. 248.
9. John McCrae, *In Flanders Fields and Other Poems* (New York: Putnam's, 1919), p. 3.
1. A. J. P. Taylor, *English History, 1914–1945* (Harmondsworth: Penguin, 1970), pp. 126n, 165–66.
2. Virginia Woolf, *Jacob's Room* (London: Hogarth, 1971), pp. 95–96. Other page references to this volume in the Hogarth Press Uniform Edition are incorporated in the text. [Bracketed page numbers refer to this Norton Critical Edition.]
3. For a detailed chronology, see Avrom Fleishman, *Virginia Woolf: A Critical Reading* (Baltimore: Johns Hopkins, 1975), pp. 49–50.

for war become direct. The ministers in Whitehall lift their pens and alter the course of history (p. 172) [139]; and the young men die. Woolf's only description of the fighting is remarkable for its contained rage, its parody of reportorial detachment: "Like blocks of tin soldiers the army covers the cornfield, moves up the hillside, stops, reels slightly this way and that, and falls flat, save that, through field-glasses, it can be seen that one or two pieces still agitate up and down like fragments of broken match-stick" (p. 155) [125].

Many readers have seen that such references to the war are significant and that *Jacob's Room* is a response to that event even though it records the years before it begins. Winifred Holtby, in the first book-length study of Virginia Woolf, suggested that Woolf was less interested in trench warfare (about which she knew nothing) than in the group identity of its victims: "When such a young man was killed, she seems to ask, what was lost then? What lost by him? What was lost by his friends? What exactly was it that had disappeared?"[4] These still seem to me the essential questions to ask in reading *Jacob's Room*, and I hope to show that they also illuminate the book's technical innovations and experiments in portraiture as well as Woolf's puzzling shifts in tone.

The question of what might have become of the Jacobs is asked by Woolf herself in a review of a book on Rupert Brooke, that classic symbol of the gifted young man killed before his time: "One turns from the thought of him not with a sense of completeness and finality, but rather to wonder and to question still: what would he have been, what would he have done?"[5] As her questions suggest, the image of such men provokes doubt rather than certainty. "Promising" they surely were. But their early deaths only magnified the absence of achieved identity and real accomplishment. As she puts it in another review about a different young casualty, "What the finished work, the final aim, would have been we can only guess."[6] Such questions are unanswerable, and Woolf does not really deal with them in *Jacob's Room*. Rather, she writes the book largely to give us a sense of what this particular stage in a young man's life— the promising stage—is like.

4. Winifred Holtby, *Virginia Woolf* (London: Wishart, 1932), p. 116. More recent critics who have commented on the significance of the war in the book include Josephine O'Brien Schaefer, *The Three-Fold Nature of Reality in the Novels of Virginia Woolf* (The Hague: Mouton, 1965), pp. 70–71; Carolyn G. Heilbrun, *Towards Androgyny: Aspects of Male and Female in Literature* (London: Victor Gollancz, 1973), p. 164; Nancy Topping Bazin, *Virginia Woolf and the Androgynous Vision* (New Brunswick, N.J.: Rutgers University Press, 1973), pp. 92–93; and Fleishman, p. 54. See also the excellent essay on Woolf's critical depiction of prewar British culture by Carol Ohmann, "Culture and Anarchy in *Jacob's Room,*" *Contemporary Literature* 18 (1977), 160–72.
5. Virginia Woolf, "Rupert Brooke," *Books and Portraits: Some Further Selections from the Literary and Biographical Writings of Virginia Woolf*, ed. Mary Lyon (London: Hogarth, 1977), p. 89.
6. "These Are the Plans," *Books and Portraits*, p. 96.

The major obstacle in her way was the almost universal impulse to sentimentalize the subject. Obituaries for the war dead are not notable for their realism, and she was determined to write an honest account rather than a heroic one. She does not avoid the possibility that such young men, for all their native gifts and youthful promise, were likely to be confused and immature. Her novel emphasizes the image of Jacob *adrift*, moving rapidly but lightly from one social set to another, from one romantic attachment to another, without either the intention or the ability to "settle." In his own rather despairing words, "One must apply oneself to something or other—God knows what" (p. 71) [56].

Woolf's fragmented narrative creates a kaleidoscopic picture of the range of Jacob's opportunities. Particularly in the London chapters, she gives us the sense that the world is all before him. His family connections, his education and his good looks provide him with an entry into many different social circles—bohemian, professional, aristocratic. And his romantic experiments suggest a similar smorgasbord: the amiable, promiscuous Florinda, the romantically unstable Fanny Elmer, the steady but frozen young heiress Clara Durrant, the "sophisticated" older married woman Sandra Wentworth Williams. These opportunities and experiences are deliberately presented in an incoherent way because for Jacob they do not add up, they cannot be thought of as sequential steps leading to his definition as an adult human being. Unlike the classic *Bildungsroman, Jacob's Room* lacks a teleology. Woolf's hero remains an essentially molten personality interrupted by death at the stage of experimenting upon himself, a young man by turns brashly self-confident and utterly confused. The novel treats this situation as an inevitable but early stage of growing up. Woolf's perspective is that of an older person who can describe "the obstinate irrepressible conviction which makes youth so intolerably disagreeable—'I am what I am, and intend to be it,' for which there will be no form in the world unless Jacob makes one for himself" (p. 34) [26]. But as the last part of her sentence suggests, it is by no means certain that such attempts to define oneself will be successful, no matter how long we are given. There is always the possibility, perhaps even the likelihood, that our rebellious adolescence will give way not to strong adult individuality but to a stale despairing conformity.

No one has written about this stage of life better than Erik Erikson, and though Woolf could not, of course, have read him, certain passages in his work illuminate Jacob's situation because both writers focus on the same phenomenon. In *Childhood and Society* (1950) and more fully in *Identity: Youth and Crisis* (1968), Erikson defines a stage of deliberately prolonged adolescence which he calls a *"psychosocial moratorium,"* a period in which "the young adult through free role experimentation may find a niche in some section of his society, a niche which is firmly defined and yet seems to be uniquely made for him." Before he is expected to take on any of his life commitments—in love, in work—the young man is offered a legitimate period of delay "often characterized by a combination of prolonged immaturity and provoked precocity."[7] His reluctance to bind himself vocationally or to choose a mate is honored or at least tolerated for a period of years because his society accepts his need for self-exploration and social mobility before demanding that the ultimate choices be made.

By its very nature, such a stage cannot be a record of triumphs, and those who are going through it often seem simply confused and self-indulgent to their elders, particularly those with short memories. Furthermore, a person in this position remains in some sense a blank, undefinable, unknowable—and therefore not an easy subject for fiction. A novel is expected to give us characters who have an identity or whose progressive change we can follow sequentially—as in the *Bildungsroman*. In *Jacob's Room*, however, Woolf was faced with the problem that this fictional convention does not hold good for all human beings at all stages of life. She had tried to deal with a similarly inchoate personality in her first novel, *The Voyage Out*, and would do so again in *The Waves*. All three of these characters (Rachel, Jacob, Percival) die young, before they have been fully defined. But it is notable that in trying to depict such people, Woolf's technique becomes more and more stylized, until in Percival she creates a mythical rather than a realistically conceived character.

Why did she move in this direction? Why did she deliberately avoid the technique of interior monologue that might have given her readers a vivid sense of the inner turmoil in which such people find themselves? In certain obvious ways, the record of a fictional character's thoughts is ideally suited to depicting identity confusion, yet in *Jacob's Room* (and even more in *The Waves*) the characters who might have been illuminated by it are never presented in this way. Their inner lives remain a mystery. In *The Waves*, this is clearly a deliberate choice, since the six major characters surrounding Percival all soliloquize at length. Only Percival has no voice. It is sometimes assumed that Woolf depicts Jacob without recording his inner life in detail because when she was writing *Jacob's Room* she had not yet perfected the techniques of rendering consciousness she learned to use so brilliantly in her later fiction. But the explanation is unconvincing, since in the first place the thoughts of many minor characters in the novel *are* consistently recorded, even if not in the

7. Erik H. Erikson, *Identity: Youth and Crisis* (New York: Norton, 1968), p. 156.

elaborate form found in *Mrs. Dalloway* or *To the Lighthouse*. Woolf deliberately minimized the reader's access to Jacob's thoughts. This is evident if one reads the holograph draft of the novel alongside the revised, final version. Again and again, Woolf eliminates the vestiges of Jacob's inner life. For example, in the potentially romantic scene in which he helps Clara pick grapes while the younger children scamper about, Woolf excises the hints of Jacob's attachment from the first version:

> "Little demons!" she cried.
> ~~"I haven't said it"~~ Jacob thought to himself.
> ~~"I want to say it. I cant say it. Clara! Clara! Clara!"~~
> They're throwing the onions," said Jacob.
>
> (holograph version, with Woolf's deletions)[8]

> "Little demons!" she cried "What have they got?" she asked Jacob.
> "Onions, I think," said Jacob. He looked at them without moving.
>
> (published version, p. 61)

As a result of such excisions, we never know exactly what Jacob feels about Clara, nor about most of the other people whose lives touch his.

There is obviously something artificial and deliberate in such narrative reticence. Any attempt to account for it must be speculative, but two reasons suggest themselves for Woolf's peculiar strategy. It is possible that she wants to give us the sense of a character still so unformed that even the relatively chaotic record of interior monologue seems too defining. The flux of feelings must be recorded in words, and words give shape. Even Jacob's conflicted "I want to say it. I cant say it. Clara! Clara! Clara!" clearly suggests romantic attachment, when it is possible that what he feels about her is less easily describable. By their very nature, words articulate confusion too neatly to be true to the extremes of the state. This is why Jacob's letters home communicate so little: "Jacob had nothing to hide from his mother. It was only that he could make no sense himself of his extraordinary excitement, and as for writing it down——" (p. 130) [105]. It is possible that Woolf refused to record Jacob's deepest feelings because such a transcript comes too close to presenting a finished product rather than a consciousness in process. She wanted to give the sense of someone who remains a

---

8. Virginia Woolf, *Jacob's Room*, holograph dated April 15, 1920–March 12, 1922, Berg Collection, New York Public Library, pt. I, p. 123. I am grateful to Professor Quentin Bell and to the Berg Collection for permission to quote from Virginia Woolf's manuscripts.

permanently unknown quantity. And so she concentrates on the conflicting impressions of Jacob among all the people he meets, and our point of view shifts abruptly every few pages as we move from one unreliable observer to another, none of them managing to fathom this young man because, as Woolf concludes, "nobody sees any one as he is. . . . They see a whole—they see all sorts of things—they see themselves" (pp. 28–29) [22].

But to pose the problem in this epistemological way does not fully explain the absence of anything resembling stream of consciousness. Mrs. Ramsay is similarly unknowable, Lily Briscoe tells us in *To the Lighthouse* ("One wanted fifty pairs of eyes to see with, she reflected. Fifty pairs of eyes were not enough to get round that one woman with, she thought.")[9] and yet this fact does not prevent Woolf from recording her character's inner life in detail. For a better explanation, we must go back to the problematic tone of *Jacob's Room*. Uninterrupted stream of consciousness tends to create sympathy and to work against satiric intent in fiction. And there are many indications in *Jacob's Room* that Woolf wanted to maintain an ironic distance between her reader and her main character. Her tone in describing him and his friends is often patronizing. For example, when Jacob first becomes involved with the brainless Florinda, Woolf describes his feelings with obvious mockery:

> Jacob took her word for it that she was chaste. She prattled, sitting by the fireside, of famous painters. The tomb of her father was mentioned. Wild and frail and beautiful she looked, and thus the women of the Greeks were, Jacob thought; and this was life: and himself a man and Florinda chaste.
>
> She left with one of Shelley's poems beneath her arm. Mrs. Stuart, she said, often talked of him.
>
> Marvellous are the innocent.
>
> (p. 77) [61]

Such ironic detachment is evident not only in the narrator's attitude toward Jacob but in her treatment of most of the young characters in the book. The narrative voice is that of an older, more experienced, highly skeptical consciousness, determined to puncture youthful illusion and undercut intense feeling of any kind. This satiric narrator often steps in to correct romantic excess, for example when describing Richard Bonamy's passion for Jacob:

> "Urbane" on the lips of Jacob had mysteriously all the shapeliness of a character which Bonamy thought daily more sublime, devastating, terrific than ever, though he was still, and perhaps would be for ever, barbaric, obscure.

9. Virginia Woolf, *To the Lighthouse* (London: Hogarth, 1967), p. 303.

What superlatives! What adjectives! How acquit Bonamy of
sentimentality of the grossest sort; of being tossed like a cork
on the waves; of having no steady insight into character; of being
unsupported by reason, and of drawing no comfort whatever
from the works of the classics?

(p. 164) [132]

The cumulative effect of such passages is to make it impossible
for the reader to sympathize fully with the character. We are, in
effect, told to keep our distance. And in one way or another, the
narrative techniques of the novel reinforce this sense of a wide gap.
Woolf frequently pretends ignorance: she is pictured as so far away
from the action that she literally can't hear the words of the characters. In one of the Cambridge scenes, for instance, the perspective
suddenly lengthens, like an aerial shot in film:

The laughter died in the air. The sound of it could scarcely have
reached any one standing by the Chapel, which stretched along
the opposite side of the court. The laughter died out, and only
gestures of arms, movements of bodies, could be seen shaping
something in the room. Was it an argument? A bet on the boat
races? Was it nothing of the sort? What was shaped by the arms
and bodies moving in the twilight room?

(pp. 42–43) [33]

In such passages the omniscient narrator suddenly and rather dis-
turbingly pleads ignorance, becomes at best "semiscient." There are
also many instances in the book in which our involvement with and
understanding of the characters is made more difficult because our
view is filtered through an alien consciousness, for example that of
Richard Bonamy's charwoman, who gives us an obviously garbled
version of what she overhears the young friends saying in the next
room as she washes up the scullery: " 'Objective something,' said
Bonamy; and 'common ground' and something else—all very long
words, she noted. 'Book learning does it,' she thought to herself"
(p. 101) [80]. The effect is to deflate the intellectual pretensions of
these budding philosophers and bring them down to earth.

Is this any way to treat a young man whose life is about to be
snuffed out? Why does Woolf challenge the ancient wisdom that
dictates "*de mortuis nil nisi bonum*"? Is there some meanness of spirit
evident in the games she plays with her characters? Such irreverence
might well have seemed offensive to a generation of readers trained
to think about the dead soldiers by the literature World War I produced. Those works, written during and immediately after the conflict, convey a sense of high idealism or heroic indignation or
romantic intensity. One has only to recall some of the classic passages:

If I should die, think only this of me:
 That's there's some corner of a foreign field
That is for ever England.
       (Rupert Brooke, "The Soldier")

What passing-bells for these who die as cattle?
 Only the monstrous anger of the guns.
 Only the stuttering rifles' rapid rattle
Can patter out their hasty orisons.
    (Wilfred Owen, "Anthem for Doomed Youth")

Have you forgotten yet? . . .
Look down, and swear by the slain of the War that
       you'll never forget.
    (Siegfried Sassoon, "Aftermath")

*Massacres of boys! That indeed is the essence of modern war. The
killing off of the young. It is the destruction of the human inheritance, it is the spending of all the life and material of the future
upon present-day hate and greed.*
    (H. G. Wells, Mr. Britling Sees It Through)[1]

Whether the sentiment is patriotic or bitterly disillusioned, such passages treat the war dead with absolute seriousness, in a style that is
characteristically intense and even reverent and that works at a high
level of generalization.

By contrast, Woolf's elegiac novel is persistently small-scaled, mis-
chievous and ironic.[2] She had an instinctive distrust for reverence
of any kind, feeling it was a fundamentally dishonest mental habit
that turned flesh-and-blood human beings into symbolic creatures.
She was no more interested in a cult of war heroes than she had
been in a religion of eminent Victorians. For one thing, such attitudes indirectly glorified war, even if the writer was, like Wilfred
Owen, consciously working against the martial myth. Woolf's elegy
for the young men who died in the war is revisionist: there is nothing
grand about Jacob; the sacrifice of his life seems perfectly pointless,
not even a cautionary tale. *Jacob's Room* is a covert critique of the
romantic posturing so common in the anthems for doomed youth.

1. *The Poetical Works of Rupert Brooke*, ed. Geoffrey Keynes (London: Faber and Faber,
1946), p. 23; *The Collected Poems of Wilfred Owen*, ed. C. Day Lewis (Norfolk, Conn.:
New Directions, 1964), p. 44; Siegfried Sassoon, *Collected Poems 1908–1956* (London:
Faber and Faber, 1961), p. 119; H. G. Wells, *Mr. Britling Sees It Through* (New York:
Macmillan, 1916), p. 431–32.
2. Carol Ohmann's finely judged description of Woolf's tone in *Jacob's Room* is worth quoting: "Neither is the novel an angry one. It is elegiac, rather, in its treatment of Jacob, and
serenely so, mourning in tranquility its hero's death and the end of what appeared to be
his promise" (Ohmann, p. 171).

Its author's attitude anticipates Dylan Thomas' World War II poem, "A Refusal to Mourn the Death, by Fire, of a Child in London":

> I shall not murder
> The mankind of her going with a grave truth
> Nor blaspheme down the stations of the breath
> With any further
> Elegy of innocence and youth.[3]

Woolf's bedrock pacifism, then, helps to account for her ironic distance from Jacob and his contemporaries. But she would probably have felt much the same about the milieu that produced him if he had never fought in the war at all, since there was something about his whole life pattern that she disliked intensely. Jacob Flanders is a paradigmatic young man of his class. Handsome, clever, and well-connected if not rich, his credentials are impeccable and his future course apparently secure. Rugby; Trinity College, Cambridge; a London flat; a couple of mistresses; the Grand Tour: everything in his life is a traditional step on the road to establishment success. The class was Woolf's own, but the sex was not; and between the training and expectations of its young men and young women, there was a great gulf. Woolf's satiric detachment is in part attributable to her feeling that Jacob's world was created by men for men, and essentially excluded her. She reacted with a characteristic mixture of condescension and apprehension. As she says in describing her own attitude toward him, "Granted ten years' seniority and a difference of sex, fear of him comes first" (p. 93) [74].

The fear is not so much of Jacob himself but of the "patriarchal machinery" that guaranteed him a powerful position in his society. Woolf describes the rites of passage for such young men in an illuminating autobiographical essay written shortly before her death. She considers the career of her illustrious cousin, H. A. L. Fisher: "What, I asked myself the other day, would Herbert Fisher have been without Winchester, New College, and the Cabinet? What would have been his shape had he not been stamped and moulded by the patriarchal machinery? Every one of our male relations was shot into that machine and came out at the other end, at the age of sixty or so, a Headmaster, an Admiral, a Cabinet Minister, a Judge."[4] Jacob too appears to be on such a trajectory. Woolf's feelings about her exclusion from this world are quite complex. She envies the men their guaranteed success (assuming they follow the rules) while pitying them their lack of freedom. The whole exploratory stage of life

3. *The Collected Poems of Dylan Thomas* (New York: New Directions, 1953), p. 112.
4. Virginia Woolf, "A Sketch of the Past," *Moments of Being: Unpublished Autobiographical Writings*, ed. Jeanne Schulkind (Sussex: The University Press, 1976), p. 132.

through which Jacob is passing is subtly undermined by the preor-
dained, mechanical program he is acting out; and the machinery that
would have assured him a place in *Who's Who* sends him off to war
instead. In *Jacob's Room*, Woolf describes a "dozen young men in
the prime of life" whose battleship has been hit "descend with composed faces into the depths of the sea; and there impassively (though
with perfect mastery of machinery) suffocate uncomplainingly
together" (p. 155) [125].

The public schools and ancient universities were the training
grounds for such complaisant attitudes, and Woolf's feelings about
these institutions differed sharply from those of the Bloomsbury
males. When people like Lytton Strachey and Leonard Woolf looked
back on their undergraduate years, they saw paradise lost. Strachey
wrote in an ecstatic letter to Leonard about a visit to Cambridge:
"Good God! The Great Court is the most thrilling place in the world,
it's no good trying to get over it; whenever I come in through the
great gate my heart thumps, and I fall into a million visions."[5] By
contrast, Virginia Woolf's picture of Cambridge in *Jacob's Room*
stresses its pretension and provinciality: "It is not simple, or pure, or
wholly splendid, the lamp of learning. . . . How like a suburb where
you go to see a view and eat a special cake! 'We are the sole purveyors
of this cake' " (p. 38) [29–30].

Her critical distance was a response to feeling shut out, a reaction
she would examine at length in the first of her feminist books, *A
Room of One's Own*. The Cambridge suburb admitted women only
on sufferance, and it taught its male products to patronize them. So
Jacob fails to understand why women are allowed to attend service
at King's College Chapel: "No one would think of bringing a dog into
church," he reflects, "a dog destroys the service completely. So do
these women" (p. 31) [23]. It is interesting that Woolf's first draft
version of the novel included a chapter about a young woman student at Cambridge which in some ways parallels the Jacob portions
of the narrative. But the chapter was excised from the final version,
probably to underline the fact that the university was still a young
man's world, despite the presence of a few female interlopers.[6]

From Woolf's point of view, Jacob fits all too easily into this world.

---

5. Lytton Strachey, letter to Leonard Woolf, 17 September 1908, Berg Collection, New York
   Public Library. I am grateful to The Society of Authors as Agents for the Strachey Trust
   and to the Berg Collection for permission to quote from Strachey's letters, copyright 1981
   Lytton Strachey.
6. See chapter X of the *Jacob's Room* holograph version (pt. I, pp. 85–91), Berg Collection,
   New York Public Library. The chapter was later revised for publication as a short story,
   "A Woman's College from Outside," in *Atalanta's Garland: Being the Book of the Edinburgh
   University Women's Union 1926* (Edinburgh: Edinburgh University Press, 1926), pp. 11–
   16, and is reprinted in *Books and Portraits*, pp. 6–9. On Woolf's irreverent attitude toward
   Cambridge, see Irma Rantavaara, *Virginia Woolf and Bloomsbury* (Helsinki: Annales Aca-
   demiae Fennicae, 1953), p. 102.

His rebellious gestures are relatively superficial, and the picture of him at Cambridge stresses his confident appropriation of his position: "He looked satisfied; indeed masterly; which expression changed slightly as he stood there, the sound of the clock conveying to him (it may be) a sense of old buildings and time; and himself the inheritor; and then to-morrow; and friends; at the thought of whom, in sheer confidence and pleasure, it seemed, he yawned and stretched himself" (p. 43) [34]. His Cambridge training reinforces the sense of membership in an elite, and there is more than a hint of arrogance in his makeup. The attitude provokes Woolf's sarcasm, though the tone remains good-humored: "The flesh and blood of the future depends entirely upon six young men. And as Jacob was one of them, no doubt he looked a little regal and pompous as he turned his page" (p. 106) [85].

There are many indications that Jacob is far from extraordinary, despite his membership in this exclusive fraternity. The novel records the classic events in the life of a presentable young man. Jacob's thoughts and experiences are treated as typical rather than unique, and his individual identity is made to merge with that of a group. Woolf's descriptions of him at Cambridge, in London, and on the Continent often seem to efface his defining characteristics and turn him into a representative figure, as in this passage:

> But Jacob moved. He murmured good-night. He went out into the court. He buttoned his jacket across his chest. He went back to his rooms, and being the only man who walked at that moment back to his rooms, his footsteps rang out, his figure loomed large. Back from the Chapel, back from the Hall, back from the Library, came the sound of his footsteps, as if the old stone echoed with magisterial authority: "The young man—the young man—the young man—back to his rooms."
>
> (p. 45) [35]

They move in packs, these young men, and their most antisocial ideas are quickly ratified by their fellows. For Jacob's friend Richard Bonamy, life is "damnably difficult" because he feels the world neglects its gifted youth; "but"—the narrator comments—"not so difficult if on the next staircase, in the large room, there are two, three, five young men all convinced of this—of brutality, that is, and the clear division between right and wrong" (p. 42) [33].

In such ways, the unexamined idea of the promising young man is challenged by Woolf's vision of incipient conventionality. It is instructive to contrast Jacob's rather banal and predictable effusions on Greece with Woolf's own first vision of that country. His thoughts are not individualized but reflect the familiar romantic Hellenism of his society and set: "He could live on bread and wine—the wine in straw bottles—for after doing Greece he was going to knock off Rome. The Roman civilization was a very inferior affair, no doubt. But Bonamy talked a lot of rot, all the same. 'You ought to have been in Athens,' he would say to Bonamy when he got back" (p. 134) [108]. Contrast this with a passage from a diary Woolf kept on her first trip to Greece in 1906, when she was, like Jacob, in her mid-twenties. Her description of the Acropolis is clearly the product of a keen observer who does not rely on potted history or Baedeker's sense of the sublime:

> No place seems more lusty and alive than this platform of ancient dead stone. The fat Maidens who bear the weight of the Erectheum on their heads, stand smiling tranquil ease, for their border is just meet for their strength. They glory in it; one foot just advanced, their hands, one conceives, loosely curled at their sides. And the warm blue sky flows into all the crevices of the marble; yet they detach themselves, and spring into the air, with edges, unblunted, and still virile and young.[7]

A description like this, though it has a self-conscious air and is clearly an attempt at fine writing, stands out as genuinely "promising" because it suggests freshness of observation and expression. It makes us aware how far Jacob still was from finding his own voice.

What would have happened to such young men had they been permitted to live out their term? It is a question the novel constantly raises but can never, of course, answer. Woolf's attempts at prediction are cut short by her sense of their group fate, which makes her hastily withdraw the question: "Behind the grey walls sat so many young men, some undoubtedly reading, magazines, shilling shockers, no doubt; legs, perhaps, over the arms of chairs; smoking; sprawling over tables, and writing while their heads went round in a circle as the pen moved—simple young men, these, who would—but there is no need to think of them grown old" (p. 41) [32]. There are, however, a few passages in the novel in which Woolf allows herself to imagine a future life for Jacob and some of his companions, and the picture is seldom radiant with hope. Respectability, responsibility, establishment success: that is the image in the crystal ball. As Jacob rails against women in youthful fervor, the narrator comments drily in a parenthesis: "This violent disillusionment is generally to be expected in young men in the prime of life, sound of wind and limb, who will soon become fathers of families and directors of banks" (p. 150) [121]. And after giving us a sense of his "desperate" infatuation with

---

7. Virginia Woolf, Diary Typescript, Sept. 14 (1906)–April 25, 1909, Berg Collection, New York Public Library, p. 9. The forthcoming edition of Woolf's early diaries by Mitchell Leaska and Louis DeSalvo may correct some of the obvious errors of transcription in the Berg Collection typescript.

Sandra Wentworth Williams, Woolf notes that Jacob "had in him the seeds of extreme disillusionment, which would come to him from women in middle life" (p. 158) [128].

Such passages make it clear that *Jacob's Room* is much more a novel about a stage of life than a particular person. The fate that lies ahead for her young man is extinction in the war. But the fate from which he is saved is not presented as much more attractive: middle age, in the novel, is a kind of slow death or betrayal of youthful promise. The book is filled with poignant images of the brevity of youth: "And for ever the beauty of young men seems to be set in smoke, however lustily they chase footballs, or drive cricket balls, dance, run, or stride along roads. Possibly they are soon to lose it" (p. 116) [93]. The very intensity of the experimental stage is too violent to be sustained, as Woolf suggests in a vivid metaphor: "Why, from the very windows, even in the dusk, you see a swelling run through the street, an aspiration, as with arms outstretched, eyes desiring, mouth agape. And then we peaceably subside. For if the exaltation lasted we should be blown like foam into the air" (p. 119) [96]. And even those who do not agree to fit themselves into the comfortable niches society has prepared when the season of youth is over are not presented as heroic rebels. In one of her predictive passages, Woolf draws a bleak picture of what lies ahead for a young bohemian painter whose work so excites Jacob in Paris:

> . . . and as for Cruttendon and Jinny, he thought them the most remarkable people he had ever met—being of course unable to foresee how it fell out in the course of time that Cruttendon took to painting orchards; had therefore to live in Kent; and must, one would think, see through apple blossom by this time, since his wife, for whose sake he did it, eloped with a novelist; but no; Cruttendon still paints orchards, savagely, in solitude.
>
> (p. 130) [104]

An elegy is a work of consolation as well as desolation. If anything in Jacob's early death can be thought of as consoling, it is the fact that he is spared the disillusionment that awaits him. Never to be defined means never to be bounded. Middle age in Woolf's work is regularly seen as a diminution. In *The Waves*, the novel in which she follows her characters through all their life stages from childhood to old age, one of them sums up the difference between youth and "maturity" in this bleak way: "Change is no longer possible. We are committed. Before, when we met in a restaurant in London with Percival, all simmered and shook; we could have been anything. We have chosen now, or sometimes it seems the choice was made for us—a pair of tongs pinched us between the shoulders."[8] Jacob's life

8. Virginia Woolf, *The Waves* (London: Hogarth, 1972), p. 151.

does not reach the treadmill stage, and he seems fixed forever at the moment of infinite possibility, before the seeds of conventionality Woolf notices in him have sprouted. In her preliminary notes for the novel, there is a cryptic notation: "Intensity of life compared with immobility."[9] She never explains what this means; but it is possible that her terms define the two life stages her book consistently contrasts: the experimental intensity of youth, the fixity of what follows. Jacob dies young, but he never dwindles into the banal life he sees ahead of him, that of "settling down in a lawyer's office, and wearing spats" (p. 49) [38].

Woolf's sharp sense of the brevity of life, of the universality of death, puts Jacob's "tragic" fate in longer perspective. To die young, to die later: the book seems to say that the distinction borders on the trivial. From the first page of her novel, we hear the note of mortality. Mrs. Flanders weeps for her husband, long since dead. Though Seabrook Flanders was no war victim, he too died young, before the world knew what to call him. And Woolf comments, "Had he, then, been nothing? An unanswerable question, since even if it weren't the habit of the undertaker to close the eyes, the light so soon goes out of them" (p. 14) [10]. The book's focus on the present moment constantly blurs to give us a sense of time past and time future. For Julia Eliot, walking down Piccadilly, "the tumult of the present seems like an elegy for past youth and past summers, and there rose in her mind a curious sadness, as if time and eternity showed through skirts and waistcoats, and she saw people passing tragically to destruction" (p. 168) [135]. This elegiac note is not connected exclusively to the carnage of the war but seems rather a response to the inescapable fact of mortality. It is, Woolf says, a sorrow "brewed by the earth itself. . . . We start transparent, and then the cloud thickens. All history backs our pane of glass. To escape is vain" (p. 47) [37]. The sense of death broods over the novel, and Woolf's images constantly reinforce it: Jacob finding the sheep's skull on the beach; the momentary illumination of faces on Guy Fawkes night, before the fire is extinguished "and all the faces went out" (p. 73) [58]; a mason's van passing "with newly lettered tombstones recording how some one loved some one who is buried at Putney" (p. 111) [89–90]; Mrs. Jarvis walking through the cemetery or telling her friend, "I never pity the dead" (p. 130) [105].

This atemporal awareness of mortality Woolf carried with her always. She asks herself in her diary as she works on *Jacob's Room*, "Why is life so tragic; so like a strip of pavement over an abyss. I look

---

9. Virginia Woolf, "Reflections upon beginning a work of fiction to be called, perhaps, Jacobs Room," *Jacob's Room* holograph, Berg Collection, New York Public Library, pt. I, p. 1.

down; I feel giddy; I wonder how I am ever to walk to the end" (*AWD*, 29). Though she says later in the same entry that this tragic sense is pervasive "for us in our generation," her novel's repeated stretching of time and space suggests a fundamentally religious perception of the issue, though without a religious consolation. Her vision recalls the "Ithaca" chapter in *Ulysses*, in which Joyce's sense of cosmic time nearly obliterates his characters. He sees the "socalled fixed stars, in reality evermoving from immeasurably remote eons to infinitely remote futures in comparison with which the years, threescore and ten, of allotted human life formed a parenthesis of infinitesimal brevity."[1] Similarly, in *Jacob's Room*, one of the guests at the Durrants' evening party examines the constellations through the telescope only to find herself suddenly deserted by all her companions: " 'Where are you all?' she asked, taking her eye away from the telescope. 'How dark it is!' " (p. 59) [46].

This sense of the universal darkness surrounding us both elevates and trivializes Jacob's death. From the aspect of eternity, individual death is meaningless, and even the annihilation of a million young men in battle is a fact that history will swallow without special effort. But at the same time, the extinction of any life inevitably recalls the fate that awaits us all and is invested with that resonance. This is why the lament for Jacob becomes, for all the novel's irony, so moving: "Ja-cob! Ja-cob!" his brother calls in the novel's first scene; and Woolf comments: "The voice had an extraordinary sadness. Pure from all body, pure from all passion, going out into the world, solitary, unanswered, breaking against rocks—so it sounded" (p. 7) [4]. "Jacob! Jacob!": it is a refrain that will be heard again and again in the book, from Mrs. Flanders, from Clara Durrant, from Richard Bonamy, from all those fellow mortals who make the mistake of attaching their deepest feelings to someone who precedes them into the earth. For all Woolf's ironic distance and critical awareness of Jacob's limitations, she knows that such composure dissolves when our emotions are engaged. Her complex attitude is conveyed in an important reflective passage in the book:

> In any case life is but a procession of shadows, and God knows why it is that we embrace them so eagerly, and see them depart with such anguish, being shadows. And why, if this and much more than this is true, why are we yet surprised in the window corner by a sudden vision that the young man in the chair is of all things in the world the most real, the most solid, the best known to us—why indeed? For the moment after we know nothing about him.

1. James Joyce, *Ulysses* (New York: Random House, 1946), p. 683.

Such is the manner of our seeing. Such the conditions of our
love.

(pp. 70–71) [56]

This double awareness of the sharpness of grief and its absurdity
gives Woolf's satiric elegy its special edge and accounts for the
novel's rapid shifts in tone. She worked hard to avoid sentimental-
izing her subject and casting her book in the romantic mold. As
Strachey wrote her after reading *Jacob's Room*, romanticism was "*the*
danger for your genre"; and she agrees that he has put his "infallible
finger upon the spot."[2] But Strachey was hardly the standard of feeling in such matters, as some of his own letters attest. When Thoby
Stephen, Virginia's brother and Strachey's intimate friend, died of
typhoid fever at the age of 26, Strachey's letter to Leonard Woolf
exemplifies the uninhibited and unreflecting expression of grief Virginia Woolf came to distrust: "I don't understand what crowning
pleasure there can be for us without him, and our lives seem deadly
blank. There is nothing left remarkable beneath the visiting moon.
It is idle to talk; but it is only to you that I can say anything, that he
was the best, the noblest, the best—oh god! I am tired out with too
much anguish. Oh god!"[3]

Such threnodies, Woolf came to feel, were finally self-serving and
insincere, a rhetorical exercise in pulling out all the stops. The literary allusions, the exaggerated sense of Thoby's qualities, the indulgence of intense emotion would have struck her as more like a public
performance than a private expression of loss. Her own very different
style of lament deliberately understates or withholds such sentiment.
In the book's last scene, Bonamy can say no more than "Jacob!
Jacob!" and Mrs. Flanders unpredictably focuses on a pair of her
son's old shoes, as though their emptiness conveyed everything:
"What am I to do with these, Mr. Bonamy?" (p. 176) [143]. The
significance of the scene is clarified by an anecdote about Woolf
recalled by one of her friends: "The only other remark I remember
from that afternoon was when she was talking about the mystery of
'missing' someone. When Leonard went away, she said, she didn't
miss him *at all*. Then suddenly she caught sight of a pair of his empty
shoes, which had kept the position and shape of his feet—and was
ready to dissolve into tears instantly."[4]

"Such is the manner of our seeing. Such the conditions of our
love." Jacob's death, like his life, has no intrinsic significance. He is
not clearly "the best, the noblest, the best." Rather, he is an engaging

2. Woolf and Strachey, *Letters*, pp. 103, 104.
3. Lytton Strachey, letter to Leonard Woolf, 21 November 1906, Berg Collection, New York
   Public Library.
4. Frances Marshall, in *Recollections of Virginia Woolf*, ed. Joan Russell Noble (London:
   Peter Owen, 1972), p. 76.

young man, in many ways typical of his class and training, who has unintentionally managed to secure the love of a few human beings. His absence, like his presence, is not likely to alter the world significantly. His youthful promise might well have been betrayed, his eager ambition have turned into the ordinary life choices. It is only on the small canvas appropriate to such a view, rather than the grand frescoes of the heroic imagination, that Woolf could allow herself to sketch—in a deliberately halting and fragmented style and in a tone that is conspicuously impure—her vision of a permanently inscrutable young man.

KATE FLINT

Revising *Jacob's Room*: Virginia Woolf, Women, and Language†

Jacob's Room, as we know it, opens with a woman writing. Betty Flanders, on the beach, is composing a letter, a quintessentially private form of expression; one which, in this case, is redolent of emotion. The fluids of composition and of sentiment seem interchangeable: 'Slowly welling from the point of her gold nib, pale blue ink dissolved the full stop; for there her pen stuck; her eyes fixed, and tears slowly filled them.'[1] Jacob, on the other hand, is missing: a foreshadowing both of his final absence from the text, and of the half-unformed, half-enigmatic presence which he is to emanate throughout. ' "Where *is* that tiresome little boy? . . . I don't see him" ' (5) [3]. Yet in Woolf's original draft of the novel, Jacob was clearly visible from the start. Mrs Flanders did not assume such an immediate position of centrality. Rather, the opening foregrounded Jacob's own anxious perception, his fears of isolation and the repulsion which rewards his attempt to seek security in a woman:

> Beyond the rock lay something on the sand. A few small fish left by the tide beat up & down with their tails. On the edge of the wave, paddling their feet, stood a single line of gulls, &, Jacob was trotting towards them when the light came across the waves. He then saw that the beach went on & on; he saw that there was a new line of hills above it; in short he was lost. He trotted along by the waves & one after another the gulls rose;

---

† From *Review of English Studies*, n.s., 42 (1991): 361–79. Reprinted by permission of Oxford University Press.
1. Virginia Woolf, *Jacob's Room* ([London: Hogarth Press, 1922] London: Grafton Press, 1986), 5. Subsequent page references in the text are to this edition. [Bracketed page numbers refer to this Norton Critical Edition.]

but in the distance he saw a woman sitting; & as the gulls rose
he ran faster & faster to reach her. But oh the waves came round
her. She was a rock. She was covered with seaweed that pops
when it is pressed. She was slimy. 'Nanny, nanny!' he cried;
Nanny! nanny! Now he sobbed it out mechanically as he ran.
Nanny! Nanny![2]

The figurative rock of security towards which Jacob hurries proves,
as in the final version, to be a sinister emanation of the world existing
outside his household sphere: a world against which, in both its
material and social forms, we are to see him tentatively testing and
asserting his identity until he is finally swallowed up by the War, a
fate prefigured through a very marker of identity, Flanders, his family
name.

One may take these two openings of the novel as indicative of a
shift in Woolf's focus as she wrote *Jacob's Room*: a shift, indeed, in
her construction of her own identity as a novelist during the period
of its composition. She had previously written of the lives of *individual* women, of their position within their families and during court-
ship, and, in the case of Mary Datchet in *Night and Day*, in relation
to the suffrage movement—though not, here, without a certain sardonic suggestion that Mary was involving herself in 'the Cause' as a
substitute for a satisfying emotional life. But when revising *Jacob's
Room*, Woolf came to organize her text around a more generalized
perception of difference between the sexes. Such differences, she
demonstrates with regard to attitudes, opportunities, and values,
were crucial to the maintenance of the dominant ideology of a society
which was capable of sending 'young men in the prime of life' (151)
[125] off to their death on battlefields or under the sea. To make
this point is initially to shift the focus which Woolf's revisions to the
novel have hitherto received from questions of form to those relating
to content and argument. As ever with Woolf, however, the question
of *what* she writes as a woman is inseparable from her own consideration of the difference which gender makes to *how* she writes.

Jacob's Room, more stylistically adventurous than Woolf's earlier
two novels, has conventionally been treated as her first sustained
attempt at presenting the fragmented nature of consciousness and
perception; representing, as Charles Hoffmann, one of the few critics to look in any detail at the text's revisions, put it, 'the turning
point in her art of the novel, marking the shift from traditional patterns of narration and style which dominated her first two novels

2. Holograph manuscript of *Jacob's Room*, Henry W. and Albert A. Berg Collection, New
York Public Library, Notebook 1, p. 3. Subsequent references in the text will take the form
Notebook 1/Notebook 2, plus page number. The manuscript of *Jacob's Room* consists of
three notebooks. Almost all the draft of *Jacob's Room* is to be found in the first two notebooks, the third containing—among other pieces of writing, including preliminary notes
for *Mrs Dalloway*—only a draft of the final chapter (Notebook 3, 61–5).

toward the narrative technique and lyrical style of the later novels'.[3]

Hoffmann indicates, through examining the drafts and final texts of *The Voyage Out* and *Night and Day*, that this shift was not sudden. But he uses the revisions to *Jacob's Room* itself, drawing attention to such factors as the cancellation of quotation marks, to indicate that in this text in particular, Woolf was aiming towards an associative prose which would 'give the moment whole', moving 'almost imperceptibly into impressionistic internality and out again to the external world.'[4] His conclusions are amplified by E. L. Bishop's thorough, thoughtful article on the revisions, which draws attention to a deliberate excision of the representation of Jacob's consciousness, the diminution of a complicity between narrator and reader, and the sharpening of our sense of the novel's scenes as discrete units.[5] Certainly the jottings on the first page of the manuscript suggest that formal experiment was one of Woolf's starting-points:

> I think the main point is that it should be free.
> Yet what about form?
> Let us suppose that the Room will hold it together.
> Intensity of life compared with immobility.
> Experiences.
> To change style at will.   (Notebook 1, 1) [167]

Taking a slightly different tack, Alex Zwerdling has attempted to demonstrate that the revisions contribute to our impression of what he terms Jacob's unformed personality, by suppressing 'the vestiges of Jacob's inner life', thus keeping an ironic distance between narrator and Jacob, reader and main character.[6] The distance of 'an older, more experienced, highly skeptical consciousness, determined to puncture youthful illusion and undercut intense illusion of any kind', Zwerdling calls it: the distance, the difference, one might say in the context of the novel, of the woman's narrative voice from the male persona. Such an effect may be considered in relation to the disconnections in the novel which Rachel Bowlby has appropriated as 'a feminine form of narrative', decentring the subject, satirizing 'the standard format of the biography of the exceptional man'.[7] But more than formal considerations are at stake. It is noticeable that neither Hoffmann nor Zwerdling, in their utilization of the manuscript notebooks, examines the substance of the passages which are added or lost, and that when Bishop does so, he is most interested

3. Charles G. Hoffmann, ' "From Lunch to Dinner": Virginia Woolf's Apprenticeship." *Texas Studies in Literature and Language*, 10 (1969), 609.
4. Ibid. 623.
5. E. L. Bishop, 'The Shaping of *Jacob's Room*: Woolf's Manuscript Revisions', *Twentieth Century Literature*, 32 (1986), 115–35.
6. Alex Zwerdling, *Virginia Woolf and the Real World* (Berkeley and Los Angeles, 1986), 69.
7. Rachel Bowlby, *Virginia Woolf: Feminist Destinations* (Oxford, 1988), 101, 112.

in Jacob himself. With their eye on form and on the enigmatic young man, they ignore the reworking of *women*'s consciousness throughout the novel. It is through the arrival at a particular conjunction of content and expression in the final version of *Jacob's Room* that we may trace what it meant for Woolf to be developing 'a woman's voice' at this stage of her career.

II

G. Thomas Tanselle has distinguished between vertical and horizontal axes in the revision of texts.[8] Horizontal revision—'that which aims at intensifying, refining, or improving the work as then conceived'—of course takes place within Woolf's reworking of *Jacob's Room*. But it is to vertical revision—that which 'aims at altering the purpose, direction, or character of a work'—that I shall be paying the most attention. Whilst much of the horizontal revision is not concerned in any way with issues which affect women, a significant proportion of the vertical revision reworks precisely this area. We should note, however, that privileging issues of gender renders 'vertical' those alterations which might not appear significant to a critic approaching *Jacob's Room* with different priorities: Tanselle's dividing line is necessarily redrawn by the critical ends which each textual analysis serves.

The 'vertical' revisions to the novel are on different scales: several pages, paragraphs, individual words and phrases. First, consider the instances where whole sections were deleted or added. I have already remarked on the distancing of Jacob which the altered opening enforces: indeed, the original first chapter continued to develop Jacob's perspective, following him directly back to his bedroom, and his speculations about the horse's—not sheep's—jawbone. Nor is this the only place in the novel where we are deprived of substantial reference to Jacob. Originally, the manuscript contained far more detail about his reflections whilst staying in Paris, and an extended description of his train journey south through Italy, including a conversation with a horse-dealer, Guiseppe Bandelli. This whole section emphasized the enthusiastic self-preoccupation of the young man at this stage of his life in a way which, whilst suggesting his naïvety, simultaneously indicates, almost indulgently, that this is a relatively endearing quality. Yet on the other hand we gain, in Chapter 2, the pages relating Jacob's pursuit of moths and butterflies; his childhood quests for the natural, the beautiful, the ephemeral in a manner which combines the destructive with the scholarly are now brought into closer focus than his manhood. Moreover, the first six and a half

<hr>

8. G. Thomas Tanselle, 'The Editorial Problem of Final Authorial Intention', *Studies in Bibliography*, 29 (1976), 167–211.

pages of Chapter 4, describing the idle masculine camaraderie of Jacob and Timmy Durrant sailing past the Scilly Isles ('What's the use of trying to read Shakespeare . . . against the rocks' (44–9) [35]), is also essentially an addition to the final version, although some scraps of it can be found at the end of the first manuscript notebook (Notebook 1, 207–9).

The overall impression of the relative distancing of Jacob's consciousness, however, persists. Yet it would be too simplistic a generalization to suggest that *all* the revisions axiomatically foreground women's consciousness at the expense of that of men. The sections relating to Mrs Flanders's home life are, in fact, considerably cut. Her particularity is diminished, especially at the opening of Chapter 11, which originally contained a depiction of her alertness to the natural world, and her thoughts of her sons, set against the mundanity of her daily life in Yorkshire (Notebook 2, 109–15). The more distanced recording of Mrs Flanders's conversation with Mrs Jarvis about Jacob's letters, and the description of the Yorkshire night which conclude Chapter 11 are substituted ('No—Mrs Flanders was told nothing of this. . . . The church clock, however, strikes twelve' (126–30) [104–107]). We also lose, from Chapter 10, a substantial section giving Fanny Elmer's thoughts as she passes Jacob's house, and as she visits Nick Bramham's studio: a passage which merges with an extended meditation about 'life itself', and how we are lifted:

> up, down: up, down, Why from the very windows, even in the dark, you [seem to] see a [wave in] swelling run through the street, an aspiration, a rising up, as with arms outstretched, [mouths] eyes deserving mouths agape—Down, down again—[For to the] for if this exultation lasted, we should be blown like [the soft foam] foam right into the air. The stars would shine through us. We should go down the gale in salt drops. As sometimes happens. For the impetuous spirits [have done with life leapt the bridge, or snatched the razor] have [stepped off the are not to be tampered with] will have none of this cradling. Off they fly, from the waves' crest; [never again to be sucked back lulled, soothed, aimlessly swaying straight at the] Never any swaying, or aimlessly lolling for them. (Notebook 2, 105) [153][9]

Even more noticeable, in the context of a gender-oriented argument, is the fact that the original Chapter 9 disappears, to be reprinted in *Atalanta's Garland: Being the Book of the Edinburgh University Women's Union* (November 1926), 11–16 as 'A Woman's College from Outside'. Within the final structure of *Jacob's Room*,

---

9. Here, and in subsequent quotations from the Notebooks, manuscript deletions are enclosed in square brackets, and manuscript additions are enclosed in half square brackets, whether interlinear or not.

the inclusion of this section's optimism about 'this good world, this
new world, this world at the end of the tunnel' would have weakened
the presentation of Cambridge as a bastion of male social and educational privilege, since it stresses the possibilities of the future, with
women's companionship 'pouring forth'; the 'laughter of mind and
body floating away rules, hours, discipline': a woman's counterpart
to the magical 'intimacy' which 'without need of movement or speech
. . . rose softly and washed over everything, mollifying, kindling, and
coating the mind with the lustre of pearl' when Jacob stood with
Simeon in the latter's room (43–4) [35]. In the printed version of
the novel, education and literature are generally deployed far more
deliberately and forcefully than in the manuscript as indicators of
the cultural and social separation of the sexes. 'Books', claims Woolf,
in a brief passage in fact deleted from the final text, 'so people say,
are an infallible guide to character. Thus we might be worse occupied
than in examining the works of Shakespeare, the plays of Ben Jonson—Mrs. Aphra Behn's Lyrics' (Notebook 2, 75). In manuscript,
Jacob gives Florinda, in Chapter 6, Jane Austen and Peacock's *Gryll
Grange* to read: in the final version, this becomes Shelley, and in
particular 'Adonais'. Florinda's difference from Jacob comes to be
underscored by her inability to feel anything other than boredom
and incomprehension when faced with male passion and grief: however, as in most of the writing concerning Florinda, one senses the
narrator's scorn for brainless women such as she represents—and
concomitant scorn for the young men who appear interested in them
only for their bodies. More telling is the section in Chapter 10 when
Fanny struggles to understand Jacob through his liking for *Tom
Jones*: a substitution for the continuous extended lyric passage partially quoted above, in which Fanny and the narrator's voices merge
in a consideration of the ebb and flow of

> life, this dark eyed mother, with all her violence, spurning us,
> bidding us fly, vanish, never learn to grow old, yet if you press
> close to her murmurs; some secret. What? Only one word. Lis-
> ten, Another. No sense to it. No. But lean closer. Follow after
> down the great hall, dimly lit with the curved ceiling, resonant
> with echoes, alarming, tapers blown out; cold gusts from what
> sea? Life, life, booming, & the lightning. (Notebook 2, 107)

The omission of this whole section works against Hoffmann's and
Zwerdling's claims for the increased experimentalism in narrative
voice demonstrated through the revisions of *Jacob's Room*. However,
if attention is paid to the content, it can be noted that cultural relations have taken the place of private, maternal ones. It is superficially
tempting to describe the alternating fluid and broken rhythms, the
associationism, the oral and exclamatory qualities of the manuscript

passage as an attempt to develop a distinctive 'feminine voice' in writing which would accord neatly with Luce Irigaray's description of woman's language[1] and which appears to illustrate Julia Kristeva's brief description of Woolf as 'Haunted by voices, waves, lights, in love with colours—blue, green—and seized by a strange gaiety'.[2] But Woolf ultimately chooses to replace intimate, uncertain fears and desires, the two barely divisible, with images belonging to a fragmented London social world. These suggest a preoccupation with lacunae in cultural communication between classes, between women, as well as between the sexes.

The tendency to employ literary signification is continued when, even more conspicuously, the eventual Chapter 9 gains the section which prefigures Woolf's treatment of the British Museum Reading Room in *A Room of One's Own*. Julia Hedge, the feminist, waiting for her books to arrive, observes the formal celebration of England's literary heritage in the gilded names inscribed here: 'she read them all round the dome—the names of the great men which remind us— "Oh damn," said Julia Hedge, "why didn't they leave room for an Eliot or a Brontë?" ' (102–3) [84]. The composite 'enormous mind' of the British Museum, containing Plato, Aristotle, Shakespeare, and Marlowe, contains no officially sanctioned women's thought.[3]

Let us now move to a consideration of the *shorter* passages which were deleted or changed. A significant proportion of these, too, involve the presentation of women. Whilst there are fewer examples of alterations relating to intellectual and literary issues, the excisions are notable, like some of the longer passages, for the way in which they work to exclude references to women's private, individualizing, even sexual lives. Three examples are particularly telling. In Chapter 2 of the published text, Mrs Flanders receives, and politely rejects, Mr Floyd's letter proposing marriage: a page later, she strokes the cat which Mr Floyd had given the family 'and she smiled, thinking how she had had him gelded, and how she did not like red hair in men' (20) [15]. At one level, this is, effectually, an example of horizontal revision: a condensing of the connection between the two ideas which is spelt out explicitly in the manuscript, far more forthright about Betty Flanders's rejection of the proposal and about the cat's emasculation: ' "How could I think of marriage!" she thought to herself almost bitterly . . . It was, probably, that the idea

1. ' . . . c'est continu, compressible, dilatable, visqueux, conductible, diffusible, . . . Que ça n'en finit pas, puissant(e) et impuissant(e) de par cette résistance au nombrable; que ça jount et pâtit d'être plus sensible aux pressions' (Luce Irigaray, in her chapter 'La "Méca-nique" des Fluides', *Ce sexe qui n'en est pas un* (Paris, 1977), 109).
2. Julia Kristeva, 'About Chinese Women', trans. Seán Hand, in *The Kristeva Reader*, ed. Toril Moi (Oxford, 1986), 157.
3. The added section runs from 'Not so very long ago' to 'stood by the pillar-box, arguing' (101–6).

of copulation had now become infinitely remote from her. She did not use the word; & yet as she sat darning the boys clothes that night it annoyed her to find that it was so' (Notebook 1, 23). Moreover, of the cat, 'she had not used the word "gelded" or [consciously connected the two ideas in her mind],—indeed she never used words when she thought indecent thoughts' (Notebook 1, 25). But whilst the revision here may be read as an example of Woolf tidying up a character's thought process, explicating the links between conscious and unconscious before compressing them, it also indicates the ultimate impossibility of dividing horizontal from vertical axes. Specifically, it offers a removal of traditional associations of women and prudery from the text—leaving Mrs Flanders with a more triumphant air at having executed a vicarious castration—and, more broadly, once again Woolf diminishes our knowledge of the precise operations of an individual woman's consciousness.

A more conspicuous example occurs in the description of the Cornishwoman, Mrs Pascoe, whose cameo appearance in Chapter 4 of the printed version largely serves to emphasize the rather haughty class self-consciousness of Mrs Durrant, set against the taciturn self-sufficiency of the Cornishwoman, a figure about whom one might speculate, but only in terms which accentuate the tourist/narrator/reader's own class assumptions: that such a woman inevitably dreams wistfully over society weddings in the picture papers. She remains as impervious as the local granite to the inquisitive gaze: 'Like a miser, she has hoarded her feelings within her breast' (52) [41]. Not so, however, in the manuscript, in a passage which indicates as powerfully as anything that Woolf ever wrote that she was not herself hesitant, at least when writing privately, at using 'words when she thought indecent thoughts'. First, a connection is made between the sea at which Mrs Pascoe gazes, and the continuity of the life of which she is part. 'For the millionth time she looks at the sea. Probably this last look confirms or alters something always growing in her. It is part of the ringings, scourings, copulations, births, & deep glooms & scoldings, which have gone on for sixty years perhaps in the four rooms of the cottage. But no body knows' (Notebook 1, 97). The geological metaphor, implicit in the printed text, is made explicit: 'the black rocks of the sea testified to the endurance of this solitary crag of human life, fronting its waves' (Notebook 1, 99). Most telling of all is the deleted description of the impression made—on Mrs Pascoe's senses? by the narrator's speculative imagination?—when she enters her cottage.

> Owing perhaps to the small size of the room, & the rich musty smell of the geraniums in the window, the body became very emphatic. [Two bodies would] [She] Mrs Pascoe wore a dirty

white cloth of some kind round her neck & the creases [of] in her skin were marked by black grains. [When her husband came in, the] Two bodies together would [create an intolerable sense of] [be] make it impossible to think of anything except the body. One might go into the scullery, the other stumble up the stairs to the bedroom, but there would be no escaping the body. [Its functions are detestable] An earth closet out in the rain—sick-ness—a woman's period—copulation upstairs in the double bed, [or here before the fire perhaps]—childbirth—[all] [all that veils & places in the shadows these natural functions of the body are all] [bodies] as the room filled with bodies. [There functions & desires would assert themselves. all these functions and desires would press become prominent] [in their four roomed cottage on] It would be impossible not to think solely of these functions and desires. (Notebook 1, 99–101) [146]

Of course, various reasons can be postulated for Woolf's decision to leave this out of the printed text. She may have found it personally embarrassing: it is a very heavily revised passage, indicating her dif-ficulties, of whatever kind, in writing it in the first place. Moreover, Woolf might have been anxious to avoid critical attention falling on such a passage: her review of D. H. Lawrence's *The Lost Girl*, pub-lished in the *Times Literary Supplement* on 2 December 1920, betrays a hint of potential embarrassment when she describes her preconception of Lawrence as a writer 'for whom the body was alive and the problem of the body insistent and important. It was plain that sex for him had a meaning which it was disquieting to think that we, too, might have to explore.'[4]

But I am not here concerned with possible authorial motive, but with textual effect. Again, the revision has worked to suppress an individual woman's connection with sexuality. And we see this again in a final example, when the sexuality in question is not the woman's own, but her son's. The passage near the beginning of Chapter 8 is, as it now stands, revelatory enough about Betty Flanders's sense of maternal distance as expressed through anxious, lonely clichés, tell-ing how 'mothers down at Scarborough scribble over the fire with their feet on the fender, when tea's cleared away, and can never, never say, whatever it might be—probably this—Don't go with bad women, do be a good boy; wear your thick shirts; and come back, come back to me' (87) [71]. Yet this archetypicality, with its almost ballad-like refrain, is a product of revision: previously, despite an attempt to make Betty representative, the emphasis falls on her individual concern, and its specific direction, ironically offset in the

4. Virginia Woolf, 'Postscript or Prelude?', *The Essays of Virginia Woolf. Vol. III: 1919–1924*, ed. Andrew McNeillie (London, 1988), 271.

narrative by the immediate juxtaposition of Jacob casually disappearing to the bedroom with Florinda: 'poor Betty Flanders!', laments the manuscript. 'Poor mothers—poor women—poor anyone indeed who lives in ignorance, & must hint at what they want to ask instead of asking it. This question of her son's chastity . . . ' (Notebook 2, 5).

The substitution of general issues for particular concerns, or the reduction of personal, intimate thoughts which is demonstrated through the mid-length revisions to *Jacob's Room* is upheld by a significant number of small alterations which Woolf made between manuscript and printed text. Again, direct references to sexuality and intimate relations are diminished in importance. More importantly, however, it is very noticeable how much the public and literary aspects of sexual politics are foregrounded. Examples of sentences not found in the published text include the remark about the four people of disparate ages and genders in Miss Perry's sitting room: 'It is impossible to imagine them naked' (Notebook 2, 41); or the aside concerning Clara Durrant: 'More than any young man in the world, she loved her mother' (Notebook 1, 189); or—confirming an important point about Bonamy—Jacob, in Greece, thinks of 'Bonamy mugging up Roman Law in his rooms in Gower street—to Bonamy who couldn't fall in love, [he saw] with any woman, & had such fine taste in the classics' (Notebook 2, 201–3). Jacob's acknowledgement of Bonamy's homosexuality is replaced, at the equivalent point in the final text, by the more delicate hint of the scholar's genteel trip to talk about Jacob with Clara Durrant, 'pausing to watch the boys bathing in the Serpentine' (144) [122] on his way home. Conversely, examining the additions, one finds that the patriarchal emphasis of Jacob's Cambridge education is underscored. A list of future potential occupations for undergraduates is insinuated into Mr Plumer's thoughts, as he carves the mutton at his luncheon party: they will 'become lawyers, doctors, members of Parliament, businessmen' (31) [24]. We are newly informed that Jacob himself 'was a young man of substance' (33) [26]. At the same time, his own consciousness of the institutionalization of the world which he is entering is intensified: 'sure enough the cities which the elderly of the race have built upon the skyline showed like brick suburbs, ⌜barracks and places of discipline⌝ against a red and yellow flame' (33) [26]. Woolf appends to Chapter 3 the title of the essay which Jacob is writing: 'Does History consist of the Biographies of Great Men?' (36). The discussion the young men are having in a room, it is suggested, may be a particularly trivial one: 'Was it an argument? ⌜ A bet on the boat races?⌝ Was it nothing of the sort?' (42) [33]. She emphasizes the force of the end of the chapter, where 'the old stone echoed ⌜with magisterial authority⌝: 'The young man—the young [man] ⌜men⌝—the young man—⌝back to his rooms⌝' (44) [35]. Notoriously, throughout the novel, Jacob has not just one, but a whole set of rooms of his own. Around such rooms, life, inevitably, circles. In the manuscript, we read of a dismal London January night, with 'up there behind the blind,—[making the world into shape.] a young man alone in his room' (Notebook 2, 17–19), whilst in the final version this suggestion is made specific. All the distracting elements of the street are '(so outright, so lusty)—yet all the while having for centre, for magnet, a young man alone in his room' (92) [75].

These additions, emphasizing the pompous masculine sphere in and for which Jacob is educated, do not just occur in those parts of the text directly bearing on Jacob's life. A similar mild satiric intensification takes place when Woolf describes the Opera House in Chapter 5:

> The autumn season was in full swing. Tristan was twitching his rug up under his armpits twice a week; Isolde [now] waved her scarf in miraculous sympathy with the conductor's baton. In all parts of the house were to be found [stout hearts, & keen ears] ⌜pink faces and glittering breasts⌝. When a Royal hand [depending from] ⌜attached to⌝ an invisible body slipped out and withdrew the red and white bouquet reposing on the scarlet ledge, the Queen of England [someone to die for] ⌜seemed a name worth dying for⌝. Beauty, in its hothouse variety (which is none of [its] ⌜the⌝ worst), flowered in box after box; ⌜and though nothing was said of profound importance,⌝ and though it is generally agreed that wit deserted beautiful lips about the time that Walpole died—at any rate when Victoria [ascended the throne] ⌜in her nightgown descended to meet her ministers⌝, the lips (through an opera glass) remained [divine] ⌜red⌝, adorable. Bald ⌜distinguished⌝ men with gold-headed canes strolled down the crimson avenues between the [acts] ⌜stalls⌝, and only [tore] ⌜broke⌝ from [their] intercourse with the boxes when the lights [going] ⌜went⌝ down, [and the bows were raised] ⌜and the conductor, first bowing to the Queen, next to the bald-headed men, swept round on his feet and raised his wand⌝. (65; Notebook 2, 135) [52]

Even more notably, in that well-known conjunction of militarism, government, and masculinity towards the end of Chapter 12, the 'other side' mentioned in the manuscript, who maintain that 'character drawing is a frivolous fireside art', are specifically identified as 'the men in clubs and Cabinets'. The feminine associations with which these dignitaries invest character drawing when they describe it as something 'accomplished with pins and needles' are underscored by the addition of the further descriptive phrase, 'exquisite outlines enclosing vacancy, flourishes, and mere scrawls'. In the following paragraph, which opens with the battleships raying out over the North Sea, Woolf accentuates the impersonal military precision through the phrase 'the master gunner counts the seconds, watch in hand—at the sixth he looks up', and enhances the bathos of the patriotic sacrifice by substituting the idea that the dozen young men in the prime of life 'suffocate uncomplainingly together' for the less dramatic 'accept their fate'. Even more tellingly, at the beginning of the next paragraph, where Woolf lists the factors which, in addition to war, 'oar the world forward'—the works of banks, laboratories, chancelleries, and businesses (a list which originally, incidentally, included one of her favourite masculine roles, 'keepers of light-houses')—in the final text she presents this opinion at a distance: 'These actions . . . are the strokes which oar the world forward, *they say*' (151–2; Notebook 2, 213) [125].

III

'They say': the question of difference between men and women's preoccupations, language, style, and political priorities had increasingly interested Woolf in the period immediately preceding the composition of *Jacob's Room*. 'A woman's writing is always feminine,' she wrote in a review of R. Brimsley Johnson's *The Women Novelists* (*TLS*, October 1918); 'the only difficulty lies in defining what we mean by feminine.'[5] It will entail recognizing 'infinite differences in selection, method and style', but she does not, on this occasion, press the point further. She takes it up again when reviewing Léonie Villard's *La Femme anglaise au XIXème siècle et son evolution d'après le roman anglais contemporain* (*TLS*, 18 March 1920): a review, incidentally, in which Woolf mentions, as she did on the earlier occasion, the difficulty of a woman writing successfully about a man, or vice versa, a theoretical and emotional problem with which she grapples in *Jacob's Room*. The issue for women writers, she makes plain, is one of the need for a particular kind of experimentation. She cites Bathsheba's words in *Far From the Madding Crowd*: 'I have the feelings of a woman, but I have only the language of men.' The energy of women's feelings has been liberated for the novelist to use, Woolf says, but 'into what forms is it to flow? To try the accepted forms, to discard the unfit, to create others which are more fitting, is a task that must be accomplished before there is freedom or achievement.'[6]

Doubtless many factors influenced the processes of discarding and creation which lay behind the composition of *Jacob's Room*, but I wish to emphasize one particular conjunction of circumstances which I believe aided Woolf in her development of a form suitable for the conveyance of women's feelings, and also which determined

---

5. Virginia Woolf, 'Women Novelists', *The Essays of Virginia Woolf. Vol. II: 1912–1918*, ed. Andrew McNeillie (London, 1987), 316.
6. Woolf, 'Men and Women', *Essays III*, 195.

that the feelings she chose to emphasize related more to the public than to the private sphere.

Writing in her diary on 26 September 1920, Woolf recorded how 'somehow Jacob has come to a stop, in the middle of that party too, which I enjoyed so much'.[7] She puts forward various hypotheses: fatigue, since she has been working solidly at her writing for two months; or perhaps she has not thought through her plan carefully enough. Most significant seems to have been a visit from T. S. Eliot on 19 September, when he professed his admiration for Wyndham Lewis and Pound as the most important modern writers, and when the conversation revolved around Joyce's new novel, *Ulysses*. As Woolf noted on 20 September, 'Joyce gives internals',[8] precisely her aim in *Jacob's Room*, and she reflected on the 26th 'how what I'm doing is probably being better done by Mr Joyce'.[9] Moreover, she recorded a sense of unease, on 20 September, that Leonard showed up better in this literary conversation than she did, and, rather cryptically, remarks on the 26th, describing her inability to concentrate on Jacob: 'An odd thing the human mind! so capricious, faithless, infinitely shying at shadows. Perhaps at the bottom of my mind, I feel that I'm distanced by L. in every respect.'[1]

Yet during the latter half of September 1920, Woolf was concerned with women's difference from men in terms which went beyond the personal: terms which, I wish to argue, were ultimately to become linked with her development of a form of modernist writing which was distinct from that of the men with whom she was implicitly and explicitly comparing herself. Although she had temporarily ceased working on the novel, her imaginative concentration had not evaporated: she was composing a *TLS* piece on another diarist, John Evelyn, and wrote on 26 September that she was 'even making up a paper upon Women, as a counterblast to Mr Bennett's adverse views reported in the papers'.[2] Arnold Bennett had been, of course, a target for Woolf's criticism in her aesthetic manifesto of the previous year, 'Modern Novels', where she condemned him for being concerned with the body rather than the spirit, taking 'too much delight in the solidity of his fabric', in well-built villas and softly padded first class railway carriages.[3] She had already indirectly countered such faults of emphasis and structure in relation to her

---

7. Virginia Woolf, *The Diary of Virginia Woolf. Vol. II: 1920–1924*, ed. Anne Olivier Bell assisted by Andrew McNeillie (London, 1978), 68. Woolf is referring to the party at the Durrants, in Chapter 7 of the published novel.
8. Woolf, *Diary II*, 68.
9. Ibid. 69.
1. Ibid. 69.
2. Ibid. 69.
3. Woolf, 'Modern Novels', *Essays III*, 32.

current novel, when writing in her Diary on 26 January 1920 that in
Jacob's Room there will be 'no scaffolding; scarcely a brick to be
seen':[4] a sustained attempt at utilizing the prose style of 'The Mark
on the Wall' and 'Kew Gardens'. Moreover, that such principles are
directly related to her developing concept of a woman's style is clarified by reference to her review (*TLS*, 19 February 1919) of *The
Tunnel*, the fourth book in Dorothy Richardson's *Pilgrimage* series,
where she commended the novelist for her ability to present the core
of consciousness, the oyster within the shell, rather than the 'odd
deliberate business', the obvious formal structure which characterizes a man's fictional compositions. 'We want to be rid of realism,'
she claimed, 'to penetrate without its help into the regions beneath
it.'[5]

   In September 1920, however, Woolf's anger was stirred less by
inadequate formal criteria than by the views put forward by Bennett
in his book of essays, *Our Women*, and by the relatively favourable
review which this volume had received from the 'Affable Hawk'—
alias Desmond MacCarthy—in the *New Statesman*. Bennett himself
was fascinated by women's psychology in a manner which veered
between the voyeuristic and the identificatory. During the early
1900s he kept a private journal of observations about women, as well
as making plenty of comments about them in the pages of his regular
journal. In 1911 we find him writing in a letter to Hilda Hellman
'. . . I am partly a woman, à mes heures.'[6] Women and the social
restrictions surrounding their lives are at the centre of many of his
fictions. *Our Women*, however, shows up the limitations and contradictions of his views, claiming, as he does: 'I am not an old-
fashioned man. I am a feminist to the point of passionateness. But
at the risk of being ostracised and anathematised by all the woman-
feminists of my acquaintance, I shall continue to assert not only that
even in this very advanced year women as a sex love to be dominated,
but that for some thousands of years, if not for ever, they always will
love to be dominated.'[7] Bennett's views should be seen not so much
as idiosyncratic, however, but as symptomatic of opinions current
within society at that time. They must be read in the context of a
rash of books which came out in the years immediately following the
First World War, reconsidering the position of women within society.
Such works reflected economic as well as social anxieties about the
increased independence which women had gained during the war
years: 'a money-grubber', Bennett called 'the salary-earning girl'

   4. Woolf, *Diary II*, 13.
   5. Woolf, ' "The Tunnel" ', *Essays III*, 12.
   6. Arnold Bennett to Hilda Hellman, 30 Nov. 1911, *Letters of Arnold Bennett. Vol. II 1889–1915*, ed. James Hepburn (London, 1968), 295.
   7. Arnold Bennett, *Our Women: Chapters on the Sex-Discord* (London, 1920), 106. Subse-quent references in the text are to this edition.

(141), for example, maintaining that 'The root of modern feminism is, of course, the desire for money' (125). *Our Women* tended to be reviewed alongside other works which, whilst more daring in their sexual frames of reference than most pre-war treatises, none the less fostered a belief in the traditional role of woman as wife and mother, advocating the maintenance of a traditional hierarchy within a relationship. This generalization fits both the gushing prose of the romantic novelist Elinor Glyn's *Philosophy of Love* (1920), offering advice on how to capture and keep one's partner, and the slightly more ostensibly liberal, yet condescendingly phrased study of woman's changing social position, Orlo Williams's *The Good Englishwoman* (1920).

On the one hand, Bennett welcomed the greater social freedom which women now had. 'The present change in girls signifies a *rapprochement*, a fraternisation [*sic*], of the sexes . . . She can meet the male companion in a hundred matters on common ground. Their mutual interests are not confined to passion and pleasure, but stretch over about two-thirds of life' (140–1). But it is the other third which concerned Woolf, and us. In terms which echo D. H. Lawrence, Bennett writes in *Our Women* of the everlasting 'discord between the sexes' (1) which can never be eliminated, although he elaborates on this in terms which, in most un-Lawrentian fashion, tame and domesticate the struggle: though it may be the most exasperating thing in existence, 'it is by general agreement the most delightful and the most interesting' (3–4). Partly, this struggle depends on the way in which men and women frequently have no comprehension of each other's point of view, and he dramatizes this at the end of the book, showing the escalation of a petty quarrel about a gardener and some chrysanthemums. But this preposterous debate was one in which more than one reviewer thought that Bennett had not been entirely fair to the woman's side, regarding his unfairness as based on the principles which he had already articulated in the book and which so riled Woolf when she read of them: that men were not only superior to women in terms of physical strength, but in the power of their imagination; that 'intellectually and creatively man is the superior of woman' (101); that 'no amount of education and liberty of action will sensibly alter' (104) this fact; and that woman's indisputable 'desire to be dominated is . . . a proof of intellectual inferiority' (106).

There is no evidence that Woolf ever read all of *Our Women*; indeed, she opens her letter to the *New Statesman*, published on 9 October 1920 under the heading 'The Intellectual Status of Women', with the claim that 'Like most women, I am unable to face the depression and the loss of self respect which Mr Arnold Bennett's blame and Mr Orlo Williams' praise—if it is not the other way

about—would certainly cause me if I read their books in the bulk.'[8]
She continues by making a set of comparisons designed to show that
woman's intellectual power is, in fact, unmistakably advancing along
paths designed to show the effects of improved education and
increased liberty, placing Aphra Behn against Charlotte Brontë, Eliza
Heywood against George Eliot. Having questioned Bennett's reason-
ing, she proceeds to turn his argument on its head, claiming, with
characteristic satiric understatement, that 'though women have
every reason to hope that the intellect of the male sex is steadily
diminishing, it would be unwise, until they have more evidence than
the great war and the great peace supply, to announce it as a fact'.[9]
The reply of 'Affable Hawk' to Woolf's letter showed him to be
unconvinced, and Woolf wrote again at more length, in a letter published on 16 October. She reintroduces the topic of the history of
women's writing. If, for some two thousand years, there was no second Sappho, no more, until the seventeenth or eighteenth century,
was there Marie Corelli or Mrs Barclay. 'To account for the complete
lack not only of good women writers but also of bad women writers
I can conceive no reason unless it be that there was some external
restraint upon their powers.' The clearest elaboration of her objec-
tions against Bennett and his belief that 'the mind of woman is not
sensibly affected by education and liberty' is found in her final paragraph. It is not just education that women need—although the
masculine 'privilege' of a Cambridge education is clearly enough
depicted in *Jacob's Room*:

> It is that women should have liberty of experience; that they
> should differ from men without fear and express their difference
> openly (for I do not agree with 'Affable Hawk' that men and
> women are alike); that all activity of the mind should be so
> encouraged that there will always be in existence a nucleus of
> women who think, invent, imagine, and create as freely as men
> do, and with as little fear of ridicule and condescension.[1]

This combating of Arnold Bennett's ideas should be regarded not
so much as a direct influence feeding into the composition of *Jacob's
Room*, but as symptomatic of the increasing attention which Woolf
was coming to pay to the position of women within society. The
occasion enabled Woolf, however, to put publicly into print for the
first time the direction of her thoughts on this matter. Her fiction
came to be less explicitly vehement on the point, although Susan
Dick has plausibly hypothesized that the polemical short story, 'A

---

8. Woolf's letters to the *New Statesman* are published as Appendix III, 'The Intellectual
   Status of Women', *Diary II*, 339.
9. Ibid. The Great War was, of course, central to *Jacob's Room*.
1. Woolf, *Diary II*, 342.

Society,' which Woolf published in *Monday or Tuesday* (1921), may
well 'be in part a fictional response to Bennett's views on the intellectual inferiority of women.'[2] None the less, when Woolf returned
to the composition of *Jacob's Room*, an interest in women's writing
became immediately apparent. After the conclusion of Chapter 7,
we find that Chapter 8 contains a discussion of Mrs Flanders's letters
in particular, and of letters in general as a means of communication:
letters, 'the unpublished works of women', Woolf calls them, 'written
by the fireside in pale profusion'. Unlike Jacob's own letters—'about
art, morality, and politics to young men at college', a form of contact
with Bellamy which breaks down later in the novel under the seeming impossibility of his retaining a masculine impersonality under
the force of the impressions of Greece, of Sandra Wentworth—
women's letters deal with the ephemeral, with gossip, with emotion;
they show a desire to communicate, to give of the self. Woolf
describes them as an intimate expression of the primitive fear of the
isolation of mind and body, '(for letters are written when the dark
presses round a bright red cave)' (90) [73].

More important than this immediate reference to women and writing is the fact that when Woolf came to revise the whole text, it was
with an alertness to sexual politics, to the conventions and power
structures which restrain women's abilities. She was more alert to
the public pressures which they faced, whilst deflecting attention
from the private fears and inhibitions centring around women's sexuality and maternity: fears which link vulnerability with the body of
the woman, not with her social position. The problematic links
between the two were to remain largely underexplored in her fiction
until she came to write *The Years*. 'There's no doubt in my own mind
that I have found out how to begin (at 40) to say something in my
own voice; & that interests me so that I feel I can go ahead without
praise', Woolf wrote on 26 July 1922, three days after Leonard first
read, and delivered a response which mingled enthusiasm ('amazingly well written . . . a work of genius') with puzzlement ('he says it
is very strange: I have no philosophy of life he says; my people are
like puppets').[3] The content, as well as the style, of Woolf's new-
found voice was to enable her to define herself against her male
contemporaries.

Any analysis of the revisions to *Jacob's Room* is bound to be incomplete: not all the evidence is available. The notebooks contain drafts
of the text only as far as the middle of Jacob and Sandra's encounter
in Greece: there is no first version corresponding to the section
between 'But to return to Jacob and Sandra' (157) [129] and 'Her

2. *Virginia Woolf: The Complete Shorter Fiction*, ed. Susan Dick (London, 1985), 407.
3. Woolf, *Diary II*, 186.

hens shifted slightly on their perches' (172) [143]. Moreover, according to her diary, Woolf made a fair copy of the manuscript in June 1922, which she gave to Leonard Woolf's secretary Minna Green to type out. Leonard himself, as noted above, did not read the novel until 23 June. But the location of this fair copy is unknown, and moreover the eight separate sheets of the typescript which do exist in the Monk's House collection indicate that Woolf, as was her custom, carried on revising even when the text had been typed up.[4] The absence of typescript impedes us from placing a more exact chronology on the development of Woolf's thought. I foreground the idea of a conceptual chronology not to reassert the importance of intentionality, whether in establishing a satisfactory text for the novel, or when coming to interpret it. Rather, by tracing the changes in emphasis which took place during the novel's composition and revision we can place it more firmly within the social and intellectual circumstances of its production. Its textual history does not stop, of course, with its final draft. The first full-length book to be published by the Hogarth Press, it was, in its cinnamon and black printed dust-jacket designed by Vanessa Bell, materially different from *The Voyage Out* and *Night and Day,* published by Duckworth, and bearing on their dust-jackets the publishers' own floral device and motto.[5] Not only did its home production remove it from the possibility of external advice and emendations being proposed during the publishing and production stages (unless one counts Leonard's probable comments); visually, it stood as a symbol of aesthetic independence and self-assertion from established connections—including the uncomfortable connection between Woolf and her half-brother.[6] As Jerome J. McGann writes, 'the concrete forms and specific moments in which literary works emerge and re-emerge are defining constituents of their modes of aesthetic existence.'[7]

The word 're-emerge' should be stressed here, with an eye on certain recent feminist attempts to appropriate Woolf's linguistic exper-

4. Monk's House Papers B/12, University of Sussex, consists of eight sheets of non-consecutive typescript, annotated in Woolf's own hand.

5. For details of the appearance of the three novels, see B. J. Kirkpatrick, *A Bibliography of Virginia Woolf,* 3rd edn. (Oxford, 1980), 3, 12, 16.

6. My consideration of textual revision is particularly indebted to Peter L. Shillingsburg's comprehensive and judicious survey of recent debates concerning textual criticism; 'An Inquiry into the Social Status of Texts and Modes of Textual Criticism', *Studies in Bibliography,* 42 (1989), 55–79. In this article Shillingsburg, summarizing the positions of Jerome McGann and D. F. McKenzie, writes: 'Any legal contract which the author signs with a publisher is . . . merely a confirmation of a predetermined contract that exists, whether acknowledged or not, among authors, publishers, and readers' (62–3). The terms of the 'predetermined contract' between Woolf and Gerald Duckworth, where violation of personal autonomy had already occurred at a sexual level, are peculiarly difficult to determine.

7. Jerome J. McGann, *The Beauty of Inflections: Literary Investigations in Historical Method and Theory* (Oxford, 1985), 96.

imentation without linking it to a materialist politics.[8] For the revisions to *Jacob's Room*, and the circumstances surrounding them, act as a reminder that Woolf's often-quoted remarks about the desirability of finding a woman's sentence, of employing a language not made by men for their own uses, are misleading if taken as some kind of prefiguration of New French Feminist thought. Rather, they emphasize that, for Woolf, women, language, and consciousness intertwine in a way which is ultimately inseparable from social context.[9]

KATHLEEN WALL

Significant Form in *Jacob's Room*: Ekphrasis and the Elegy†

In the first chapter of *Jacob's Room*, we meet one of the novel's numerous painters, Charles Steele. Faced with the prospect that his subject, Mrs. Flanders, might move, he "struck the canvas a hasty violet-black dab. For the landscape needed it. It was too pale—greys flowing into lavenders, and one star or a white gull suspended just so—too pale as usual" (2) [4]. While Mr. Steele is certain that the critics will condemn his work, he feels that his hasty dab is just what his canvas needed—"it was just *that* note which brought the rest together" (3) [4]. The effect of Mr. Steele's black dab suggests a vision of the work of art that bears a considerable resemblance to that which Clive Bell articulated in his 1914 book on aesthetics, *Art*. Attempting to define the characteristics that are shared by those works we consider art, Bell concludes that it is their significant form:

> What quality is shared by all objects that provoke our aesthetic emotions? What quality is common to Santa Sophia and the windows at Chartres, Mexican sculpture, a Persian bowl, Chinese carpets, Giotto's frescoes at Padua, and the masterpieces

8. Notable among critics who attempt to write of Woolf's ideas about women and language without looking closely at their social context is Makiko Minow-Pinkney, claiming, for example, in *Virginia Woolf and the Problem of the Subject* (Brighton, 1987), 23, that 'Woolf's argument . . . has an affinity . . . with Kristeva's theory of poetic language'.

9. The author would like to thank Professor Quentin Bell, and the Henry W. and Albert A. Berg Collection, The New York Public Library, Astor, Lenox and Tilden Foundations for their kind permission to publish the material from the holograph of *Jacob's Room*, and the British Academy for making funds available which enabled her to consult this material in New York Public Library.

† From *Texas Studies in Literature and Language* 44.3 (2002): 302–23. Copyright © 2002 by the University of Texas Press. All rights reserved. Reprinted by permission of the publisher. [Bracketed page numbers refer to this Norton Critical Edition.]

of Poussin, Piero della Francesca, and Cezanne? Only one
answer seems possible—significant form. In each, lines and colours combined in a particular way, certain forms and relations
of forms, stir our aesthetic emotions. (8)

In his chapter on "The Aesthetic Hypothesis," Bell contrasts works
like Frith's "Paddington Station," whose detailed representation is
meant to convey ideas and information, with nonrepresentational
work that conveys the "aesthetic emotion":

> Let no one imagine that representation is bad in itself; a realistic
> form may be as significant, in its place as part of the design, as
> an abstract. But if a representative form has value, it is as form,
> not as representation. The representative element in a work of
> art may or may not be harmful; always it is irrelevant. For, to
> appreciate a work of art we need bring with us nothing from
> life, no knowledge of its ideas and affairs, no familiarity with its
> emotions. Art transports us from the world of man's activity to
> a world of aesthetic exaltation. For a moment we are shut off
> from human interests; our anticipations and memories are
> arrested; we are lifted above the stream of life. (25)

Woolf's letters, written in response to her friends' reactions to
Jacob's Room, raise precisely this issue of her novel's lack of representation. She tells Lytton Strachey that some of the romanticism
he accuses her of "comes from the effort of breaking with complete
representation. One flies into the air" (II, 569). To David Garnett
she confesses that she had doubts about the novel's form, whether
it "did keep together as a whole" without the "realism" that we traditionally expect of a novel (II, 571). In the context of R. C. Trevel-
yan's criticisms of *Jacob's Room*, she admits that "the effort of
breaking with strict representation is very unsettling, and many
things were not controlled as they should have been" (II, 588). Mr.
Steele's painting and her choice of words in these letters suggest that
Jacob's Room constitutes Woolf's attempt to find a "significant form"
for her elegy for her brother and for the generation of young men
who died in the war.

Numerous critics have commented upon Woolf's unusual and
fragmentary treatment of both plot and character in *Jacob's Room*,
viewing these as the novel's most notable formal innovations. But
two important aspects of this "significant form" which have not been
sufficiently explored are the narrator's uneven authority and incon-
sistent relationship to the textual world, and the text's saturation with
visual images that frequently seem almost ekphrastic, both of which
are related to her elegiac purpose.[1] Her narrator's placement within

1. Other critics have also viewed *Jacob's Room* as an elegy. See Alex Zwerdling, "*Jacob's Room*:

the world of the text yet outside of it and her claims to omniscience that are so frequently undercut by her emphasis upon what she doesn't know create two important effects. First, they interrogate the unequivocal distinction between the textual world and the represented world, or, moving up another level of abstraction, between the world of art and the world of life. They also create the perception that the world, particularly its human inhabitants, is only partially knowable, a perception that is part of the narrator's elegiac design. Precisely because her subject is loss, and thus she feels compelled to foreground the fleeting and inscrutable aspect of the textual world, Woolf's narrator seeks, through the use of vivid, composed descriptive passages which resemble verbal paintings (and recall some painterly conventions like the still life or the impressionist landscape), to create both a momentary timelessness and an almost tragic fall back into time, in order to fix images of Jacob and of his world in her text, just as Mr. Steele sought to capture Mrs. Flanders before she fled.[2]

But far from wholeheartedly adopting Bell's concept of significant form, complete with visual counterparts, Woolf also interrogates Bell's ideas about the distinction between art and life, both through the form the narrator takes and through her use of painterly descriptions. In so doing, she challenges a modernist tenet. While one must, of necessity, speak of modernism's multiple and often contradictory poetics, its often aestheticized response to the chaos, fragmentation, discontinuity, and alienation of modernity (particularly after the Great War) was to create a formal order that was meant both to reveal and transcend the particularities of individual experience. By maintaining that art exists only for its own sake, some modernists, Bell and his mentor, Roger Fry, included,[3] disconnected it from the public sphere. Since it was not the task of art to represent anything, much less to provide social critique, art was confined to the individ-

---

Woolf's Satiric Elegy," *Virginia Woolf and the Real World* (Berkeley: University of California Press, 1986), 62–83, and Roger Moss, "*Jacob's Room* and the Eighteenth Century: From Elegy to Essay," *Critical Quarterly* 23.3 (Autumn 1981): 39–54. My treatment differs in numerous ways, particularly in my consideration of the generic characteristics of elegy and my linking of the text's elegiac qualities to the novel's narration and its use of ekphrasis.

2. Francesca Kazan has also observed the set descriptions in *Jacob's Room* and the way they "explore both movement and stasis" (703). Kazan argues that frames around these depictions, expressed by devices like the white spaces that sprinkle the text, create questions about "the relation and the boundaries between art and life" (701). Rather than turning to the poetics of ekphrasis, Kazan uses Hagstrum's notion of pictorial writing (1958) which "must be, in its essentials, capable of translation into painting or some other visual art" (702). While Kazan and I are both viewing Woolf's novel as questioning the relationship between art and life, Kazan's argument foregrounds textual frames as effecting this interrogation, and relates the question neither to the poetics of the elegy nor to Bell's concept of significant form.

3. In her essay on Roger Fry, Woolf comments that "He wanted art to be art; literature to be literature; and life to be life" (102). See "Roger Fry," in *The Moment and Other Essays*, 99–105. Leonard Woolf will later criticize Woolf's "essay-novel" *The Pargiters* because it introduces too many political issues into the fiction.

ual's private aesthetic experience of it. But I would argue that such a putative separation can function only for some privileged men, those whose public and private lives are fluidly coterminous, whose lives do not daily reinforce the arbitrary distinction between the public and private spheres. Woolf, on the other hand—whether in the aesthetics she espouses in *Room of One's Own*,[4] in her drafting of *The Pargiters*, the precursor to *The Years*, as a "novel essay" that explored the social context influencing her characters; in her view of the similarities between the patriarch of the private house and the public dictator explored in *Three Guineas*; or in her insertion of marriage plots in Miss La Trobe's "island history" (*BTA*, 60)—sought consistently to question the very possibility of such a distinction between art and life or between the private and public spheres. Art, for her, was not disconnected from social questions about the relations between men and women, or about the way in which an individual's experience of war affects his inner and intimate life as it does in *Mrs. Dalloway*. So while these experiments with narration and ekphrasis express an attempt to create a significant aesthetic form that will embody the postwar experience of grief, they also constitute an argument with the aspect of Bell's aesthetics which asserts that it is art's task to lift us "above the stream of life" (*Art*, 25).

Jahan Ramazani and Melissa Zeiger, studying the relationship between the elegy and its historic context, observe that generic elements of the elegy reflect literary *and* social codes of mourning. Ramazani observes that between 1880 and 1920 periods of mourning shortened significantly and the rituals attached to mourning were simplified; the elegy, as if in a struggle against this attempt to suppress thoughts about death and mortality, was redefined and reinvigorated: "It would seem that creative writers perceived the dying of death-consciousness around them and sought to embalm it in their work" (11–12). The Great War further changed the elegy's tone and function. The fact that the bodies of British soldiers were not returned to England for burial necessitated some kind of public memorial to the dead.

If we situate the autobiographical sources of *Jacob's Room* in the context of this change in the form and character of the elegy, we can see the way in which the novel is emblematic of this conflict between the work of mourning and the social rites that provide a vehicle for that work and the elegy's response to that conflict. Woolf's brother, Julian Thoby Stephen, died on November 20, 1906, having contracted typhoid on a trip to Greece with Virginia, Vanessa, Adrian, and Violet Dickinson, a family friend who had nurtured Woolf after

---

4. See my essay, "Frame Narratives and Unresolved Contradictions in Virginia Woolf's *Room of One's Own*," *Journal of Narrative Theory* 29.2 (1999) 184–207.

her mother's death and who encouraged Woolf's writing. His obituary in *The London Times* on November 21, 1906, is characteristically terse, in keeping with "modern" ideas of mourning and memorial:

> STEPHEN—On the 20th Nov., at 46 Gordon-square, W.C., Julian Thoby, elder son of the late SIR LESLIE STEPHEN K.C.B., aged 26. The Funeral will take place on Thursday, at 10 o'clock at Golder's-green.

Thoby's death produced an early instance of Woolf's fictionalizing. In order to protect Violet, who was also ill, from shock, Woolf wrote letters that created Thoby's everyday, convalescent life for a full month after he died, reporting on his temperature, his diet (he longed for chopped chicken but could only have soft things like chocolate), his flirtations with his nurses, his interest in the books that Clive Bell was reading aloud to him, his inquiries about Violet's own progress (*Flight*, 247–66). They are poignant and fanciful creations: as if careful not to deviate from the darting and informal quality of her letters, Woolf does not overdo her fiction, but—self-consciously, one suspects—drops in chatty, fragmentary details of Thoby's convalescence.

Sixteen years later, when she finished the draft of *Jacob's Room*, she wrote across the bottom of the final page

> Atque in perpetuum, frater, ave atque vale
> Julian Thoby Stephen
> (1880–1906)
> Atque in perpetuum, frater, ave atque vale. (Lee, 227) [167]

As numerous commentators have pointed out, the general shape of Jacob's career conforms to Thoby's: education at Cambridge, work of a faintly literary kind in London, a trip to Greece. But in *Jacob's Room*, as in *To the Lighthouse*, Woolf has changed the time frame of the novel so that the young men, Jacob Flanders and Andrew Ramsay, die in the war, thus transforming her elegy for her brother into an elegy for a generation of young men, for an age, and for its worldview. Because of the "generic modulations" to the elegy that occurred in the late nineteenth century (Fowler, 211), Woolf can cast that elegiac impulse in the form of a lyric novel.[5] One can thus place *Jacob's Room* in the context of the changes to the elegy observed by Ramazani and Zieger, viewing it as a complex, problematized, postwar response to Thoby's death, the substitution of an

---

5. For Woolf's awareness of such a "generic modulation," consider her diary entry on 27 June, 1925, about her work on *To the Lighthouse*: "I have an idea that I will invent a new name for my books to supplant 'novel.' A new——by Virginia Woolf. But what? Elegy?" (*Diary*, Vol. III, 34).

enigmatic, problematic novel for the public, terse certainty of Julian Thoby Stephen's obituary, as Woolf situates her text between the unspeaking reticence of the obituary and the anger of postwar aesthetics.

But one can also view the recasting of Thoby's death in the period of the Great War as another of Woolf's efforts to trouble the distinction between public and private, and to transform private loss into public experience and text. The formal requirements of elegy dictated a preoccupation with conventions which typically mediated between the private experience of loss and its public expression through codifying and suggesting what could be said but casting this content in the richly suggestive, indeterminate language of poetry. But while late Victorian social conventions made grief a more private matter, the postwar, modernist aesthetics of the elegy had foregrounded public experience, anger, and outrage. The modern(ist) elegy thus became, as Ramazani observes, "a compromise-formation in its response to the privatization of grief. Often representing itself as private utterance, it offers refuge from the social denial of grief; yet as published discourse, it carries out in the public realm its struggle against the denial of grief" (15–16).

Theories of mourning and of the elegy help us to understand not only the social dimensions of Woolf's elegy but its stylistic characteristics—its significant form—as well, suggesting why it is so idiosyncratic, characterized as it is by a narrator who questions the possibility of writing a novel even while she is driven to do so; by the preponderance of visual images in the novel (Kiely, Kazan);[6] by the Jacob-shaped hole that is often articulated by the limitations of the narrator's perspective, which focus more attention on a fragmented social context than on his character; and by empty rooms and empty shoes, closed doors and unknown thoughts. In her study of melancholia, *Black Sun,* Kristeva comments upon the relationship between grief and the drive to create, observing that "loss, bereavement, and absence trigger the work of the imagination and nourish it" (9). Just as the original loss catapults the child into the world of signs and symbols, so do subsequent instances of grief and loss encourage the individual to create some kind of elegiac memorial (Kristeva, 41; Sacks, 9), a kind of fetish that, in Freud's words, "while it fills the gap . . . nevertheless remains something else" (qtd. in Sacks, 7). The *attempt* to translate a visual image into words in an ekphrastic moment constitutes, I would argue, an appropriate monument to the

6. Kiely's attention to the visual images in the novel also emphasizes their likeness to painting and locates the source of this phenomena to Woolf's relationships with Bell and Fry. Like Kazan, he notes the tension between perishability and permanence in these descriptive passages (150), but these aspects of Woolf's poetics are not related either to Bell's idea of significant form or to the elegy. As I will do later in my argument, Kiely points to Woolf's repeated descriptions of Jacob's rooms as "the major set pieces of the novel" (154).

object of loss or grief.[7] As Mr. Steele's rush to include the departing Mrs. Flanders in his painting suggests, the visual image defies time, that medium of mortality, by providing a monument to its fragmentary and fleeting immobility—an immobility Mr. Steele seeks precisely because time and change, and thus death, are inevitable.

Aside from providing a powerful motive for creating and memorializing, the loss that generates the elegiac gesture pushes the boundaries of language and genre in precisely the directions Woolf has taken in her text, toward a paradoxical effort to represent absence, both of the loved one and of any knowledge of death. David Shaw, considering the generic qualities of elegy observes that "Since death is not an experience inside life, but an event that takes place on its boundary, every elegy sooner or later reaches the limits of language" (5). In modernist elegies, those interrogated boundaries give rise to "open sites of fracture and breakdown" (Shaw, 147), and, finally, silence (103), as the elegist discovers, as do Mrs. Flanders and Bonamy (and most of the other characters, for that matter), that the person for whom they call is beyond the reach of their cries. As Bishop points out, Woolf's revisions of *Jacob's Room* both minimized Jacob's characterization and suppressed uncertainty about other characters, so that, so to speak, it is *his* absence and not the inscrutability of the human character that is foregrounded in the text (*Shaping*, 127). If we include Woolf's narrator among the mourners, we realize that the absence and inscrutability of Jacob from the outset represent her elegiac treatment of his career. By creating a kind of synecdochal *bildungsroman* that requires us to read a single, uncontextualized, reticent scene for an entire phase of Jacob's development, Woolf emphasizes what we do not know about our ostensible hero, Jacob, and foregrounds the elegiac fractures and silences in the text.

The illimitable unknown of death is often answered by what Peter Sacks refers to as elegiac questioning, in which the mourner poses questions that range from the guilt-ridden "Where was I?" to teleological queries about the meaning of an indifferent universe. Language, the conventional medium of mourning, is also called into question, since the elegist's substitution of signifier for signified is so relentlessly unsatisfactory (Sacks, 4–5 and 8–9); by extension, the elegiac genre itself is revealed to be inadequate to the task, thus "[e]very elegy is an elegy for elegy" (Ramazani, 8). Kristeva, exploring the literature of mourning from a psychoanalytic perspective, observes that the writer's struggle to express grief often results in the translation of affect into "rhythms, signs, forms" (Kristeva, 22) by a

---

7. See W. J. T. Mitchell's essay, "Ekphrasis and the Other," in *Picture Theory* (Chicago: University of Chicago Press, 1994) for a thorough discussion of the problems created by the attempt to "translate" a visual image into words.

"dissociation of form" (Kristeva, 27), by form that is fragmented, form that questions the terms of its own existence, form that is brought to a halt in moments of silence and self-questioning (Shaw). As a modernist writer concerned with form's potential to *mean*, to fuse with content, Woolf articulates the fractures and silences of mourning and its elegiac expression in part through an omniscient narrator who embodies loss in the limitations to her omniscience and in the ekphrastic moments that freeze time momentarily, only to emphasize its inexorability. It is as if the form does not merely reflect loss but marks the traces of that loss on the novel's textual skin.

One of the most significant aspects of Woolf's form is her narrator, who sometimes abrogates to herself a great deal of authority, though who more frequently acknowledges and laments her lack of knowledge.[8] As if to emphasize the silences, questions, and fragments in her text, Woolf allows her narrator to reveal, through anticipations or prolepses, that she possesses enough authority to know how the story ends. In Chapter Two, as a kind of coda to the scene in which Mr. Floyd gives departing gifts to the three Flanders boys, the narrator notes that Mr. Floyd met "Jacob in Piccadilly *lately*, [note this diectic marker] [and] recognized him after three seconds," [p. 15] thus situating the time of the narration at least as late as the last page of the penultimate chapter, where the same scene is recorded in its proper place in the chronology.[9] Meditating upon the activities of the young men at Cambridge, Woolf's narrator engages in a strategy that both indicates her authority and yet constitutes an elegiac site of fracture that anticipates their deaths in the war when she describes the reading and writing of "simple young men, these, who would—but there is no need to think of them grown old" (44) [32]. In this single, authoritative, yet elegiac gesture, Woolf evokes the promise of young men and alludes to its future destruction in the war. Midway through the novel, in one of the fragments of social life that recounts the undeveloped romance between Helen and Jimmy, the narrator comments that "now Jimmy feeds crows in Flanders and Helen visits hospitals" (107) [76], again undercutting ideas about youthful romance and promise while establishing the fact the narration is undertaken part way through the war. These prolepses suggest that the text's elegiac gestures and form are present from the outset. We do not have a character-focalizer who discovers only near the end that the story she has been relating closes with Jacob's death.

8. Judy Little reads this "inconsistency" of the narrator as a contribution to the humor and gaiety that Woolf hoped to incorporate into the work (106), whereas Olin-Hitt sees this strategy as an attempt to rebel against conventional narration and the power relations that inhere in the conventionally authoritative narrator.
9. See Gerard Genette, *Narrative Discourse: An Essay in Method* for his discussion of order (33–85).

This observation, of course, raises the issue of the focalization. Woolf's narrator early establishes her presence within the world of the text through diectic markers that place her, for example, in Scarborough during Jacob's youth as she suggests to an invisible narratee, "Let's to the museum" or "And now, what's the next thing to see in Scarborough?" (16) [12], as if the narrator and the implied reader were both visiting the seaside town. In these instances, she is a character-focalizer who functions simply as a witness,[1] and as such, her knowledge is limited; Jacob and Florinda close the door in her face, and she loses Jacob and Sandra on their evening walk to the Parthenon. But Woolf's narrator also possesses the authority of the omniscient narrator or narrator-focalizer who is outside the textual world.[2] This position gives her the power to shape enormous generalizations and to speak directly to the implied reader (who is also outside the text) in observations about the sky above Cambridge, for instance:

> They say the sky is the same everywhere. Travellers, the ship-wrecked, exiles, and the dying draw comfort from the thought, and no doubt if *you* are of a mystical tendency, consolation, and even explanation, shower down from the unbroken surface. But above Cambridge—anyhow above the roof of King's College Chapel—there is a difference. (31; italics added) [22]

Or, in a moment when the narrator is both the character-focalizer who cannot open the door that has been closed behind Florinda and Jacob, and the overt, omniscient narrator who can make generalizations about the world of the text and the world outside the text, she muses "Let us consider letters" (102) [73]. These two types of focalization, external and internal, are certainly at odds here, but they are going to be most at odds when we consider the narrator's reporting of characters' thoughts. A character-focalizer simply cannot know the unexpressed thoughts of other characters, which Woolf's narrator-focalizer clearly does, as demonstrated when she reports Jacob's unarticulated impressions of the women who have invaded the service of King's College Chapel but who shouldn't be there because "thought Jacob, they're as ugly as sin" (33) [24].

The scene in which Mrs. Norman meets young Jacob on his way to Cambridge provides a compact example of this narrative anomaly.

---

1. It can be complained that narratology has coined far more technical terms than are necessary. Rather than use Rimmon-Kenan's distinction between extradiegetic vs. intradiegetic and homodiegetic vs. heterodiegetic, I have decided to employ the simpler terminology used by Mieke Bal and refer to character-focalizers or narrator-focalizers (or, in some cases, simply narrators). Character-focalizers who do not perform actions in the text are simply termed witnesses. See the section on focalization in Mieke Bal's *Narratology*, 2nd ed., 142–60.
2. See Seymour Chatman's *Story and Discourse* for a discussion of the prerogatives of the overt omniscient narrator vis a vis such things as commentaries and generalizations.

Initially, Woolf's narrator assumes full knowledge of Mrs. Norman's thoughts as the older woman reaches into her dressing-case to clutch the novel from Mudie's and her scent bottle as ammunition against this "powerfully-built young man" who enters her carriage quite suddenly. Gaining courage, she looks at him more carefully: "Taking note of socks (loose), of tie (shabby), she once more reached his face. . . . All was firm, yet youthful, indifferent, unconscious—as for knocking one down! No, no, no!" (29) [21]. This last bit of direct discourse assures us of the narrator's full access to Mrs. Norman's mind, as does the narrator's observation, toward the end of this scene, that Mrs. Norman forgot her meeting with Jacob because she met so many young men during her weekend in Cambridge. Had the omniscient narrator not plucked the thought, as it were, from Mrs. Norman's head just as it occurred, it could never have been recorded. Yet, undermining this omniscience, Woolf's narrator follows up with the observation that "One must do the best one can with her report," once again suggesting that the narrator is a witness within the world of the text who must get some of her information about Jacob from others—a strategy she invokes again with Bonamy's char (30; 113–14) [22; 80–81].

In her omniscient guise, the narrator follows this reference to Mrs. Norman's "report" with a narrative meditation upon our knowledge of other people—a meditation which undermines the very possibility of omniscience: "Nobody sees any one as he is, let alone an elderly lady sitting opposite a strange young man in a railway carriage. They see a whole—they see all sorts of things—they see themselves. . . . It is no use trying to sum people up. One must follow hints, not exactly what is said, nor yet entirely what is done" (30; ellipses in original) [22]. In his discussion of the elegy's silences, questions, and use of sound, Shaw observes that "When the odd assortments of sound and sense in a poem send a reader in search of its silent or unspoken meanings, the interplay between what is heard and what is intimated or half said creates a polyphony that gives the poet a chance to speak with a divided mind upon a subject" (126). Woolf's narration is the novelistic version of this poetic strategy: while the omniscient narrator asserts a knowable, explicable world, the character-focalizer laments the half-knowledge and fragments that must suffice. We can read this conflict between perspectives as a variation on the elegiac question, which becomes "What can I know about this ever-changing world of people whose thoughts are so seldom articulated and who disappear before I can observe them carefully enough?"

But the narrator's care in examining the various kinds of limitations that bedevil her full knowledge of characters' behavior and motives suggests that Woolf's broader purpose is to explore and exemplify the epistemological crisis of authority that in part characterizes modernism. The character-focalizer is aware of all the perspectival limitations on our knowledge of our world—of the ways in which our feelings distort our vision; of the fact that, looking at others, we see ourselves and our own expectations; of the way our distance from a scene dictates what we see; of our need to rely upon the experience of others to fill in the gaps created by our inability to be in more than one place at a time. As if to emphasize the way in which perspectival limitations are one of the novel's preoccupations, its first scene opens by describing the way in which feelings—in this instance, loss—distort perceptions. Betty Flanders's tears, as she thinks about the death of her husband, change the view before her: "The entire bay quivered; the lighthouse wobbled; and she had the illusion that the mast of Mr. Connor's little yacht was bending like a wax candle in the sun" (1) [3]. Thus, loss creates an epistemological crisis, both for the characters and for the narrator.

When Jacob is at Cambridge, the narrator's perspective, and thus her authority, varies widely: at one moment, she must guess what the young men are reading; at another, she knows that they are "holding their books as if they had hold in their hands of something that would see them through" (45) [32]. At still another, her physical perspective gives her difficulty: surveying a scene from outside the window, it would seem, she can see only the most exaggerated gestures of arms moving and hear only the loudest voices; the young men might be engaging in either an enthusiastic discussion or an argument (46) [32]. She intuitively understands the youthful iconoclasm that allows the university-aged Jacob to be horrified at the stodginess of the university establishment and its wives and that is reflected in his ability to assert " 'I am what I am, and intend to be it,' for which there will be no form in the world unless Jacob makes one for himself" (36) [26], yet she does not understand his romantic naiveté. Similar and dramatic changes in perspective occur within a single scene when Jacob watches Florinda "turning up Greek Street upon another man's arm." Although the narrator can observe "the pattern on his trousers; the old thorns on his stick; his shoe laces; bare hands; and face" she recognizes that "what was in his mind is another question" (104) [74]; a question she cannot answer because of "ten years' seniority and a difference of sex" (104) [74].

These perspectival limitations suggest the epistemological crisis, the difficulty of summing people up, that the narrator invokes first in the scene in which Mrs. Norman observes Jacob, and then reiterates as Evan and Sandra engage in "character-mongering" (30, 174) [21–22, 123–24]. This undermining of authority and foregrounding of the problems of perspective can be seen as a distinctly modernist practice, one that recognizes the individual as the only site of authority, even while problematizing the individual's knowledge. But, as is the case with Mrs. Flanders's distorted vision at the novel's outset, it is loss that intensifies this epistemological problem, making it a version of the elegiac question that haunts much post-war literature.

In her meta-commentary, the narrator suggests that part of her limitation resides in language itself. As a character-focalizer, observing Jacob chat with Bonamy, she tries to classify him, having noted that our classifications of people are a means of sorting through the cacophonous information with which the world assaults us (75) [53]. Was he "A writer? He lacked self-consciousness. A painter? There was something in the shape of his hands . . . which indicated taste. Then his mouth—but surely, of all futile occupations this of cataloguing features is the worst. One word is sufficient. But if one cannot find it?" (77) [55]. By foregrounding these limitations of language and perspective in the text, by creating a dissonance between the limited knowledge of a character-focalizer and the theoretically unlimited knowledge of a casually omniscient narrator, Woolf is creating a significant [narrative] form which is always already elegiac because it must encompass both our feelings and our observations, both the known and the inferred, both what is present and what is absent:

> In any case life is but a procession of shadows, and God knows why it is that we embrace them so eagerly, and see them depart with such anguish, being shadows. And why, if this and much more than this is true, why are we yet surprised in the window corner by a sudden vision that the young man in the chair is of all things in the world the most real, the most solid, the best known to us—why indeed? For the moment after we know nothing about him.
>
> Such is the manner of our seeing. Such the conditions of our love.
>
> (78) [56]

If the point of these narrative anomalies or contradictions is to emphasize what we do not know, we have no real need for the omniscient narrator, except perhaps as a leftover, a reminder of the novel's old potential for coherent characters and representable culture texts. Thus the narrator-focalizer whose omniscience is consistently questioned, compromised, or undercut, is itself an elegiac gesture insofar as it evokes an earlier, more authoritative and confident world view not imbued with loss and change.

But while narration's fluctuation between omniscience and the perspectival limitations of a character-focalizer is one aspect of Woolf's self-consciously crafted "significant form," this is also a moment at which she critique's Bell's notion that the aesthetic emotion lifts us above the stream of life. For the two kinds of narration in combination create a permeable membrane between text and world. If the perspective of the narrator can be both inside and outside the text, then the distinction between *inside* and *outside* becomes open to question, as does the distinction between life and art. Just as Shaw suggests elegy tests the boundaries of language, *Jacob's Room* explores the boundaries of the textual world created by the author.

Both Kiely and Kazan note that *Jacob's Room* is characterized by an unusual use of description. Kazan argues that located amongst the "narrator's reflections and digressions," the "snatches of events" and the "disembodied voices" of the text are "pictorial compositions that seem to interrupt the text in an arbitrary fashion and cut through the reflections and the dialogue" (702). Using Jean Hagstrum's work (1958), Kazan argues that these are instances of pictorial writing, which must be " 'capable of translation into painting or some other visual art . . . must be imaginable as painting or sculpture' " (Hagstrum xxii; qtd. in Kazan, 702). Kazan argues that these moments are textually framed (by the blank spaces in the text, for instance), and that the frame "functions as a protean device to explore both movement and stasis" (703). Kiely suggests that Woolf's interest in such painterly moments has its source in her relationships with Clive Bell and Roger Fry and the general discussion of aesthetics amongst the Bloomsbury group, which would have inevitably included conversation about Fry's 1910 Postimpressionist exhibition. Like Kazan, Kiely observes a tension between perishability and permanence in these textual moments (150) and suggests that they are similar to the painter's composition of a still life (154).

These observations suggest that Woolf is working in some way within the tradition of ekphrasis. Simply put—though the poetics of ekphrasis are anything but simple—ekphrasis is "a verbal representation of a visual artwork" (Carrier, qtd. in Wagner, 10–11). The first instance of this translation from one art medium to another occurs in the *Iliad*, with the extended description of Achilles's shield. Many subsequent definitions of this practice insist on the pre-existence of the artwork that is being described; we might imagine, for instance, a writer looking at a Cezanne still life and describing what she sees. Both Homer and Keats (in "Ode on a Grecian Urn"), however, described objects that they themselves have imagined into being. Thus W. J. T. Mitchell suggests that

> The narrowest meanings of the word ekphrasis as a poetic mode, "giving voice to a mute art object," or offering "a rhetorical description of a work of art," give way to a more general application that includes any "set description intended to bring per-

son, place, picture, etc. before the mind's eye." (153; quoting Jean Hagstrum, *The Sister Arts*, 18)

Such a definition, of course, doesn't make much distinction between garden-variety description and ekphrasis. For help here, we can turn to Murray Krieger, who suggests that a description invokes the "ekphrastic principle" when "the poem takes on the 'still' elements of plastic form which we normally attribute to the spatial arts" (107). Our experience of a text is temporal: it takes time to read words. But our experience of a painting has the capacity to occur in a single, "still" moment. Moreover, the painting itself has captured (unless we are thinking here of Duchamp's "Nude Descending a Staircase") a single, stilled moment.

Anyone who has read *Jacob's Room* will quite rightly point out that, while there are numerous painters in Woolf's novel, there are few art-works that have been described, though there are frequent references, for example, to the Elgin Marbles. Why, then, would I want to use the theory of ekphrasis to examine this text? The answer to that might well be that Kiely, Kazan, and I experience certain moments of the text foregrounding this exchange between text and picture, "movement and status," (Kazan, 703), "perishability and permanence" (Kiely, 150). Such moments are elegiac by virtue of the way in which they temporarily freeze time, and then, upon releasing it, remind us that their timelessness is a fiction.

Woolf was, admittedly, an enthusiastically visual writer, a quality that Clive Bell first observed in his review of *Jacob's Room*, where he asserts that her "almost painterlike vision is Virginia Woolf's peculiarity: it is what distinguishes her from all her contemporaries" (Bell, 138). Bell's review, published in the *Dial* of December 24, 1924, goes on to raise exactly the issue that theorists of ekphrasis raise. Can one "translate" from one medium to another? What is lost in the translation? What is added?

> Of course a first-rate literary artist can never really be like a painter; for it is out of words that literary artists have to create the forms that are to clothe their visions, and words carry a significance altogether different from the significance of lines and colours. Certainly Mrs Woolf's vision, and superficially her style, may remind any one . . . of the French impressionists—of their passion for the beauty of life, loved for its own sake, their abhorrence of symbolism, their reputed inhumanity, technically of their little touches and divisions of tones. To our joy we are all familiar with the way in which Renoir and Claude Monet express their sense of a garden blazing in the sun. It is something which comes to them through shapes and colours, and in shapes and colours must be rendered. (*Critical Heritage*, 144).

For Bell, the entire structure of the novel, its dependence upon "fragmentary revelations, glimpses, glances, and scraps of glances" evokes the Impressionists, particularly the way in which Woolf builds up the sense of her hero through "other people's reactions to him": "Here is impressionism with a vengeance: if the technique consisted in 'little touches', the composition is a matter of 'frank oppositions' and the whole will dawn on us only when the last harmony is established" (146).

But Bell's observations, while they assert the painterly effect of Woolf's text, hardly establish an ekphrastic aesthetics. For that, we must turn to Woolf's later nonfiction, her essays "The Leaning Tower," and "Walter Sickert." In "The Leaning Tower," (1940) she asserts and then undoes the similarity between the painter and the writer when she defines a writer as

> a person who sits at a desk and keeps his eye fixed, as intently as he can, upon a certain object—that figure of speech may help to keep us steady on our path if we look at it for a moment. He is an artist who sits with a sheet of paper in front of him trying to copy what he sees. What is his object—his model? Nothing so simple as a painter's model; it is not a bowl of flowers, a naked figure, or a dish of apples and onions. Even the simplest story deals with more than one person, with more than one time. (128)

Woolf's metaphor implicitly addresses one of the difficulties inherent in translating between the visual image and words: they deal with different temporalities. For this reason, no rendering will ever be exact. Indeed, her metaphor, while suggesting that we will understand the writer better if we consider the task of the painter, problematizes the relationship and points out the very inequivalency that she explores in *Jacob's Room*.

It is in her essay on the painter Walter Sickert, however, that Woolf most fully explores the relationship between words and paint. In this essay, which gathers together a hypothetical group of commentators, Woolf arranges an argument between one individual who sees Sickert as "among the best of biographers" and another who asserts that "to me Sickert always seems more of a novelist than a biographer" (176). In an ekphrastic moment, one of these speakers suggests that they "go on living in the world of words a little longer" and creates a narrative that seems to unfold from Sickert's image:

> Do you remember the picture of the girl sitting on the edge of her bed half naked? Perhaps it is called *Nuit d'Amour*. Anyhow, the night is over. The bed, a cheap iron bed, is tousled and tumbled; she has to face the day, to get her breakfast, to see about the rent. As she sits there with her nightgown slipping

from her shoulders, just for a moment the truth of her life comes over her; she sees in a flash the little garden in Wales and the dripping tunnel in the Adelphi where she began, where she will end, her days. So be it, she says, and yawns and shrugs and stretches a hand for her stockings and chemise. Fate has willed it so. (178)

But the translation or transaction between words and paint can go both ways. Not only is the painter like the novelist, the novelist is also like the painter: "Let us hold painting by the hand a moment longer, for though they must part in the end, painting and writing have much to tell each other: they have much in common. The novelist after all wants to make us see" (181).[3] Thus Woolf's poetics suggests a reciprocal relationship between paint and words that is manifested in ekphrasis.

The dissimilarity between the two seems to be their relationship to time. I have already suggested through my exploration of Mr. Steele's work that a visual image freezes a moment in time, yet frequently acknowledges the mortality of the original. Nowhere is this tension clearer than in the English term "still life" and the French expression, *nature morte*, the English term capturing the stasis that presumably keeps something alive by immortalizing it, the French term highlighting the mortality of the plants or fruit (not to mention skulls and dead birds) that are depicted. But once the frozen moment of the visual image is translated back into a temporal medium—words—does the same relationship to time apply? In the essay on Sickert, she suggests not: his "figures are motionless, of course, but each has been seized in a moment of crisis" (177). I'd suggest, then, that the moments I have identified below as ekphrastic are those in which Woolf has, like Keats or Homer, created a visual image precisely to stop narrative time through the engaged contemplation of a particular scene. But, because the novel is elegiac, the temporal effect is not quite this simple: although time is temporarily stopped, its resumption and inexorability is emphasized.

Woolf's inclusion of movement in her still lives occurs early in the novel, in a tableau she constructs around the effluvia of Mrs. Flanders's daily life with her sons: "There were her large reels of white cotton and her steel spectacles; her needle-case; her brown wool wound round an old postcard. There were the bulrushes and the *Strand* magazines; and the linoleum sandy from the boys' boots. A daddy-long-legs shot from corner to corner and hit the lamp globe" (7) [7]. Like most of the ekphrastic moments in Woolf's novel, this one contains movement, here of the daddy-longlegs, which undoes

---

3. Thus we might see Woolf engaged in what W. J. T. Mitchell terms "ekphrastic hope." See "Ekphrasis and the Other," in *Picture Theory*.

the momentary timelessness and reveals its status within time, not outside of it. Or consider another intensely visual description of the sea, which sounds, for all the world, like a series of Monet paintings—his Houses of Parliament or facades of the Cathedral at Rouen:

> By six o'clock a breeze blew in off an icefield, and by seven the water was more purple than blue; and by half-past seven there was a patch of rough gold-beater's skin round the Scilly Isles, and Durrant's face, as he sat steering, was of the colour of a red lacquer box polished for generations. By nine all the fire and confusion had gone out of the sky, leaving wedges of apple-green and plates of pale yellow; and by ten the lanterns on the boat were making twisted colours upon the waves, elongated or squat, as the waves stretched or humped themselves. (55) [39]

Once again, though we have descriptions of moments that would be frozen in time in their visual translations, here the passing of time is foregrounded.

As the narrator's lengthy description of the Parthenon suggests, these moments of visual beauty have the potential to be immortal, outside of time and daily life. In Bell's words, "A good work of visual art carries a person who is capable of appreciating it out of life into ecstasy: to use art as a means to the emotions of life is to use a telescope for reading the news" (29–30). Thus, (in Woolf's words,) the Parthenon's

> durability exists quite independently of our admiration. Although the beauty is sufficiently humane to weaken us, to stir the deep deposit of mud—memories, abandonments, regrets, sentimental devotions—the Parthenon is separate from all that; and if you consider how it has stood out all night, for centuries, you begin to connect the blaze . . . with the idea that perhaps it is beauty alone that is immortal. (167–68) [119]

Both Bell and Woolf (in this passage, at least) argue that whether or not the work of art is elegiac, it ought to be above the emotional or the personal, above our inconsequential reactions to it.

Except that in the penultimate chapter, Greek art is used to figure forth Jacob's mortality and other characters' sense of loss. In order to keep her "idea of Jacob" alive, Fanny Elmer has taken to sneaking up on the stature of Ulysses in the British Museum; consequently her image of Jacob becomes "more statuesque, noble, and eyeless than ever" (193) [137]. Julia Eliot's visit to look at the statue of Achilles gives her the "rapt look of one brushing through crowds on a summer's afternoon, when the trees are rustling, the wheels churning yellow, and the tumult of the present seems like an elegy for past youth and past summers, and there rose in her mind a curious sadness, as if time and eternity showed through skirts and waistcoats, and she saw people passing tragically to destruction" (191) [135]. What Julia manages to see in the statue of Achilles is not outside time, but is the precise historical moment in which she lives, a moment in which "sixteen gentlemen, lifting their pens or turning perhaps rather wearily in their chairs, decreed that the course of history should shape itself this way or that way" (195) [139], suggesting that our experience of a work of art has a context that we cannot elude.

Among the most important ekphrastic images are those of Jacob's rooms in Cambridge and his flat in London which are lifted out of their chronological context to recur in the final chapter, both of which are related by a character-focalizer whose lack of omniscience emphasizes Jacob's inaccessibility to her. In Chapter 3, the character-focalizer rushes up the stairs in Neville's Court, arriving "a little out of breath" to find that Jacob is not there—"Dining in Hall, presumably" (39) [28]. There, attempting to capture his character, perhaps, she looks over his books and papers and observes his "incredibly shabby [slippers] like boats burnt to the water's rim" (40) [29]. We're given much visual information about the room, its photographs, mezzotints, the "cards from societies with little raised crescents, coats of arms, and initials" (39) [28], and his emblematic pipe. It is the final image that is important to us here: "Listless is the air in an empty room, just swelling the curtain; the flowers in the jar shift. One fibre in the wicker arm-chair creaks, though no one sits there" (40) [29]. In this description of Jacob's room, movement and sound evoke his absence by implying a presence; the still life of the room enters time through its evocation of the creaking of the wicker. Chapter 5 includes a description of his flat, again provided by the character-focalizer (as is indicated by what she does not know):

> This black wooden box, upon which his name was still legible in white paint, stood between the long windows of the sitting-room. The street ran beneath. *No doubt* the bedroom was behind. The furniture—three wicker chairs and a gate-legged table—came from Cambridge. These houses . . . were built, say, a hundred and fifty years ago. The rooms are shapely, the ceilings high; over the doorway a rose, or a ram's skull, is carved in the wood. The eighteenth century has its distinction. Even the panels, painted in raspberry-coloured paint, have their distinction. . . . (76–77; final ellipses in original; italics mine) [54]

Lifting these passages verbatim from earlier points in the novel suggests, initially, a timelessness to the scenes they describe and an absence of change. But, just as you cannot step in the same river twice, so the meaning of these words is not the same once their context has changed. Placed in the final chapter where Mrs. Flanders and Bonamy sorrowfully sort through Jacob's things, the images reveal that everything has changed.

Writing of ekphrasis, Murray Krieger observes that many of the objects of ekphrastic description partake of "a specially frozen sort of aesthetic time" (105), that the formal recurrences used to create this kind of time arrest movement even while the objects are still—that is, always—moving. (Consider, for example, the paradox of Keats's urn, in which the stilled figure is also continuously in motion.) In an elegiac context, then, such recurrences represent that which is already beyond representation, that which is no longer there to represent. Consequently, what represents the lost object, as Eliot articulated in "Burnt Norton," is form, perhaps Bell's significant form:

> Words move, music moves
> Only in time; but that which is only living
> Can only die. Words, after speech, reach
> Into the silence. Only by the form, the pattern
> Can words or music reach
> The stillness, as a Chinese jar still
> Moves perpetually in its stillness.

Such stately, measured ambiguity, implying a formal balance between cycles and dead ends, might well articulate an appropriate response to *the novel Jacob's Room*. But for the narrator, who is both inside and outside the world of the text, what is the distinction between the appropriate "aesthetic emotion" invoked by a work of art and the inferior "emotion of life" that Jacob's death elicits?

The war seems to have destroyed such a tidy distinction between art and life. As Sandra and Evan Williams consider the character of Jacob, who has just (in a kind of synecdoche) stepped out of sight, the narrator comments upon the futility of "character-mongering." Opening out of this discussion, without any subject-shifting white space, Woolf's narrator presents us with the vision of battleships on the North Sea and one group of young men blowing up their targets, another group "descending impassively into the sea and suffocating uncomplainingly together," a third group working its way through a cornfield. These are the unseizable forces that now "oar the world forward" (176) [125]: "They say that the novelists never catch it; that it goes hurtling through their nets and leaves them torn to ribbons. This, they say, is what we live by—this unseizable force" (176) [125]. Thus, the war is the force that has killed Jacob, problematized "character-mongering," and torn Woolf's own elegiac text to ribbons.

Woolf was always self-conscious about her formal innovations; her diaries bristle with descriptions of the experiments she was planning in her next work. Having found a different approach to fiction with the short stories she was writing between 1917 and 1920, she conceived *Jacob's Room* as

> entirely different this time: no scaffolding; scarcely a brick to
> be seen; all crepuscular, but the heart, the passion, humour,
> everything as bright as fire in the mist. Then I'll find room for
> so much—a gaiety—an inconsequence—a light spirited stepping
> at my sweet will. Whether I'm sufficiently mistress of
> things—thats the doubt; but conceive mark on the wall, K[ew].
> G[ardens]. & unwritten novel taking hands & dancing in unity.
> What the unity shall be I have yet to discover: the theme is a
> blank to me; but I see immense possibilities in the form I hit
> upon more or less by chance 2 weeks ago. (*Diaries*, 2, 13–14)

In the case of *Jacob's Room*, her paradoxical and elegiac attempt to
represent Jacob's absence so powerfully that his presence, though
one of the "shadows" (78) [56], is felt and inferred, dictates the use
of formal devices that can mediate between contradictions. Thus she
creates a narrator who is inside and outside the text; who possesses
omniscience, but whose efforts to understand the world are troubled
by her limited perspective; and whose shift from narrator- to character-focalizer
reveals the arbitrariness of the world which has
destroyed both Jacob and her authority. Her use of ekphrasis questions
the boundaries between the visual and the verbal and requires
the creation of a new kind of temporality, one which momentarily
asserts its timelessness only to accede to the flow of time and change
more elegiacally because of time's momentary cessation. In doing so,
she creates a significant form for the postwar elegiac novel that Bell,
judging from his review, approved.

At the same time, however, her form implicitly poses questions—
and suggests answers—about the relationship between art and life
that would have troubled many of her contemporaries. In Bell's
terms, can we separate the "emotions of art" from the "emotions of
life?" Do we really bring to every work of art no knowledge of life,
its vagaries, its challenges, its traumas? In this novel—whose time
frame has been shifted to include "life" in the form of the Great
War—Woolf suggests not. Thus *Jacob's Room* becomes, as it were,
an aesthetic argument in which she grasps precisely those "unseizable
forces," allowing them elegiacally to tear the whole implied by
the omniscient narrator "to ribbons," in order to defy the very idea
that the novelists can't catch the effects those forces have had on
life and on art. Her conception of "significant form," then, does not
elude history or daily life; rather, historical circumstances have
brought it into being, just as they have brought the form of her novel
into being.

WORKS CITED

Bal, Mieke. *Narratology*. 2nd Ed. Toronto: University of Toronto Press, 1997.

Bell, Clive. *Art*. London: Chatto and Windus, 1931.

———. "On Virginia Woolf's Painterly Vision." In *Virginia Woolf: The Critical Heritage*, ed. by Robin Majumdar and Allen McLaurin, 138–47. London: Routledge & Kegan Paul, 1931.

Bishop, Edward L. "The Shaping of *Jacob's Room*: Woolf's Manuscript Revisions." *Twentieth Century Literature*, 32.1 (Spring 1986): 115–35.

———. "The Subject in *Jacob's Room*." *Modern Fiction Studies*, 38.1 (Spring 1992): 147–75.

Chatman, Seymour. *Story and Discourse*. Ithaca: Cornell University Press, 1978.

Fowler, Alastair. *Kinds of Literature: An Introduction to the Theory of Genres and Modes*. Cambridge: Harvard University Press, 1982.

Freedman, Ralph. "The Form of Fact and Fiction: *Jacob's Room* as Paradigm." In *Virginia Woolf: Revaluation and Continuity*, ed. by Ralph Freedman, 123–40. Los Angeles: University of California Press, 1980.

Froula, Christine. "War, Civilization, and the Conscience of Modernity." In *Virginia Woolf: Texts and Contexts*, ed. by Beth Rigel Daugherty and Eileen Barrett. New York: Pace University Press, 1996. 280–95.

Fussell, Paul. *The Great War and Modern Memory*. New York: Oxford University Press, 1975.

Genette, Gérard. *Narrative Discourse: An Essay in Method*. Trans. Jane E. Lewin. Ithaca: Cornell University Press, 1980.

Handley, William R. "War and the Politics of Narration in *Jacob's Room*." In *Virginia Woolf and War*, ed. by Mark Hussey, 110–33. Syracuse: Syracuse University Press, 1991.

Kazan, Francesca. "Description and the Pictorial in *Jacob's Room*." *ELH*, 55 (1988): 701–19.

Kiely, Robert. "*Jacob's Room* and Roger Fry: Two Studies in Still Life." In *Modernism Reconsidered*, ed. by Robert Kiely, 147–66. Cambridge: Harvard University Press, 1983.

Krieger, Murray. *The Play and Place of Criticism*. Baltimore: Johns Hopkins, 1967.

Kristeva, Julia. *Black Sun: Depression and Melancholia*. New York: Columbia University Press, 1989.

Lawrence, Karen. "Gender and Narrative Voice in *Jacob's Room* and *A Portrait of the Artist as a Young Man*." In *James Joyce: The Centennial Symposium*, ed. by Morris Beja. Urbana: University of Illinois Press, 1986. 31–38.

Lee, Hermione. *Virginia Woolf*. New York: Knopf, 1997.

Lilienfeld, Jane. " 'Must Novels Be Like This?': Virginia Woolf as Narrative Theorist." In *Virginia Woolf: Texts and Contexts*, ed. by Beth Rigel Daugherty and Eileen Barrett, 123–28. New York: Pace University Press, 1996.

Little, Judy. "Feminizing the Subject: Dialogic Narration in *Jacob's Room*." *Literature-Interpretation-Theory* 3.4 (1992): 241–51.

———. "*Jacob's Room* as Comedy: Woolf's Parodic *Bildungsroman*." In *New*

Feminist Essays on Virginia Woolf, ed. by Jane Marcus, 105–24. Lincoln: University of Nebraska Press, 1981.

McNichol, Stella. *Virginia Woolf and the Poetry of Fiction*. New York: Routledge, 1990.

Mitchell, W. J. T. *Picture Theory*. Chicago: University of Chicago Press, 1994.

Morgenstern, Barry. "The Self-Conscious Narrator in *Jacob's Room.*" *Modern Fiction Studies* 18 (Autumn 1972): 351–61.

Moss, Roger. "*Jacob's Room* and the Eighteenth Century: From Elegy to Essay." *Critical Quarterly* 23.3 (Autumn 1981): 39–54.

Newman, Herta. *Virginia Woolf and Mrs. Brown: Toward a Realism of Uncertainty*. New York: Garland, 1996.

Olin-Hitt, Michael R. "Power, Discipline, and Individuality: Subversive Characterization in *Jacob's Room.*" In *Virginia Woolf: Texts and Contexts*, ed. by Beth Rigel Daugherty and Eileen Barrett, 128–34. New York: Pace University Press, 1996.

Ramazani, Jahan. *Poetry of Mourning: The Modern Elegy from Hardy to Heaney*. Chicago: University of Chicago Press, 1994.

Rimmon-Kenan, Shlomith. *Narrative Fiction: Contemporary Poetics*. New York: Routledge, 1990.

Ruotolo, Lucio P. *The Interrupted Moment: A View of Virginia Woolf's Novels*. Stanford: Stanford University Press, 1986.

Sacks, Peter M. *The English Elegy: Studies in the Genre from Spenser to Yeats*. Baltimore: Johns Hopkins University Press, 1985.

Shaw, W. David. *Elegy and Paradox: Testing the Conventions*. Baltimore: Johns Hopkins University Press, 1994.

Stewart, Garrett. *Death Sentences: Styles of Dying in British Fiction*. Cambridge: Harvard University Press, 1984.

Wagner, Peter. *Icons, Texts, Iconotexts: Essays on Ekphrasis and Intermediality*. New York: de Gruyter, 1996.

Woolf, Virginia. *Between the Acts*. London: Grafton Books, 1987.

———. *Diary of Virginia Woolf*. Vol. II. ed. Anne Olivier Bell. London: Hogarth Press, 1978.

———. *The Flight of the Mind: The Letters of Virginia Woolf*. Vol. I: 1888–1912. Ed. Nigel Nicolson. London: Hogarth Press, 1975.

———. *Jacob's Room*. New York: Signet, 1998.

———. "The Leaning Tower." In *The Moment and Other Essays*, ed. by Leonard Woolf, 128–54. New York: Harcourt Brace, 1975.

———. *The Question of Things Happening: The Letters of Virginia Woolf*. Vol. 11: 1912–22. Ed. Nigel Nicolson. London: Hogarth Press, 1976.

———. "Walter Sickert." In *The Captain's Death Bed and Other Essays*, 172–85. London: Hogarth Press, 1950.

Zeiger, Melissa F. *Beyond Consolation: Death, Sexuality, and the Changing Shapes of Elegy*. Ithaca: Cornell University Press, 1997.

Zwerdling, Alex. "*Jacob's Room*: Woolf's Satiric Elegy." *ELH* 48 (1981): 894–913.

EDWARD L. BISHOP

Mind the Gap: The Spaces in *Jacob's Room*†

Classical pianist Alfred Brendel says, "I like the fact that 'listen' is an anagram of 'silent'. Silence is not something that is there before the music begins and after it stops. It is the essence of the music itself, the vital ingredient that makes it possible for the music to exist at all. It's wonderful when the audience is part of this productive silence" (Alvarez 53). He is speaking of piano concerts, but the same could be said of *Jacob's Room*. So much of the effect of this book depends upon the spatial silence, the white space of the gaps on the page. They are, to paraphrase Brendel, the essence of the text itself, the vital ingredient that makes it possible for the narrative to exist at all. And it is indeed wonderful when the audience is part of this productive silence. In *Mimesis*, Eric Auerbach talks about the narrative of the Bible and how the mind swarms into the dark spaces between the events that are lit up by the narration. The gaps, then, do not merely pace the reader, they allow her or his mind to move into the silence.[1] This is what happens, or at least can happen, in *Jacob's Room*.

Throughout her career Woolf was concerned by the conjunction of space and silence. At the end of 1921 as she was finishing the first draft of *Jacob's Room*, she concluded "A Glance at Turgenev" with the observation that in his stories Turgenev fuses his elements "in one moment of great intensity, though all round are the silent spaces" (*E3* 317). Two decades later, in a diary note on *The Years* she writes, "I think I see how I can bring in interludes—I mean spaces of silence" (*D4* 332; 17 July 1935). And in the *Pointz Hall* typescript she refers to "That feeling slipped between the space that separates one word from another; like a blue flower between two

---

† From *Woolf Studies Annual* 10 (2004): 31–49.

1. "Since so much in the story is dark and incomplete [. . . the reader's] effort to interpret it constantly finds something new to feed upon" (15). Auerbach is arguing that the styles of the *Iliad* and the Bible represent the two basic styles in Western literature of representing reality: "on the one hand [the *Iliad*] fully externalized description . . . all events in the foreground; on the other hand [the Bible], certain parts brought into high relief, others left obscure, abruptness, suggestive influence of the unexpressed" (23). See also pp. 9–11.

Auerbach is talking about elements of style, but as Roger Chartier insists, forms produce meaning, and with the early printings of the Bible the "visual articulation of the page" was a vexed issue. The sixteenth to the eighteenth centuries saw "the opening up of the page through the multiplication of paragraphs that broke the uninterrupted continuity of the text common in the Renaissance [. . .]. This textual segmentation (*découpage*) had fundamental implications when it was applied to sacred texts. The story of Locke's anxiety regarding the practice of dividing the text of the Bible into chapter and verse is well known. For him such a division presented a considerable risk of obliterating the powerful coherence of the word of God" (51–52).

stones" (36). The notion of silence as an essential element of Woolf's work has been recognized by Woolf critics for decades. Back in 1970 Harvena Richter argued that Woolf "approached this aspect of form in the same way as does an architect, painter, or composer—to use negative 'blank spaces' or 'intervals' in a positive way so as to make them contribute to subjective feeling" (229), and Richter drew attention to Woolf's comment that Sterne is a "forerunner of the moderns" because of his "interest in silence rather than in speech," which makes us "consult our own minds" (CE 1 98).[2] So gaps are essential, and if they are to be truly productive in engaging the audience they must be more than merely visual cues like paragraph indents. It is surprising, therefore, that while the linguistic text of *Jacob's Room* has been comparatively little altered through the various editions, the space breaks which are one of the most distinctive features of the book have been shrunk, paved over, and ignored altogether.

Students who want a machine-searchable text, or perhaps simply don't want to buy the book, can find *Jacob's Room* on the net at sites such as Project Gutenberg. The problem, however, is that in the online texts every paragraph is double-spaced and the space breaks Woolf wrote into her book are eliminated altogether. As Mark Hussey noted of the hypertext *Mrs. Dalloway* in "How Should One Read a Screen?" "the spaces on the page that contribute to the rhythmic context of the words on the page are insignificant, 'unreadable,' in effect, by the machine" (254).[3] But these days, when electronic texts are still in their infancy, we almost expect them to be flawed, and for most readers they are still things to be consulted, not read.[4] More interesting are the variations in the print editions, variations that have been there since 1923.

The first English edition of *Jacob's Room* was published by the Hogarth Press—their first novel, and the largest production to date for the young publishing company—on October 27, 1922. Three months later, on February 8, 1923, in New York, Harcourt Brace brought out the American edition. There are very few changes to the

2. Patricia Laurence's excellent *Reading of Silence* reproduces the black page from Sterne's *Tristram Shandy* and states, "Sterne's black page calls attention to the materiality of the text. Silences are marked. This forerunner of Woolf, with his modern interest in silence— the blank spaces, the white and black pages, the typography (asterisks, ellipses, dashes, parentheses)—illuminates the unsaid" (30). She only mentions *Jacob's Room* in passing, but the whole book provides a useful commentary on the silences of the gaps.
3. Hussey reiterates the point that Woolf was "concerned not only with the sound of her words, but also with their visual display upon the page"; her use of space breaks all contributed "to the effort Woolf made to shape the *reading* of her fiction after about 1917— the date of her and Leonard's acquisition of the Hogarth Press and, not merely coincidentally I think, of her earliest experimental fictions" (253).
4. John Thompson, writing in the introduction to *Books and Bibliography*, addresses this problem: "A year or so ago I searched the Web for copies of Rudyard Kipling's poem 'If.' There were many hundreds. I took the first eight hits my search engine produced: all eight were textually different. There is no answer to what a library, any library, should do faced with this digital tidal wave" (11).

linguistic text between the English and the American editions and these are for the most part variations in hyphenation and capitalization; they could have been made by a typesetter, and in any case none is substantive enough to give authority to the American text as an improvement over the English text. Woolf did no rewriting between editions.[5] Nevertheless, considerable variation *does* exist between the first British and the first American editions in the handling of the space breaks. In every chapter except chapter seven and the short final chapter there are more divisions in the English text, with the result that in the book as a whole the English edition has twenty-five more sections than the American edition: 148 as opposed to 123.[6] So how did this happen?

Woolf seems to have been a victim of Harcourt Brace's house style in page design. If you look at an English first edition you will see that many of the space breaks occur at the top or bottom of the page. In the American text no spaces are left at the top or bottom of the page; thus if a break in the English edition is due to occur at either point the American typesetters silently collapse it.[7] In fifteen of the cases this seems to be what happened. In another five instances the English text indicates only a small break at the top or bottom of its page, difficult for the typesetters to judge unless they compared it closely with a full page. Finally, there are five breaks clearly marked in the English edition that would not have fallen at the top or bottom of the page in the American edition, yet inexplicably do not make it into that edition.

5. In preparing the text for the Shakespeare Head Edition I let inconsistencies between accepted spellings of the same word stand, such as *Flanders'* and *Flanders's*; and I did not make changes based on felicitous phrasing: the "smoothly sculptured" policeman on p. 156, therefore, was not altered to "sculpted"; and I noted but did not change Woolf's idiosyncratic spelling of Van Gogh and Boulevard Raspail (*JR* 61, 206). In a letter to Jacques Raverat on 10 December 1922, she says, "Raspail was spelt wrong owing to Duncan and Vanessa, whom I consulted. A letter more or less means nothing to them" (*L2* 591–2). I did, however, correct three obvious misprints that appear in both 1E and 1A, and I included the two emendations that Woolf requested in the 4 October 1922 letter to Donald Brace quoted in Appendix A.

6. Howard Harper, in *Between Language and Silence: The Novels of Virginia Woolf* (Louisiana State University Press, 1982), p. 88, n.3, notes that "Interesting patterns, almost musical in their rhythmic arrangement and in their effects, are involved in the distributions of chapters and sections in *Jacob's Room*," and argues that the twelve subdivisions in the first two chapters constitute a sort of base line from which the later chapters depart. My findings differ (he documents only eight lost sections between the first English and the first American editions, some of which in fact are there), but I am grateful to him for drawing attention to the differences in format between the first editions. I am also grateful to the Harry Ransom Humanities Research Center, U of Texas at Austin, for making the first editions of *Jacob's Room* available to me, and for the Andrew Mellon Fellowship which enabled me to study the texts.

7. With *The Waves* on the other hand, the printers were actively attentive. J. H. Willis notes, "The managing director of R. & R. Clark, with the kind of attention to detail that endeared him to the Woolfs, soon wrote back to Leonard in July 1931 explaining that while he had allowed a half-inch space in the seven places indicated in the text by their directions to 'leave larger space,' he believed there were other places where there were distinct breaks in the narrative, perhaps requiring two kinds of space (HP 575). He sought clarification before putting the text into page proofs" (198).

There is another change: in the Hogarth edition there are four
different sizes of breaks, ranging from one to four-line spaces, where
in the Harcourt Brace edition they are all regularized as one-line
spaces. Why should we care? Woolf herself did not seem concerned
about the variations in the U.S. edition. She makes no note of these
matters in the brief correspondence we have between her and Harcourt and Brace.[8]

Woolf could be casual about the fate of her texts once they made
it into print, but in developing *Jacob's Room* she did care very much
about the space breaks. When she began writing the novel in April
of 1920 she had been setting Hope Mirrlees's *Paris: A Poem* (published May 1920), a complex text in which, as Julia Briggs points
out, Mirrlees had "learned from Apollinaire, Cocteau and Reverdy
that the placing of a line of poetry itself constituted a form of punc-
tuation, and that the spaces on the page were a crucial part of a
poem's rhythm."[9] Also, the year before she had hand-set T. S. Eliot's
Poems (1919). So she was aware of the potential of space, but she
did not use it immediately in the writing of *Jacob's Room*. At first
Woolf divided her text only with numbered chapter divisions. After
three months of writing she began using a row of 'x's to indicate
subdivisions, and after six months she began to use space breaks in
her manuscript book; thus the gaps, deliberate and considered, were
part of the evolving shape of her novel.[1]

I will not weary the reader by analyzing all of the missing gaps,
nor the nearly eighty instances where the English text has a space
four times greater than that of the American text, but what I want
to do below is draw attention to six pivotal moments in *Jacob's Room*
and very briefly suggest how the absence of a space break, or even a
variation in the size of the space break, can affect our response to
the text. The argument here is not for a particular reading but for a
modified practice: I believe critics of whatever theoretical persua-
sion, whether they are analyzing typography or investigating trauma,
would find it productive to examine the first editions. For ease of
access I have indicated the chapter and the page numbers in the first
British, first American, and current Harcourt Brace paperback editions. [Bracketed page numbers refer to this Norton Critical Edition.]

---

8. See Appendix A.
9. " 'Printing Hope': Virginia Woolf, Hope Mirrlees, and the iconic imagery of 'Paris'," In
   press; I am grateful to Dr. Briggs for allowing me to read the typescript. J. H. Willis notes,
   "Their typesetting skill was tested at least twice[. . .]. T. S. Eliot's *Waste Land* (1923)
   required adroit spacing, and *Paris* (1920) by Hope Mirrlees was self-consciously modern
   in its typographical configuration, one line running vertically down the page (34).
1. See my Introduction to Jacob's Room: *The Holograph Draft* p. xxi and *passim*.

The Conspiracy of Hush and Clean Bottles

(12A, 13 HBJ) [6–7]
She had her hand upon the garden gate.
    "The meat!" she exclaimed, striking the latch down.
She had forgotten the meat.
There was Rebecca at the window.

    The bareness of Mrs. Pearce's front room was fully displayed
at ten o'clock at night when a powerful oil lamp stood on the
middle of the table.

_____

(15E) [6–7]
She had her hand upon the garden gate.
    "The meat!" she exclaimed, striking the latch down.
She had forgotten the meat.
There was Rebecca at the window.

    The bareness of Mrs. Pearce's front room was fully displayed
at ten o'clock at night when a powerful oil lamp stood on the
middle of the table.

The first big (four-line) gap in the English text occurs after "There
was Rebecca at the window." It comes shortly after the narrator's
reflection "who shall deny that this blankness of mind, when combined with profusion, mother wit, old wives' tales [. . .] who shall
deny that in these respects every woman is nicer than any man."
Where the smaller gap in the American text allows the eye to skip
easily into the next paragraph and Mrs. Pearce's front room, the large
gap isolates Rebecca in the window, situates her as an object of
Betty's gaze, and distinguishes her from the minor characters we
have already met or heard of—Mr. Connor who owns the yacht,
Charles Steele the painter, Mr. Curnow who lost an eye. Thus we
are expectant when Rebecca returns two pages later "bending over
a spirit-lamp in the small room next door," the small flame of which
burns quietly while the wind rushes outside. The two women murmur "over the spirit-lamp, plotting the eternal conspiracy of hush
and clean bottles."

(14A, 13 HBJ) [8]

"Good night, Rebecca" Mrs. Flanders murmured, and Rebecca called her ma'am, though they were conspirators plotting the eternal conspiracy of hush and clean bottles.

Mrs. Flanders had left the lamp burning in the front room. There were her spectacles, her sewing; and a letter with the Scarborough postmark. She had not drawn the curtains either.

(17–18E) [8]

"Good-night, Rebecca" Mrs. Flanders murmured, and Rebecca called her ma'am, though they were conspirators plotting the eternal conspiracy of hush and clean bottles.

Mrs. Flanders had left the lamp burning in the front room. There were her spectacles, her sewing; and a letter with the Scarborough postmark. She had not drawn the curtains either.

The flame of female friendship, quietly subversive (it is a "conspiracy") assures the continuity of the household while the wind, associated with the male world of Captains and steamers, "rages" outside. The theme of female friendship will become important, and Woolf wanted to set off this intimate exchange over the spirit-lamp (which, interestingly, burns volatile liquid fuel to produce its quiet light). In the English text, the start of the scene is signalled by a two-line gap at " 'I thought he'd never get off—such a hurricane' " (17E, 13A, 12HBJ) [7]. The scene still has resonance in the first American edition, but it is absorbed into the longer tri-partite scene of putting Archer to bed, Betty discussing the baby with Rebecca, and the narrator's description of the house after all have gone to sleep. We end with the famous image of the crab in the bucket (19E, 16A, 14 HBJ) [9] and we lose the conspiracy of hush and clean bottles as a countervailing force to the confinements, and violence, of the male world.

What's the Next Thing to See in Scarborough?

(24A, 19HBJ) [12]

But there was a time when none of this had any existence [. . .]. Fix your eyes upon the lady's skirt [. . .]. It changes; drapes her ankles—the nineties [. . .].

And now, what's the next thing to see in Scarborough?

Mrs. Flanders sat on the raised circle of the Roman camp, patching Jacob's breeches[. . .].

(27E) [12]
But there was a time when none of this had any existence
[. . .]. Fix your eyes upon the lady's skirt [. . .]. It changes;
drapes her ankles—the nineties [. . .]. And now, what's the
next thing to see in Scarborough?

Mrs. Flanders sat on the raised circle of the Roman camp,
patching Jacob's breeches [. . .].

At the end of the well-known time-travel passage the narrator asks,
"And now, what's the next thing to see in Scarborough?" In the first
American edition the next line, "Mrs. Flanders sat on the raised circle of the Roman camp," immediately answers the question. The
narrative gaze swivels from the Roman artefacts in the museum to
Betty sitting at the Roman camp. But with the gap, and it is the
largest, a four-line gap, the question hangs over the white space. The
effect is subtly different now: the text instead of providing an answer
for us asks us to speculate on our own. The gap is for us to fill in.
The question takes us back to the imperative at the beginning of the
interlude, "Fix your eyes upon the lady's skirt," and invites meditation
on the palimpsestic quality of this historic town and of life itself.
These are at once unique events, and rituals where the participants
change but the actions remain the same. Thus when the line "Mrs.
Flanders sat [. . .]" comes after the gap it does so as a resumption
of the narrative, not the answer to the question, and we see her now
not as "the next thing to see in Scarborough" but as one of many
figures through the ages who have "sat on the raised circle of the
Roman camp." The spatial configuration is crucial: with the gap we
continue our tunnelling into the past, without it we slip easily back
into the unfolding present.

One Word Is Sufficient. But if One Cannot Find It?

(117A, 71HBJ) [55]
Then his mouth—but surely, of all futile occupations this of
cataloguing features is the worst. One word is sufficient. But if
one cannot find it?
    "I like Jacob Flanders," wrote Clara Durrant in her diary. "He
is so unworldly. He gives himself no airs, and one can say what
one likes to him, though he's frightening because . . ."

(114E) [55]

Then his mouth—but surely, of all futile occupations this of cataloguing features is the worst. One word is sufficient. But if one cannot find it?

"I like Jacob Flanders," wrote Clara Durrant in her diary. "He is so unworldly. He gives himself no airs, and one can say what one likes to him, though he's frightening because . . ."

Jacob's Room is filled with reflections on writing and the (im)-possibility of capturing character. The narrator has been musing on Mrs. Durrant's phrase for Jacob ("distinguished-looking") and trying to apply it. In the English edition the reflection ends poised on the question, "But if one cannot find it?" followed by a large gap. The first American edition moves right on to Clara and her diary, where the concern is less for precision in language than for prescribed space: "Mr. Letts allows little space in his shilling diaries. Clara was not the one to encroach upon Wednesday." The point of the scene in the American text becomes the mild humor at Clara's expense ("But then, this is only a young woman's language") rather than, as in the English edition, the narrator's self-reflexive observation. It is a serious question—what indeed is the point of writing if one cannot find the right word, if perhaps it does not exist? This obsession with linguistic slippage dogs the narrator in her project throughout.

Whether She Had a Mind . . . Turning up Greek Street

(132A, 79HBJ) [62]

But it did occur to Jacob, half-way through dinner, to wonder whether she had a mind.

They sat at a little table in the restaurant.

Florinda leant the points of her elbows on the table and held her chin in the cup of her hands.

(128E) [62]
But it did occur to Jacob, half-way through dinner, to wonder whether she had a mind.

They sat at a little table in the restaurant.
Florinda leant the points of her elbows on the table and held her chin in the cup of her hands.

Here again the American text collapses a large gap. On the previous page Florinda has been wrestling with Shelley ("What on earth was it *about*?") and Jacob has been wrestling with chastity ("Whether or not she was a virgin seems a matter of no importance whatever. Unless, indeed, it is the only thing of any importance at all"). Then for Jacob a larger question looms, one that follows from what we've seen of Florinda's encounter with Shelley, not whether or not she's chaste but "whether she had a mind."

With the paragraph break Woolf has already shifted from the indeterminate space of authorial reflection to the scene at the restaurant (Jacob and Florinda are "half-way through dinner") but she more emphatically sets off her one-line paragraph. The gap renders Jacob's sudden apprehension of just how vacuous Florinda is. Between the manuscript and the published text Woolf made the decision to deny her narrator any access to Jacob's mind at all, and so rather than internal monologue it is the gaps that render the emotion. The white space is where Jacob's horror sinks in. Or where time stops, as it does in Greek street:

(158A, 94HBJ) [74]
Then he saw her turning up Greek Street upon another man's arm.

The light from the arc lamp drenched him from head to toe. He stood for a minute motionless beneath it.

(152E) [74]
Then he saw her turning up Greek Street upon another man's arm.

The light from the arc lamp drenched him from head to toe. He stood for a minute motionless beneath it.

Two chapters later we find Jacob still trying to rationalize his attraction to Florinda. He has come to terms with the fact that she is not chaste, but has convinced himself that she has an "inviolable fidelity." Then his delusion is violated by seeing her turning into Soho, up the notorious Greek Street, which a police commission in 1906 had called the worst street in the West End. (We might wonder what Jacob is doing in the area, but he sees her turning off Shaftesbury Avenue, a main thoroughfare, as he walks back to Bloomsbury from central London.) When the famous Italian libertine Giacomo Casanova (1725–98) came to London in 1763–4 he lived in Greek Street, and conceived a disastrous passion for an innocent-looking prostitute, Marianne Charpillon, who swindled him. Jacob is no Casanova but he is as devastated as the Italian was (who, like Jacob, knew better even as he slipped deeper into his obsession), and that sense of time standing still is rendered by the gap.

There is no break in the narrative, no shift in point of view or subject. There is in the American edition a one-line gap, but it is of course one of many. The four-line gap, on the other hand, imposes a moment of arrest upon the reader that corresponds to the blankness in Jacob's mind. Woolf's narrator tries in a series of similes—"as if a stone were ground to dust; as if white sparks flew from a livid whetstone which was his spine; as if the switchback railway, having swooped to the depths, fell, fell, fell"—to render what Jacob must feel. The passage turns to a reflection by the narrator on the impossibility of entering another's consciousness: "Whether we know what was in his mind is another question. Granted ten years' seniority and a difference of sex, fear of him comes first; this is swallowed up by a desire to help—overwhelming sense, reason, and the time of night [. . .]" (153E, 158A, 94HBJ) [74–75], but the gap allows Woolf to have it both ways, at once rendering the emotion and then talking about the impossibility of capturing or articulating it.

Darkness Drops like a Knife

(300A, 175HBJ) [142]
    Darkness drops like a knife over Greece.

    "The guns?" said Betty Flanders, half asleep, getting out of bed and going to the window, which was decorated with a fringe of dark leaves.

(288E) [142]
    Darkness drops like a knife over Greece.

    "The guns?" said Betty Flanders, half asleep, getting out of bed and going to the window, which was decorated with a fringe of dark leaves.

As in the Greek Street passage, at the end of the book when war enters the text—the war that will kill Jacob—the four-line gap in the English edition leaves the line hanging, letting the ominousness of the metaphor (however clichéd the phrase "drops like a knife" might be) emerge fully. Similarly, at the end of chapter three the line, "Jacob Flanders, therefore, went up to Cambridge in October, 1906," which marks the beginning of the process that will lead Jacob to war, is set off by a four-line gap in the English edition, giving it a portentousness it does not have in the American volume. The editions that regularize the size of the gaps mute these effects, even if they do not obliterate them completely; they direct and foreclose the reader's response, rather than engage it. *Jacob's Room* is a novel full of fissures, ruptures, gaps, and chasms, and the intent of the novel is not just to tell the story of Jacob but to make us aware of these spaces.

Chasms in Our Ways

(161A, 96HBJ) [76]
    As frequent as street corners in Holborn are these chasms in the continuity of our ways. Yet we keep straight on.
    Rose Shaw, talking in rather an emotional manner to Mr. Bowley at Mrs. Durrant's evening party a few nights back, said that life was wicked because a man called Jimmy refused to marry a woman called (if memory serves) Helen Aitken.

(155–6E) [76]

As frequent as street corners in Holborn are these chasms in the continuity of our ways. Yet we keep straight on.

Rose Shaw, talking in rather an emotional manner to Mr. Bowley at Mrs. Durrant's evening party a few nights back, said that life was wicked because a man called Jimmy refused to marry a woman called (if memory serves) Helen Aitken.

At the end of chapter eight Woolf's narrator speaks of the chasms that exist in our daily lives, but which we remain unaware of and "keep straight on." This is the opposite of the cataclysmic rupture for Jacob in Greek Street. Here Woolf posits an encounter with an old busker on the street, whose tale, if you stop to talk to him instead of brushing by, will bring "you one winter's day to the Essex coast" and ultimately to the tropics, to "the verge of the marsh drinking rum-punch, an outcast from civilization." The first American edition closes over the gap and so the notion of the "chasm" is immediately reduced to the fact that someone named Jimmy has refused to marry someone called Helen, but in the British edition the gap episode testifies to the contingency of life, where a single chance occurrence can take your life in a completely different direction. In *Jacob's Room* Woolf is seeking to articulate these fissures not only through the discourse but with the page design, and where the first British edition renders the chasms, too often the first American edition keeps straight on.

There are chasms in everyday life, and *Jacob's Room* makes us aware of those, but there is also the larger chasm underlying the novel: that of the Great War. I have spoken elsewhere of the freeze-frame effect of the narration in the novel (Bishop xx), and Susan Sontag in her recent *New Yorker* article, "Looking At War: Photography and Violence," argues that, "Non-stop imagery (television, streaming video, movies) surrounds us, but, when it comes to remembering, the photograph has the deeper bite. Memory freeze-frames; its basic unit is the single image." She goes on,

> In an era of information overload the photograph provides a quick way of apprehending something and a compact form for memorizing it. The photograph is like a quotation, or a maxim or proverb. Each of us mentally stocks hundreds of photographs, subject to instant recall. [. . .] Conscripted as part of journalism, images were expected to arrest attention, startle, surprise. As the old advertising slogan of *Paris Match*, founded in 1919, had it: 'The weight of words, the shock of photos.' (87)

The format is part of the memorializing impulse in *Jacob's Room*: the sections are like individual photographs; the book as a whole is like an album of snapshots. To remove or reduce the gaps then is not to alter something inconsequential, but to tamper with something that lies at the very core of the book.

Much has been made of the fluidity of Woolf's prose, but we are only now becoming aware of the fluidity of Woolf's texts. Woolf allowed both versions of *Jacob's Room* to stand, as she did some of the famous cruxes in her other novels (*To the Lighthouse* and *Mrs Dalloway*). And the issue is still with us: the current HBJ edition now incorporates most of the spaces but it does not give the variations in size; the Penguin text uses two sizes of gaps; the Oxford Classics edition provides the variation from one- to four-line gaps. The forthcoming Shakespeare Head Edition (2004) follows the page design of the first English edition and lists the variants from the first American edition. I would argue that readers in England and America, even though they may be reading the same words, are reading very different texts. And anyone who is reading a print edition is reading something radically different from those who are reading online editions. As textual studies of Woolf become more sophisticated we must be alert to more than the variations in the linguistic text: we must also mind the gaps.

*   *   *

WORKS CITED

Alvarez, A. "The Playful Pianist," *New Yorker*, 1 April 1996, 49–55.

Auerbach, Eric. *Mimesis: The Representation of Reality in Western Literature*. Trans. Willard Trask. Princeton: Princeton UP, 1971, 1953.

Bishop, Edward L. *Virginia Woolf's* Jacob's Room: *The Holograph Draft*. NY: Pace UP, 1998.

Chartier, Roger. "Labourers and Voyagers: From the Text to the Reader." In David Finkelstein and Alistair McCleery, eds. *The Book History Reader*. London: Routledge, 2002. 47–76.

Harper, Howard. *Between Language and Silence: The Novels of Virginia Woolf*. Louisiana State UP, 1982.

Hussey, Mark. "How Should One Read a Screen?" Pamela L. Caughie, ed. *Virginia Woolf in the Age of Mechanical Reproduction*. New York and London: Garland, 2000. 249–265.

Laurence, Patricia Ondek. *The Reading of Silence: Virginia Woolf in the English Tradition*. Stanford: Stanford UP, 1991.

Richter, Harvena. *The Inward Voyage*. Princeton: Princeton UP, 1970.

Sontag, Susan. "Looking At War: Photography and Violence." *New Yorker*, 9 December 2002, 82–98.

Thomson, John, ed. *Books and Bibliography: Essays in Commemoration of Don McKenzie*. Wellington: Victoria UP, 2002.

Willis, J. H. *Leonard and Virginia Woolf as Publishers: The Hogarth Press, 1917–41*. Charlottesville and London: UP of Virginia, 1992.

Woolf, Virginia. *Jacob's Room*. London: Hogarth Press, 1922.

———. *Jacob's Room*. New York: Harcourt Brace, 1923.

———. *Jacob's Room*. New York: Harcourt, Harvest Books, n.d. [Reprint of the 1960 ed. which was published together with the author's *Waves* by Harcourt Brace & World]

———. *Jacob's Room*. Project Gutenberg. http://ibiblio.org/gutenberg/etext04/jcbrm10.txt. 6 August 2002; accessed 17 September 2003.

———. *POINTZ HALL: The Earlier and Later Typescripts of BETWEEN THE ACTS*. Edited, with introduction, annotations, and afterword by Mitchell A. Leaska. New York: University Publications, 1983.

Virginia Woolf: A Chronology

1878 March 26	Marriage of Virginia Woolf's parents, Leslie Stephen and Julia Duckworth
1879 May 30	Birth of Vanessa Stephen
1880 September 8	Birth of Julian Thoby Stephen
1882 January 25	Birth of Adeline Virginia Stephen
1883 October 27	Birth of Adrian Leslie Stephen
1895 May 5	Julia Stephen dies suddenly of influenza
Summer	Virginia's first breakdown, aged thirteen
1897 July 19	Death of Stella Duckworth, Virginia's half-sister
1898 October	Virginia starts Latin and Greek lessons
1899 October 3	Thoby becomes a student at Trinity College, Cambridge, where Virginia frequently visits him
1902 October	Adrian becomes a student at Trinity College, Cambridge
1904 February 22	Leslie Stephen dies after a long illness
May	Beginning of Virginia's second long breakdown
November	The Stephen children move from 22 Hyde Park Gate to 46 Gordon Square, Bloomsbury
December 14	Virginia's first publication, an unsigned review in *The Guardian*
1906 September 8	Virginia, Vanessa, and their friend Violet Dickinson depart for Greece, where they meet Thoby and Adrian
November 20	Thoby dies of typhoid fever
1907 February 7	Vanessa marries Clive Bell
April	Virginia and Adrian move to 29 Fitzroy Square
October	Virginia works on her first novel
1911 July 3	Virginia meets Leonard Woolf at the Bells' house
November	Virginia moves into a shared house at 38 Brunswick Square
1912 January	Leonard Woolf proposes to Virginia
May 29	Virginia agrees to marry Leonard; her mental health again becomes unstable

August 10	Virginia and Leonard marry
1913 September 9	After months of illness, Virginia attempts suicide and remains unstable for the next couple of years
1915 January 25	The Woolfs decide to set up a printing press and to move into Hogarth House, Richmond
March 26	Publication of *The Voyage Out*, Virginia's first novel; by Duckworth Press
1917 July	Hogarth Press publishes its first books: *The Mark on the Wall* (by Virginia) and *Three Jews* (by Leonard)
1919 May 12	*Kew Gardens* published by the Hogarth Press
July 1	The Woolfs buy Monk's House, Rodmell, where they will spend almost every summer from now on
October 20	*Night and Day* published by Duckworth Press
1920 Fall	Virginia works on *Jacob's Room*
1921 Summer	Virginia has a minor breakdown
1922 October 27	*Jacob's Room* published by the Hogarth Press, which will publish all Virginia's subsequent novels
1924 March	The Woolfs move into 52 Tavistock Square
October 30	*Mr Bennett and Mrs Brown* published
1925 April 23	*The Common Reader* published
May 14	*Mrs Dalloway* published
December 17–20	Virginia stays with Vita Sackville-West, and the two women begin an intermittent sexual relationship
1927 May 5	*To the Lighthouse* published
1928 October 11	*Orlando*, a mock biography of Vita Sackville-West, published
October 20	Virginia goes to Cambridge and delivers the lectures that will become *A Room of One's Own*
1929 March	Virginia works on the final version of *A Room of One's Own*
October 24	*A Room of One's Own* published
1930 March	Virginia writes *The Waves*
1931 October 8	*The Waves* published
1932 October 13	*The Common Reader: Second Series* published
1933 October 5	*Flush* published
1934, 1935	Virginia's mental health is uncertain for much of this time, while she writes *The Years*
1936 November	Virginia starts writing *Three Guineas*
1937 March 15	*The Years* published

July 18	Virginia's nephew, Julian Bell, is killed in the Spanish Civil War
1938 June 2	*Three Guineas* published
1939 September 1	Germany invades Poland
September 3	England declares war on Germany. Woolfs start living full-time at Monk's House
1940 July 25	*Roger Fry* published
September	Woolfs' house in Mecklenburg Square, London, bombed and severely damaged. Hogarth Press moves to Letchworth, Hertfordshire
1941 February 26	Virginia finishes *Pointz Hall (Between the Acts)*
March	Virginia's mental health deteriorates
March 28	Virginia drowns herself in the River Ouse
July 17	*Between the Acts* published

Selected Bibliography

WORKS BY VIRGINIA WOOLF

Novels

The Voyage Out. London: Duckworth, 1915.
Night and Day. London: Duckworth, 1919.
Jacob's Room. London: Hogarth, 1922.
Mrs Dalloway. London: Hogarth, 1925.
To the Lighthouse. London: Hogarth, 1927.
Orlando: A Biography. London: Hogarth, 1928.
The Waves. London: Hogarth, 1931.
Flush: A Biography. London: Hogarth, 1933.
The Years. London: Hogarth, 1937.
Between the Acts. London: Hogarth, 1941.

Nonfiction

A Room of One's Own. London: Hogarth, 1929.
Three Guineas. London: Hogarth, 1938.
Moments of Being. Autobiographical essays. Ed. Jeanne Schulkind. 2nd ed. New York: Harcourt Brace, 1985.

Collections

Collected Essays. Ed. Leonard Woolf. 4 vols. New York: Harcourt Brace, 1966–67.
The Complete Shorter Fiction of Virginia Woolf. Ed. Susan Dick. 2nd ed. New York: Harcourt Brace, 1989.
The Diary of Virginia Woolf. Ed. Anne Olivier Bell and Andrew McNeillie. 5 vols. New York: Harcourt Brace, 1977–84.
The Essays of Virginia Woolf. Ed. Andrew McNeillie. 3 vols. New York: Harcourt Brace, 1986–88.
The Essays of Virginia Woolf. Ed. Andrew McNeillie. Vol. 4. London: Hogarth, 1994.
The Letters of Virginia Woolf. Ed. Nigel Nicolson and Joanne Trautmann. 6 vols. New York: Harcourt Brace, 1977–82.
A Passionate Apprentice: The Early Journals of Virginia Woolf, 1897–1909. Ed. Mitchell Leaska. New York: Harcourt Brace, 1990.

BIOGRAPHIES OF VIRGINIA WOOLF

Bell, Quentin. *Virginia Woolf: A Biography*. New York: Harcourt Brace, 1972.
Briggs, Julia. *Virginia Woolf: An Inner Life*. New York: Harcourt, 2005.
Lee, Hermione. *Virginia Woolf*. New York: Knopf, 1997.
Poole, Roger. *The Unknown Virginia Woolf*. 4th ed. New York: Cambridge University Press, 1995.
Rose, Phyllis. *Woman of Letters: A Life of Virginia Woolf*. New York: Oxford University Press, 1978.

CRITICAL STUDIES OF VIRGINIA WOOLF

Abel, Elizabeth. *Virginia Woolf and the Fictions of Psychoanalysis*. Chicago: Chicago University Press, 1989.
Auerbach, Eric. "The Brown Stocking." *Mimesis: The Representation of Reality in Western Literature*. Trans. Willard Trask. Princeton: Princeton University Press, 1953. 16–34.
Beer, Gillian. *Virginia Woolf: The Common Ground*. Ann Arbor: Michigan University Press, 1996.
Black, Naomi. *Virginia Woolf as Feminist*. Ithaca: Cornell University Press, 2004.
Bowlby, Rachel. *Feminist Destinations and Further Essays on Virginia Woolf*. Edinburgh: Edinburgh University Press, 1997.
Caramagno, Thomas C. *The Flight of the Mind: Virginia Woolf's Art and Manic-Depressive Illness*. Berkeley: University of California Press, 1992.
Caughie, Pamela. *Virginia Woolf and Postmodernism*. Urbana: University of Illinois Press, 1991.
Cuddy-Keane, Melba. *Virginia Woolf, the Intellectual and the Public Sphere*. New York: Cambridge University Press, 2003.
Dalgarno, Emily. *Virginia Woolf and the Visible World*. New York: Cambridge University Press, 2001.
DeSalvo, Louise. *Virginia Woolf: The Impact of Childhood Sexual Abuse on her Life and Work*. Boston: Beacon, 1989.
Froula, Christine. *Virginia Woolf and the Bloomsbury Avant-Garde: War, Civilization, Modernity*. New York: Columbia University Press, 2005.
Glenny, Allie. *Ravenous Identity: Eating and Eating Distress in the Life and Work of Virginia Woolf*. New York: St Martin's, 1999.
Goldman, Jane. *The Feminist Aesthetics of Virginia Woolf: Modernism, Post-Impressionism and the Politics of the Visual*. New York: Cambridge University Press, 1998.
Levenback, Karen L. *Virginia Woolf and the Great War*. Syracuse: Syracuse University Press, 1999.
Marcus, Jane. *Virginia Woolf and the Languages of Patriarchy*. Bloomington: Indiana University Press, 1987.
Meisel, Perry. *The Absent Father: Virginia Woolf and Walter Pater*. New Haven: Yale University Press, 1980.
Minow-Pinkney, Makiko. *Virginia Woolf and the Problem of the Subject*. New Brunswick, N.J.: Rutgers University Press, 1987.
Roe, Sue. *Writing and Gender: Virginia Woolf's Writing Practice*. New York: St Martin's, 1990.
Silver, Brenda R. *Virginia Woolf Icon*. Chicago: Chicago University Press, 1999.
Snaith, Anna. *Virginia Woolf: Public and Private Negotiations*. New York: St Martin's, 2000.

Squier, Susan M. *Virginia Woolf and London: The Sexual Politics of the City.* Chapel Hill: University of North Carolina Press, 1985.

Zwerdling, Alex. *Virginia Woolf and the Real World.* Berkeley and Los Angeles: University of California Press, 1986.

COLLECTIONS OF ESSAYS

Caughie, Pamela, ed. *Virginia Woolf in the Age of Mechanical Reproduction.* New York: Garland, 2000.

Clements, Patricia, and Isobel Grundy, eds. *Virginia Woolf: New Critical Essays.* Totowa, NJ: Barnes and Noble, 1983.

Haule, James M., and J. H. Stape, eds. *Editing Virginia Woolf: Interpreting the Modernist Text.* New York: Palgrave, 2002.

Hussey, Mark, ed. *Virginia Woolf and War: Fiction, Reality and Myth.* Syracuse: Syracuse University Press, 1986.

Marcus, Jane, ed. *New Feminist Essays on Virginia Woolf.* Lincoln: University of Nebraska Press, 1981.

Roe, Sue, and Susan Sellers, eds. *The Cambridge Companion to Virginia Woolf.* New York: Cambridge University Press, 2000.

CRITICAL STUDIES OF *JACOB'S ROOM*

• indicates a work included or excerpted in this Norton Critical Edition.

Bazin, Nancy Topping. "*Jacob's Room* and *Mrs Dalloway*." *Virginia Woolf and the Androgynous Vision.* New Brunswick, N.J.: Rutgers University Press, 1973. 89–123.

Beattie, Thomas C. "Moments of Meaning Dearly Achieved: Virginia Woolf's Sense of an Ending." *Modern Fiction Studies* 32 (1986): 521–41.

•Bishop, Edward L. "Mind the Gap: The Spaces in *Jacob's Room*." *Woolf Studies Annual* 10 (2004): 31–49.

———. "The Shaping of *Jacob's Room*: Woolf's Manuscript Revisions." *Twentieth-Century Literature* 32 (1986): 115–35.

———. "The Subject in *Jacob's Room*." *Modern Fiction Studies* 38 (1992): 147–75.

Booth, Allyson. "The Architecture of Loss: Teaching *Jacob's Room* as a War Novel." *Re: Reading, Re: Writing, Re: Teaching Virginia Woolf: Selected Papers from the 4th Annual Conference on Virginia Woolf, Bard College, New York, June 9–12, 1994.* Ed. Eileen Barrett and Patricia Cramer. New York: Pace University Press, 1995. 65–72.

Bradshaw, David. *Winking, Buzzing, Carpet-Beating: Reading* Jacob's Room. London, England: Virginia Woolf Society of Great Britain, 2003.

Dobie, Kathleen. "This is the Room that Class Built: The Structures of Sex and Class in *Jacob's Room*." *Virginia Woolf and Bloomsbury: A Centenary Celebration.* Ed. Jane Marcus. Bloomington: Indiana University Press, 1987. 195–207.

Dowling, David. "Virginia Woolf's Own Jacob's Room." *Southern Review: Literary and Interdisciplinary Essays* 15 (1982): 60–72.

•Flint, Kate. "Revising *Jacob's Room*: Virginia Woolf, Women and Language." *Review of English Studies,* n.s., 42 (1991): 361–79.

Handley, William R. "War and the Politics of Narration in *Jacob's Room*." *Virginia Woolf and War: Fiction, Reality, and Myth.* Ed. Mark Hussey. Syracuse: Syracuse University Press, 1991. 110–33.

Harris, Susan C. "The Ethics of Indecency: Censorship, Sexuality, and the Voice of the Academy in the Narration of *Jacob's Room*." *Twentieth-Century Literature* 43 (1997): 420–38.

Kazan, Francesca. "Description and the Pictorial in *Jacob's Room*." *English Literary History* 55 (1988): 701–19.

Kiely, Robert. "*Jacob's Room* and *Roger Fry*: Two Studies in Still Life." *Modernism Reconsidered*. Ed. Robert Kiely and John Hildebidle. Cambridge: Harvard University Press, 1983. 147–66.

•Little, Judy. "*Jacob's Room* as Comedy: Woolf's Parodic *Bildungsroman*." *New Feminist Essays on Virginia* Woolf. Ed. Jane Marcus. Lincoln: University of Nebraska Press, 1981. 105–24.

Neverow, Vara S. "The Return of the Great Goddess: Immortal Virginity, Sexual Autonomy and Lesbian Possibility in *Jacob's Room*." *Woolf Studies Annual*, 10 (2004): 203–31.

Schlack, Beverly Ann. "*Jacob's Room*." *Continuing Presences: Virginia Woolf's Use of Literary Allusion*. University Park: Pennsylvania University Press, 1979. 29–164.

•Wall, Kathleen. "Significant Form in *Jacob's Room*: Ekphrasis and the Elegy." *Texas Studies in Literature and Language* 44 (2002): 302–23.

•Zwerdling, Alex. "*Jacob's Room*: Woolf's Satiric Elegy." *English Literary History* 48 (1981): 894–913.